JAPANESE SUCCESS? BRITISH FAILURE?

JAPANESE SUCCESS?
BRITISH FAILURE?

Comparisons in Business Performance Since 1945

Edited by

ETSUO ABÉ
and
TERRY GOURVISH

OXFORD UNIVERSITY PRESS

1997

Oxford University Press, Great Clarendon Street, Oxford OX2 6DP

Oxford New York
Athens Auckland Bangkok Bogota Bombay
Buenos Aires Calcutta Cape Town Dar es Salaam
Delhi Florence Hong Kong Istanbul Karachi
Kuala Lumpur Madras Madrid Melbourne
Mexico City Nairobi Paris Singapore
Taipei Tokyo Toronto Warsaw
and associated companies in
Berlin Ibadan

Oxford is a trade mark of Oxford University Press

Published in the United States by
Oxford University Press Inc., New York

© the various contributors 1997

British Library Cataloguing in Publication Data
Data available

Library of Congress Cataloging in Publication Data
Japanese success? British failure? : comparisons in business
performance since 1945 / edited by Etsuo Abe and Terry Gourvish.
Includes bibliographical references (p.).
1. Industrial management—Japan. 2. Industrial management—Great
Britain. 3. Industrial policy—Japan. 4. Industrial policy—Great
Britain. 5. Japan—Economic conditions—1945– 6. Great Britain—
Economic conditions—1945–1993. 7. Great Britain—Economic
conditions—1993–   I. Abe, Etsuo, 1949– . II. Gourvish, T. R.
(Terence Richard)
HD70.J3J3946 1997 97–5483
338.941'009'045—dc21

ISBN 0-19-829058-6

1 3 5 9 10 8 6 4 2

Typeset by Best-set Typesetter Ltd., Hong Kong
Printed in Great Britain by Biddles Ltd., Guildford and King's Lynn

PREFACE

This book arose from the Business History Unit's long-established and close links with Japanese business historians. In discussions it emerged that a theme of considerable interest to both sides was the apparent over-simplification represented by the 'declinist' literature on the modern economic history of Britain and the 'miracle' literature on modern Japan. A conference was then convened by the Unit at the London School of Economics in April 1994 with the title 'British and Japanese Performance Since the War (Reassessing the Japanese Economic Miracle)'. The papers given at the conference provided the raw materials for the chapters which appear in this book.

The authors would like to thank all those who assisted in the preparation of the volume, and in particular: Mrs Sonia Copeland, who organized the BHU Conference; the conference delegates; Phillipa Wall; The Daiwa Anglo-Japanese Foundation; the Baring Foundation; the Japanese Business History Society; and last, but certainly not least, David Musson, Leonie Hayler, John Callow, and the team at Oxford University Press.

T. G.
E. A.

London and Tokyo
January 1997

CONTENTS

PART IV: FINANCE 139

**PART V: CASE STUDIES: AUTOMOBILES
AND ELECTRONICS** 185

LIST OF FIGURES

LIST OF TABLES

NOTES ON CONTRIBUTORS

ETSUO ABÉ is Professor of Business Administration at Meiji University. His publications include *Daiei Teikoku no Sangyo Haken* (The Industrial Supremacy of the British Empire) (1993) and *Keieishi* (Business History) (with S. Suzuki and Y. Yonekura, 1987). He has edited a number of books on business history, including *The Origins of Japanese Industrial Power* (with R. Fitzgerald, 1995) and *Changing Patterns of International Rivalry* (with S. Suzuki, 1991). He is a subject editor of the *International Encyclopedia of Business and Management* (1996).

MARTIN CAMPBELL-KELLY is Reader in Computer Science at the University of Warwick, where he specializes in the history of computing and technology policy. His publications include *ICL: A Business and Technical History* (1989) and *Computer: A History of the Information Machine* (1996).

FORREST CAPIE is Professor of Economic History in the Department of Banking and Finance at City University Business School, London. He has written or edited several books on monetary, banking, and trade topics, including *Tariffs and Growth* (1994), *The Future of Central Banking* (with C. Goodhart and S. Fischer, 1995), and *Asset Prices and the Real Economy* (ed. with G. E. Wood, 1997). He is editor of the Economic History Review.

TERRY GOURVISH is Director of the Business History Unit at the London School of Economics and Political Science. His publications include *British Railways 1948–73* (1986) and *The British Brewing Industry* (with Richard Wilson, 1994). He has edited a number of books on business history, including *Management and Business in Britain and France* (with Y. Cassis and F. Crouzet, 1995) and *The International Bibliography of Business History* (with F. Goodall and S. Tolliday, 1997). He has won the Newcomen, Wadsworth, and Basil Yamey prizes for work in business history.

CHIKAGE HIDAKA is Professor of Economics at Musashi University. Her publications include *Eikoku Mengyo Suitai no Kouzu* (The Decline of the British Cotton Industry) (1995).

HIDEMASA MORIKAWA is Professor of Business History in the Faculty of Management Information at Toyohashi Sozo College. His publications include *Zaibatsu* (1992) and *Nihon keieishi* (Japanese Business History) (1978). He has edited a number of books, including *Nihon Keieishi* (Japanese Business History), v (with S. Yonekura, 1996) and *Keieisha Kigyo no Jidai* (The Age of Managerial Enterprise) (1991).

TAMOTSU NISHIZAWA is Professor of Economics in the Institute of Economic Research at Hitotsubashi University. His publications include *Itan no Ekonomisuto Gunzo* (Heretical Economists) (1994).

GEOFFREY OWEN is Director, Business Policy Programme, Centre for Economic Performance, London School of Economics and Political Science. He was editor of the *Financial Times* from 1981 to 1990. His publications include *Industry in the USA* (1966).

MARY BRENNAN ROSE is Senior Lecturer in Business History in the Department of Economics at Lancaster University. She specializes in business and textile history, and has written or edited a number of books, including *The Gregs of Quarry Bank Mill: The Rise and Decline of a Family Firm* (1986) and *The Lancashire Cotton Industry: A History since 1700* (1996).

HIROMI SHIOJI is an Associate Professor in the Faculty of Economics at Kyoto University. His publications include *Jidosha Dealer no Nicibei Hikaku* (A Comparison of Japanese and American Automobile Dealers (with T. D. Keeley, 1994).

NICK TIRATSOO is Senior Research Fellow in History at the University of Luton and a Visiting Research Fellow at the Business History Unit, London School of Economics and Political Science. His many publications include *Industrial Efficiency and State Intervention: Labour 1939–51* (with J. Tomlinson, 1993) and *'England Arise!' The Labour Party and Popular Politics in 1940s Britain* (with S. Fielding and P. Thompson, 1995).

JIM TOMLINSON is Reader in British Politics and Head of the Department of Government at Brunel University, West London. He is the author of several books on economic and business history, including *Government and the Enterprise Since 1990* (1994) and *Democratic Socialism and Economic Policy: The Attlee Years* (1997).

SEIICHURO YONEKURA is Professor of Business History, the Institute of Business Research, Hitotsubashi University. His publications include *The Japanese Iron and Steel Industry* (1994). He has edited *Nihon Keieishi* (Japanese Business History), v (with H. Morikawa, 1996).

1. Introduction: *Japan's 'Miracle' in Perspective*

TERRY GOURVISH

The significance in business and economic history of Japan's startling rise in international competitiveness since the mid-1950s has not only given business historians much food for thought but has also served to expand considerably the amount of English-language writing on modern Japan.[1] Such work increased enormously from the 1960s, and included 'miracle' identifiers such as Hewins, Stone, Khan, and Vogel, who used Japan to make criticisms of Britain and the United States.[2] They anticipated an army of researchers who since then have sought to dissect the 'miracle', isolating a wide range of 'key' variables, including: the national character; 'consensus'; an emphasis on human resources; unique structural elements; government policy; the favourable conjunction of market forces; and a 'free ride' based on American support and free trade.[3] In the business history field, Alfred Chandler's impressive though American-centred stage-theory of corporate development, demonstrated to good effect in the *Visible Hand*, and *Scale and Scope*, has recently been the subject of intense criticism, and one of the important areas in the debate has been the need to incorporate American failure and Japanese success into his model.[4] Chandler's basic approach, which in essence emphasized the 'three-pronged investment' in production, marketing, and management by large-scale, integrated corporations with the relative absence of government intervention, has been held to have limited applications in the late twentieth century, with the rise of Japan, and the Asian tigers of Korea, Taiwan, and Singapore, where government intervention and planning were more important, and with the emergence of alternatives to mass production, notably the 'flexible specialization' of small and medium-sized enterprises in countries such as Italy.[5]

Michael Porter's ambitious assessment of mid-1980s competitiveness, *The Competitive Advantage of Nations*, gave more attention to Japan. He pointed out that while Japan's rise had often been attributed to the role of government and the distinctiveness of her management practices, competitive advantage was attained in some industries but not in others. There were spectacular successes, such as electronics and transportation equipment; equally, there were notable weaknesses, such as services, consumer-packaged goods, and chemicals. This indicated that some commonly advanced explanations of Japan's success do not have blanket coverage.

Government policy may have given certain Japanese industries a competitive edge; in others it clearly did not.[6] Porter's work, together with that of
Western analysts in general, has opened up the debate about the secrets (if
any) of Japan's economic miracle.

Most of the existing literature involves comparisons of Japan and the
United States, but there also is much to be said for comparisons of *Britain*
and Japan. The latter have been rare. It is true that as early as 1973 Ronald
Dore, in his well-known book *British Factory—Japanese Factory*, chose to
compare industrial relations practices in the two countries. More recently,
John Zysman's study of British and French financial systems drew valuable
insights from further comparisons with other countries, including Japan.[7]
However, the primary focus of scholarship remains the Japanese–
American comparison. At first sight the differences between Britain and
Japan appear great. The periodization of industrial growth in the two countries has clearly been very different, with Britain following a 'Rostovian'
take-off in the late eighteenth century, and Japan providing a good example
of 'Gerchenkronian late start'.[8] Human and raw material resource endow-
ments have also been dissimilar.[9] But there are similarities also. Both countries are island nations with imperialist traditions and an emphasis in their
economic activity on trade. Both have been closely allied for much of the
twentieth century, and the Japanese presence in the contemporary British
economy is very striking indeed. In the present decade the two countries
seem to be displaying some signs of convergence, as Japan comes to terms
with the appreciation of the yen, the rise in its debt/GDP ratio, and an end
to manufacturing 'catch-up' based on comparatively low wage costs. Major
problems have surfaced in banking and manufacturing industry. All this suggests that economic 'miracles', like other types of economic phenomena,
are subject to vicissitudes. However, in any case, differences are just as
important in national comparisons as similarities, and it is certainly true that
late-starting countries can provide important lessons for early-starting ones.
The fact that in Japan the emergence of the large-scale business enterprise
coincided with a more egalitarian thrust in human resource management
provides an important lesson for Britain, where a more paternalistic industrial relations system had ossified before the onset of the 'managerial revolution'.[10] Other elements worth examining include the importance of
cultural differences, where Britain's Christian traditions contrast with
Japan's mix of Taoism and Zen Buddhism, and Britain's relatively open con-
stitution, which contrasts with Japan's more secretive approach. All this has
led some writers at least to suggest that Britain has as much to learn from
contemporary Japan as from contemporary America.[11]

In the aggregate, the economic experience of Britain and Japan has been
very different since the War. British GDP growth amounted to 3.0 per cent
per annum 1950–73, then fell to 1.7 per cent 1973–94, while Japanese GDP
increased by 9.3 and 3.5 per cent over the same periods. British GDP growth

per capita was also modest in comparison with Japan's: annual rates were 2.5 per cent, 1950–73 and 1.5 per cent, 1973–94, compared with 8.0 and 3.8 per cent.[12] And Japan has more of the world's largest industrial companies than the UK—eight in the top twenty compared with only two.[13] On the other hand, the relative maturity of the two economies obviously played some part in the disparity. Catch-up and convergence were clearly at work. In 1950, for example, Japanese GDP per capita was only $1,873 (in constant 1990 $), while in Britain it was over 3.5 times higher at $6,847. Japanese GDP per capita did not exceed that of the UK until 1980.[14] In fact, Britain's post-war performance has been close to that of the United States. Turning to industrial sectors, experience in Britain and Japan has been very different. Japan has clearly outperformed Britain in electronic and optical products (e.g. television sets and cameras), heavy equipment, and transport-related industries (cars, motorcycles, tractors, and lorries), but aerospace, consumer-packaged goods such as food and drink and toiletries, services such as banking and insurance, and pharmaceuticals have proved much more competitive and dynamic in the UK than in Japan. Porter is quite right to point out the disparity in the record. It encourages us to make a more critical evaluation of the various components which contributed to Japan's economic success. In so doing we follow in the footsteps of many scholars, who, from both Western and Eastern perspectives, have examined the major components of Japanese performance, viz. management structures, the characteristics of production systems and industrial organization, the government–industry relationship, institutional elements, such as education and training, finance and technology, and cultural elements. Thus, it was entirely fitting that the organizers of the Anglo-Japanese Business History Conference should choose as the theme of their fourth meeting, held at the London School of Economics in April 1994, 'British and Japanese Performance Since the War (Reassessing the Japanese Economic Miracle)'. The aim was to attempt a reinterpretation of the miracle by juxtaposing British and Japanese responses over the fifty years from the end of World War II to isolate the meaningful elements in Japan's rise from others which were not unique or even important. By making comparisons both at a thematic and sectoral level with the UK, often judged to be a 'failure' in the same period, new insights into the components of international competitiveness in the globalizing economy were sought. This book is the product of the conference proceedings.

The first section is devoted to one of the core issues, Government and Industry. Etsuo Abé provides a critical evaluation of the state as the 'Third Hand', while Jim Tomlinson poses the question 'Why no MITI in Britain?' Abe's contribution may be said to be part of the critical reaction to Eugene Kaplan's *Japan: the Government–Business Relationship* of 1972, and Chalmers Johnson's *MITI and the Japanese Miracle*, published in 1982.[15] The latter, important bench-mark work argued that post-Meiji Japan was first and foremost a 'developmental state', a tradition which culminated in the key post-war role of MITI, the Ministry of International Trade and Industry. MITI was particularly effective (and dominant) in the 1950s, but continued to contribute to economic growth in the 1960s, when its role was less pervasive, being characterized by the terms 'administrative guidance', 'controlled competition', and 'creative umpire'.[16] Johnson's thesis has inspired a substantial response from scholars, much of it directed at the precise character of Japan's industrial policy. Some of it unfairly associates Johnson with the view that industrial policy in general, and MITI in particular, was entirely responsible for Japan's economic success. All of it extends our understanding of the complex processes of Japan's government–industry relations, though the more that is published, the muddier the waters seem to become, at least to this writer. Three recent examples underline the point. Daniel Okimoto's *Between MITI and the Market*, which focuses on high technology activities, is representative of a relatively sympathetic reaction to Chalmers Johnson. Focusing on high technology industries, he places less emphasis on MITI as the plank of industrial policy. It is pointed out that Japan was a 'minimalist' state in terms of taxation, expenditure, equity ownership, and regulatory apparatus, and that several areas of industrial policy were characterized by failure. Nevertheless, Okimoto emphasizes the positive role played by government in sustaining a favourable business environment, one in which the private sector is encouraged to flourish. He stresses the importance of a complex web of government–industry networks, which characterize the 'synergistic interplay of the state and private enterprise' and provide a 'framework for communication and consensus building'. On the other hand, David Friedman's *The Misunderstood Miracle*, which deals primarily with computer-controlled machine tools, rejects both the 'bureaucratic regulation' approach of Johnson and the 'market regulation' alternative. He dismisses MITI's role, pointing out that few of its interventions produced the anticipated results. Instead, he draws on Piore and Sabel to emphasize the importance of the flexible manufacturing strategies of small and medium-sized firms and also highlights Japan's 'politics structuring industrial behaviour at all levels of the economy'. Odagiri's recent survey of Japanese management and the economy, *Growth through Competition*, is equally agnostic, suggesting that Japan's success rested on less regulatory intervention, not more, and arguing that an effective competitive environment and good management systems were more important than industrial policy.[17] Responding to the current intellectual climate and building on earlier work, notably his survey with Bob Fitzgerald of the factors making for Japan's economic success,[18] Abé argues that it is not particularly sensible to ask whether MITI's role was decisive or limited, whether the market or industrial policy was the crucial factor in industrial development. Rather, it is the way in which government and market forces interacted that was crucial. Japan should be seen neither as an example of the 'invisible hand' of the market nor of the 'visible hand' of corporations à la Chandler. Instead, argues Abé, the state acted as a 'third hand'.[19] The precise nature of state intervention should be clearly understood, of course. Japanese industrial policy had many facets: an 'arm's-length' approach to the private sector; the incorporation of trade associations, business groups, and councils in the decision-making process; the virtual exclusion of trade unions; protectionism as a temporary and preparatory stage for trade liberalization; financial aid; research support; government purchasing; and the advantages of political stability. But the essential feature was that it preserved the competitiveness of domestic firms. It failed when it lost sight of this objective. There was thus no simple government–business relationship. Referring to the interactions of MITI and the private sector in iron and steel, the motor industry, and electronics (computers and semiconductors), Abe favours a 'tripartite' analysis, distinguishing government, the leading or 'mainstream' firms and 'maverick' companies. This provides a more satisfactory backcloth for understanding the ramifications of industrial policy in the periods of tight control (to *c*.1960) and decreasing intervention (*c*.1960–80). The government's leverage clearly diminished with the rise of large modern enterprises and the easing of foreign exchange controls.

Jim Tomlinson explores the comparison between British and Japanese industrial policy, focusing on the period 1945–70. Like Abé he concludes that it is unhelpful to use the 'role of government v. role of the market' framework. 'Comparative economic history', he observes, 'is not well served by the use of the "cartoon images" of the all-powerful state or unfettered competition.' Tomlinson notes that in the realm of industrial policy both countries had their successes and failures; and any comparative analysis must take account of their relative economic positions. Political differences were nevertheless important. Drawing on Okimoto's work, he observes that in Japan's long period of one-party government, MITI was left free to attend to the larger, internationally competitive sectors of the economy. In two-party Britain, on the other hand, there was more political interference, and, in the critical period of the 1950s, more difficulty in making industrial regeneration an issue of sufficient priority. There were other contrasts too. In Japan there were more cordial relations with employers; trade policy was used to further industrial policy; and a greater resistance was shown to the entry of foreign-based MNEs. As regards competition policy, Japan's 'protection without and competition within' is contrasted with Britain's ambivalent and shifting stance. Finally, Tomlinson identifies a more positive approach in Japan to what would now be called 'human resource management', which contrasts with Britain's disappointing record in this area.[20]

In Part II, Management comes under the microscope, with essays by Hidemasa Morikawa on 'The Top Management of Large-scale Enterprises in Post-war Japan', and Nick Tiratsoo on 'British management 1945–64:

Reformers and the struggle to improve standards'. Much academic effort has gone into dissecting Japanese organization and management in order to isolate the ingredients of 'success'. Interest has focused on business organization itself, and in particular on the way Japan's larger enterprises diverged from Chandler's large-scale model with their *keiretsu*, the post-war successors of the pre-war, family-led *zaibatsu*, vertically integrated conglomerate holding companies which were aped in modified form by the South Korean *chaebol*.[21] Yoshitaka Suzuki has even gone so far as to posit another third hand or way—the Japanese corporation, with its defining principle—to co-ordinate internal labour resources. If Chandler's ideal American corporation was production-driven and Britain's holding company type was finance-driven, then the Japanese enterprise, which gave operating units and factory managers greater accessibility to head office, was driven by human resource management.[22] However, scholars such as Geoffrey Jones, in observing the global dynamism of both Japan's trading companies, known as *soga shosha*, and Britain's free-standing companies, see as many similarities as contrasts in the two institutions.[23] Clearly, organizational forms in themselves are not a sufficient explanation of contrasting performance. Both Britain and Japan diverged from Chandler's American typology, since conglomerate holding companies were a popular form of organization. However, in Britain holding companies such as Imperial Tobacco and the Calico Printers Association, which emerged at the turn of the century, have been frequently criticized for their large boards, loose control, and inadequate professional management.[24] It is not the *form* but the *substance* that matters. We must take account of the way in which Japanese institutions worked; the use of inter-firm networks, which blended co-operative and competitive impulses;[25] the way subsidiaries interacted with the centre, including 'just-in-time' targeting; the goal-setting, or culture of the enterprise, embracing on-the-job training, promotion by seniority, and life-time employment; the emphasis on the integration of production with human resource management and on product improvement—*kaizen*;[26] and last, but not least, the emphasis on quality, where Japan apparently seized on the emphasis placed by Dr Edwards Deming on the importance of quality attainment and controls in production.[27]

Morikawa's contributions to the study of the development of Japanese management are widely known.[28] Here he looks at the rise of 'managerial capitalism' in Japan's large-scale businesses since the War and seeks explanations for the difficulties facing the corporate sector since the appreciation of the yen in the mid-1980s. Developing a preliminary paper published in *Business History* in 1995, he provides data on the recruitment of corporate presidents, while noting the continuing importance of family-owned enterprises. The impetus to use professional salaried managers was greatly enhanced by the dissolution of the *zaibatsu* under the Allied Occupation. Morikawa underlines the importance which top management attached to harmonious working relations with its skilled work-force, building up 'skilled workers' networks' with the familiar characteristics of co-operativeness, OJT training, and 'bottom-up' communication. These networks are seen to have contributed to the quality and productivity achievements in the precision engineering and machinery industries in particular. However, looking at the post-'Miracle' period, Morikawa finds a situation of 'incumbent inertia'. Japanese companies are criticized for their complacency. They failed to reform their organizational networks in response to changed market conditions, and this was particularly serious in view of the weakness of such networks in relation to innovation. These deficiencies are attributed to a substantial increase in the size of boards of directors, the inability of managers to act decisively despite the wealth of their information base, and the inadequacies of an educational system which, it is argued, tended to sap student motivation. In a section redolent of scholarly criticisms of *British* industrial performance at an earlier date, Morikawa provides much food for thought about the future challenge for Japanese top management.

In an equally provocative contribution, Nick Tiratsoo examines the opportunities to reform British management practices which existed after 1945. In contrast with the situation in Japan, where managers applied American ideas with enthusiasm, in Britain the 1950s were very much years of wasted opportunity. Focusing on manufacturing, where the post-war record was particularly disappointing, Tiratsoo finds that the initiatives taken to reform British management in the period 1951–64 failed to have much impact. This was not because the programmes were either unambitious or defective. Rather the explanation lay in the fact that the reforms ran counter to conservative and deeply ingrained management attitudes and were subverted by employers' associations such as the Federation of British Industry and the Institute of Directors.

The issue of education is examined by Tamotsu Nishizawa and Mary Rose. The linkage between education and industrial competitiveness is not a clear-cut one, of course, and it is unsurprising to find that both the Japanese and British education systems have had their fierce critics and staunch defenders. In Japan the role of education in fostering human resource development and the work ethic within institutions (and especially firms) is admired, but, as Morikawa has noted (see above), its penchant for stereotypical learning and learning by rote has fewer supporters.[29] In the UK, the apparent gulf between the educators and the 'practical' needs of business has attracted considerable research attention, notably by Michael Sanderson and Robert Locke.[30] Tamotsu Nishizawa pays particular attention to in-firm training. In his chapter he points out that while Japan quickly moved to a meritocratic emphasis based on educational achievements, the vast majority of school and graduate recruits to business had no prior vocational qualifications (here there is a similarity with the position in Britain before

the rapid expansion of business schools in the 1980s). Educational attainment was largely confined to a first degree from a good university, leaving
further training to corporate initiatives, including in-firm courses. Here the
role of business leaders as lobbyists from the 1950s was crucial. The Japan
Society for Industrial Training and the Japan Productivity Center were also
important in filling the gap left by the universities in vocationally oriented
post-graduate education, and providing a platform for in-house training by
the major companies.

Mary Rose is concerned with the deficiencies in the provision of human
capital in Britain since 1945. Only in sectors where scientific knowledge
rather than practical skill was at the root of international competitiveness—
e.g. pharmaceuticals—was formal education, rather than shop-floor training, valued. Like Tiratsoo (see Chapter 5) she is critical of British
businessmen for their indifference to formal education and training, but she
observes that workers' organizations also tended to doubt that educational
training could provide direct benefits. While government expenditure on
education increased steadily after 1945, little of this was applied to education of direct relevance to business. British in-firm training was also rather
limited; in this context the tendency to short-termism encouraged by a
dependence on the stock market for funds and the importance of mergers
in corporate growth strategies may be relevant. However, the key point is
not the extent of in-firm training. Rather it is that such training should have
the requisite quality and be incorporated into appropriate corporate strategies. Here, Japan appears to have scored much more heavily than Britain.
Rose's wisely tentative conclusion is that the implications for Britain
include a management stratum less equipped to cope with the complexity
of modern large-scale corporations, and a productivity gap which was particularly evident where skill deficiencies were critical.

The finance sector and the degree of support it offered to business are
examined in the essays by Chikage Hidaka and Forrest Capie. There has
been much debate in recent years on the issue of the historical provision of
bank finance to industry and the implications of the various institutional
arrangements for successful international competitiveness.[31] Hidaka provides a detailed case-study of the complex ways in which the finance sector
responded to the investment needs of post-war Japanese industry in the
period to *c*.1970. In spite of the severe difficulties facing the financial sector
after the War, the Japanese successfully introduced a system of long-term
industrial lending, in which, at first, the government's presence was very
pronounced. But as complex mechanisms were developed in the 1950s,
adapted to the requirements of industrial rationalization and innovation,
the banks grew in strength and confidence and were able to establish more
of an arm's-length relationship with government. Thus, the mechanism
driving the successful buildup of industrial financing is here seen in terms
of aggressive lending by banks anxious to expand their deposit base. In so
doing they may have contributed to Japan's 'economic miracle' but their

efforts were scarcely conducive to improved risk awareness and greater financial responsibility.

In Britain, of course, the financial sector has been historically dominant in terms of global competitiveness, though its precise contribution to British industrial lending has been the subject of much debate. Forrest Capie locates himself firmly in this context when he asks: 'has the British economy failed, and if so can the blame for failure be placed at the door of finance?' In a speculative, but insightful, piece he finds that the post-1945 role of the banks was if anything stronger than it had been in the past and that the performance of the sector compared favourably with that of other European countries. Rejecting the more gloomy notions of Britain's post-war failure, he notes that financial intermediation has been often cited as a weakness, especially in terms of long-term finance. But several widely held notions are challenged, including the idea that investment must always be positively correlated with economic growth, and the view that the British were damagingly short-termist. He shows how the commercial banks extended medium-term lending after 1945, while several new institutions, including ICFC/3i, emerged to ease the financing problems of the small and medium-sized sector.

Two sets of case-studies complete the volume. In the first the motor industry is examined, a field in which there has been a great deal of recent comparative work and much talk of Japanese rise and British decline.[32] Hiromi Shioji provides a detailed analysis of a key aspect of Toyota's famous system of outsourcing or subsidiary component supply. His essay on the *itaku* system reveals how Toyota orchestrated its growth in the 1960s by careful management of its relationship with subsidiary assemblers as well as parts-suppliers. *Itaku* firms such as Toyota Shatai, Kanto, and Hino were used to assemble trucks, luxury, and specialist vehicles with lower production runs, leaving the main Toyota plant to optimize use of its main assembly lines. Later on, as private motor cars began to dominate production, the subsidiary firms were used to manufacture models in a flexible manner, enabling Toyota to respond quickly to fluctuating demand for particular models by adjusting production levels at the various plants. The British, meanwhile, did not enjoy the same degree of organizational capability and clear strategic direction. Geoffrey Owen, developing one of the themes in his conference paper on the experience of the British motor industry since 1945, focuses on the case of Britain's 'national champion', British Leyland, a sad story of failure and lost opportunity. The merger which in 1968 produced the British Leyland Motor Corporation was a critical moment in Britain's post-war manufacturing history. The subsequent failure of British-managed volume-car production provides a case in which most of the widely held traits of British post-war failure were present: inept corporate strategies, poor industrial relations, government interference, poor marketing, and inadequate pricing and costing. BL was the third largest European car producer and also had competitive advantages in 4WD vehicles, trucks, and buses. But it was unable to penetrate the continental European market and its share of the domestic market fell from 40 to 15 per cent, 1968–94. Owen pays particular attention here to the impact of management weaknesses on marketing, the fatal consequences of a combination of 'wishful thinking and confused organization', the numerous attempts to inject a sense of realism into product strategy, and the company's subsequent and painful rationalization.

Electronics industries are considered in the final two chapters. Seiichiro Yonekura shows how by spinning off divisions a major Japanese company was able to optimize innovation and growth. Fuji Denki began life in 1923 as a joint venture of Furukawa and the German giant Siemens, with the purpose of manufacturing electrical plant and telecommunications equipment. The synergy between the two was limited, however. In 1935 Fuji Denki separated its telephone division and established Fuji Tsushinki Kabushi Kaisha (later Fujitsu) as an entirely separate independent concern. The move gave considerable impetus to innovation, and Fujitsu subsequently became the leading Japanese computer manufacturer. In turn, Fujitsu did the same with its numeric control division, which was spun off as Fanuc in 1972. The case is an interesting one, contributing to the debate about the post-Chandlerian corporation and the time-old debate about the appropriateness of diversification v. core strategies, which have provided so much fruitful employment for management consultants. Much is made here about the significance of the spin-off strategy, but more than equal weight should be given to the role of key individuals inside the organization, which was critical to the move into computers. Fuji Denki may have done the right thing in hiving off its telephone and telegraph activities, but without innovative engineers and managers of vision little would have been achieved. Martin Campbell-Kelly's essay on ICL charts an entirely different story of corporate change. Here, ICL, Britain's leading computer company, and like British Leyland the product of a merger in 1968, made the transition from much-vaunted national champion to a less prestigious though more effective position as a subsidiary of Fujitsu in its drive to international competitiveness. Building on his well-known case-study of the company, Campbell-Kelly provides an illuminating account of the history of information technology activity in Britain. ICL tended to follow rather than lead developments in computing, which until the 1980s were dominated by IBM. It was also influenced by the supply-side, mainframe computer obsessions of successive British governments. Like Leyland, its product range required rationalization. Like Leyland, it suffered from weak management (though this was improved by an injection of American expertise) and chose an over-ambitious strategy, one which proved ruinous in the recession of the early 1980s. The outcome was a government rescue operation, an agreement with Fujitsu in 1981, a take-over by STC in 1984, and sale to Fujitsu in 1990.

This book provides a series of insights into most of the key elements affecting comparative economic performance in modern economies: the role of the timing of the initial spurt of industrialization; the relative importance of resources broadly defined, including human resources; the relevance of corporate capabilities and strategies; the role of institutional infrastructure, including government; the ability to capture technological gains; and the part played by contingency. The chapters presented here do not of course pretend to be comprehensive, nor to present a quantitative assessment of the relative positions of the two economies.[33] Rather their aim is to provide more focused analyses and information useful to those seeking to refine judgements, and quantitative judgements in particular, made at a macroeconomic level. Everywhere in Anglo-Japanese comparisons since 1945 apparently marked contrasts seem to evaporate on closer inspection. For example, the differences in the education/business linkage in the two countries are not as pronounced as is sometimes claimed, and the performance gap in financial services is now much narrower since the entry of the major Japanese banks into the City of London.[34] Debates about Japanese secrets and myths of British failure will continue. The essays in this volume are intended to serve as a starting-point for further research which, it is hoped, will shed light on the critical aspects of modern corporate behaviour and national competitiveness which affect the two countries.

NOTES

1. I am grateful to Etsuo Abé, Ian Nish, Nick Tiratsoo, and Jim Tomlinson for their helpful comments on this introduction.
2. Ralph Hewins, *The Japanese Miracle Men* (London, 1967); Peter B. Stone, *Japan Surges Ahead: Japan's economic rebirth* (London, 1969); Herman Khan, *The Emerging Japanese Superstate* (Englewood Cliffs, NJ, 1970); and Ezra Vogel, *Japan as Number One: Lessons for America* (Cambridge, Mass., 1979). These and other works are cited by Chalmers Johnson, *MITI and the Japanese Miracle: The Growth of Industrial Policy, 1925–1975* (Stanford, Calif., 1982), 7.
3. Johnson, *MITI and the Japanese Miracle*, ch. 1.
4. Alfred D. Chandler, Jr., *The Visible Hand: The Managerial Revolution in American Business* (Cambridge, Mass., 1977), *Scale and Scope: The Dynamics of Industrial Capitalism* (Cambridge, Mass., 1990).
5. Cf. Leslie Hannah, 'The American Miracle, 1875–1950 and After: A View in the European Mirror', *Business and Economic History*, 24/2 (Winter 1995), 197–220; Michael J. Piore and Charles F. Sabel, *The Second Industrial Divide: Possibilities for Prosperity* (New York, 1984); Ezra F. Vogel, *The Four Little Dragons: The Spread of Industrialization in East Asia* (Cambridge, Mass., 1991). Chandler did try to incorporate Japan into some of his analyses. Cf. 'The Emergence of Managerial Capitalism', *Business History Review*, 58/4 (1984), 473–503.

6. Michael Porter, *The Competitive Advantage of Nations* (1990), 384, 394, 416.
7. Ronald Dore, *British Factory—Japanese Factory: The Origins of National Diversity in Industrial Relations* (Berkeley and Los Angeles, 1973); John Zysman, *Governments, Markets, and Growth: Financial Systems and the Politics of Industrial Change* (Ithaca, NY, 1983).
8. W. W. Rostow, *The Stages of Economic Growth* (Cambridge, 1960); A. Gerschenkron, *Economic Backwardness in Historical Perspective* (Cambridge, Mass., 1962).
9. In 1992 the population and land area of the two countries were: UK: 57.8m., 24.4m. ha; Japan: 124.3m., 37.8m ha.
10. Cf. Dore, *British Factory—Japanese Factory*, 339–40.
11. Stephen Wilks and Maurice Wright, 'Introduction', in Stephen Wilks and Maurice Wright (eds.), *The Promotion and Regulation of Industry in Japan* (Basingstoke, 1991), 1–2.
12. Data from Angus Maddison, *Monitoring the World Economy 1820–1992* (OECD, Paris, 1995), tables C-16(a) and D-1(a).
13. *Times 1000, 1996.*
14. Maddison, *Monitoring the World Economy*. GDP is expressed in constant Geary-Khamis 1990 dollars.
15. E. J. Kaplan, *Japan: the Government–Business Relationship* (Washington, DC, 1972); Johnson, *MITI and the Japanese Miracle*.
16. Cf. Ronald Dore, *Flexible Rigidities: Industrial Policy and Structural Adjustment in the Japanese Economy 1970–80* (London, 1986), ch. 6; Zysman, *Governments, Markets, and Growth*, 237; Takashi Wakiyama, 'The Implementation and Effectiveness of MITI's Administrative Guidance', in Stephen Wilks and Maurice Wright (eds.), *Comparative Government–Industry Relations: Western Europe, the United States, and Japan* (Oxford, 1987), 211–27.
17. David Friedman, *The Misunderstood Miracle: Industrial Development and Political Change in Japan* (Ithaca, NY, 1988); Daniel I. Okimoto, *Between MITI and the Market: Japanese Industrial Policy for High Technology* (Stanford, Calif., 1989); Hiroyuki Odagiri, *Growth through Competition, Competition through Growth: Strategic Management and the Economy in Japan* (New York, 1992). See also Robert Wade, *Governing the Market: Economic Theory and the Role of Government in East Asian Industrialization* (Princeton, 1990).
18. Etsuo Abé and Robert Fitzgerald, 'Japanese Economic Success: Timing, Culture, and Organisational Capability', *Business History*, 37/2 (Apr. 1995), 1–31.
19. Abé derived the term 'third hand' from Leslie Hannah, who gave the term a different meaning. Hannah was apparently referring to the *keiretsu*-type business groups, drawing on Ken-ichi Imai, 'The Corporate Network in Japan', *Japanese Economic Studies* (Winter 1987–8), who noted that the corporate groups were 'an intermediate institution that exists between the market and the organization' (p. 18).
20. Cf. also an earlier list of contrasts assembled by G. C. Allen, 'Industrial Policy in Japan', in Charles Carter (ed.), *Industrial Policy and Innovation* (London, 1981), 85–7.
21. Cf. Hidemasa Morikawa, 'The View from Japan', Chandler's Scale and Scope Symposium, *Business History Review*, 4 (1990), 716–25; Odagiri, *Growth*

Through Competition, 161–4; Kenichi Miyashita and David Russell, *Keiretsu: Inside the Hidden Japanese Conglomerates* (New York, 1994); Richard M. Steers, Yoo Kuen Shin and Gerardo R. Ungson, *The Chaebol: Korea's New Industrial Might* (London, 1990).

22. Y. Suzuki, *Japanese Management Structures, 1920–80* (London, 1991), ch. 1; Imai, 'Corporate Network', 34.

23. Cf. Geoffrey Jones, 'Diversification Strategies and Corporate Governance in Trading Companies: Anglo-Japanese Comparisons since the Late Nineteenth Century', *Business and Economic History*, 25/2 (1996), 103–18.

24. Cf. P. L. Payne, 'The Emergence of the Large-scale Company in Great Britain 1870–1914', *Economic History Review*, 20 (1967), 527 ff; Leslie Hannah, *The Rise of the Corporate Economy* (London, 1983), 21–2; John F. Wilson, *British Business History, 1720–1994* (Manchester, 1995), 103–5. However, more recent research has cast some doubt on the apparent lack of post-merger reform. The Distillers Company, for example, established an efficient centralized organization. See R. B. Weir, *The History of the Distillers Company, 1877–1939* (Oxford, 1995), 231–51.

25. Cf. W. Mark Fruin, *The Japanese Enterprise System: Competitive Strategies and Co-operative Structures* (Oxford, 1992).

26. Masaaki Imai, *Kaizen: the Key to Japanese Competitive Success* (New York, 1988). See also James C. Abegglen and George Stalk, Jr., *Kaisha, The Japanese Corporation* (New York, 1985).

27. Cf. W. Edwards Deming, *Out of the Crisis: Quality, Productivity, and Competitive Position* (Cambridge, 1986); Raphael Aguayo, *Dr Deming: The American Who Taught the Japanese About Quality* (New York, 1990); and Takeshi Yuzawa (ed.), 'Japanese Business Strategies in Perspective', in Takeshi Yuzawa (ed.), *Japanese Business Success: The Evolution of a Strategy* (London, 1994), 8–18. For a more critical stance on Deming's contribution and the quality control process see William M. Tsutsui, 'W. Edwards Deming and the Origins of Quality Control in Japan', *Journal of Japanese Studies*, 12/2 (Summer 1996), 295–325; Toshihiro Wada, 'The Introduction and Development of Quality Control in the Communications Equipment Industry, 1945–1955', in H. Shiomi (ed.), *Japanese Yearbook on Business History*, 12 (1995), 73–98; and Izumi Nonaka, 'The Development of Company-Wide Quality Control and Quality Circles of Toyota Motor Corporation and Nissan Motor Co. Ltd.', in H. Shimo and K. Wada (eds.), *Fordism Transformed: The Development of Production Methods in the Automobile Industry* (Oxford, 1995).

28. E.g. H. Morikawa, *Zaibatsu: the Rise and Fall of Family Enterprise Groups in Japan* (Toyko, 1992); 'The Education of Engineers in Modern Japan: An Historical Perspective', in Howard F. Gospel (ed.), *Industrial Training and Technological Innovation: A Comparative and Historical Study* (1991), 136–47; 'The Role of Managerial Enterprise in Post-War Japan's Economic Growth: Focus on the 1950s', *Business History*, 37 (Apr. 1995), 32–43.

29. Cf. Ikuo Amano, 'Japanese Schooling in Historical Perspective', *Economic Eye*, 14/1 (Spring 1993), 3–8.

30. M. Sanderson, 'Social Equity and Industrial Need: A Dilemma of English Education Since 1945', in Terry Gourvish and Alan O'Day (eds.), *Britain Since 1945* (London, 1991), 159–82; and *The Missing Stratum: Technical School Education*

in England, 1900–1990s (London, 1994); Robert Locke, *Management and Higher Education since 1940* (Cambridge, 1989).

31. E.g. Håkan Lindgren, Alice Teichova, and P. L. Cottrell (eds.), *European Industry and Banking Between the Wars: A Review of Bank–Industry Relations* (Leicester, 1992); Forrest Capie and Michael Collins, 'Have the Banks Failed British Industry?', *IEA Hobart Paper*, 119 (1992); Alice Teichova, Terry Gourvish, and Agnes Pogány (eds.), *Universal Banking in the Twentieth Century Finance Industry and the State in North and Central Europe* (Aldershot, 1994).

32. Cf. Steven Tolliday and Jonathan Zeitlin (eds.), *The Automobile Industry and its Workers: Between Fordism and Flexibility* (Oxford and Cambridge, 1986); Karel Williams, John Williams, and Colin Haslam, *The Breakdown of Austin Rover* (Leamington Spa, 1987); Koichi Shimokawa, *The Japanese Automobile Industry: A Business History* (London, 1994); Roy Church, *The Rise and Decline of the British Motor Industry* (Basingstoke, 1994); Yoshiro Miwa, 'Subcontracting Relationships: The Automobile Industry', in Kenichi Imai and Ryutaro Komiya (eds.), *Business Enterprise in Japan: Views of Leading Japanese Economists* (Cambridge, Mass., 1994), 141–58; Shimo and Wada, *Fordism Transformed*; and James Foreman-Peck, Sue Bowden, and Alan McKinlay, *The British Motor Industry* (Manchester, 1995).

33. For a start here cf. Ryoshin Minami, *The Economic Development of Japan: A Quantitative Study* (Basingstoke, 2nd edn., 1994) and Nicholas Crafts and Gianni Toniolo (eds.), *Economic Growth in Europe Since 1945* (Cambridge 1996).

34. Cf. Sir Paul Newall, *Japan and the City of London* (London, 1996).

PART I
Government and Industry

2 The State as the 'Third-Hand': *MITI and Japanese Industrial Development After 1945*

ETSUO ABÉ

Since the publication of Chalmers Johnson's *MITI and the Japanese Miracle*, the view that Japanese industrial development was made possible by MITI (Ministry of International Trade and Industry) activities and policy-making, has become, rightly or wrongly, widespread.[1] Some Japan-bashers regard MITI as one of the strongholds for maintaining unfair trade practices and structures; by contrast, others, rejecting the notion of 'notorious MITI', argue that the role of MITI was fairly limited throughout the post-World War II period and was losing its dominant influence over Japanese industry with time. Instead of MITI's role, they stress the importance of market forces and business firms' initiatives and capabilities. Which is right? Or should we find other factors for the development?

In the debate at the present time, it is a plausible explanation that private firms did play a major role in industrial development, and MITI, a supplementary one. However, my conclusion is different. It seems to me that it does not make very much sense to ask which factor is more important. Rather it is worthwhile to combine both market forces and industrial policy. Put differently, did industrial policy promote or hinder competition between private business? How did such a policy function, and through what kind of mechanism?

Therefore, along with the effectiveness of industrial policy by MITI, the mechanism-implementing policy is important. In Japan, intermediate organizations, such as trade associations, cartels, and *keiretsu* networks,[2] falling in the category between market and organization in Oliver Williamson's words, are a prominent feature. How did MITI stand in relations to these? How did MITI as the 'third hand'[3]—distinct from the invisible and visible hand—promote or hinder the development of Japanese industry? This chapter traces the trajectory of MITI's industrial policy between 1945 and 1980 and tries to make clear how successful or unsuccessful the policy was and what its functional mechanism was, focusing on several well-known episodes. In the process, the historical implication of some aspects of MITI's policy will be revealed, by reference in the main to the iron and steel, automobile, and electronics (computers and semiconductors) industries which are considered to have been crucial in building industrial Japan. Needless to say, though there are other industries such as shipbuilding, machine tools, chemicals, and so on, it is not possible to describe all other industries in such a limited space, and the basic characteristics of Japanese industrial policy will be clarified by the analysis of the three industries mentioned above.

The Pros and Cons of MITI's Role in Japanese Industrial Development

One of the books which stressed the importance of MITI's industrial policy was *Japan: The Government–Business Relationship* published by the US Department of Commerce in 1972.[4] Ten years later, Chalmers Johnson published *MITI and the Japanese Miracle*, arguing that government organization was instrumental in developing the Japanese economy and Japan was the 'developmental state', quite different from the market-orientated Western countries. Afterwards, a flood of studies on Japanese industrial policy appeared.[5] In the same vein as Johnson, Patricia O'Brien contended that MITI 'facilitated the emergence of a globally competitive Japanese steel oligopoly' and made an 'economic environment in which firms were sheltered from the inherent risks attending the huge investment typical of the steel industry'. Japanese steel firms were allowed 'to manage and shape their industry structures', co-operating with MITI. O'Brien attaches importance to MITI's role as the 'unique' factor, not seen in other countries.[6] In addition, C. V. Prestwitz, who wrote *Trading Places: How We Allowed Japan to Take the Lead*, maintained that policy and planning brought Japan strong and continuous economic activity.[7] Furthermore, Thomas McCraw seems to underline the difference in policy-making and its effects in America and Japan.[8] Among these proponents, some argue that the United States should adopt industrial policies similar to those of Japan in order to take advantage of such an approach; others insist that Japan discard them because they are unfair trade practices and structures, contradictory to the 'legitimate' free trade doctrine.

However, by and large, the recent academic trend is moving in the opposite direction. It is argued that the contribution of MITI's policies and coordination was not crucial for the development of the Japanese economy; alternatively, entrepreneurship, corporate endeavours, the fierce competition among domestic firms, and Japan's management system played a momentous role. For instance, P. H. Trezise wrote that 'the impressive economic growth and social stability of post-war Japan are not owing in any decisive degree to the microeconomic decision-making [by MITI]'.[9] K. Zinsmeister strongly attacked the supporters of industrial policy, insisting that 'The great economic lesson of the last generation is that earnest centralized management—even in as mild a form as existed in post-war Japan—always will bring less prosperity than open market competition' and 'the most important factor driving the nation's [Japan's] success is the fierce market competition'. He criticizes the Clinton administration's economic change 'in the direction of the managed capitalism found in Japan and Western Europe, where governments play a larger role than Washington in shaping industries and markets'.[10] Michael Porter also emphasized the pivotal importance of domestic rivalry for economic success and concluded that in every country the role of governments is not the major factor to obtain competitive advantage in international competition.[11] Furthermore, Alfred Chandler came to the conclusion that organizational capabilities of firms are crucial for growth and prosperity in the long run, regarding the legal system and governmental role as supplemental.[12] David Friedman, who studied the Japanese machine tool industry, made the claim that the industry had not benefited from the government, although he did not agree that Japanese development was the result mainly of market forces in the neo-classical sense.[13]

As an intermediate position between these two poles, a mixture of government activity and market forces is the third interpretation. To give an example, Yasusuke Murakami's concept of 'compartmentalized competition' falls into this category. He contends that some Japanese firms are selected as players, and are compelled to compete fiercely on the basis of equal opportunity. The selection process is the role of government, which determines the membership, and subsequent competition is determined by market forces, based on each company's strength. Accordingly, the ingredients of industrial policy and market forces are distinct. In Murakami's explanation, however, the location of the boundary between the two may still be questioned.[14] In some cases, new entry into the industry may be somewhat easy, despite MITI's intention to suppress it; in other cases it may be quite difficult owing to MITI's regulation. The writer will demonstrate this facet in this chapter, but before that it would be useful to take a look at the theoretical and actual significance of industrial policy.

The Theoretical and Actual Significance of Industrial Policy

First of all, there is the oft-cited argument about the comparative theorem of David Ricardo. Countries should not produce all types of goods but rather should specialize. Production costs will be determined by the relative availability of factors such as labour and capital. Furthermore, countries should engage in free international trade. In this way, the output, consumption and welfare of the world will be maximized.[15] None the less, this explanation of the international division of labour and free market economics is, in essence, a static theory, inviting the objection that it would be likely to cement countries inside an existing division of international activities which they might not find to their long-term benefit, without regard to the international mobility of capital and human resources. In addition, it ignores the possibility of creating new industries which may have higher

income elasticities of demand and productivity growth, in a word, technological innovation. Consequently, the theorem does not fit late-developing
countries, leaving them in a relatively unfavourable state. On the contrary,
a dynamic theory must be produced. Friedrich List is quite often mentioned
as the guardian of protectionism for latecomers and infant industries, particularly among Japanese academics and policy-makers.[16] Infant industries
of strategic importance, thus, will be provided with the basis for protective
policy-making. In particular, a targeting policy may be effective for late-
coming countries.

Second, the problem of 'market failure' should be examined. The market
may be frustrated due to higher transaction costs than with internal (corporate) organization. Oliver Williamson, theoretically, and Chandler, historically, made it evident that organization (the visible hand) is essentially
preferable to and more workable than the market (the invisible hand), and
over time organization has been taking the place of the market by dint of
lower transaction costs.[17] This is partly because of scale economies which
are found inside firms. Yet a different kind of organization, that is, 'government', can accelerate this process from market to organization, by investing in infrastructure, education, research and development, stimulating a
new demand for novel products, signalling a new developmental direction
with essential information, and appealing to the necessity for mergers. We
may call this organization 'the third hand' since it differs from enterprise
organizations.[18] (see Fig. 2.1.)

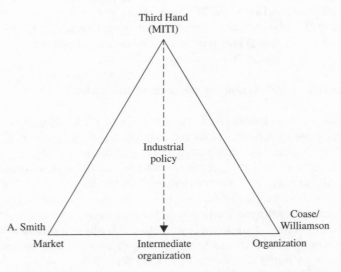

FIG. 2.1. Relationship between market, organization, and intermediate organization (the 'Third Hand').

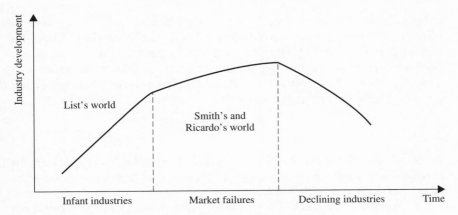

FIG. 2.2. Areas of industrial policy.

Third, in the case of multiple-equilibria by virtue of Marshallian externalities, the attainment of a better equilibrium via government policy can be more favourable than an equilibrium in a market economy. This occurs in industries where strategic complementarity produces a *co-ordination failure* caused by pessimistic forecasting. These cases typically take place in an oligopolistic structure, while existing economic theories on competition tend to be concerned with perfect competition. Here is another theoretical basis for government intervention.[19]

From a different view, there are some realistic reasons for industrial policy. In addition to the three reasons above, another of importance is the reduction of problems in declining industries such as coal by a government policy which seeks to transfer people and resources into other, growing, sectors. This approach usually has a political motivation. By the same token, when a huge imbalance stems from international trade, countries may assume the right to rely on protectionism. A country cannot continue with international trade when it experiences a large trade deficit. In such a case, the government is obliged to intervene and take measures to improve the trade balance even if it might be guilty of 'managed trade'.[20] Figure 2.2 summarizes the basis for industrial policy.

The Japanese Experience, 1945–c.1980

Japanese economic development in the post-war period is divided into three periods: recovery (1945–55); high growth (1955–73); stable growth (1973 to the present). According to the nature of industrial policy, the following three periods may be identified: the period of tight control

(1945–*c*.1960); decreasing intervention, and adaptation to the demand of foreign countries for liberalization (*c*.1960–80); and the period of international harmonization (*c*.1980 to the present). In this way, there is a time-lag between intended policies and actual economic development, which was partly the result of the policies executed. In this chapter, the first and second periods relating to industrial policy will be examined.

Ideology

To clarify the historical significance of industrial policy, it is necessary to make observations on the ideological background, organization (mechanism), and extent of industrial policy.

The period of economic recovery was a turbulent but preparatory stage for high growth. After defeat in World War II, Japan faced serious difficulties, political, economic, and social. But as Chalmers Johnson has stressed, the bureaucratic system, surprisingly enough, did not undergo a drastic change. Rather, the continuity of personnel and system from the pre-war time period was remarkable.[21] The same people planned, directed and monitored private companies. The basic rationale behind the industrial policy and the bureaucracy of MITI was a mix of ideas, not based on any single ideology. Before and during the War, what were called 'innovative bureaucrats', influenced by Nazi Germany's totalitarianism or the rationalization movement (one of them was Nobusuke Kishi, later Prime Minister in the 1950s), and even affected by Soviet Russia's Gosplan, were at the heart of planning.[22] Such a tradition remained after the War. In addition, as a new ideology, Keynesianism, i.e. the notion of 'modified capitalism', which justified the active intervention of the government, found wide support among not only bureaucrats but also people at large. In fact, one of the four big business associations in Japan, Keizai Doyukai (the Japanese counterpart of the Business Round Table in the US) was established on the basis of this idea in 1946. By the same token, a substantial number of GHQ/SCAP (the General Headquarters of the Supreme Commander of the Allied Powers) staff were left-wing New Dealers. Furthermore, it is said that the Japanese had views similar to the corporatism in Europe, which lead to communitarianism in Japan and became the basis for permeating governmental guidance. In the 1950s, some bureaucrats were strongly influenced by French industrial planning. Moreover, the traditional ideas of 'okaminiwa katenai' (the overwhelming power of the government over its citizens) persisted among the population. Taken together, the *Zeitgeist* of the period was quite favourable to positive government intervention.

However, actual performance under the control economy was not satisfactory, so that even during the War the way the economy was run had to be changed in the direction of respecting private sector initiatives. The bureaucrats of MITI—at that time, correctly speaking, the Ministry of Commerce and Industry 1925–43, 1945–49) and the Ministry of Armaments (1943–45)—learned the lesson that a simple command economy did not work. This experience was applied to the direction of industries in the post-war period.

To conclude, the ideology shared by MITI's bureaucrats comprised a variety of ideas, including the relics of the command economy, Keynesianism, corporatism, and historical tradition. This amounted to a complex ideological background.[23] However, there was a strong belief that the simple command economy could not be effective and the initiatives of the private sector should be respected.

Organization

In order to control the economy, an appropriate organization is indispensable. In the pre-war period, MITI set up Control Associations (Toseikai), partly governmental, partly private organizations, so that its intentions would smoothly permeate industries. On top of this, there were a large number of trade associations because those trade associations functioning as cartels were in fashion. Cartel behaviour was not illegal in pre-war Japan; on the contrary it was encouraged to establish order within industry. Accordingly, a hierarchy comprising MITI, the Control Associations, trade associations, and firms was established. After the War, Control Associations were dissolved by GHQ. Instead, an Industrial Rationalization Council (Sangyo Gorika Shingikai) was established in 1949. This organization was the virtual successor of the pre-war Control Associations. MITI utilized the Council as the linkage organization for communication between itself and the trade associations. Thus, the post-war system had characteristics which were very similar to that of pre-war. There was a virtual continuity of personnel between both organizations because MITI was not dissolved by GHQ, unlike the Ministry of Home Affairs (Naimu Sho).[24] The persons in the pivotal positions in the pre-war organization occupied similar posts after the War. Yet the Rationalization Council has a more open character, accentuating the *interaction* function which was underpinned by the 1972 publication by the US Department of Commerce referred to above.[25] This interaction was typical of the Japanese government–business relationship, different from the completely planned or command economy.

The period 1945–60 may be further divided into two parts: the first the period of direct control, 1945–52, the second, 1952–60, one of relatively indirect control. In the first period, the direct control of the government and GHQ dominated. Commodity prices were controlled by the Price Control Ordinance (Bukka Tosei Rei), and many industrial products were regulated by the Temporary Materials Supply and Demand Adjustment Act (Rinji Busshi Jukyu Chosei Ho) of 1946. During the Allied occupation (1945–52), the Japanese government exerted a tight control over industry subject to

GHQ directives. However, around 1950 most of the regulation ordinances were removed and after 1952 when the Temporary Materials Supply and Demand Adjustments Act lapsed, direct control over manufactured goods lost its legal support.[26]

Measures for Control and Promotion

With regard to the mechanisms for conducting industrial policy in the 1950s, the major elements were: the regulation of foreign exchange and inward investment; tax allowances; financing through special banks based on fiscal investment and loans (Zaisei Toyushi); and *ad hoc* laws for designated industries. In 1949, the Foreign Exchange and Trade Administration Act (Gaitame Ho), and the Foreign Capital Act (Gaishi Ho) were passed. These two acts were the effective measures to realize MITI's intentions. Most of the major firms had to obtain foreign currency to import raw materials which were desperately needed for manufacture in almost all important industries because of the paucity of natural resources in Japan. In addition, the introduction of technology from foreign countries was imperative in Japan because her technical level was far behind the world standard in those years. Japan relied heavily on technology imports as the statistics show (technology exports from Japan amounted to only 1 per cent of imports, 1955–65). To introduce advanced technology, Japanese firms had to pay large royalties in foreign currency at MITI's discretion. As a consequence, MITI had the authority to decide which technology was beneficial to Japan. MITI was very severe about giving permission for the payment of royalties and even intervened in relation to the rate. Even where the firms concerned accepted a certain royalty rate, e.g. 6 per cent, MITI insisted on 5 per cent. It put pressure on the firm to the effect that if it did not follow this rate, the technology introduction contract would not be granted. Firms occasionally took advantage of MITI's tough stance to reduce royalties in negotiation on the pretext that MITI would not permit it. This was one of the reasons why the description 'notorious MITI' emerged.[27]

Under the Foreign Capital Act, MITI was *de facto* able to exclude foreign capital, by refusing foreign firms permission to set up subsidiaries except in special cases. It reluctantly conceded the setting up of foreign subsidiaries only if it was conducive to the improvement of foreign exchange through exports and the bringing of important technology to Japan by the firms concerned.

In addition to these regulations, MITI had specific tools for financing. Through the fiscal investment and loan plan, and the Japan Development Bank (Nihon Kaihatsu Ginko), the successor of the Reconstruction Finance Corporation (Fukko Kinyu Kinko), it could channel funds into specific industries which it judged vital for industrial development. Funding through the Development Bank was relatively small, e.g. 12 per cent of all equipment investment in the iron and steel industry between 1951 and 1955, but, if the Japan Development Bank made a loan to a firm on MITI's recommendation, usually with a lower interest rate than a commercial one, the firm was in a position to obtain more funds from one of the commercial banks thanks to the prestige of the Development Bank. This pump-priming effect mattered in the Japanese industrial context where a chronic shortage of capital was a serious problem in those years.[28]

By the same token, MITI was the prime initiator of special laws considered to be helpful in the development of the industries concerned. Among such laws, the Temporary Measures Act for the Promotion of the Machinery Industry (Kikai Kogyo Shinko Rinji Sochi Ho) in 1956, and the Temporary Measures Act for the Promotion of the Electronics Industry (Denshi Kogyo Rinji Sochi Ho) in 1957 are well known. These laws aimed at the deliberate promotion of the industries in question, and played an integrative role in the development of various functions, and especially finance and information supply. In the next section, we briefly consider each industry in turn.

Case Studies

The Iron and Steel Industry

The iron and steel industry is often mentioned as the successful example of Japanese industrial policy. Although the sound performance of an industry does not necessarily imply a sound industrial policy, the growth of iron and steel was spectacular. In fact, the production of steel ingots was only 500,000 tons in 1946 just after the War. Japan's production then grew rapidly, surpassing that of West Germany in 1964, and thereby becoming second only to the USA. Production reached 100 million tons in 1971 and was higher than that of the USA in 1980. In the export market, Japan had already attained the strongest competitiveness in the 1960s. At the present time, NIEs (Newly Industrializing Economies) such as South Korea and Taiwan are catching up with Japan in terms of international competitiveness, but Japan may still be considered the leader if quality as well as price is taken into account.

Was this industry the object of a targeting policy? Let us look at its progress since the War. Along with the end of tight legal control of the economy, most direct economic regulations had been abolished by *c.*1950. The price control of finished steel was terminated in 1950 by directive of GHQ, followed by pig-iron in 1951. At the same time, MITI devised a policy entitled 'On the Reduction of the Price of Iron and Steel Products' in May 1951, subject to a report from the Industrial Rationalization Council. The policy aimed at the reduction of Japan's high domestic steel prices to the international price level through an energetic rationalization, the aim being to achieve international competitiveness and to supply cheap steel to other industries such as shipbuilding, machinery, and so on. In accordance with MITI's policy, the Industrial Rationalization Council published a further report on the rationalization of the iron and steel industry in February 1952. This report, entitled 'The First Rationalization Plan', covered the three years 1951–3, but was extended to 1955, thus becoming a five-year plan. Steel firms already had a 'go-go' attitude towards investment partly because of the Korean War which broke out in 1950. MITI co-ordinated these vigorous investment intentions, which were based on a forecast of long-term demand growth. As a result of this rationalization, a trimming of costs was achieved—14 per cent in the pig-iron sector, 12 per cent in steel. The fund from the Development Bank was instrumental in this successful rationalization. Following the first five-year plan, the second (1956–60) and third (1961–5) plans were implemented. With the first, MITI's guidance was relatively strong in determining the size and type of investment for each firm, but afterwards private-sector initiatives increased in importance over time. Eventually, a fourth plan became unnecessary, and was not introduced. However, throughout the whole period, and especially before the liberalization of iron and steel products in 1961, MITI was able to use the Foreign Exchange Act effectively to control the import of raw materials and the introduction of new technology such as LD converters, the continuous-casting process, and hot-strip mills. [29]

The iron and steel industry, which was not well established in the late 1940s, became one of Japan's major exporting industries in the 1960s. Many scholars have thus argued that this was the typical product of MITI's targeting policy. None the less, the truth is not quite so clear-cut since in the early 1950s MITI had not necessarily thought that this industry would grow to become a major exporting industry. On the contrary, a pessimistic feeling was predominant as the technical gap between the advanced steel-producing countries and Japan was so tremendous that it was thought to be impossible to draw level with them. In fact, MITI's view on the future of the industry, expressed in the 'New Export Programme' in September 1954, was that the steel industry was not suited to exporting. From the outset, however, it is apparent that MITI tried to foster the industry as the basis for other industries such as machinery, which was expected to grow into a major exporting industry. In that sense, it would be not too much to say that it was the object of a targeting policy.[30]

The relationship between MITI and the steel firms was not altogether smooth. MITI wanted to exert a tight control over the industry, but the firms, which had experienced the pre-war control associations, did not desire it. They simply wanted the freedom to form *voluntary* cartels to suppress cut-throat price competition, and consequently they disliked the Fair Trade Commission (Kosei Torihiki Iinkai) which was established in the American fashion after the War. Sometimes the interests of MITI and the firms were in accord, at other times they were not. To give a few examples, a government bill entitled 'The Rationalization of the Iron and Steel Industry', submitted in August 1949, contained a clause giving MITI the authority to authorize new equipment investment and the exemption of cartels formed in the industry from the Anti-monopoly Act. The steel firms were in favour of the exemption, but felt that MITI would have too strong a regulatory power. Consequently, the bill was not passed. In 1956, when a 'Bill to Stabilize the Supply and Demand of Steel Products' (Tekko Jukyu Antei Hoan) was discussed in an office of MITI, the Heavy Industries Bureau (Jukogyo Kyoku), the steel firms objected on the grounds that the bill would give MITI the power to order the formation of *compulsory* cartels.[31]

Needless to say, there were also examples of co-operation, for example in the adoption of LD converters. This revolutionary process for steel-making was invented in Austria in 1952. To obtain the patent, two companies, Nippon Kokan (NKK) and Yawata Steel competed. MITI was afraid that the rivalry between Japanese firms would make royalties higher, so it intervened in the negotiation for the patent. Due to its mediation, NKK became the sole licensee, and Yawata and other Japanese steel firms sublicensees, with cheap royalties. As a result, NKK's royalties to the Austrian company remained relatively low, and the Japanese steel industry as a whole benefited from MITI's intervention. It is quite surprising to learn that MITI's officers went all the way to Austria with the NKK negotiation team to back them up. Furthermore, a joint technical research association for stimulating the wider use of the process was set up thanks to MITI's influence over Japanese steel firms.[32] The research association was important in securing the improvement of the process.

The following example is more complicated. By a GHQ directive the Japan Steel Corporation was divided into Yawata Steel and Fuji Steel in April 1950. This division epitomized an American-style competitive policy. Before the War, only two integrated iron and steel firms were operating in Japan. GHQ attempted to make the industry more competitive in accordance with an anti-trust policy. But until then the Japan Steel Corporation was a state-owned firm, though a joint-stock company. Accordingly, the firm had a responsibility more or less to supply pig-iron to non-integrated firms. But as a result of the division, two newly created, purely private firms appeared as serious rivals of the non-integrated firms. One such non-integrated company, Kawasaki Steel, which was separated from Kawasaki Heavy Industries in August of the same year, started the construction of a new integrated works in Chiba near Tokyo in the following February. This project was so ambitious—the investment for it was estimated at 16.3 billion yen (in comparison with the company's existing capital of 4.9 billion yen)— that the reaction of the financial sector such as the Bank of Japan was basically negative. Within MITI as a whole there was a considerable debate

about the Kawasaki project.³³ Some of the young section managers supported this project, but top bureaucrats, including the Director of MITI,
were against. The Director apparently objected to it because the mainstream
powers in the industry felt that a gigantic, modern integrated works would
encourage over-production and had lobbied the government accordingly.
However, it would be incorrect to state that MITI opposed the project, since
the younger bureaucrats supported it and such section managers usually had
the actual decision-making power. MITI's permission was eventually
granted in February 1952.³⁴ This move by Kawasaki stimulated other steel
firms so that Sumitomo Kinzoku (Metals) and Kobe Seiko (Steels) followed
suit in building new integrated steel works. In this way, encouraged by
GHQ's anti-trust policy as a detonating fuse, and MITI's semi-positive
support, the Japanese steel industry acquired a very competitive structure,
with a 'Big Six' (Yawata, Fuji, Kawasaki, NKK, Sumitomo, and Kobe).

Another well-known example concerning the relationship of MITI and
a steel firm was the Sumitomo Metals incident. A sharp antagonism
between MITI and Sumitomo Metals developed in 1965. At this time, the
steel industry was in the depth of a depression. For that reason, MITI
decided on a reduction of steel production, following an agreement among
the major steel companies including Sumitomo. The reduction was a
uniform one of 10 per cent for every steel company based on prior production. But this decision was advantageous to the older firms, and newer
firms such as Sumitomo and Kawasaki were critical of it. Sumitomo wanted
to change the reduction allocation on the basis of exports and more recent
performance and created an unusual antagonism with MITI. The decision,
known as 'administrative guidance' (gyosei shido), in fact 'administrative
directive', had no legal force, but it was very difficult to resist or decline this
kind of 'guidance'. In Japan, a maverick was hard to live with. MITI took
its revenge by curtailing the import allocation of coal which was indispensable for production, although the allocation was originally intended to
protect the domestic coal industry, with its low productivity, from overseas
competition. On the other hand, the mainstream and long-established firms
such as Yawata and Fuji supported MITI's decision since they considered
it profitable to keep order in the industry. Finally, Sumitomo agreed to co-
operation after persuasion by companies such as Kawasaki.³⁵

How should we interpret the Sumitomo incident? To regard it as a simple
confrontation between MITI and private firms would be wide of the mark.
The tripartite antagonism between MITI, the mainstream firms, and a maverick is a more accurate representation of the facts. If order in an industry
was threatened, the mainstream firms tended to appeal to MITI, and a maverick was compelled to succumb to MITI's intentions. Therefore, a simple
dichotomy between government and business is not very useful to an understanding of the Japanese situation. Rather, the notion of a tripartite relationship is conducive to a more accurate understanding.³⁶

From a different angle, however, this incident seems to symbolize the weakening of MITI's power as contrasted with the increase in the strength of private firms, because this incident created an unusual social confusion, aside from the fact that Sumitomo Metals was a leading member company of the Sumitomo group, one of the most influential of the old *zaibatsu*. Shortly after this incident, steel industry leaders began to emphasize the necessity of mergers. Exposed to the growing pressures of trade and capital liberalization, they called for merger in order to strengthen international competitiveness. MITI supported the idea, and in the event a merger between Yawata and Fuji, the first and second largest companies, became a reality in 1970 (a policy which would never have been allowed in the USA). The new firm was named the New Japan Steel Corporation, the world's largest steel company. At first the Fair Trade Commission took a tough stance over the merger, but it ultimately accepted it under pressure from the government. This was a sort of 'national champion' policy which is thought to have led to the stagnation of the Japanese steel industry. As Michael Porter has noted, a national champion policy tends to lead to failure.[37] Shortly afterwards, ironically, the growth of the Japanese steel industry ended, the statistics showing the peak of steel output in 1973.

To sum up, it is fair to say that the rapid growth of the steel industry in the 1950s and 1960s was mainly due to the on-going drive of private firms, but on top of this, MITI's policy and role, embracing the Development Bank, which was able to utilize the funds of fiscal investment and loan which amounted to about half of the general budget, were substantially conducive to the development. Basically MITI was the co-ordinator of private interests and the supplier of information and guidance, not the almighty director. By acting in this way, MITI contributed to lessen the ups and downs of the industry and served to lead the industry along a long-term growth path.

The Automobile Industry

As with the iron and steel industry, the Japanese automobile industry grew rapidly from an insignificant position to become one of the major industries with strong competitiveness. In 1980 the number of cars produced in Japan outran that of the USA, making Japan the largest automobile-producing country. But oddly enough, the industrial policy of restructuring the industry largely failed and MITI's policy of preventing new entrants was frustrated also. In the pre-war period, the government tried to exert a strong control over the industry by passing the Automobile Manufacturing Industry Act (Jidosha Seizo Jigyo Ho) in 1936, which aimed to restrict the number of automobile firms to only two, Toyota and Nissan. Accordingly, in the late 1940s there were still only a handful of automobile companies.[38] But later on, new firms entered the industry, resulting in eleven firms altogether, despite MITI's policy of restricting new entrants in order to secure economies of scale. Why did new entrants emerge in spite of MITI's intentions?

In the automobile industry, there were three notorious failures or unsuccessful efforts by MITI. In 1955 MITI planned the expansion of the automobile industry, announcing the 'National Car Plan'. This aimed at designing a standard car like Volkswagen in Germany and selecting *only one* firm to manufacture the car, enabling it to secure full economies of scale. However, this plan encountered vehement opposition from the automobile manufacturers, each fearing to be ruled out. The trade association, the Japan Automobile Association, formally stated its objection to MITI's plan, though such clear dissent was quite unusual. Consequently, the plan was discarded. This case is from time-to-time recalled as an absurd strategy by MITI's officials, although some have argued that it had the beneficial effect of initiating car standardization.[39]

The next episode was the 'Grouping Plan', announced a little later in 1961. According to this plan, the industry was to be restructured into three groups, the mass-produced type, the special type, and the very small type. Each group was to have two or three firms. The most important group was the mass-produced type. Toyota and Nissan were in favour of the plan because it was quite probable that both firms would have been chosen as members of the group. However, other firms were insistent that the plan should be abandoned. In the end, the plan was never realized. The third example was MITI's enthusiastic support for mergers in order to realize economies of scale. In the later period several promotions of this kind were made. Some mergers succeeded under MITI's guidance, such as Nissan and Prince Automobile in 1966. However, the Honda case is well known as an unfortunate example. In 1963 Honda, which had established its reputation in the motor-cycle market, expressed its intention to enter the automobile market. Honda's head at the time, Soichiro Honda, a legendary entrepreneur, vehemently confronted a MITI official, who was also a famous bureaucrat, Shigeru Sahashi. Sahashi tried to persuade Honda not to enter the automobile market, but the latter was so stubborn that he refused to accept MITI's guidance. As this case exemplified, MITI was unable to restrain a new entrant, and there were others as well—Suzuki in 1955, Daihatsu in 1957, Fuji in 1958, Matsuda in 1960. Consequently, the industry came to have a very competitive structure of eleven firms including bus and truck manufacturers.[40]

On the other hand, there were successes in two areas, that is, the protection of the industry from overseas firms in the import of products and capital. In this industry, unlike steel, foreign companies, with their advantage in quality and price, were a serious threat to Japanese manufacturers. MITI therefore erected a high barrier to foreign manufacturers through the Foreign Exchange Act and the Foreign Capital Act. Thanks to this protection, Japanese automobile firms had an opportunity to invest in equipment and to strengthen their competitiveness. On account of foreign pressure, the liberalization of both products and capital became a critical issue. The import of passenger vehicles was liberalized in 1965, but that of engines, i.e. the key components, was only achieved in 1972. Even after that, high tariffs on imported cars were levied, in spite of the fact that the export proportion of total Japanese production was well over 20 per cent in 1970. The liberalization of capital was effected in 1971. However, Japanese firms had established an unassailable position by then so that foreign companies found it very difficult to enter Japan's market. Taken altogether, it is evident that Japanese automobile firms drew many benefits from MITI's protectionist policy. Yet it should be noted that these measures were destined to be temporary, and all automobile firms faced pressure sooner or later when they had to compete with foreign firms in the Japanese market. To survive this challenge, they had to invest in plant modernization.

Another field where MITI's policy succeeded was in the automobile-parts industry. The Japanese vertical *Keiretsu* is well known for its multilayered structure, putting assemblers on top of a pyramid of component-makers, usually subsidiaries, and associated firms. Thanks to the Temporary Measures Act for the Promotion of the Machinery Industry (Kishin Ho) in 1956, the components industry enjoyed generous subsidies and tax benefits in comparison with assemblers. It is a characteristic of Japan that there have been, and are even today, a host of medium- and small-sized firms. In general terms, they were liable to be short of funds and suitable information and knowledge. MITI provided funds through tax allowances and subsidies, and information through the Industrial Rationalization Council (since 1964, the Industry Structure Council) which was, as mentioned before, the advisory council to MITI. Components-makers were more or less able to enjoy economies of scale by increasing their size under this act.[41]

To sum up, apart from protectionism and the components industry, which received substantial help from MITI, the Japanese automobile industry, and in particular assemblers, benefited little from MITI's policy; just on that account, we may say that the automobile industry was able to achieve international competitiveness through the fierce *domestic* rivalry among eleven automobile firms, a factor emphasized by Michael Porter as critical to the creation of competitive advantage. If MITI's policy had been successful, it would have damaged the industry's competitive advantage. A policy designed to 'eliminate domestic competition' or 'the national champion theory' was obviously harmful for industrial development when an industry was growing. It is likely that 'Industries that ignore this government "assistance" succeed, while those that rest on it drag down national productivity.'[42] The experience of the Japanese automobile industry clearly demonstrates this. Ironically, just as British industrial policy toward the automobile industry succeeded in producing a national champion—British

Leyland—the industry lost international competitiveness, in spite of the fact that the industry had foreign automobile firms like British Ford and Vauxhall.[43]

The Electronics Industry (Computers and Semiconductors)

Many scholars have argued that the electronics industry was a case in point of success via MITI's policies. But Daniel Okimoto has insisted that whereas Japanese industrial policy was helpful in advancing the steel industry, it did not contribute to high-tech industry very much. Rather, market forces were the price factor. In contrast with the steel industry, where MITI co-ordinated investment and prices, there was no clear co-ordination of such elements in the electronics industry.[44] However, MITI provided a variety of generous measures to promote the electronics industry, which were rarely seen in other industries.

In fact, Japan's share of high-tech exports, calculated across thirteen OECD countries, increased from 13 per cent in 1970 to 21 per cent in 1990. In contrast, that of the USA fell from 31 to 26 per cent over the same period. Again, with regard to the import penetration ratios of high-tech products, while that of Japan remained at the same level (5 per cent) between 1970 and 1989, that of the USA rose sharply from 4 to 18 per cent over the same period. The situation was similar with Western European countries.[45] This makes it clear that Japan's high-tech industries, and especially the electronics industry, stepped up their competitive advantage. This may not naturally lead to the conclusion that industrial policy was instrumental in the industry's rapid expansion, but it could still be the major factor. So, let us examine how Japan's high-tech industry developed, or, to put it another way, how deeply industrial policy affected the development.

The Japanese government identified at an early stage the strategic importance of the electronics industry, compared with France, West Germany, and the UK. These countries had an industrial policy to promote the industry in the late 1960s, but Japan had a Temporary Measures Act for the Promotion of the Electronics Industry (Denshin Ho) as early as 1957.[46] The law provided a favourable impetus to an industry where a number of firms such as Sony were operating vigorously to introduce advanced technology from the USA and develop new products. Thanks to the law, electronic firms could garner subsidies, tax allowances, special loans from the Development Bank, and moreover, exemption from the Anti-monopoly Act. The impressive exemplar was a digital electronic computer which was the most successful of a list of many research projects undertaken under MITI's guidance. This suggests that the importance of computers was well understood by MITI's officials. In the same year (1957), MITI persuaded the major firms to form a joint R&D project for computers which functioned as a body to receive subsidies from the government. Seven companies participated in the project; Toshiba, Oki, Nippon Denki (NEC), Fujitsu, Hitachi, Hokushin, and Sony. In addition, MITI decided a 'Five Year Plan for the Promotion of the Electronics Industry'. Its policy was inclined to give weight to industrial electronics; by comparison it played down consumer electronic products such as TV, radio, etc., because emphasis was placed on the needs of 'the nation', not consumers.[47]

The Act, operative for seven years, was renewed in 1964 for a further seven years. In 1971 it was replaced by the Temporary Measures Act for the Promotion of Designated Electronics and Machinery Industries (Kiden Ho). Together with Kishin Ho (Temporary Measures Act for the Promotion of the Machinery Industry), the new act was influenced by the tendency for the machinery and electronics industries to merge. In 1978, when the act lapsed, MITI submitted another new law called the 'Temporary Measures Act for the Promotion of the Machinery and Information Industries' (Kijo Ho). As is evident from its name, the act included the software industry so as to respond to the growing importance of IT. As the above path indicates, MITI's legislative responses kept pace with trends in society, providing varying types of assistance. The reason why it was able to provide appropriate advice and information was that it had bureaucrats called *Gikan* who specialized in natural science. The *Gikan* who worked for MITI's ETL (Electro-Technical Laboratory) were crucial in providing sound information for private companies.[48]

On the other hand, the history of computers in Japan was that of rivalry with IBM, the world-wide computer giant. In the attempt to catch up with IBM, MITI and the electronics firms formed several kinds of association. The joint R&D project for computers, mentioned earlier, aimed at countering the IBM 650 which sold well across the world. In 1962 MITI promoted the Technical Research Association for Computers to counter the IBM 7000 series, a large-sized computer for scientific calculation. Fujitsu, Oki, and NEC took part in this association, which produced a newly designed computer called FONTAC, the starting point for later Japanese mainframes. Next, in 1964, IBM announced System 360, which proved to be a revolutionary innovation in the history of computers. MITI responded by initiating the Very High Performance Computer Development Project in 1967. Once again, in 1970, when IBM announced System 370 using LSI (Large Scale Integration), this provided a shock to MITI and Japanese firms. In the following year MITI attempted to merge the computer-producing companies into two or three firms. As in the automobile industry, this attempt failed because of strong opposition from private interests. As a compromise, however, the firms agreed to constitute three groups which were intended to exchange technical information and conduct joint research. The three groups were: Fujitsu-Hitachi; NEC-Toshiba; and Mitsubishi-Oki. Each group functioned in the main as a technical linkage. Evaluation of this grouping has varied, but some have judged it to be fruit-

ful in elimination over-lapping R&D investment and in improving information exchange.[49]

In 1973 it emerged that IBM was planning the 'Future System', a fact dis-
covered by accident from documents which IBM submitted to a US court.
The plan was to produce one mega chip as the start of a completely new
epoch. Stimulated by this plan, MITI encouraged the five major firms
(Fujitsu, Hitachi, NEC, Toshiba, Mitsubishi) to start a research programme
for VLSI (Very Large Scale Integration). As a result of this initiative, the
Very Large Scale Integrated Circuit Research Association started in 1976.
In the four years 1976–80 70 billion yen was spent on this project, 30 billion
financed by the government and 40 billion from the private sector. The
results were judged to be the most successful even in comparison with parallel projects.[50]

As the above cases show, IBM's position in the computer world was overwhelming. In Western countries, IBM's power was even more well established. IBM's market share in the USA was 71 per cent in money terms in
1970, 57 per cent in France (1971), 62 per cent in West Germany (1971), and
only in the UK was the share lower—at 33 per cent thanks to the then-
successful domestic maker, ICL (1971). In Japan, IBM's share was only 32
per cent in 1970, where the proportion of computers manufactured in Japan
by foreign firms dropped from 93 per cent in 1958 to 43 per cent in 1969.
Likewise, imports fell sharply from 80 per cent in 1959 to 20 per cent in
1968. What is more, Fujitsu surpassed IBM in Japanese sales of all elec-
tronic-information products in 1979, and in the trade in integrated circuits
Japan's exports to the USA in 1980 outran imports from the USA for the
first time. In 1986 Japan's production of integrated circuits surpassed that
of the USA.[51] Why was Japan's amazing growth possible?

Let us begin with the IBM Japan story. IBM Japan was confiscated as an
enemy asset during the War. In 1949 it was re-established as a corporation,
but the Foreign Capital Act of 1950 ensured that IBM Japan could not remit
profits and royalties to its parent company. Unless subsidiaries of foreign
companies were authorized under the Foreign Capital Act, they could not
remit overseas. Such firms were called yen-based firms. The conditions for
authorization were so strict that it was difficult to get authorization except
in such cases where a company could prove that its activity would improve
the trade balance by exports, or where the technology was indispensable
for industrial development. Japan was tough not only in relation to product
imports but also to capital under the control of foreign companies, unlike
some Western countries. Consequently, IBM Japan could not remit royalties and profits. It tried without success to get authorization from 1956
onwards. On the other hand, Japanese firms as users of computers wanted
to use the IBM 650 which was useful for their office modernization. Eventually, MITI and IBM compromised in 1960. IBM Japan provided its patents
to any Japanese firm, in return for which it began to remit royalties (later,

profits) to the parent company and commenced the manufacture of computers in Japan. The price for providing its patents to Japanese firms was a 5 per cent royalty to computers and 1 per cent on components. But the start of manufacturing had to be postponed for two years to enable Japanese firms to go ahead and IBM Japan was obliged to purchase components from Japanese companies as far as possible. IBM, however, opened only basic patents, so that Japanese firms had to get know-how from other sources. Japanese firms contracted with several American companies, for example, Hitachi with RCA, and NEC with Honeywell. In doing so, IBM Japan succeeded in remaining a 100 per cent subsidiary of American IBM, despite MITI's preference for joint ventures with no more than 50 per cent foreign capital.[52] But in general it was difficult to set up a 100 per cent subsidiary. Another large computer maker, Sperry Rand, was compelled to form a joint venture with Oki, and set up Oki-Univac with Oki having a 51 per cent and Sperry Rand a 49 per cent stock-holding in 1963. Through these processes, the Japanese computer industry took off commercially, although original research and development started much earlier.

At a critical time, i.e. the 1960s, MITI took the next step, which was to form the Japan Electronic Computer Corporation (JECC) in 1961. This was a financing company to assist computer firms which were financially weak in comparison with IBM, in obtaining funds to support a rental service. At the time, users were short of money for computers so that leasing was imperative. Since IBM had adopted the rental service in principle, Japanese firms faced a potentially unfavourable situation unless they took it up also. MITI led the way in setting up an institution which could provide the money necessary for the service. JECC comprised seven computer firms, backed by the Development Bank, and this institution was so successful that it expanded the demand for computers, and *pari passu*, manufacturers grew rapidly. Between 1961 and 1981, some 650 billion yen flowed into this institution as government aid. One of the reasons JECC succeeded was that it was a mere rental company and actual marketing relied on producers' efforts. Manufacturers had to obtain orders from users, so competition was not reduced.[53] Another example was the VLSI Research Association, previously mentioned. This organization produced about 1,000 patents which member companies could use freely. Furthermore, it was engaged only in basic and peripheral research on VLSI, not in commercial or applications research. As a consequence, the association did not rule out competition among companies, especially in marketing and applications research.

MITI, together with another government organization, also played a unique role in the semiconductor industry. The Ministry of Communications' Electric Laboratory was dissolved in 1948 and split into the Electro-Technical Laboratory (ETL) of the Industrial Technology Agency under MITI, and the Electrical Communications Laboratory (ECL) of the Telegraph and Telephone Corporation (Dendenkosha). Both ETL and ECL assisted technical development, focusing on basic fields, signalling new directions and disseminating information. On the other hand, the Telegraph and Telephone Corporation itself set a high standard for its purchasing. In particular, the DEX 2 plan (Dendenskosha Electric Exchange) for the telephone system in 1964–9 insisted that the semiconductor makers called the 'Denden Family' (such as Hitachi, Toshiba, NEC, Mitsubishi and Fujitsu) adhered to strict product quality. This high quality demand stepped up the technological level of firms, an example of the importance of upgrading quality by a demanding purchaser, as Porter has pointed out.[54]

On the aspect of finance such as subsidies and tax allowances, there is some disagreement among scholars. Daniel Okimoto held that judging from the sum of total investment, and also in comparison with Europe and the USA, the subsidies in Japan were not unusually high; government funding of plant equipment investment fell from 2.5 per cent in the early 1960s to a mere 0.8 per cent in the later 1970s. However, Marie Anchordoguy gives the following numbers: from 1961 to 1969, estimated subsidies and tax benefits ($132.6 million) were equivalent to 46 per cent of what the private sector was investing in R&D and plant and equipment; if we include government loans, total aid ($542.8 million) was equal to 188 per cent of what the firms were investing. This was 'relatively large in proportion to what the firms were investing'.[55] Consequently it is difficult to reach a clear-cut conclusion on this point.

Needless to say, there were not always success stories. The well-known case is that of the transistor. Sony, which was endeavouring to manufacture transistors, tried to buy the patent from Western Electric of USA. The first payment of several instalments was $25,000. MITI, however, did not give its permission because it could not judge the possibilities of the transistor which was too revolutionary an innovation. Another reason was that Sony was too small and virtually an unknown firm. MITI's officials treated Sony with indifference, revealing strong objections to permitting the use of valuable foreign currencies for the patent. Nevertheless, the then-president, Ibuka, was so stubborn, continuing to lobby MITI officials for six months, that he eventually managed to obtain permission. Morita, the present chairman of Sony, and the author of *Made in Japan*, looked back on the incident and observed: 'MITI has not been the great benefactor of the Japanese electronics industry that some critics seem to think it has'.[56] Taken together, however, it is fair to conclude that industrial policy as a whole was vitally important in expanding the industry.

The Synthetic Fibre Industry

Lastly, let us take a brief glance at the synthetic fibre industry for a better understanding of the competition-oriented character of Japanese industrial policy. In the adoption of nylon, MITI showed a precise judgement. In 1951 the Toyo Rayon Company, then the leading synthetic fibre in Japan, wanted to introduce nylon technology from Du Pont of America. But the patent royalties were so exorbitantly expensive that the company had to obtain MITI's tough permission. At that time, Toyo Rayon's paid-up capital (shi-honkin) was 705 million yen, yet royalties amounted to 1.08 billion yen (3 million dollars). Toyo Rayon was supposed to pay the sum by instalment (the first payment was $500,000). MITI, which judged the technology to be very significant for the Japanese economy, supported the firm by means of tax allowances, along with permission to use foreign currencies. Taxes on profits were waived completely between 1951 and 1958 under the Tax Exemption System of Important Commodities (Juyo Bussan Menzei Seido). To benefit from this system, firms had to achieve profits, otherwise they were not able to derive any gains at all. In fact, Toyo Rayon made its first profits in 1954, and very soon the amounts became enormous, all tax-free. The then-president of the firm, Tashiro, judged MITI's policy for synthetic fibres as 'unprecedentedly excellent'. On account of the paucity of nylon, a great number of dealers came to the head office of Toyo Rayon to buy nylon, and because of this Toyo Rayon was called 'Muromachi MITI' named after the head office's address.[57] Toyo Rayon was a substantively large firm and a leading member of big *zaibatsu*, Mitsui. Although the *zaibatsu* had been dissolved, the conglomerate still retained great prestige and therefore was in a favourable position to get permission to use foreign currencies. In contrast, Sony was a negligible firm in those days. It is probable that this difference in size accounted for the differing response from MITI.

Conclusion

In this chapter we have analysed industrial policy in a number of industries which experienced rapid growth in the post-war period. Of the three industries examined in detail, it would be safe to say that the automobile industry benefited least from government policy, the electronics industry benefited most, and the iron and steel industry fell in between. Here, we summarize some of the overall characteristics of industrial policy.

First, the regulation in Japanese industrial policy was not basically tight—in other words, it was an 'arm's-length regulation', respecting the initiative of the private sector. Because of pre-war experience, a direct and tight control by the government was not favoured by private firms, and in addition its defects were accepted by some bureaucrats, whereas free competition, which was believed to lead to 'excessive competition', was not welcomed either. Excessive competition was very often deplored by industrialists. The outcome was that they preferred voluntary cartels which were effective in excluding outsiders including foreign companies. From time to time they took advantage of the government's help to suppress new entries and to maintain stability in the industry, indirectly putting pressure on a maverick. To list only a few, the Idemitsu Oil, Bijikon (Business Computers, Inc), and Lions Oil cases are well known,[58] together with Sumitomo Metals which has been dealt with above. Needless to say, by rebuffing the pressure of MITI and the mainstream firms, there were successful new entrants such as Honda Automobile.[59] These episodes prove that a simple dichotomy between government and business is not adequate enough to explain the Japanese business situation. Focusing on the tripartite relationship of government, mainstream firms, and mavericks provides deeper understanding.

Second, the relationship between trade associations and the government was enhanced by the intervention of numerous councils. This structure helped to interconnect the government with private firms through bilateral communication, not via simple top-down commands. As a result, various plans were made in councils, which took into account the expectations of the private sectors. By the same token, the personal interaction of bureaucrats and businessmen was activated. Put differently, government as the 'third hand' provided an influence not merely to firms directly, but also to intermediate organizations such as trade associations, making use of councils which included representative persons from the business world, in addition to academics.

Third, there were various means for funding, such as subsidies, tax benefits, special loans from the Development Bank, and loan guarantees from the government. In particular, the tax exemption system on profits was very effective in stimulating corporate incentives.

Fourth, varying types of research associations were conducive to technical development, specifically in the electronics industry. With the support of MITI, such associations were able to gain exemption from the anti-trust act, and these associations did not usually reduce competition among firms because their main purpose was to develop basic or peripheral R&D, leaving firms to compete in marketing and applications of R&D.

Fifth, in organizing the above technical associations, the judgement of MITI itself was important in the sense that a minimum ability in evaluation was required. Otherwise it was quite difficult to suggest which direction of technological development would be promising. Fortunately, there were two organizations in the electronics industry such as ETL and ECL. These served to advise on the rough path for future development.

Sixth, the exacting nature of government purchasing was helpful in securing quality improvement in automobiles, computers, and other communication equipment, as shown in the DEX 2 plan.

Seventh, the strong protectionism in trade and capital investment alike succeeded in defending the domestic market. And because such protective policies invariably presumed that liberalization of trade and capital was inevitable, they provided an effective pressure on domestic makers. Yet the success of protectionism *per se* stimulated the dissatisfaction of foreign countries and provoked a demand to open the Japanese market, which led to trade and investment friction, inclusive of non-tariff barriers.

Eighth, as in the protective policies, the domestic laws to foster manufacturing industries in most cases had a time limit, as demonstrated by the inclusion of the word 'temporary' in many of their titles. This time limit also provided another pressure on firms to modernize their plants and improve products.

Finally, in prosecuting these policies, administrative authorities were, relatively speaking, immune from political lobbying and could keep a political independence. This was due to the historical tradition of a high prestige for élite bureaucrats. This kind of tradition was deeply rooted in Japanese policy-making, probably analogous to French bureaucracy. Politically good or bad, the conservative party (Liberal Democratic Party) continued to hold power in the Diet for about forty years, which produced political stability. In this regard, the British political situation was quite different, and political power changed hands frequently. It is certain that the continuity in Japan contributed to the increased effectiveness of industrial policy.

Taken all together, these factors contributed to the conditions under which industrial policy functioned well.

Returning to the first question—did market forces or industrial policy play the major role in accelerating industrial development—it does not seem to make sense to raise the question in this way. Rather, how were market forces and industrial policy combined would be the right question. In that sense, it is quite certain that Japanese industrial policy served to activate market forces, not to undermine them. To paraphrase this, whether an industrial policy is good or not, is the crucial matter. But what, then, is good industrial policy? It would be a policy which promotes competition among firms. A mix of market forces and industrial policy, not a simple dichotomy, should be judged from the viewpoint of its stimulating competition. Above all, to help create several rival firms in an industry and to facilitate competition on *equal* terms was of vital importance to enhance international competitiveness. It is natural that the roles of government may be both positive and negative. In Porter's words, 'governments do not control national competitive advantage; they can only influence it'.[60] Not unlike other countries' experience, the history of Japanese industrial policy is a chequered one as shown in the failure of the petrochemical industry[61] and other industries, but it seems that it was more effective than some advanced countries in the sense of *competition-promoting policy*, largely because Japan was in the fledgeling state with the potential for rapid growth, facing rising domestic demand and an open world trade system.[62]

Yet as the measures toward IBM Japan reveal, such a protectionist stance would only be allowed when Japan was a backward country and faced a difficult balance of payments situation. As Japan has emerged as a major industrial power with substantive competitive advantage, these kinds of policies have lost ground. Paradoxically, because of the very success of industrial policy, the importance of it is now decreasing. As early as the late 1950s, some foreign countries began to claim that Japan should open its market more widely,[63] and at the moment the liberalization of trade and capital has become the focal point of industrial policy debates. But this is quite another issue.

NOTES

1. Chalmers Johnson, *MITI and the Japanese Miracle* (Stanford, Calif., 1982).
2. On the *Keiretsu*, see T. Kikkawa, 'Kigyo Shudan: the Formation and Function of Enterprise Groups', in E. Abé and R. Fitzgerald (eds.), *The Origins of Japanese Industrial Power* (London, 1995); M. Shimotani, 'The Formation of Distribution *Keiretsu*: The Case of Matsushita Electric', in Abé and Fitzgerald (eds.), *Origins*.
3. The author acquired the term 'the third hand' from a presentation at Hitotsubashi University by Professor Leslie Hannah. According to Hannah, the third hand can embrace an intermediate organization such as a network or group, but I should like to confine its application to the government only. Consequently, my definition is not the same as his.
4. US Department of Commerce, Bureau of International Commerce, *Japan; the Government–Business Relationship* (Washington, DC, 1972).
5. There are many studies of Japanese industrial policy, as the recent work, James E. Vestal, *Planning for Change: Industrial Policy and Japanese Economic Development, 1945–1990* (Oxford, 1993) shows with its comprehensive bibliography. The works by a British scholar, Ronald Dore, *Flexible Rigidities: Industrial Policy and Structural Adjustment in the Japanese Economy, 1970–1980* (London, 1986); and idem, *Taking Japan Seriously: A Confucian Perspective on Leading Economic Issues* (London, 1987) are thought-provoking. For a comparison of Japanese and British industrial policy see Jim Tomlinson, 'British Industrial Policy in a Japanese Mirror: Why no MITI in Britain?', in this volume; Leslie Hannah, 'British Industrial Policy, 1945–1995: Effective but Inefficient Intervention', paper for the conference on European Industrial Policy, Pisa, 20–3 Apr. 1995. I have not attempted a full comparison of both countries' industries policy in this chapter.
6. Patricia O'Brien, 'Industry Structure as a Competitive Advantage: The History of Japan's Post-War Steel Industry', *Business History*, 34/1 (1992), 152, 154–5.
7. C. V. Prestwitz, *Trading Places: How We Allowed Japan to Take the Lead* (New York, 1988).
8. Thomas, K. McCraw, 'America Versus Japan', in idem (ed.), *America Versus Japan* (Boston, 1986).
9. P. H. Trezise, 'Industrial Policy is Not the Major Reason for Japan's Success', *The Brookings Review* (Spring 1983), 13.

10. Karl Zinsmeister, 'MITI Mouse: Japan's Industrial Policy Doesn't Work', *Policy Review*, 64 (Spring 1993), 28.
11. Michael Porter, *The Competitive Advantage of Nations* (London, 1990), 126–8.
12. Alfred D. Chandler, Jr., *Scale and Scope: The Dynamics of Industrial Capitalism* (Cambridge, Mass. 1990), 498.
13. David Friedman, *The Misunderstood Miracle: Industrial Development and Political Change in Japan* (Ithaca, NY, 1988), 3–6. Although Friedman rejects 'the market regulation thesis', it seems to depend on the definition of market forces. He is thinking of the American type of mass production when he uses the words 'market forces', and distinguishes it from the flexible production system whose importance was stressed by M. J. Piore and C. F. Sabel, *The Second Industrial Divide: Possibilities for Prosperity* (New York, 1984). According to Friedman, Japan belongs to the latter type.
14. Yutaka Kosai, 'Kodo Seichoki no Keizai Seisaku' (Economic Policy in the High Growth Economy), in Y. Yasuba and T. Inoki (eds.), *Kodo Seicho, Nihon Keizaishi* (Japanese Economic History), 8 (1989), 252.
15. Keith Smith, *The British Economic Crisis: Its Past and Future* (rev. edn., 1989). 218–19.
16. For the impact of List on Japanese economists and policy-makers, see Charles J. McMillan, 'The State as Economic Engine: Lessons from the Japanese Experience', *Journal of Far Eastern Business*, 1/3 (Spring 1995), 5.
17. Alfred D. Chandler, Jr., *The Visible Hand: The Managerial Revolution in American Business* (Cambridge, Mass., 1977), 1–14.
18. Oliver Williamson, *Markets and Hierarchies: Analysis and Anti-Trust Implications* (New York, 1975).
19. K. Suzumura and M. Okuno, 'Nihon no Sangyo Seisaku: Tenbo to Hyoka' (Industrial Policy of Japan: Perspective and Evaluation), in H. Itami, T. Kagono and M. Itoh (eds.), *Nihon no Kigyo Shisutemu* (Enterprise System of Japan) (Tokyo, 1993), 149–50. See also K. Suzumura, 'Industrial Policy of Japan: Whither Now?', Discussion Paper Series A, No. 246, Institute of Economic Research, Hitotsubashi University (1991), 3–7. M. Itoh, K. Kiyono, M. Okuno-Fujiwara, and K. Suzumura, *Economic Analysis of Industrial Policy* (San Diego, 1991).
20. The author would like to stress this point, considering the recent Japan–US trade conflicts. Managed trade can be allowed under some conditions.
21. Johnson, *Japanese Miracle*, 306.
22. R. Komiya, 'Josho' (Introduction), in R. Komiya, M. Okuno and K. Suzumura (eds.) *Nihon no Sangyo Seisaku* (Industrial Policy of Japan) (Tokyo, 1984), 7.
23. Regarding the Marxist tradition among policy-makers, some have argued that 'Marxists in fact did play a key role in Japanese policy formulation in the immediate post-war period' (Tomlinson, 'British Industrial Policy in a Japanese Mirror'). But it seems that the importance of Marxism's influence should not be overvalued. A *mixture* of various ideologies should be emphasized.
24. T. Okazaki, 'Nihon no Seihu-kigyo kan Kankei' (Business–Government Relationship in Japan), *Soshiki Kagaku* (Organization Science), 26/4 (1993), 120.
25. US Department of Commerce, *Japan*, ch. 4.
26. Suzumura and Okuno, 'Sangyo Seisaku', 162.

27. Y. Miyake, 'Gijutsu Donyu Kyoso' (Competition in Technology Introduction), in Ekonomisuto Henshubu (ed.), *Shogen: Kodo Seichoki no Nihon* (Evidence: Japan in the Age of Rapid Growth) (Tokyo, 1984), 298.
28. Tsusho Sangyo Seisakusi Hensan Iinkai (ed.), *Tsusho Sangyo Seisakushi* (History of Policies in Commerce and Industry), vi (Tokyo, 1992), 473.
29. Ibid. 451; ibid., x (1990), 134–40.
30. S. Yonekura, 'Tekko: Sono Renzokusei to Hirenzokusei (Iron and Steel: Its Continuity and Discontinuity), in S. Yonekawa, K. Shimokawa and H. Yamazaki (eds.), *Sengo Nihon Keieishi* (Business History in Post-War Japan), i (Tokyo, 1991), 305, 312. M. Udagawa and E. Abe, 'Kigyo to Seihu' (Firms and Government), in H. Morikawa and Y. Yonekura (eds.), *Nihon Keieishi* (Japanese Business History), v (Tokyo, 1995), 261–5.
31. *Tsusho Sangyo Seisakushi*, vi. 439–41, 457.
32. Leonard H. Lyon, *How Japan Innovates: A Comparison with the US in the Case of Oxygen Steelmaking* (Boulder, Colo., 1982), ch. 4; interview with Mr Keizo Kojima, an ex-MITI official.
33. S. Yonekura, 'Sengo Nihon Tekkogyo niokeru Kawaski Seitetsu no Kakushinsei' (Innovativeness of Kawasaki Steel in the Japanese Post-War Iron and Steel Industry), *Hitosubashi Ronso*, 90/3 (1983), 396–410.
34. Ibid. 408; Interview with Mr Keizo Kojima; Kazuo Noda, 'Kigyo Seicho no Ketteiteki Shunkan, Kawashaki Seitetsu' (The Decisive Moment of Enterprise Growth, Kawasaki Steel), *Ekonomisuto* (24 Sept. 1963), 74. Noda wrote as follows: 'Kawasaki Steel put to MITI its proposal to build a new steelworks in November 1950, and at the same time announced it publicly. *As expected*, the mainstream steel companies which became aware of Kawasaki Steel's plan lobbied MITI, and, explicitly and tacitly, began impeding the plan' (my italics).
35. *Tsusho Sangyo Seisakushi*, x. 150–4.
36. As regards the drive of large private firms, Dennis J. Encarnation interestingly underlined the importance of Japanese oligopolists rather than MITI: 'The government could limit foreign ownership, but it could not deny foreign access to the local market without the support of Japanese oligopolists . . . these Japanese oligopolists pressured MITI to approve direct investment in Japan by Texas Instruments' (D. J. Encarnation, *Rivals Beyond Trade: America versus Japan in Global Competition* (Ithaca, NY, 1992), 69, 75. Oligopolists in his terms are similar to my 'mainstream firms'; hence his view and mine coincide in affirming that large firms have the final say.
37. Porter, *Competitive Advantage*, 620.
38. On pre-war conditions in the Japanese automobile industry see M. Udagawa, 'Business Management and Foreign-Affiliated Companies', in T. Yuzawa and M. Udagawa (eds.), *Foreign Business in Japan before World War II* (Tokto, 1990).
39. Motoshige Ito, 'Onshitsu no nakadeno Seicho Kyoso: Sangyo Seisaku no Motarashita Mono' (Growth Competition in a Hothouse: What Industrial Policy Brought About), in H. Itami, T. Kagono, T. Kobayashi, K. Sakakibara, and M. Itoh (eds.), *Kyoso to Kakushin: Jidosha Sangyo no Kigyo Seicho* (Competition and Innovation: Enterprise Growth in the Automobile Industry) (Tokyo, 1988), 188.
40. Ibid.
41. *Tshuso Sangyo Seisaku*, vi.

42. Porter, *Competitive Advantage*, 620.
43. In my view, there are two types of competition. One is 'visible competition' which means domestic rivalry where competing firms know each other's manufacturing process, investment policy, and R&D activities more or less. The other is 'invisible competition', which is competition between domestic firms and imported products. The domestic firms may know the products themselves but can scarcely know the manufacturing process or those companies' strategy concerning investment or R&D activities. The competition between multinationals and domestic firms falls into an intermediate category as 'semi-visible competition'. Multinationals may have a substantive effect on domestic firms in labour management, production techniques, and management methods as American and Japanese multinationals did in Britain, but the effect might be limited. It seems that the British automobile industry could not produce effective domestic rivalry, which led to its relatively weak competitiveness.
44. Daniel Okimoto, *Between MITI and the Market: Japanese Industrial Policy for High Technology* (Stanford, Calif., 1989), 57. See also Marie Anchordoguy, 'Mastering the Market: Japanese Government Targeting of the Computer Industry', *International Organisation*, 42/3 (1988).
45. *Financial Times*, 11 July 1994.
46. Kiyoshi Nakamura, 'Sangyo Seisaku to Computer Sangyo' (Industrial Policy and the Computer Industry), in H. Morikawa (ed.), *Bijinesuman no tameno Sengo Keisishi Nyumon* (The Post-War Business History for Businessmen) (Tokyo, 1992), 210–16.
47. *Tsusho Sangyo Seisakushi*, vi. 588–612.
48. Ibid., x. 267–8, xiv. 334–41.
49. Nakamura, 'Sangyo Seisaku'.
50. Yutaka Aida, *Denshi Rikkoku Nihon no Jijoden, Kanketsu Hen* (Autobiography of Electronic Japan), iv (Tokyo, 1992), 14–23, esp. p. 21.
51. Kazuichi Sakamoto, *Computer Sangyo* (The Computer Industry) (Tokyo, 1992), 80–97; Anchordoguy, 'Mastering in Market', 516.
52. IBM Japan, *Nihon IBM 50 Nenshi* (A Fifty-Year History of IBM Japan) (Tokyo, 1988), 158–62; Anchordoguy, 'Mastering the Market', 516; IBM Japan, *Joho Shori Sangyo Nenpyo* (Chronology of the Information Processing Industry) (Tokyo, 1988), 76.
53. Anchordoguy, 'Mastering the Market', 517–20, Sakamoto, 'Computer Sangyo', 62–4.
54. Porter, *Competitive Advantage*, 644–5.
55. Okimoto, *Between MITI*, 76–85; Anchordoguy, 'Mastering the Market', 523.
56. Akio Morita, *Made in Japan: Akio Morita and SONY* (London, 1987), 65–6.
57. Hidemasa Morikawa (ed.), *Sengo Sangyoshi eno Shogen*, 2 (Evidence For the Post-War Industrial History), ii (Tokyo, 1977), 159–61. In this case, a group manager of MITI played an important role in prompting the introduction of nylon. See Tsuneo Suzuki, 'Sengo Gata Sangyo Seisaku no Seiritsu' (The Rise of The Post-War Industrial Policy Pattern), in H. Yamazaki and T. Kikkawa (eds.), *Nihon Keieishi*, iv (Tokyo, 1995), 302–8.
58. For Idemitsu Oil see Yoshiki Ogawa, 'Sekiyu Sangyo' (The Petroleum Industry), in Institute for Japan Energy Economy (ed.), *Sengo Enerugi Sangyoshi* (History of the Post-War Energy Industry) (Tokyo, 1986), 156–60: for Bijikon,

Aida, *Denshi Rikkoku Nihon*, iii. 175–80, for Lions Oil, *Nihon Keizai Shinbun* (Japan Economic Times), 28 Dec. 1984.

59. Honda embarked on the production of small-sized cars in 1963 to escape a law which was intended to provide tight MITI regulation of specific industries including the automobile industry. If the law had been passed, it would have made it extremely difficult to enter the automobile industry. However, the law, *Tokutei Sangyo Shinko Rinji Sochi Ho* (the Temporary Measures Act for the Promotion of Designated Industries) was not passed in the Diet on account of strong objection by the business world.

60. Porter, *Competitive Advantage*, 617.

61. For the failure of MITI's policy in the petrochemical industry, see Takeo Kikkawa, 'Enterprise Groups, Industry Associations, and Government: the Case of the Petrochemical Industry in Japan', *Business History*, 37/3 (1995), 89–110.

62. Boltho positively evaluates MITI's role in developing industry. Andrea Boltho, 'Was Japan's Industrial Policy Successful?', *Cambridge Journal of Economics*, 9 (1985), 199.

63. For the historical process and its implications for the liberalization of capital investment in Japan, see D. J. Encarnation and M. Mason, 'Neither MITI nor America: The Political Economy of Capital Liberalisation in Japan', *International Organisation*, 44/1 (1990), 31, 50–1.

3   British Industrial Policy in a Japanese Mirror: *Why no MITI in Britain?*

JIM TOMLINSON

'The very intimate and manifold connections at all levels between Government and industry are a most important factor in the attitudes and policies of both.'[1]

'We do not need to choose between cartoon images of Japan Inc. or a land of unfettered competition. It is the particular interaction of state and market in Japan that is interesting.'[2]

An almost constant feature of the debate about Britain's industrial decline over the last century has been admiring reference to seemingly superior performance and policy in other countries. The model held out for admiration and emulation has varied significantly over the period. Before World War I it was often Germany, and after an understandable eclipse in mid-century, she came into favour again from the 1960s; in the 1920s and 1950s especially, the US model was commonly deemed attractive. More recently Japan has found favour as the country which has discovered a formula which should perhaps be copied.

As an approach to understanding, let alone rectifying, decline this 'they do things better abroad' approach has had a number of obvious difficulties. First, commentators have often been unable to agree what feature(s) of the foreign economy accounted for the difference in performance, and which therefore it might be helpful for Britain to emulate. Judgements on this issue have been affected by the current concerns of commentators and/or by their theoretical allegiances.[3] Second, it has commonly been pointed out that even if one particular feature could be isolated as having 'caused' a superior performance, it did not follow that such a feature could be grafted on to what might be a wholly alien economic and social situation in Britain.

Despite these pitfalls, the comparative approach to the history of economic policy and performance can yield significant insights, even if the translation of these into policy proposals is best avoided. In this chapter the comparison explored is that between Japanese and British industrial policy in the post-war period, focusing on the period 1945–70. The chapter is essentially about Britain, but uses Japanese experience to try and illuminate features of British policy which might not stand out so clearly if looked at from a purely national perspective.

The chapter makes no attempt to arbitrate the issue of whether Japanese industrial policy has played a key role in Japan's post-war industrial growth, or whether within that policy MITI has been the crucial instrument. Rather it starts from the seemingly incontrovertible points that Japan has had a quite distinct industrial policy in this period, and that MITI has figured largely in that policy, though opinions are divided on the efficacy of both the general policy and MITI's particular contribution.[4]

The English language literature on MITI has suggested a number of features of that institution which would seem to contrast with anything that has happened in Britain. These will provide the 'mirror' to be held up against British experience. As noted above, in looking into that mirror, this paper attempts to avoid a normative approach to British/Japanese differences.

In looking at the contrasts outlined below, it should be emphasized that they may too readily give the impression that everything done in this area in post-war in Japan has been a complete success, whilst the story of Britain is one of unrelieved failure. Such a conclusion should be resisted. Japanese policy and performance has had its failures even within an overall success. Similarly, Britain has made significant economic advances, even if, measured by industrial growth compared with Japan, these have tended to be overshadowed by a sense of overall weakness. To reiterate, the aim here is to note and perhaps explain *differences* rather than offer judgements.

I

At the most general level it seems striking that MITI was part of a 'developmental' state, where government policy was dominated by the objective of industrial growth. Many have noted (and lamented) the absence of precisely such a state in Britain.[5]

Such a difference raises enormous problems of explanation. It could be argued that it arises simply from different starting-points—that Japan in 1945 was a poor and defeated country, which had a strong motive to 'catch up', whilst the gap between itself and the leading industrial countries specially USA offered a clear opportunity to make that 'catch-up' happen. As a late entrant to industrialization, Japan recognized the need for a state role in industrial modernization as most previous 'catching-up' nations had done (France, Germany, Russia for example). Britain after the War, by contrast, it may be argued, was a mature industrial economy that, whilst beset with short-run macroeconomic difficulties, still had an income per head far ahead of most, and could reasonably be regarded as the second most important industrial economy in the world in 1945. Consequently, immediate macroeconomic stabilization was imperative, but the predominant policy concerns were political (e.g. restoring Britain's status as a 'world power') rather than to do with economic expansion.

In short, the difference in policy objectives and apparatuses to pursue these may be explained as part of a 'situational logic' of economic development. But is this adequate? Some qualifications, at least, may be suggested.

First, whilst it was undoubtedly true that, viewed in terms of income per head, as of the late 1940s Britain was close to the top of the league, it is also clear that even in that period there was wide recognition both in and outside government of the gap between US and British achievements, in industry in particular. Second, this recognition, coupled to the compelling short-term need to expand production, led to a range of policy initiatives to raise the productive efficiency of the economy.[6] In the 1940s the answer to the question 'why didn't Britain have a developmental state' is to a significant extent about the *political* problems of mobilizing sufficient support for, and facing down opposition to, such policies of industrial modernization.

In the 1950s the situation was different. The immediate macroeconomic problems of the 1940s did not recur,[7] and economic efficiency and expansion slid down the government policy agenda, only to be clearly revived in the sudden enthusiasm for 'growth' from 1960 onwards. That at least is the conventional story.[8] However, the government archives suggest that recognition of long-term relative economic decline was a persistent if not preeminent issue in government discussions from the early to mid-1950s.[9] The difficulty was that such recognition of decline could not be readily translated into policies to reverse the process. On the one hand there were those who advocated the classic liberal routes to faster growth—free trade abroad, free competition at home—but they did not gain political ascendancy.[10] On the other hand, the non-liberals were generally attached to notions of Empire and the Sterling Area rather than to *dirigiste* programmes for industrial reform. Again, the *political* obstacles within the government to any move to a 'developmental' state appear very strong.

In the 1960s economic growth and efficiency did undoubtedly dominate much of the rhetoric of economic policy. The agenda for growth generated in that decade deserves to be taken rather more seriously than is often the case. In particular, and a point returned to below, it seemed to involve a set of policies which were largely 'market conforming' and pro-competitive. Nevertheless, they faced obvious difficulties.[11] Essentially, under Labour from 1964, the attempts at changes in labour market and technology policy, which were at the heart of the contemporary modernization agenda, were squeezed by the deflation which both preceded and followed the devaluation of the pound in 1967. Commitment to such modernization was compromised by the basically *political* objective of defending the value of the pound and the role of London as a financial centre.

Overall, in looking at Britain's failure to build a 'developmental' state it may be helpful to adhere to the precept 'Away With All Great Arches'.[12] Too often, analysis of this issue has fallen back on grand sweeps of largely sociological history, rather than on the rather 'lower' level issues of political ideology and organization, which would seem able to give a surer purchase on the problems of the period.

In this light it is instructive to read Okimoto's highly persuasive account of the *political* conditions for MITI's role.[13] As he points out, a key condition for that role has not just been the predominance of one political party, the LDP, but that this party, courting its (gerrymandered) constituencies, especially in the rural and suburban areas, was able to arrive at a division of labour with MITI. Whilst the LDP has been able to feed the demands of its constituencies in agriculture and low-tech industry, MITI has been left free of all that log-rolling activity to focus its attention on the larger-scale, high-tech, internationally competitive sectors. So one-party rule has not prevented MITI from being in a position to pursue the economic growth which has in turn enabled that party to pursue its successful clientist politics.

II

The role of MITI in Japan has been in the context of quite particular political relations between government and employers. This relationship has been amicable and co-operative to an extent which can be exaggerated, but which would certainly seem far greater than in Britain. Partly, and obviously enough, this relationship has been grounded on the predominance of the LDP, so that the question of the relationship between employers and other political parties has not been raised. In Britain, by contrast, the 1945–70 period saw alternation in government between the dominant political parties. But even allowing for this, it does seem striking the extent to which in Britain employers have been politicized, such that they have to a large extent acted in alliance with one political party, the Conservatives, at least when the Labour party has been in power.

Such a high level of political commitment of employers is evident in the 1940s, under the Attlee Government. Despite the assertions of Blank, the Federation of British Industries was *not* in practice co-operative with the government, but in fact mobilized its members against the government on a number of key policy issues.[14] It may be argued that this is unsurprising, given that the Attlee Government nationalized 20 per cent of British industry. But against this assumption must be weighed: (1) these nationalizations could reasonably be seen as a way of 'socializing losses' and supplying cheap electricity, coal, and transport to the privately owned sector; (2) not only was the Attlee government strongly rhetorically committed to industrial efficiency, but its policies allowed the private sector to make 'frightfully high profits' in the late 1940s conditions of buoyant demand.[15]

The anti-Labour position of British business largely remains to be investigated. It may be that in the 1960s it was less pronounced than in the 1940s, though the picture revealed by the archives when they become available may, like that for the 1940s, differ significantly from that suggested by public pronouncements. In any event, Labour has often been a 'disappointed suitor' of employers and it would be useful to know why this has been so.[16] Has it, for example, reflected the lack of knowledge of industry on the part of Labour ministers, the internal politics of employers organizations, or what?

The amicability of relationships between government and employers in Japan has not only involved political parties, but also ministries, notably in the current context, MITI. This is not to say that the relationship between that body and Japanese employers has always been amicable; there have been important differences, and on some issues employers have clearly not done as MITI hoped. A famous example is the car manufacturers' development of links with US multinationals at variance with the strategy of MITI.[17] But what is interesting in this and other examples of divergence between MITI and employers is that the differences were not 'politicized', they were not made into arguments of *principle* about the role of government in the economy.[18] In contrast, discussion of industrial policy in Britain has always tended to become generalized into an ideological/political dispute, thus hampering effectiveness and continuity in such policy. The Japanese system of 'administrative guidance'[19] requires 'high trust' relations, with employers willing to treat government bodies as disinterested agents of public policy (even if they think the policy misguided). Such relations were little apparent in the post-war decades in Britain.

III

MITI was at the peak of its power in the 1950s and 1960s.[20] Its role in that period depended in part on its control of Japan's commercial policy in the period before Japan liberalized much of its foreign trade in the 1970s.[21] What is striking in Japanese policy in this period of continuing trade controls is the extent to which that country used commercial policy as an instrument of industrial policy. Broadly speaking, the pattern of controls and the pattern of eventual liberalization was guided by concerns to sustain and develop Japanese positions in what were deemed the key industries. Whilst external pressure undoubtedly forced liberalization faster than many desired, by and large that liberalization was acceptable because previous commercial policies had helped to secure competitiveness in key sectors.

Britain's history in this area is again in sharp contrast. British trade was, like Japan's, highly controlled in the 1940s, but liberalized more rapidly in the late 1950s and 1960s. But if we examine the debates in the period either of controls or of liberalization what is striking is the extent to which they did *not* link commercial policy to industrial policy.

Under Labour, controls were deemed essential to protect the balance of payments and so to avoid a deflationary response to payments problems. Such liberalization as took place largely reflected pressure from the USA, coupled to a growing realization that such liberalization did not threaten full employment. Policy development on the international economy in this period was *ad hoc*, but what emerges from the overall pattern is the predominance in decision-making of macroeconomic and political concerns. When some Labour ministers became worried about the extent to which liberalization was being pushed, it was because they wanted to hang on to controls for macroeconomic reasons, not because they wanted to sustain particular sectors or build up 'infant industries'.[22]

In the 1950s the same negative conclusion seems appropriate—commercial policy was not seen in the light of industrial development, but in the light of political pressures for liberalization and macroeconomic problems. Also important in the debates of the 1950s was the impact of liberalization on trade relations with the Empire, and the slow pace of liberalization was partly conditioned by considerable worries on this issue, as well as the weakness of the balance of payments.

Of course to some extent trade liberalization in Britain could be offset by other instruments not so widely used in Japan e.g. public procurement. But the point still remains that especially in the period when controls were extensive, in the 1940s and early 1950s, their pattern was seemingly determined in a separate compartment from industrial policy. The only partial exception to this was under Thorneycroft at the Board of Trade in the 1950s who saw liberalization *per se* as an industrial policy i.e. as a source of efficiency stemming from competition.[23] But this was exceptional and *not* the typical policy of Britain in this period.

IV

Part, and arguably a very large part, of MITI's role in its heyday was to formulate and pursue a technology policy. Freeman argues that 'it is clear that a large part of the Japanese success must be attributed to the management of technical change by numerous Japanese enterprises, but this success was related to social and institutional changes promoted and sometimes initiated by MITI, and to the persistent pursuit of long-term strategic goals.'[24]

For Freeman the character of MITI was defined by consistent goals and pragmatic and eclectic means. Those goals were based on a clear perception of the sectors to be privileged at different times. Hence the priority of steel, chemicals, and electricity in the 1950s linked to the idea of fast development of resource-intensive mass- and flow-production technologies. This was followed in the 1960s by a focus on goods characterized by (a) high income elasticities and (b) high productivity potential.

We may say that Japanese policy in this period had a clear perception of 'technological paradigms', also evident in the shift beginning away from energy and material intensive technologies even *before* OPEC I in the early 1970s.

By contrast, policy in Britain lacked any clear sense of technological developments in the *civilian* sector. As is well-known, Britain in the post-war period was not a low spender on R&D, rather its characteristic pattern was high state expenditure compared with the private sector, particularly because of very big spending on defence-related and 'big science' projects.[25] This was a pattern to persist well into the 1960s when for the first time its detrimental effects on civil R&D, especially via the employment of such a large proportion of all trained scientists and technologists, was seriously addressed. (This focus was obviously in part the result of Britain's pursuit of 'world power' status and the military capacity to achieve it.)

The Attlee Government did take seriously the perceived technological deficiencies of British industry, and expanded the DSIR (created 1916) and set up the National Research and Development Corporation especially to encourage the development of inventions and innovations made in the public sector. But these efforts did not amount to a technology *policy*. The Advisory Council on Scientific Policy, also established soon after the War, focused very much on basic research and showed little interest in industrial technology. Again, this only began to change in the 1960s when the level of public expenditure on the military was challenged, and the style of R&D expenditure this had encouraged came to be looked at more critically. How significant the changes of the 1960s were remains a matter of dispute. Organizational change rather than policy formulation seems to have figured highly, though Coopey *et al.* have argued that MinTech's role has been unfairly denigrated by many commentators.[26]

Part of the slow recognition by British policy-makers of the key role of technological development in the civilian sector for economic expansion is undoubtedly due to the pursuit of 'world power' status. Such illusions were only slowly given up—a process perhaps beginning after Suez, but not really having much impact until the late 1960s. The impact of this on the pattern of R&D (as well as on the overall high level of military expenditure) is an old story but also it would seem a broadly accurate one.

However there is perhaps a different angle from which the absence of a civilian-oriented technology policy in Britain can be addressed. Allen notes half-seriously that in Japan the government in the early post-war period did not consult economists about policy because most senior academic economists were Marxists.[27] This meant they turned to administrators whose policy advice was not based on Japan's existing pattern of comparative advantage linked to labour-intensive techniques. Rather it was based on a notion of acquiring *foreign* technologies necessary to achieve high growth and income levels. Others have suggested that Marxists in fact did play a key role in Japanese policy formulation in the immediate post-war period, and that they, in classic Marxist fashion, wanted to emphasize the development of a heavy industrial base. Certainly Japanese industrial policy looks similar to that proposed by Labour governments in Britain rather than the Conservatives.

In looking at British policy in this period it is striking that in so far as economic growth and efficiency were concerns of public policy, the advice available on these issues from economists was very limited. The economic analytics of the time tended to emphasize three routes to efficiency: (i) competition; (ii) economies of scale; (iii) higher investment. Competition will be returned to below, but it is a quite striking feature of the debate about British industrial efficiency, back to at least the 1920s and forward to the 1970s, how much faith was put in scale economies and higher investment. This in part was the economists agenda; before the 'growth-accounting' explosion of the 1960s, it seems to have been generally assumed amongst British economists that the importance of capital accumulation and downward-sloping average cost curves were the main contributions they could make to the striving for greater industrial efficiency. It was only with that growth-accounting work (and the theoretical work which tried to make sense of its results) that technological change came to play a much larger role in economists beliefs about economic growth. This seems to form a striking contrast with the Japanese experience.

The point is not that British economists were in any sense remiss in this regard. The literature on growth was in fact by the 1950s mainly American, and the evolution of the debate was similar in the two countries. But the point is that even in so far as British governments did seek to raise growth, the arguments offered by the economists tended on the whole to play down technological change in comparison with a rather simple 'big is beautiful' approach. It is probably also fair to note that the most growth-oriented governments of this period were Labour, and this kind of approach to growth seems to have been congenial to the Left, a Left, it should be noted, with rather limited knowledge of industry on which to base an alternative diagnosis.

V

To return to the issue of competition. Japanese policy in the 1950s and 1960s may be characterized as 'protection without and competition within'.[28]

Whilst protecting domestic industry from both imports and any influx of multinational corporations (a point returned to below), and putting limits on the anti-trust policies imposed by the US occupation authorities after the War, Japanese policy clearly recognized the benefits of competition. One way of seeing Japanese policy at this time is to compare it to a football league, where the league authorities determine the membership, lay down the rules, and then encourage all the teams to compete as vigorously as possible.[29]

In Britain, by contrast, competition was a problematic issue for public policy, reflecting in part the ambivalence of both major political parties on the issue.

On the Labour side, one of the striking features of its rhetoric in 1945 was the commitment to an anti-monopoly policy, fuelled by the belief that monopoly and restrictionism had damaged economic activity in the 1930s and also underlay the rise of aggressive Right-wing regimes in that decade.[30] In the event little was done to back-up this rhetoric. The 1948 Monopolies and Mergers Act was marginal in its impact, partly because of business opposition, but also because enthusiasm for competition was always problematic for Labour. Whilst hostile to private monopoly, many in Labour's ranks saw the solution to lack of competition as public ownership, not more competition, though this attitude was waning by the late 1940s.[31]

Under the Conservatives after 1951 a similar ambiguity was evident. Whilst some Conservatives were strong believers in competition, others were worried by its consequences for particular groups (e.g. small traders/retailers) and the passing of the 1956 Restrictive Practices Act, creating a Restrictive Practices Court, was the occasion of considerable debate in the Conservative government. The genesis of the Act lay as much in the (unrealized) hopes that a legal body like the RPC would go easier on anti-competitive practices than the Monopoly Commission. Conservative ambivalence on competition continued after 1956, as evidenced by the debate over the abolition of Retail Price Maintenance in the early 1960s.[32]

After 1964, with the return of Labour, policy continued in its ambivalence. Whilst eventually passing a law strengthening the Monopolies Commission in 1968, Labour also pursued a policy of developing 'national champions', where the aim was to create *one* domestic firm for example, International Computers Ltd., or the British Motor Corporation, which could compete internationally. 'Big is beautiful' ideas were not easily meshed with a coherent policy on competition.

VI

One of the characteristics of Japanese industrial policy in the early post-war years was the resistance to entry into the country by foreign multinationals.[33] This policy led to a much lower level of penetration by multinationals (especially, at this time, American multinationals) probably than in any other major industrial countries. Between 1945–60 it has been estimated that foreign investment in production industry was only 2–2.5 per cent of the total of such investment.[34] The policy eventually broke down in the 1960s and 1970s largely because major Japanese companies acted as a powerful lobby for a relaxation.

This policy forms a striking contrast to the British experience where, irrespective of political colours, successive governments encouraged the entry of multinationals, a policy which went back well before World War II. The arguments for such a liberal policy (leaving aside the political pressure from the USA) and the technological advance it was deemed to generate, was above all the balance of payments advantages of large capital inflows. Also important was the fact that, as a large capital exporter herself, Britain was disinclined to pursue any policy which might threaten liberal movement of capital. As a result of this stance, by 1963 foreign-controlled companies accounted for around 10 per cent of output in manufacturing in the UK, and about 13 per cent of investment.[35]

Britain's policies in this area have not excited a great deal of comment. The first official study of these investment flows was in the early 1970s and focused on the balance of payments consequences, reflecting the emphasis of policy on this aspect of their impact.[36] The *industrial policy* aspect of this influx of multinationals seems rarely to have gone much beyond generalities in the official discussions. Yet it may be argued that a Japanese-style emphasis on restriction of direct investment, coupled to encouragement of licensing and joint ventures might have provided superior outcomes.[37] Some commentators on the Japanese economy have seen those policies as allowing the use of foreign-generated technologies in a manner integrated and compatible with the indigenous enterprise system. An obvious case is in the car industry where collaboration with US multinationals proved compatible with flourishing domestically owned production. In the UK, by contrast, the powerful presence of wholly-owned US companies hemmed-in the domestic producer and reduced the policy options available to government.

VII

Zysman has argued that the success of attempts at 'economic planning' in Western economies have been significantly affected by the nature of the financial system in each country.[38] Where ploughed-back profit and stock markets have been important in financing industrial investment this has inhibited the 'planning' of investment operating by governmental control or influence on the distribution of investment funds. Planning in the French sense of indicative planning of the 1950s and 1960s was never seriously considered in Japan, and all commentators regard the Japanese Economic Planning Agency as much less important to economic policy than MITI. Nevertheless, at one or two removes, MITI's power was based on influence over the distribution of investment funds, especially in the post-war years when such funds were in short supply.[39]

In Britain, in the early post-war years, companies were extremely liquid because of high profits in the 1940s and the physical controls over investment. This meant that it was extremely difficult for any external agency to affect investment by financial mechanisms. The Labour government of 1945–51 was pledged to create a National Investment Board to regulate investment, but from the beginning this forswore controlling internal funds of companies, so that even if such a body had been created it would have been a dead letter. There was widespread debate on this issue in the late 1940s, but the basic dilemma of how to 'plan' investment without drawing the state into a politically unacceptable level of intervention in company-level decision-making was never resolved.[40]

Like other contrasts, this one should not be overdrawn. State allocation of finance in Japan was at least complemented by an intermeshing of private financial institutions and industry, which seem to facilitate long-run investment decision-making and resistance to short-run financial market pressures. In this sense, recent work has emphasized the similarities of Japan to Germany's 'organized capitalism', and distance from Anglo-American 'arm's-length' relationships between finance and industry.[41]

In the 1950s and 1960s the government impact on company financing was largely limited to providing tax 'breaks' for investment, most of which, except for a regional aspect, did not attempt to discriminate between types or sectors of investment. The impact of this was probably very small, except that it helped stem the decline in pre-tax profits evident from the mid-1950s. Companies remained dependent on ploughed-back profits for most of their investment resources, and largely autonomous of any government influence on how those funds were spent.

VIII

Much of the recent debate about Japanese economic success has concerned the respective roles of industrial policy and the enterprise system in generating that success.[42] This debate may be said to be misconceived in the sense that, as argued persuasively by Okimoto, the enterprise system was one condition of the success of industrial policy rather than a separate source.[43] This debate leads on to the last difference between Japan and Britain to be addressed here, which is the relation between industrial policy and enterprise practices.

Clearly enterprise structure and behaviour is *never* simply a product of policy, and in neither Britain nor Japan would even the most enthusiastic advocates of industrial policy suggest that enterprises could or should be fully subordinated to the directives of a central agency. The issue is one of degrees, though in the British and Japanese comparison, arguably a large number of degrees. The basic points to make in that comparison are twofold. First, in general Japanese bodies like MITI seem to have had a much more *consistent* policy on desirable enterprise practices than is evidenced in Britain. Second, that in the particular area of 'employee relations' and its many synonyms, this consistency has avoided what might be called the pathology of the British system, obsessed as it has been with 'labour' as the source of problem in the enterprise and dealing with this 'problem' as the central strategic issue for management.[44]

One of the bodies created by MITI (in 1949) was the Industrial Rationalization Council. 'Perhaps the council's least known but later most applauded activities were in the areas of the reform of management, the institutionalization of the lifetime employment system, and the raising of the productivity of the Japanese industrial worker.'[45]

Under the aegis of this Council and its offshoots, techniques of business administration, many imported from the USA, were widely propagated, including techniques later regarded as peculiarly Japanese such as close attention to quality as an integral part of the production process. It is impossible to say how important such policy initiatives were in the formation of the 'flexible rigidities' of the Japanese enterprise, but it would seem that in general a consistent notion of the best enterprise practices by MITI and its offshoots provided at least a setting for the evolution of those practices.

By contrast, in Britain no such consistency was apparent. The Attlee Government took a range of initiatives to try and improve enterprise practices in Britain, including creating the British Institute of Management to try and spread notions of best practice by education.[46] Whether these initiatives provided a coherent package is questionable, especially given the newness of the area of concern to many Labour people, as well as the lack of enthusiasm shown by many of the intended 'customers' of such management reforms. If one over-arching notion did emerge in this field it was that of 'Human Relations' as the key to higher productivity in the enterprise. At its simplest, this approach suggested that 'the happy worker is a productive worker', and that happiness was likely to be induced by welfare provision, consultation, and above all the worker being felt to be involved in the enterprise. 'Human Relations' ideas could degenerate into a crass social psychology, in which unavoidable conflicts at enterprise level could be represented as pathological. It almost certainly exaggerated what could be achieved by consultative bodies at the enterprise level separate from other reforms. On the other hand, it did provide some handle on enterprise practices which had previously been largely outside the domain of government concern.

In the 1950s and 1960s such coherence as was present in this area in the 1940s disappeared. 'Human Relations' went into eclipse in the 1950s, to be replaced by a narrowly focused concern with 'Work Study' itself a bowdlerized version of 'Time and Motion Study', which in turn seemed to be an attempt to tear out of context one feature of US-style mass production systems.[47] It did not lead very far, and in the 1960s led into a focus on productivity bargaining, which, whatever its merits, could again only address a very narrow range of issues at the enterprise level.

What is particularly interesting is that all of the themes which came and went in at least the rhetoric of enterprise policy tended to focus on labour, whether it was labour to be 'treated better' under 'Human Relations', closely studied and cajoled under 'Work Study', or bargained with in productivity deals. This represents what might be considered the continuing obsession of British governments *and* management with the 'British Worker Question'.[48] This is the long-standing belief that Britain's economic difficulties lay in the assumed peculiar recalcitrance of British labour, with its alleged penchant for restrictivism and resistance to change.

Whatever foreign models have been offered to British management a frequent response has been to try and split off those features from the model which relate to labour. Thus with the US model of the 1950s and 1960s it was the 'Work Study' aspect which was applied in Britain, so in the 1980s and 1990s it was largely the (alleged) employment practices of Japanese enterprises which seemed to be regarded as the element importable into Britain.

This British obsession with labour as the strategic issue in the management of the enterprise cannot be said to have *originated* in policy decisions. On the other hand, it cannot be said that this approach has been in any way offset by government policy, which has tended to be driven by fads and fashions rather by any sense of how the various components of enterprise practices might 'fit' together to produce a strategic vision of the efficient firm.

IX

This chapter has plainly offered only the most summary account of some of the major differences between Britain and Japan in industrial policy. One obvious conclusion which flows from its arguments is that there are many areas of this comparison which require further explanation and research. But in making such comparisons it has been suggested that a framework of 'the role of government' *versus* 'the role of the market' is unhelpful. If the Japanese experience of industrial policy does hold out any one general lesson for Britain, it is that this dichotomy, so beloved of both politicians and economists, is ill-suited to our understanding. Comparative economic history is not well served by the use of the 'cartoon images' of the all-powerful state or unfettered competition—perhaps especially in the Japanese case where such notions appear as unhelpful as does the polar alternative of treating Japanese economic behaviour as the result of an ultimately mysterious 'cultural' difference.

NOTES

1. Federation of British Industry, *A Look at Japan: Report of Visit* (London, 1961), 5.
2. S. Cohen and J. Zysman, 'Double or Nothing: Open Trade and Competitive Industry', *Foreign Affairs*, 61 (1983), 1120.
3. *The Economist* 'Consider Japan: I', 1 Sept. 1962, and 'Consider Japan: II', 8 Sept. 1962; A. Boltho, 'Was Japan's Industry Policy Successful?', *Cambridge Journal of Economics*, 8 (1985), 187–201. The first of these is an especially striking case from a British point of view. A pioneer assessment of Japan for the British reader, it focuses almost entirely on macroeconomic policy and the role of 'indicative' planning, the big issues in British economic policy debate at this time. Visitors' tales, as always, tell us at least as much about the visitors as the place being visited.
4. For some of the range of argument about Japanese industrial policy see C. Johnson, *MITI and the Japanese Miracle: The Growth of Industrial Policy 1925–1975* (Stanford, Calif., 1982); R. Dore, *Flexible Rigidities: Industrial Policy and Structural Adjustment in the Japanese Economy* (London, 1986); D. Okimoto, *Between MITI and the Market: Japanese Industrial Policy for High Technology* (Stanford, Calif., 1989); H. Odagiri, *Growth Through Competition; Competition Through Growth: Strategic Management and the Economy in Japan* (Oxford, 1992); W. Fruin, *The Japanese Enterprise System: Competitive Strategies and Co-operative Structures* (Oxford, 1992); K. Calder, *Strategic Capitalism* (Princeton, 1993).
5. P. Hall, *Governing the Economy* (Cambridge, 1986); D. Marquand, *The Unprincipled Society* (London, 1988); C. Newton and P. Porter, *Modernization Frustrated* (London, 1988).
6. N. Tiratsoo and J. Tomlinson, *Industrial Efficiency and State Intervention Labour 1939–51* (London, 1993); J. Tomlinson, 'Mr. Attlee's Supply-Side Socialism', *Economic History Review*, 46 (1993), 1–22.
7. The balance of payments crises of the 1950s, unlike those of 1947 and 1949, did not relate to incapacity to finance a full-employment level of imports, but to problems of defending the role of the pound as an international currency with low reserves and large outstanding liabilities.
8. For example, S. Brittan, *The Treasury Under the Tories, 1951–64* (London, 1965).
9. J. Tomlinson, 'An Unfortunate Alliance: Keynesianism and the Conservatives 1945–64', *History of Political Economy*, 27 (1995), 61–85.
10. K. Middlemas, *Power, Competition and the State*, i. *Britain in Balance 1941–61* (London, 1986), 250–2.

11. J. Tomlinson, *Government and the Enterprise Since 1900: The Changing Problem of Efficiency* (Oxford, 1994), ch. 9.
12. M. Barratt-Brown, 'Away with all Great Arches', *New Left Review*, 167 (1988), 22–51.
13. Okimoto, *Between MITI and the Market*, ch. 4.
14. S. Blank, *Government and Industry in Britain, the FBI in Politics, 1945–65* (Farnborough, 1973); H. Mercer, 'The Labour Governments of 1945–51 and Private Industry', in N. Tiratsoo (ed.), *The Attlee Years* (London, 1991), 71–89.
15. T. Barna, 'Those "Frightfully High" Profits', *Bulletin of the Oxford University Institute of Statistics*, 11 (1948), 213–26.
16. W. Grant, *Business and Politics in Britain* (London, 1987), ch. 8.
17. Johnson, *MITI and the Japanese Miracle*, 287–8.
18. Ibid. 288–9.
19. Dore, *Flexible Rigidities*, 198–204; E. F. Vogel, *Japan as No. 1: Lessons for America* (Cambridge, Mass., 1979), 70–8.
20. Okimoto, *Between MITI and the Market*, p. 144; Johnson, *MITI and the Japanese Miracle*, ch. 6.
21. Japan removed many of its quotas and quantitative controls on trade around the time it joined OECD in 1964, but these changes were offset by *increases* in tariffs, which (especially in effective terms) were higher than in most of Western Europe up until the 1970s. G. C. Eads and K. Yamamura, 'The Future of Industrial Policy', in K. Yamamura and Y. Yasuba (eds.), *The Political Economy of Japan i. The Domestic Transformation* (Stanford, Calif., 1987), 430–54.
22. N. Rollings, 'The Reichstag Method of Governing? The Attlee Governments and Permanent Economic Controls?', in H. Mercer, N. Rollings, and J. Tomlinson (eds.), *Labour Governments and Private Industry: The Experience of 1945–1951* (Edinburgh, 1992), 15–36.
23. Middlemas, *Power*, 250–5.
24. C. Freeman, *Technology Policy and Economic Performance: Lessons from Japan* (London, 1987), 33.
25. On Britain see M. Peck, 'Science and Technology', in R. E. Caves (ed.), *Britain's Economic Prospects* (Washington, DC, 1968); D. Edgerton, 'British Industrial R&D, 1900–70', *Journal of European Economic History*, 23 (1994), 49–67. Japan, by contrast, has *not* had a high proportion of total R&D financed by government, even if defence is excluded. Dore, *Flexible Rigidities*, 134–6.
26. R. Coopey, M. Uttley and G. Spinardi (eds.), *Defence Science and Technology: Adjusting to Change* (London, 1993).
27. G. C. Allen, 'Industrial Policy and Innovation in Japan', in C. Carter (ed.), *Industrial Policy and Innovation* (London, 1981), 68–87.
28. A. Boltho, *Japan: An Economic Survey 1953–73* (Oxford, 1975), 129.
29. In practice, MITI and other government agencies have not always been able to control the number of players e.g. in steel. See Calder, *Strategic Capitalism*, 4.
30. H. Mercer, *Constructing a Competitive Order: The Hidden History of British Anti-Trust* (Cambridge, 1995).
31. Tomlinson, *Government and the Enterprise since 1900*, ch. 8.
32. Mercer, *Constructing a Competitive Order*, chs. 4–6; N. Harris, *Competition and the Corporate Society: British Conservatives, the State and Industry 1945–64* (London, 1972).

33. D. J. Encarnation and M. Mason, 'Neither MITI nor America: The Political Economy of Capital Liberalisation in Japan', *International Organisation*, 44 (1990), 25–54.
34. K. Inada, S. Sekiguchi, S. Yasutoyo, *The Mechanism of Economic Development: Growth in the Japanese and East Asian Economies* (Oxford, 1992), 277.
35. G. Jones, 'The British Government and Foreign Multinationals Before 1970', in M. Chick (ed.), *Governments, Industries and Markets* (Aldershot, 1990), 194–214.
36. M. Steuer, *The Impact of Foreign Direct Investment* (London, 1973).
37. N. Hood and S. Young, *The Economics of Multinational Enterprise* (London, 1979), 269–71.
38. J. Zysman, *Governments, Markets and Growth: Financial Systems and the Politics of Industrial Change* (London, 1983).
39. Calder, *Strategic Capitalism*, 130–3.
40. J. Tomlinson, 'Attlee's Inheritance and the Financial System: Whatever Happened to the National Investment Board?', *Financial History Review*, 1 (1994), 139–55.
41. Calder, *Strategic Capitalism*, ch. 8.
42. Fruin, *Japanese Enterprise System*, ch. 1.
43. Okimoto, *Between MITI and the Market*, ch. 8.
44. H. Gospel, *Markets, Firms and the Management of Labour in Modern Britain* (Cambridge, 1992), 178.
45. Johnson, *MITI and the Japanese Miracle*, 216.
46. Tiratsoo and Tomlinson, *Industrial Efficiency*, chs. 4–7.
47. For a fascinating and innovative approach to this whole episode see N. Rose, *Governing the Soul: The Shaping of the Private Self* (London, 1989), chs. 5–10.
48. T. Nichols, *The British Worker Question* (London, 1986).

PART II
Management

4. The Top Management of Large-scale Enterprises in Post-war Japan

HIDEMASA MORIKAWA

Much has been written about management in Japan and the particular contribution it has made to the success of Japanese firms. This chapter explores this contribution, focusing in particular on the top management in post-war Japan's economic miracle.

The Rise of Professional Top Management

Table 4.1 provides a comparison of the careers of the presidents of the largest enterprises in the major industries in Japan at four points in time: 1930, 1955, 1975, and 1992. For 1930, paid-up capital was used as the measure of the size of the enterprise, but for the subsequent three years, the measure was total assets. The names of the industries and enterprises have been omitted.[1] As is obvious from the table, the proportion of full-time presidents increased over the years, and there was a marked increase in the number of presidents who were salaried managers promoted from within. Full-time presidents of Type A (internal recruits) increased from 26 per cent of the total (11/43) in 1930 to 80 per cent (52/65) in 1992. Salaried managers promoted from within made similar gains, from an initial 7 per cent in 1930 to 75 per cent in 1992. By contrast, the percentage of part-time presidents declined sharply, from 51 per cent in 1930 to 13 per cent in 1955 and zero in 1992.

The figures in parentheses indicate the number of presidents with chairmen that fall into a different category (a Type A president and Type B chairman, for instance). In an increasing number of major Japanese enterprises, the board of directors, the single top management body, has both a chairman and a president. In a separate study, I found that the percentage of enterprises with both a chairman and a president has increased dramatically: from a mere 3 per cent in 1930 (4 companies with both chairman and president out of 158 enterprises) to 19 per cent in 1943 (83/433); 22 per cent in 1954 (85/387), 49 per cent in 1974 (148/305), and 64 per cent in 1991 (316/492). Since, in general, the chairman outranks the president, a president serving under a chairman of a different type (e.g. a Type A full-time president under a Type B full-time or part-time chairman, or a Type B full-time president under a part-time chairman) may be unable to manifest

TABLE 4.1. *Corporate president profiles in Japan's largest businesses, 1930–1992*

Presidents	1930	1955	1975	1992
A: Full-time (internal recruits)				
Salaried managers promoted from within	3 (1)	35 (5)	41 (8)	49 (7)
Founders	8	3	3 (1)	3
SUBTOTAL	11	38	44	52
B: Full-time (external recruits)				
Professional (non-company specific) salaried managers	4	3 (1)	3	2 (1)
Founder's family members	4	4	8 (1)	6 (1)
Former high-ranking bureaucrats (*amakudari*)	1	0	2 (1)	1 (1)
Major stockholders	1	0	0	0
Sent from bank or other financial institutions	0	2	1	1 (1)
Parent company's representatives	0	1	2	0
Salaried manager's heirs	0	1	2	3 (1)
SUBTOTAL	10	11	18	13
C: Part-time				
Founder's family members	4	0	0	0
Former bureaucrats (*amakudari*)	5	3	3	0
Major stockholders	11	2	1	0
Sent from bank or other financial institutions	0	1	0	0
Parent company's representatives	2	0	0	0
Salaried manager's heirs	0	1	0	0
SUBTOTAL	22	7	4	0
TOTAL	43	56	66	65

Sources: Shogyo Koshinsho, *Zenkoku Shokaisha Yakuinroku* (Company Directory), 1930; *Diamond-sha Kaisha Shokuinroku* (Company Directory), 1955, 1975, 1992.

the traits of his type fully. Therefore, I identified these presidents in parentheses.

The dramatic increase in the percentage of salaried managers promoted from within not only reflects the natural development of the managerial enterprise, which I will discuss later, but was also brought about by major structural changes. The first factor here was military demand during World

War II. The military authorities wanted to be in a position to give orders to and control heavy industry, including enterprises involved in producing armaments and aircraft. In consequence, they preferred presidents who were full-time and able to fulfil their production responsibilities. (The Munitions Manufacturing Company Act was implemented in December 1943.) Many owners who had been working as a part-time president, attending board of directors meetings only out of concern for protecting their investments and receiving their dividends, handed over presidential authority to salaried managers promoted from within.[2]

A second factor was the dissolution of the *zaibatsu* by the Allied Occupation immediately after the War.[3] The *zaibatsu* families, who owned the parent holding companies and many other operating enterprises, were, for all intents and purposes, stripped of them. The government bonds they were given in exchange for their shares in the *zaibatsu* company turned out to be virtually worthless, due to inflation. Members of the *zaibatsu* families were also forced to resign from top management positions. Salaried managers promoted from within, who had been in *de facto* control of the *zaibatsu* holding companies and operating companies, became the *de jure* top managers of former *zaibatsu* enterprises as well. The purge policy enforced by the Occupation was a third factor. Immediately after the War, leaders who had co-operated in the War effort were purged—i.e. barred from public office. As the purges extended to the business world, the majority of top management figures, including salaried managers promoted from within, at major enterprises designated by SCAP (Supreme Commander, Allied Powers) were forced to resign. As a result, the top management of such enterprises was filled by even greater numbers of salaried managers promoted from within. The average age of top managers also dropped by a decade.[4] This factor clearly contributed to the vigour shown by major enterprises in post-war Japan.

We can define the salaried manager group as consisting of the salaried managers promoted from within plus the professional (non-company specific) salaried managers and former high-ranking bureaucrats in Type B. The ratio of that salaried manager group to the total number of presidents increased from 19 per cent in 1930 to 80 per cent in 1992. In writing elsewhere about the rapid development of the managerial enterprises[5] in pre-war Japan, I have indicated that its development was still in a transitional stage in 1930.[6] Thus, the managerial enterprise achieved its full flowering in Japan after the War.

The Entrepreneurial Responses of Japan's Top Management

Although the managerial enterprise did develop strikingly, the role of what Chandler has called the 'entrepreneurial enterprise' cannot be underestimated. We must not forget the brilliant founders who set up their companies after 1930, successfully made the most of the many business opportunities offered by the wartime economy and post-war economic reconstruction, and built them into large-scale enterprises. These entrepreneurial enterprises include Matsushita, Sanyo, Bridgestone, YKK, Yammar, Sony, and Honda. Their founders were, of course, owners, but they were not capitalists whose interests lay only in protecting their investments and raking in dividends. These entrepreneurs were full-time presidents who made direct contributions to the development of Japanese industry and its achievement of competitive advantages.

I classified both salaried managers promoted from within and founders in Type A (internal recruits) because both are clearly distinguished from other types of full-time presidents, including professional (non-company specific) salaried managers, the founder's family members, former high-ranking bureaucrats (*amakudari*), major stockholders, those sent from banks or other financial institutions, parent company representatives, and salaried managers' heirs. What separates the two groups is long experience inside the enterprise, experience that includes a close relationship between the president and employees who have worked for years for the company. These relationships are not restricted to middle or lower managers but often include blue-collar workers as well. Both salaried managers promoted from within and founders have close relationships with their employees— especially those in groups with skills built up over time in the company— and acquire information from them. A salaried manager builds such relationships in the process of being promoted up through the company, while a founder forges them in the course of setting up and operating the company. The information flowing from these employees to their top managers concerns both the company's operations and the relationships between the individuals with the relevant skills.

The achievements of these Type A presidents were respected by the groups of skilled workers within the company. Moreover, these presidents knew the status of the company's operating units and won the trust of their employees. The result was the establishment of good relationships between top management and skilled workers in many major enterprises in post-war Japan. What is often referred to as 'Japanese-style management' is one aspect of those relationships. Good relations between top management and groups of skilled workers not only led to a healthy labour–management relationship and good morale on the work site, but also played a positive role in the investment activities of major enterprises—and investment was the biggest growth factor in the Japanese economy.

In the 1950s, major Japanese enterprises made bold investments disproportionate to their managerial resources; examples include Kawasaki Steel's construction of a new integrated steel plant in Chiba[7] and Toray's introduction of nylon technology and launch of domestic production. The top management of those enterprises was confident that their skill groups had the ability to master the necessary technology. Investments that looked excessively ambitious and risky were made in the confidence that their skill groups would definitely make a success of the technology and permit a good return on the enterprise's outlay. What Hamel and Prahalad have called 'strategic intent'[8] must not be seen as merely a question of intent; it was the relationship of trust between top management and the enterprises' skill groups that permitted top management to act on their intent. Carrying out these ambitious investment plans required huge bank loans. Many banks did agree to provide financing because the enterprises' top management persuaded them that their investment would pay off, in part because the skill groups had the abilities and the capacity to learn. (Projections of increased demand in the future were another persuasive factor.)

Obviously, the trade unions were not hostile to these substantial investments. It is true that the unions reacted against the radical, communist-led labour movement that emerged immediately after the War. Union members also realized that improving their wages and living standards would depend upon the competitiveness of the corporation for which they expected to work for many years. Above all, employees were sympathetic to their Type A full-time top managers, for they had gone through hard times together, in the post-war years or when the company was starting up.

In the early 1950s, growth in the Japanese economy was fuelled by the major capital investments of progressive enterprises. Rapid economic growth was then sustained by a virtuous cycle of investment leading to more investment and growth leading to more growth. During the two decades from 1955 to 1973, the top management of large-scale enterprises adopted multifaceted strategies aimed at achieving economies of scale and economies of scope by building up their skills and capacities to international standards and by entering new industries. However, the key to success lay in the employees who carried out these strategies improving their skills amidst intense competition. The network of skilled workers in large-scale enterprises in post-war Japan (which I will call the 'skilled workers network') had the following characteristics:

   (i) Co-operative relationships between employees who had worked, over the years, in a variety of operating units in the same company.
  (ii) Co-operative relationships between well-educated white-collar engineers and blue-collar workers on the work site.
 (iii) Rapid transfer and feedback of information and know-how beyond the boundaries of specific operations.
 (iv) On-the-job training.
  (v) A system in which bottom-up communications and overall

consensus were given more stress than bureaucratic top-down decision-making.

These characteristics did not spring up after the War. Their roots go back to the pre-war period. Co-operation between white-collar engineers and blue-collar workers at the work site, for example, goes back to the tradition of highly advanced technical education which began immediately after the Meiji Restoration.[9] However, it was after World War II that the companies systematized these characteristics and made conscious use of them. In post-war Japan, the skilled workers' network in major enterprises supported strategies for expansion and diversification from 1955 to 1973. They contributed substantially to the development of the machinery industry, including automobiles and electrical appliances, in which co-operation between workers and information sharing are essential. Precision processing and assembly technology in the Japanese machinery industry reached the world's top level by a sustained effort to cut costs in order to survive the 1973 oil crisis and the rapid appreciation of the yen, which began about that time.[10]

As many research papers have revealed, work in the Japanese machinery industry is organized in a series of work stages—development, processing, assembly, and inspection. That is not unlike the system in other countries, in which there is a highly developed division of labour, in which each stage is broken down into a number of processes. What is unique to Japan is that each worker in charge of one manufacturing process in this highly specialized division of labour can also work in several other processes. Workers often co-operate and co-ordinate with other workers in charge of other processes and with the highly educated engineers stationed on the work site. Through such exchanges, they improve their skills and become well informed about the system as a whole. The result is improved product quality and fewer mistakes: in other words, increased yield. That is the real nature of the precision processing and assembly technology that is the pride of Japan's machinery industry.[11] And, of course, it rests on skilled workers' networks which are unique to Japan.

It can safely be said that the industrial driving force behind the rapid economic growth that continued through the 1980s was Japan's outstanding precision processing and assembly technology in the machinery industry. The appreciation of the yen touched off by the 1985 Plaza Accord raised the possibility of stopping Japan's economic growth at last, but the precision processing and assembly technology managed to overcome the pressure that the soaring yen placed on Japanese industry. It should also be noted that major Japanese enterprises chose to make overseas investments as a counter-measure against the rise of the yen. Japan recorded substantial growth in overseas direct investments: from \$12,217 million in 1985 to \$47,022 million in 1988 and \$56,911 million in 1990.[12]

Strategic Mistakes After 1985

In my opinion, major enterprises in Japan made a number of significant mistakes in the course of overcoming the appreciation of the yen in the years since the 1985 Plaza Accord, which took action to rectify the over-valuation of the US dollar. It appears that many economists and other scholars lost their cool objectivity in their excitement over Japan's success in coping with the appreciation of the yen. They praised the outstanding precision processing technology possessed by the automobile industry and other parts of the machinery industry. Many scholars observed that it was the Japanese-style manufacturing system (what I refer to as Japanese skilled workers' networks) and Japanese-style management that created such excellent technology.[13] Some scholars overestimated the competitiveness of the Japanese machinery industry and arrogantly asserted that Japanese industry had nothing left to learn from American or European technology.[14]

I do not imagine that the top management of major Japanese enterprises was complacent enough to relax in that environment. It is true, however, that none of them reassessed the limits of that unique skilled workers' network or made efforts to reform the management system behind it. Therein lies a major problem. A change of environment often robs a strong person or system of its strength, even though the person or system remains unchanged. That is what has happened to the skilled workers' networks in major Japanese enterprises—the networks that gave rise to the world's top competitive advantages in the machinery industry's precision processing and assembly technology.

As we have seen, the skilled workers' network unique to major Japanese enterprises focuses on co-operation and information-sharing. The system is highly unlikely to throw up a genius or two to create a new product or new technology. To develop fields such as computer software or fine chemicals (including pharmaceuticals and biotechnology), however, requires such creative breakthroughs. And that is where Japanese skilled workers' networks are weakest. These unique networks help to make Japan strong in the machinery industry and weak in the chemical and software industries. Major Japanese enterprises are thus faced with a pressing need to re-evaluate their networks.

The need is urgent, first, because newly emerging industrial countries such as South Korea and Taiwan are rapidly catching up with Japan in the field of precision processing and assembly technology, where Japan has led the world. Add a foreign exchange rate of 100 yen to the dollar and rising protectionism in the West, and there is little warrant for optimism about the future of the Japanese machinery industry. Second, as other countries inevitably catch up with Japan's machinery industry, the Japanese economy must prepare for the future by shifting its priorities to industries that produce high value-added or integration of information, such as fine chemicals and software. Such industries, however, have shown no rapid growth in Japan. An example here would be instructive. Japan dominated the world market by increasing its semiconductor production in the latter half of the 1980s. The semiconductors that established Japan's competitive advantage were, however, general-purpose DRAM chips that required large-scale capital investment and precision processing and assembly technologies. South Korea is now moving rapidly into the DRAM market. Meanwhile, US enterprises withdrew from DRAM production in the 1980s to concentrate on MPUs, which require a higher level of integration of information. Japan's semiconductor industry, with its domination of the DRAM market threatened by South Korea, cannot defeat the US in the MPU field.[15]

An urgent task for major Japanese enterprises is thus to strengthen high value-added fields and fields that integrate higher levels of information. To achieve that goal, they should have reassessed their skilled workers' networks and begun revamping them, but top management neglected this task. They were too confident of the familiar skilled workers' network and the Japanese-style management system behind it, which had underpinned the Japanese machinery industry's competitive advantage. The managerial response was not to reform the existing system but to devote their companies to an expansion strategy along familiar lines. The soaring yen after the Plaza Accord in 1985 presented a good opportunity for them to change direction. Instead, full of confidence in the system they knew, they were also bewitched by the 'bubble economy', with its widespread speculation in stocks and lands, brought about by the ultra-low interest-rate policy adopted since 1985 as the yen appreciated. Some enterprises engaged in speculation; some made major capital investments to build productive capacity to meet the demand in the domestic market, which expanded during the bubble years. In 1990 the economic bubble burst, leaving enterprises saddled with massively excessive productive capacity. The result has made the current recession even more severe in Japan.[16]

The top managers of large-scale Japanese enterprises have also made other mistakes. One, already mentioned, was to make large-scale capital investments based on their existing strategies instead of changing direction. They did not, however, make the same scale of investment in R&D (see Table 4.2). In particular, investment in basic research was conspicuously low. They are bound to pay a price for neglecting the investment in basic research needed to build high value-added and information-integrating industries. The conclusion that they have been short-sighted is inescapable.

Even restricting our time frame, for the moment, to the years after 1985, we find that the top management of large-scale enterprises in Japan made many such mistakes.

Why were so many mistakes made by Japanese management? The strategic errors made by so many companies since 1985 cannot be attributed simply to the rise of the managerial enterprise.

TABLE 4.2. *A comparison of research expenditures in four countries, 1970–1990*

Year	Japan	US	Germany	UK
			(1971)	(1972)
1970	1.59 ⟨23.3⟩	2.57 ⟨13.5⟩	2.09 ⟨26.9⟩	2.09
			(1981) (1981)	(1981)
1980	1.91 ⟨14.5⟩	2.18 ⟨13.5⟩	2.49 ⟨20.8⟩	2.30
			(1989) (1987)	(1989)
1990	2.77 ⟨12.6⟩	2.63 ⟨15.5⟩	2.89 ⟨19.3⟩	2.25

Notes: Figures indicate the ratio of total expenditures on research to GNP for each country; figures in ⟨ ⟩ indicate the ratio of basic research expenditure/total research expenditure; figures in ( ) for Germany and the UK indicate the year.

Source: *White Paper on Science and Technology* (1992), 343–53, 367–9.

Explanations for Faltering Managerial Performance

As noted earlier, the managerial enterprise is flourishing in Japan today. It is now unthinkable for a major stockholder to take office as a chief executive of a large-scale enterprise simply by virtue of owning a large share of the stock. Even in entrepreneurial enterprises where the founders worked as full-time presidents, salaried managers promoted from within often join founding family members in the top management after the founder retires. In an increasing number of such entrepreneurial enterprises, salaried managers promoted from within are becoming core members of the top management and winning the chief executive's position. Examples include Ajinomoto, Bridgestone, Honda, Matsushita, and Shimizu. Family enterprises in which members of the founding family will not let go of the core management role—e.g. Seibu, Suntory, Kikkoman, Idemitsu, or Kajima—are growing rarer. Managerial enterprises were not, however, the only major enterprises to have blundered since 1985. It is certainly incorrect to think that deficiencies peculiar to salaried managers promoted from within led to the mistakes made at this stage.

I would like to refer to three elements as the cause of the strategic mistakes made by the top management of large-scale enterprises.

First, the number of top managers increased substantially as enterprises grew, the number of operating units increased, some units were spun off as subsidiaries, and company groups were formed and expanded to a gigantic scale. In 1954, the board of directors of a large-scale enterprise would be made up of ten to twenty persons; having eleven to fifteen persons on the board was most common. Only a handful of enterprises had fewer than ten directors, and it was rare to have more than twenty.[17] In 1975, however, most enterprises had twenty to thirty directors; ten to twenty was the next most common pattern; enterprises with fewer than ten directors were scarcely to be found.[18] By 1993, boards of directors in large-scale enterprises had swollen to the sizes shown in Table 4.3. Since it is, naturally enough, impossible for so many people to get together and carry out the various levels of decision-making, a hierarchy of directors (chairman, president, vice-president, senior executive director, executive director, and ordinary director) became widespread. With so many directors in so hierarchical a structure, it is more and more difficult for a top manager to make an individual statement based on his or her own judgement. The decision top management reaches tends to be a product of compromise. With a larger board, too, the proportion of members of average ability and conventional turn of mind increases; the result is a welcoming of risk-avoiding, safety-first behaviour that does not deviate from what competitors in the industry are doing. Large-scale enterprises have all acted along similar lines since 1985. They have reduced costs to cope with the appreciation of the yen. They have become fully involved in the 'bubble economy'. They have made large-scale investments in anticipation of market growth. They have expanded their overseas direct investments while failing to invest in R&D. They failed to reassess systems which hampered the development of high value-added industries and those that integrated research results. One reason for the sameness of their behaviour is the over-expansion of the top management group and consequent loss of individuality in top management.

Second, failures should not be attributed to a lack of information. Today we are surrounded by lavish, almost excessive amounts of information; an information shortage cannot occur. The information-related factor behind the situation was not the volume of information available but the ability of top management to understand the situation, based on that information,

TABLE 4.3. *Number of directors in leading large-scale enterprises in 1993*

Japan Steel (Shin Nittetsu)	48	Nomura Securities	40
Mitsui Bussan	52	Tokio Marine & Fire Insurance	38
Toyota	55	Tokyo Electric Power	32
Hitachi	32	NTT	36
Kajima	54	Japan Airline	36
Mitsubishi Heavy Industries	40	Asahi Chemical	36
Kirin Brewery	35	Ajinomoto	30
Sumitomo Bank	42		

Source: Toyo Keizai Shimpo-sha, *Kaisha Shikiho* (Quarterly Company Guidebook), 1993–4 edition.

and work out a strategy. Putting that together with their tendency to sup-press individual comments and act in conventional, copy-cat ways to stay in step with competitors, I am inclined all the more to comment on how far the abilities of top management have declined.

The intellectual abilities of the top management of Japan's major enter-prises did not, of course, take a nosedive in 1985. Signs of a decline had been evident for some time. It is difficult to specify the origins of this pre-cisely, but in about 1970 the behaviour of employees of large-scale enter-prises became the subject of criticism. Overseas, it was asserted, they acted rudely and arrogantly and were viewed with contempt by people there. They were alleged to be company-centred, focused only on in-house matters, and uninterested in matters outside their company. Their topics of conversation were apparently, limited to golf and their children's education. These criticisms appeared minor compared with the remarkable achieve-ments of the enterprises themselves. The intellectual ability of business people in Japan was, however, gradually declining, just as the critics stated. Is it an overstatement to note that when those who had been middle man-agers in about 1970 were promoted to top management positions in and after 1985, the results were detrimental?

Finally, to clarify the situation further, I would like to point out that this question also concerns Japanese education. The nature of university edu-cation changed after the Japanese university system was reformed in 1949. The university curriculum is classified into general and specialized educa-tion in, I assume, every country. The reforms made no critical changes in specialized education in Japan, but general education did change. In the old system, general education was acquired through individual, self-motivated study of history, literature, philosophy, and other areas of high culture; the reforms under the Occupation forcibly changed that into the study of American-style liberal arts. While called 'liberal arts', the new curriculum was liberal in form only. The new general education entailed the compul-sory study of a broad range of subjects in non-specialized courses. This cur-riculum did not motivate students. Worse, less than competent teachers were hired to cope with a rapid increase in the size of the student body. As a result, the universities' general education programmes have not met stu-dents' needs, but both the Ministry of Education and the universities have neglected to take action about the sad state of general education. Recently, at long last, the need for reform has been discussed, but without result thus far.

The result was the mass-production of students who, lacking the oppor-tunity for self-motivated cultural studies that had been so characteristic of the old university system, lost any motivation to study. They graduated, found employment with business enterprises, were promoted to middle management, and eventually moved into top management positions. Until about 1985 there were still business people in middle and top management who had trained their intellects under the old university system. They began to retire from 1985 on; only a few graduates of the old university system are still to be found in the top management of large-scale enterprises. For instance, among the seventy-nine largest companies across all industries, forty-three (54 per cent) have presidents who are graduates of the old-system university, but most of them graduated after the War, in the last years of the old system (1948 to 1953).[19] In a few years, the number of presidents who graduated from the old-system university will approach zero. There is clear evidence of this lowering in intellectual abilities, but there is room for discussion as to whether the causes are to be found only in the post-war changes in the university system I have described. I myself am not basing my argument on sufficiently reliable data to be totally confident of my conclusions. But the impact on large Japanese enterprises of the total disappearance of graduates of the old university system and their replacement throughout the management hierarchy by graduates of the new, qualitatively different education is inescapable. That will be a critical issue for the future.

Conclusion

In the first part of this chapter, I described the rise of professional top management in the large-scale enterprises that promoted the rapid growth of the Japanese economy after the War and described the characteristics of those managers' careers that permitted them to fulfil those roles. It will not always be the case, however, that the past successes of those top managers can be sustained or that Japan's managers will be up to the job of serving as the power behind the Japanese economy. That very experience of success may have produced a dulling in the response to the changes currently occurring. It is, I would argue, precisely because their predecessors were so successful that the top management of Japan's large-scale enterprises is suffering from an inability to discover better ways to respond to new challenges. I do not think that, intoxicated by the sweetness of success, managers have all become easygoing or arrogant. But they are hindered by their ties to the familiar, existing structures. The greater size of top management, its more elaborate structure, and the changes in the intellectual system in which younger managers were educated also contributed to their not responding creatively to a changed environment.

Will the top managers of large-scale enterprises in Japan be able to reinvigorate the Japanese economy and put it back on the road to growth? That will be the key factor in foreseeing whether Thurow's prediction is on the mark and the world economy of the twenty-first century will indeed be the arena for a battle between the United States, the EU, and Japan.[20]

NOTES

1. This analysis was first presented in H. Morikawa, 'The Role of Managerial Enterprise in Post-War Japan's Economic Growth: Focus on the 1950's', *Business History* 37/2 (Apr. 1995), 32–43.
2. Toyo Keizai Shinpo-sha (ed.), *Nihon Keizai Nenpo* (Japan's Economic Quarterly Review, 1943) (Tokyo, 1944), 56–65.
3. H. Morikawa, *Zaibatsu: The Rise and Fall of Family Enterprise Groups in Japan* (Tokyo, 1992), 237–9.
4. H. Miyajima, 'Zaikai Tsuiho to Shin Keieisha no Tojo' (The Purge Policy and the Emergence of New Executives in Post-War Japan), in H. Morikawa (ed.), *Sengo Keiseishi Nyumon* (A Guidebook to Post-War Japan's Business History) (Tokyo, 1992), ch. 1.
5. For a precise definition of the concept of 'managerial enterprise' see Alfred D. Chandler, Jr., 'The United States: Seedbed of Managerial Capitalism,' in Alfred D. Chandler, Jr. and Herman Daems (eds.), *Managerial Hierarchies: Comparative Perspectives on the Rise of the Modern Industrial Enterprise* (Cambridge, Mass., 1980), 14.
6. H. Morikawa, *Nihon Keiei-shi* (Japanese Business History) (Tokyo, 1981), 165.
7. S. Yonekura, 'Sengo no Ogata Setsubitoshi' (Large-scale Investment in Equipment in Post-War Japan), in Morikawa (ed.), *Sengo Keiseishi Nyumon*, ch. 4.
8. G. Hamel and C. K. Prahalad, 'Strategic Intent', *Harvard Business Review* (May–June 1989).
9. H. Morikawa, 'The Education of Engineers in Modern Japan: A Historical Perspective', in Howard Gospel (ed.), *Industrial Training and Technological Innovation* (1991), 136–47.
10. Minoru Ito, *Gijutsu Kakushin to Human Network Soshiki* (Technical Innovation and the Human Network System) (Tokyo, 1988).
11. E.g. H. Itami, T. Kagono, T. Kobayashi, K. Sakakibara, and M. Itoh (eds.), *Kyoso to Kakushin-Jidosha Sangyo no Kigyo Seicho* (Competition and innovation: The Growth of the Firm in the Automobile Industry) (Tokyo, 1988), ch. 4.
12. Economic Planning Agency, *Keizai Yoran* (Survey of Economic Statistics), 1987, 1991, 1992.
13. E.g. J. Hashimoto, *Nihon Keizai Ron* (On the Japanese Economy) (Kyoto, 1991), ch. 6; and H. Itami, 'Endaka no Kokufuku Process' (The Process of Overcoming the Impact of the High Yen Exchange Rate), in H. Itami, T. Kagono, and M. Ito (eds.), *Nihon no Kigyo System* (Japanese Business System), iv (Tokyo, 1993), ch. 12.
14. E.g., Hajime Karatsu and Shoichi Watanabe.
15. Yutaka Ueda, 'Computer Business ni okeru Kyosoryoku no Kongen' (Basis of Competitive Advantages in the Computer Business), Keio Business School MBA thesis, 1994.
16. *Nihon Keizai Shimbun*, 1 July 1993.
17. Keizai Orai-sha, *Nihon Kaisha-shi Soran* (Survey of Japanese Company History) (Tokyo, 1954).
18. Toyo Keizai Shimpo-sha, *Kaisha Shikiho* (Quarterly Company Guidebook), 1975–3 edn.

19. *Kaisha Shikiho*, 1994–1 edn; Toyo Keizai Shimpo-sha, *Yakuin Shikiho* (Directory of Top Corporate Executives), 1994 edn.
20. Lester C. Thurow, *Head to Head: The Coming Economic Battle among Japan, Europe and America* (Cambridge, 1992).

5. British Management 1945–64: *Reformers and the Struggle to Improve Standards*

NICK TIRATSOO

Introduction

One of the most striking features of Britain's post-war economic record is the comparatively poor performance of its manufacturing industry.[1] Some sectors have prospered, but these tend to be exceptions. Overall, as Barry Supple has recently observed, manufacturing and manufacturing productivity have experienced 'a relatively slow rate of expansion'. The result has been 'a dramatic fall' in Britain's share of world manufacturing output and an inability to maintain competitiveness in many markets. Indeed, the country's share of global trade in manufactured products 'fell from some 25 per cent in 1950 to 14 per cent in 1964, 9 per cent in 1973, and less than 8 per cent in the early 1980's'.[2]

This remarkable change in fortunes has provoked much comment and there is now an enormous literature that seeks to discover what went wrong. Several explanations remain controversial. On the other hand, there is growing agreement that one factor—ineffective management—can be legitimately isolated as a significant part of the problem. Michael Porter describes British firms as 'too often' having 'a management culture that works against innovation and change'. Karel Williams and associates, writing from very different assumptions, identify 'pervasive management incompetence' as 'a crucial cause' of recent manufacturing failure. Indeed, this view is now to some extent enshrined in the official diagnosis, since the 1994 Government report on competitiveness concludes that much British management outside a top cohort of companies displays significant weaknesses and thus continues to compromise the country's growth potential.[3]

However, if many now accept that management has been defective, there is little convincing discussion about how and why such a situation should have arisen. Economic historians of contemporary Britain have spent little time speculating on the subject.[4] Their colleagues in business history provide insights, though fewer than might be expected. Business historians have tended to focus on big companies, exactly those that are least likely to suffer from typical management deficiencies. Moreover, the influence of Chandler, with his stress on internal organizational form, means that what

Michael Best calls 'the inter-subjective dimension of structure' is frequently ignored. There is little exploration of managers' shared ideas and beliefs and the way these shape decision-making.[5] This leaves those who have adopted a more self-consciously sociological or cultural approach to management. The emphasis here is usually on long-term features of British society—for example, the alleged biases against industry or professionalism.[6] These accounts no doubt yield insights but they have also been widely criticized.[7] At worst, they merely amount to ahistorical and determinist generalizations. There is no room for the fluctuations, divergent traditions, and choices that are always evident in real historical situations. Given these important problems and flaws, it is difficult not to conclude, with Hirst and Zeitlin, that the whole subject of British management performance is blighted by 'a vacuity of analysis'.[8]

This chapter is an attempt to cast some new light on developments by the detailed examination of one particular episode. It focuses on initiatives that were made in the first two post-war decades to reform management practices in manufacturing industry. The objective is to trace why such efforts were made and how they subsequently fared, thereby uncovering some of the factors that have shaped the wider pattern of management attitudes and aptitudes up to the present.

Management Reformers

Criticism of British industrial management and its methods first began to be heard at the end of the nineteenth century and had become quite prevalent by the inter-war period.[9] Proponents of new methods—for example, scientific management and industrial psychology—tried to popularize their ideas, producing a proliferation of textbooks and periodicals urging change. Various organizations were created to encourage greater professionalism, However, by the end of the 1930s, it was quite evident that little of this agitation had produced any real impact. Only an 'infinitely small' proportion of managers were members of the new institutions. Moreover, most remained wedded to very traditional techniques. As John Child notes, the common response to the trade difficulties of these years involved cutting wages and lengthening hours of work, strategies which were 'completely at variance with those elementary lessons of industrial psychology which had long been absorbed by the management intellectuals'.[10]

The War ushered in a new phase of discussion about British management, with debate both more public and better informed.[11] From 1939, the government wanted maximum output of many strategic products, organizing very close relationships with business to achieve its goals. However, progress was hardly smooth and between 1940 and 1942 Britain endured a profound production crisis. A series of Select Committee reports were highly critical of management and prompted widespread comment in the press. Civil servants and ministers were especially shocked by their contacts with industry, expressing bewilderment, for example, at the technical ineptitude and autocratic attitudes displayed by managers. The situation was serious enough to convince those thinking about post-war reconstruction that major changes would have to be implemented in the future. The key need, they believed, was for more professionalism in management. The old nepotistic dynasties, which had promoted the incompetent, must be swept away and replaced by a new breed of trained specialists, well versed in technical, commercial, and industrial-relations skills. As Stafford Cripps explained in 1944, 'There was really no more right for an unqualified person to manage a factory than for an unqualified doctor to perform an operation.'[12]

After the war, the incoming Labour government, beset by economic difficulties, accepted much of this analysis, seeing management amelioration as one path to the productivity growth necessary for economic stability. Cripps created the British Institute of Management (BIM) in 1948 and action was also taken to improve management education in line with the Urwick Report, by introducing a national diploma scheme. Subsequent Conservative administrations were less keen on such state intervention but nevertheless agreed to continue Labour's policies. Treasury money was used to support the BIM until the end of the 1950s and launch the British Productivity Council, a body mainly (though not exclusively) concerned with management questions. Meanwhile, pressure was exerted from a new direction. American missions to Britain during the late 1940s agreed that the managers they met were often unimpressive. This matter became more pressing with the intensification of the Cold War, since the US government wanted all Allied powers to play their part in boosting production to defeat Communism. The result was a concerted effort to spread the kind of modern methods that had allegedly already transformed American productivity, particularly those which were broadly concerned with management skills. Early manifestations of this policy included the Anglo-American Council on Productivity team visits to the USA and an extensive technical assistance programme. After 1953, the key institution was the European Productivity Agency (EPA), set up with $2.5 million of US government funds to encourage productivity-improving schemes across the Continent. For the British manager who was committed to improvement, the EPA provided much of interest. It employed over 100 consultants who could be called upon for advice. Furthermore, it offered a variety of specially tailored educational schemes: between 1954 and 1958, there were 340 training courses and seven international conferences on management subjects alone.[13]

These various initiatives amounted to a formidable reform package. They were not identical but certainly shared much in common. All aimed to provoke change in a similar way, highlighting best practice and encouraging emulation through self-interest. More importantly, most of those in the reforming organizations were committed to the same ultimate objectives. First, like Cripps, they wanted to make managers more professional. Management, it was agreed, could only be really improved through education and training. Career advancement should therefore optimally depend upon a system of formal qualifications. Secondly, there was a pronounced belief in the importance of specialist techniques and methods. Modern manufacturing was becoming increasingly complicated. Consequently, management required input from emerging fields like production engineering, cost accounting, and marketing. The manager of the future would need to be both literate in many subject areas and willing to call on particular experts where this was appropriate. Finally, the reformers emphasized the importance of promoting good human relations. Team-working amongst managers was always preferable to the existing system of authoritarian direction from the top. Moreover, the workers' role in the firm required fresh consideration. Full employment and insights provided by social psychologists suggested that older forms of labour control were no longer applicable. In future, management would have to treat the employee as a fully-rounded person and not a mere 'hand', which meant allowing a much greater degree of shop-floor participation.[14]

The Impact of Reform

What impact did the reformers have on British managers? Some were certainly influenced for the better. A survey of the Lancashire textile industry in the 1960s concluded hopefully that deliberate attempts to improve standards had succeeded: 'Management in the industry has always been well trained in technical matters; it is now better trained than it was in the arts of management, and is better equipped to bring about and cope with change.' Similar progress was observable in the steel industry.[15] On the other hand, there is no doubt that the general situation was disappointing. One careful assessment of the reformers' efforts in 1960 asserted that 'it is difficult to avoid the conclusion that progress is slow, at least as far as a major part of British industry is concerned'.[16] A survey of the evidence suggests that even this measured assessment was somewhat over-optimistic.

To begin with, it is noticeable that some of the key institutions promoting reform were hardly considered great successes at this time. The BIM limped along for much of the 1950s, beset by financial difficulties and internal divisions. The Mead report of 1968, reviewing another decade of activity, reported increased membership but was not very reassuring about the BIM's influence and advised: 'More widespread awareness of the purposes, views, activities and achievements of the Institute is overdue and a more

positive effort should be made to make them known.'[17] The EPA appeared
no more successful. A profile in *The Economist* during 1956 described it as
'little known' in Britain. Three years later, the Cabinet Mutual Aid Committee was equally unenthusiastic. The EPA's achievements, it believed,
when balanced against cost, 'could not be regarded as outstanding'.[18] Examining how the reform movement's more specific concerns progressed during
these years confirms that such assessments were not wide of the mark.

The exhortation to increase management education and training fell
largely on deaf ears.[19] In-house schemes were organized in some big companies but continued to be rare. One estimate was that 'in 1960 only 400 of
11,000 public and 310,000 private companies in the United Kingdom had
some kind of management training, and that about 50 had residential staff
training centres'.[20] External courses were more common and a survey in
1960 referred to their 'ever-increasing diversity' at technical colleges,
universities, and specialist centres like Henley and Ashridge.[21] However,
proliferation masked problems. Most courses contained little on specialist
subjects like industrial relations and marketing.[22] Nor were they regarded
with much respect within companies. One journalist was told: 'The common
attitude is summed up by the remark "When a man is in a rut, and there's
no bigger job for him we send him on a staff course somewhere for a fort-
night or so. The lectures may be punk [sic], but he meets new people, and
the fact that he's been chosen and the firm is paying, boosts his morale".'[23]
Given such attitudes, only a small minority of firms were willing to use the
available facilities regularly. A National Economic Development Council
investigation in 1965 looked at seventy companies and found that only 14
per cent of their managers had attended an external course of any kind over
the preceding few years.[24] Finally, the various independent qualifying associations were also unsuccessful in encouraging education. In fact, most managers had not even bothered to join such bodies. An enquiry of 1951 which
looked at seven organizations found that they had enrolled only about 16
per cent of their potential memberships. During the 1950s this position
changed, but only slowly, and as late as 1963 a majority of managers were
still non-members.[25] The sum of progress, therefore, was quite modest. A
BIM report during the early 1960s painted a bleak picture: 'As a nation we
have not yet started on the task of providing trained and capable managers
in sufficient numbers.'[26] What this meant in numerical terms was spelt out
by Elizabeth Sidney, the prominent management educationalist. She estimated that there were 400,000 to 450,000 managers in British industry but
felt it would be 'optimistic' to suggest that more than 1 per cent of that
number had received 'any formal training for their job'.[27] The whole situation was summed up by the failure of the Urwick diploma scheme, which
had only managed to yield 1,500 successful candidates during its first fifteen
years of operation.[28]

The pressure to promote specialists and specialisms produced similarly meagre results. Most senior managers continued to believe that 'the specialist should be on tap but not on top', an epigram coined in 1950 by the President of the Federation of British Industries (FBI).[29] As a result, technical experts were rarely promoted to senior positions within companies. An Acton Society investigation of 1956, which focused on big manufacturing concerns, examined how different qualifications affected a manager's chances of promotion, and concluded that an arts degree from Oxbridge was five times more valuable in the competition for advancement than a technical qualification alone.[30] At the same time, there was often little real enthusiasm for boosting the overall employment of qualified personnel in firms. An official study during the late 1950s produced figures on the number of scientists and engineers in each industrial sector and found wide variation. The specified groups made up 0.8 per cent of the manufacturing labour force, but were much more numerous in oil-refining (7.0 per cent), chemicals (3.7 per cent), and aviation (2.7 per cent) than in precision instruments (1.7 per cent), machine tools (1.3 per cent), motor vehicles (0.5 per cent), shipbuilding (0.4 per cent), cotton (0.1 per cent), or clothing (0.02 per cent).[31] What especially alarmed observers was the fact that Britain's international competitors seemed to have no similar inhibitions. In 1960, the Machine Tool Advisory Council reported that qualified drawing office personnel made up 3.0 per cent of the British industry's labour-force, contrasting with equivalent figures of 6.6 per cent and 7.2 per cent in Germany and Switzerland.[32] A British delegation to the Dutch and German weaving industries in 1961 came to similar conclusions. It noted of Germany in particular:

Belief in the importance of good management was borne out in the firms visited by the unusually high proportion of technical specialist staff employed, the number appearing to be . . . very high compared with the average in Lancashire.[33]

In a comparative perspective, therefore, it could be argued that British business was in some ways unique, maintaining a 'specialist barrier' which had long since disappeared abroad.[34]

These circumstances inevitably affected the reception given to new techniques. Managers who had received little or no specialist training were often unable to evaluate specific innovations and thus disregarded them. Interfirm comparison (IFC), and early form of bench-marking, was widely and successfully applied in Europe at this time, but tended to be ignored in Britain. Commenting on this contrast, one of IFC's leading proponents suggested that the British problem was 'indifference'. He explained: 'this seems to be due mainly to a lack of imagination on the part of managers and trade association officials, who find it difficult to envisage what good a comparison can do for the industry and its firms.'[35] A similar situation was evident in relation to work study (a more advanced form of time and motion study). This had been developed in Britain, principally by experts at ICI, but was also now more commonly used in Europe than at home. Sir Thomas Hutton, President of the Work Study Society, wrote emphatically about what lay behind British backwardness: 'The main obstacle to the wider introduction of work study, as indeed of many other valuable techniques of production management, is that top management does not understand them and will not admit it.'[36] Two final examples concern marketing and selling. Some British companies had begun using market research in the inter-war years but most continued to believe it was an unnecessary complication, requiring the employment of experts when the 'feel' of the chief executive was perfectly adequate.[37] Accordingly, only about 5 to 10 per cent of consumer goods firms used the technique in the mid-1950s, while it was almost unknown in export fields.[38] This meant, in effect, that thousands of products were being 'tested on the customer'.[39] Furthermore, many companies made only sporadic efforts to encourage sales. Expenditure on advertising in Britain grew from £162 million in 1950 to £454 million in 1960, but most of the total continued to be concentrated on the promotion of a relatively small number of consumer goods.[40] Throughout industry, selling tended to be organized in very traditional ways. A report in the *Director* during 1956 castigated car manufacturers for not adopting the new practices which were being introduced in America and Europe:

Perhaps the worst failing of the British motor industry as a whole is its lack of knowledge of publicity. It ought to put itself over to the world in an altogether 'bigger' way than it does and use . . . modern methods and techniques instead of the hackneyed, old-style material . . . of long ago. But very few of the top men in the industry are publicity-minded; they leave this sort of thing to their underlings, telling them not to spend too much money.[41]

The fundamental feeling, amongst many British manufacturers, was that goods should be 'offered for sale rather than sold'.[42]

For the reformers, the position over human relations was equally disappointing. Within company managements, there was little sign of any pronounced move towards collaborative methods. A large number of companies were dominated by charismatic chief executives, in line with the generally accepted belief that the senior manager should be 'an all-powerful, thrustful personality, whose very genius overshadows and detracts from the more modest performance of his subordinates'.[43] At lower levels, managers were organized into a hierarchy of ranks, differentiated by varying privileges and badges of status. Sizeable businesses frequently operated six or seven restaurants and canteens, differentiated by price and comfort. Management lavatories, too, were another potent symbol, as the average executive apparently felt that 'to meet a junior employee in the place of common humanity would be an affront to dignity'.[44] The whole management structure was usually bound together by codes that emphasized obedience and discipline. Even as late as 1963, an FBI working party

identified 'central authoritarian control' as a typical arrangement throughout industry.[45]

On the shop-floor, too, human relations remained more talked about than
acted upon. Personnel managers were the great evangelists of the new
approach but they had not gained any significant degree of influence. The
Institute of Personnel Management grew during the 1950s but only encom-
passed 4,500 members by the end of the decade. A survey of 1959 found
the discipline of personnel management suffering from a crisis of confidence, perhaps not 'bankrupt . . . but . . . insolvent'.[46] At the British Motor
Corporation, personnel managers had been appointed but were not allowed
to attend major negotiations with the unions, and this seemed to be fairly
typical.[47] Other key components of a human relations approach also
remained undeveloped. Joint consultation in plants had spread quite widely
in the late 1940s but thereafter languished. An enquiry by the Industrial
Society in 1962, focusing on firms that were most likely 'to think in consultative terms' reported 'out of a sample of about 100, 56 per cent had no
[joint] committees, and of those that had, most thought of them as a forum
for company pronouncements and the airing of petty irritations'.[48] In
another investigation, firms were asked whether they shared financial information with their employees. The answers were equally uninspiring:

Presenting financial information is still a managerial novelty. Only about 20 per cent
of all companies are currently giving any information to their employees . . . The
methods that are being used are still tentative and experimental . . . It is significant
that, of the many companies which prepared special annual reports for their employees, only one could be found which had ever tried to find out just how many of them
had actually read it.[49]

Given such attitudes, the gap between 'us' and 'them' continued to be very
wide in many firms, a fact that was noticed by more candid observers.[50]
British workers hired by US contractors to build the ESSO refinery at
Fawley in the mid-1950s were amazed at the openness of their new employers. The American supervisors would take time to explain their plans for
any part of the operation: 'They're not afraid that you're trying to pick their
brains. English engineers are much more snooty.'[51]

Explanations

By the beginning of the 1960s, therefore, it was quite apparent that the
reform programme had only achieved minimal results. Indeed, discourses
about Britain's decline that appeared at the turn of the new decade
repeated many of the criticisms levelled against management in the late
1940s.[52] Why had the organizations promoting change achieved so little?

Part of the problem, no doubt, lay with the reformers themselves. Government interventions to improve management standards were sometimes poorly planned, inadequately financed, or insufficiently harmonized with other policy objectives. Enthusiasts in organizations like the BIM and the EPA could express themselves in a jargon that was impenetrable to the average manager. One 'improving' textbook was criticized by a reviewer for being full of 'a priori reasoning from mathematics, ratiocination about the suppositious [sic] behaviour of omniscient barrow boys . . . , self-evident propositions from the law, proverbs from the scriptures, all blended with the half-truths of the half-sciences, and the coy striptease of personal self-revelation'.[53] Secondly, the general conditions prevalent in industry during the period were in some ways hardly propitious for innovation. Industrialists were instructed to maximize output for exports under the Attlee Government, which inevitably encouraged an indifference to new methods. Subsequently, the existence of a sellers' market until well into the late 1950s produced a similar effect. Since firms were usually making good profits at this time, the incentive to experiment could appear unattractive.

However, the impact of these various factors should not be exaggerated. Most of the reform movements' output was well executed and presented. Organizations like the BIM deliberately attempted to reach the 'average' manager in the smaller firm. Moreover, the economic environment was certainly not uniformly unfavourable to innovation. A sellers' market existed after the War but its benefits did not extend to all sectors equally. From the mid-1950s, much of industry was beginning to experience pressure on margins. The *Director* remarked in 1953:

Competition is getting severe. Anyone with only the remotest connection with industry has known that for well over twelve months. Ministers have been warning us about it for years and industrialists have been saying much the same at one annual general meeting after another. But it has got beyond the talking stage in the past six months. Both at home and abroad firms are up against it and all their decisions reflect it.[54]

Anyway, it was clear throughout these years that British hegemony in overseas markets often continued to be insecurely established. Board of Trade officials and journalists in the business press warned manufacturers about the unsatisfactory nature of British methods and products from almost as soon as the War had ended.[55] Information on resurgent German and Japanese industrial power was also widely available, transmitted with some urgency from government departments to companies via their trade associations.[56] There could be no plea of ignorance about the threat that was beginning to materialize from abroad. If anything, changes in the economic environment should have reinforced the reformers' case.

In fact, to understand why the reform movement failed, it is necessary to look at various other causes. One problem for the reformers was their continuing inability to convince managers about the need for change. Some in management remained uneasy about the reasoning behind what was being suggested and argued that the new methods were not necessarily appropriate for this country. More importantly, there was an obvious dissonance between what the reformers were suggesting and the established common-sense culture shared by British managers. Finally, the reform movement also had to cope with a series of quite deliberate obstructions, co-ordinated by organizations wedded to the *status quo*. The following sections look at each of these three points in turn.

Reasoned Reservations

Those managers who argued a reasoned case against reform made two interrelated observations. Some suggested that the case for professionalizing management was correct but queried whether the means being proposed and adopted were sensible. The American system of business education was often held up as the model to follow. However, close scrutiny of the US business schools, for example, suggested that they were rather less effective than some believed. Indeed, as the more perceptive British visitors emphasized, debate about the merits of American programmes was nowhere sharper than in America itself.[57]

Elsewhere, doubt was expressed about what were taken to be the implicit assumptions underpinning the reformers' ideas about production. British companies might well need to improve manufacturing techniques and employ specialists if this would help efficiency. However, they should not accept, as some outside 'experts' were now allegedly arguing, that such innovations must in the end lead to the wholesale adoption of mass-production techniques. Complete standardization might suit American conditions but it would be disastrous if applied on this side of the Atlantic. Serving many different markets, British firms required maximum flexibility, and an ability to produce relatively small batches of customized products.[58]

These were coherent arguments, but it is also clear that they only really influenced a minority in management circles. The majority of managers who visited American companies believed that they could learn from the experience. Few worried about grand questions of strategy but most were impressed by particular aspects of their hosts' methods. The reactions of a group who attended the College of Business at the University of Cincinnati during 1952–3 were typical:

Many members of the group have noted techniques that, if applied, would be beneficial in their own work. These improvements range from, for instance, a different method of performing a clerical operation to a radical change in top management policy with regard to budgetary control.[59]

Indeed, this kind of approach, with its emphasis on selective emulation, was encouraged by both UK and American reforming organizations. Thus, when the British Productivity Council discussed standardization, it was careful to emphasize that the process should not be pushed too far: 'The objective is to cut out *wasteful* variety, not to eliminate variety altogether, for that would lead to the narrowing of consumer choice while tending to discourage skill in design and inventiveness.'[60]

There is no doubt, too, looking at the other side of the coin, that many of those who were most hostile to American methods had little grasp of the reasoned case outlined above. Some simply feared US competition and distrusted the motives of American government representatives, particularly in relation to Commonwealth markets.[61] Others adopted a more patronizing stance, arguing that Americans were like children in their naïve enthusiasms. Reviewing the American Institute of Management's *Manual of Excellent Managements*, the *Director* adopted a not uncommon tone of languid superiority:

There is something rather endearing about the business efficiency of the United States. Certainly by English standards there is something surprising about the way in which American business is willing to submit to the judgement of efficiency consultants, management experts, company doctors and professors ... of business administration. Whereas in Britain free criticism is applied to books, sports and theatrical productions, in the U.S. it extends to the management of industrial companies.[62]

This was far from any careful debate about issues like standardization.

Management Culture

In fact, the reasons why most managers felt unenthusiastic about the reform programme had little to do with any formal or technical critique. Their dislike of change stemmed from a recognition that what the reformers were suggesting contradicted long-established ideas which managers shared about management.[63] This point can be substantiated by looking in more detail at the key concerns of British management culture.

There is no doubt that most British managers of the 1940s and 1950s felt generally uneasy about abstract discussions of their occupation.[64] Nevertheless, the majority knew instinctively what good management involved. Managers must, above all, be leaders, akin to military generals. Accordingly, they needed to be 'characters', able to inspire subordinates in the firm. Additionally, they were required to possess sound judgement— a 'good brain'—and a capacity to act decisively. Prevarication was not admired, even if the consequences of quick thinking caused problems. A steel manager told the journal *Future*: 'good management is making three decisions, two right and one wrong ... I'm always making wrong decisions here, and they cost the firm a hell of a lot of money. But I don't get sacked, because I make just enough right decisions to get away with it.'[65]

Compared with the emphasis that was placed on leadership qualities, technical competence received far less attention. Although junior managers might need to know about a limited range of specific processes or functions, at the top of the firm, many felt, no such proficiency was necessary. As a correspondent to the *Director* explained with didactic wit, there was nothing intrinsically wrong with a colour-blind person being in charge of a paint factory.[66] The ascent of the management ladder was, therefore, popularly viewed as a move away from the mundane world of special skills. In this spirit, the British representative at an international conference during these years told his audience that the top executive should pursue the broader vision: 'During the weekend... [he] should not plan his time chasing... conferences but, according to his disposition, play golf or garden. Above all things, he should cultivate a balanced outlook towards contemporary life, keeping his imagination lively.'[67]

These core assumptions shaped some of the attitudes to more practical matters that have already been touched upon. For example, the high value placed on intuition in solving everyday matters produced a general scepticism about the potential for formal management training. Anyone so placed could attend 'the school of hard knocks' or 'sit at Nellie's knee', in other words, develop their aptitudes on the job. Others would no doubt be recruited from the public schools and universities—institutions that produced 'good minds'. However, little was likely to be gained from special courses simply because qualities like character could not be taught from books.[68] In such circumstances, those who persevered with management education often remained rather defensive. The Director of Welfare at BEA told the *Manager* in 1953: 'I know from my visits to the technical colleges... in... Middlesex... that the great bulk of people attending the management classes are doing so without the knowledge or encouragement of their employers... [and] the normal position is attendance *sub rosa*.'[69] Similar reasoning determined views of consultation. A belief in decisive and authoritative leadership encouraged an impatience with enforced deliberation. Advice from experts might be necessary, but most believed that discussion with the shop-floor was pointless, literally a waste of time. In private conversation, managers continued to emphasize their prerogatives and underline 'the manager's right to manage'. One told a visiting American academic that if a trade union representative came to see him about his firm's balance sheet, 'he would kick him out of the office'.[70]

Taken as a whole, therefore, the pervasive management culture was in important respects at odds with the reform programme. Managers generally held views about their calling which actively contradicted much of the new thinking. What made this situation even more disappointing for the reformers was the fact that employers seemed to be actively encouraging intransigence. Indeed, organizations like the FBI and the Institute of Directors (IoD) had continued deliberate campaigns aimed at undermining reform initiatives. This aggressive stance stemmed from events in World War II.

Employer Attitudes

During the production crisis of 1940–2, to repeat, there was much discussion about the nation's industrial underperformance. Several groups were blamed, but the most popular view was that management bore the greatest responsibility. Indeed, even the journal *Business* partly accepted this diagnosis, commenting: 'it is certainly and unfortunately a fact that however guilty officialdom may be in the way of not putting men to proper work, business management itself is in many places mishandling the good men and materials that *are* at work.'[71]

Managers and employers reacted to this criticism in a variety of ways. Some drew radical conclusions, arguing that the current system needed drastic overhaul. However, the majority were deeply shocked by what they perceived as the anti-capitalist bias inherent in the public denunciations. The consequence was a sense of insecurity but also a growing determination to defend the *status quo*, a point emphasized in Mass-Observation's exhaustive study of *People in Production*:

The people who own, organize and run war industry, are not necessarily fighting for the same thing as the much larger number who work in it. The ownership . . . side is naturally concerned with preserving freedom of private industrial enterprise . . . and the profit incentive . . . Putting it very crudely, the average employer is almost automatically, and sometimes unthinkingly, fighting for a revival of the peacetime industrial system.[72]

By 1943, the crisis in industry had largely passed, but now employers and managers became worried by a second kind of threat. The government had encouraged trade union participation in decision-making during the War so as to boost co-operation, and labour generally seemed to be becoming stronger and more confident. Some employers accepted that these changes might be advantageous while the fighting continued, but few believed they could possibly be extended into the peace. Concerted action to restore pre-war norms, it was agreed, might well be unavoidable. Given such resolve, tension began to mount in industrial areas. During late 1944, the director of the Coventry Engineering Employers Association felt that 'he was sitting on the edge of a volcano', leading a Ministry of Labour official to comment:

this may be an exaggeration, but nevertheless we feel that the atmosphere is changing to one in which industrial trouble can easily and rapidly spread. The psychological effects of cuts in production, the approaching end to hostilities and the uncertainty as to the post-war position are, without question, having a very disturbing effect in the Coventry area.[73]

In many ways, Labour's victory at the 1945 General Election hardened attitudes even further. The *Financial Times* noted the 'apprehension' which 'afflicted a wide area of private enterprise' in the weeks following the poll, while *Business*, in an edition of early 1946, referred to a 'wave of anxiety' that was passing through British industry. The issue was clear. Labour, the business community believed, might publicly declare that its plans were moderate but in the end favoured the workers and meant to nationalize large parts of the economy. Business had no alternative but to fight back.[74]

One facet of this new-found commitment was a growing willingness to join representative organizations. During the early 1940s, there were 130,000 to 140,000 firms in Britain, but less than one-tenth subscribed to any of the trade or 'peak' associations.[75] By contrast, reports after 1945 painted a very different picture. Business organizations had become better run, with higher quality staff and greater knowledge of Whitehall ways. More importantly, they were also benefiting from enhanced support. The FBI's membership doubled in size between 1942 and 1950, while other umbrella organizations, like the National Union of Manufacturers, achieved similar growth. Trade associations also prospered. Even previously moribund institutions benefited: the IoD consisted of 'a handful' of members on its relaunch in 1948, but within three years had attracted over 5,000.[76]

At the same time, many were prepared to go beyond mere organizing and support active forms of intervention. The objective was to limit state intervention on industrial matters, no matter in what form it occurred. A variety of tactics were used. An effort was made, firstly, to influence public opinion by promoting private enterprise. Pressure was exerted on the BBC hierarchy to report 'industry's problems' as 'sympathetically' as possible.[77] Money poured into the coffers of propaganda organizations like the Economic League and Aims of Industry, with the former distributing 7.6 million leaflets and organizing 7,000 meetings during the first five months of 1950 alone.[78] Meanwhile, behind the scenes, attempts were made whenever possible to undermine a range of government industrial policies through the use of procedure, obstruction, and innuendo.[79] For example, efforts to staff the fledgeling BIM dragged on because of secret manoeuvring by hostile employers. Since none of the first-choice candidates would agree to run the organization, the government ended up by installing a complete outsider as its first chief executive: the Hon. Leo Russell, an ex-Etonian, veteran of Montgomery's staff, and then Assistant Secretary at the Board of Trade and gentleman farmer, had not even considered applying for the job when it was first advertised and so was mildly surprised when subsequently appointed.[80] The general message emerging from this and other episodes was clear: industry did not welcome government reforms even when they were aimed at promoting efficiency.

Given this uncompromising stance, it was inevitable that much of business should approach the 1950 and 1951 election in something of a 'do or die' spirit. As confidential reports to the Conservative Party recorded, some companies were desperate enough to be considering the transfer of their assets abroad in case of a Labour victory.[81] However, at the second contest, with the Tories victorious, the employers could at last begin to relax, happy at the demise of what one columnist in the *Director* termed 'the "constitutional dictatorship" of the Socialist Party'.[82]

During the ensuing thirteen years of Conservative rule, relations between government and business were generally far more amicable. Employers did not always agree with the detail of Tory policy, but they appreciated the fact that the administration believed wholeheartedly in private enterprise. Nevertheless, the events of the previous years still left their mark. In 1954, for example, the journal *Scope* warned that 'a swing to the Left could occur at any future election' and continued: *'Private enterprise has not turned the corner. It still exists on sufferance. One must deplore this, but one should not forget it.'*[83] A year later, the *Director* rated the threat of a Labour victory at the polls as 'very real' and described how disastrous this would be:

A Labour Government today would be a Bevanite and extreme left-wing affair. And a left-wing Labour administration means not only more rationalization, but possibly nationalization without compensation . . . Labour's promise to 'start new public enterprises' is . . . a threat to every company, small and large.[84]

At the 1959 contest similar anxiety was evident. Business expenditure on publicity attacking nationalization was described as 'enormous'—'about four times what the Conservative party was spending on advertising in the same period and fourteen times the Labour party's outlay on public relations'.[85]

In these circumstances, attitudes on practical questions continued to be uncompromising. American officials in London, charged with encouraging the productivity drive, were frequently astonished at the negative attitudes displayed by their business contacts. They heard from the FBI and the British Employers Association, for example, that the EPA was a waste of money which had produced 'negative' results.[86] Occasionally, intransigence was such that the Americans became disheartened. Over $1.3 million was spent during the first half of the 1950s on educational programmes which took British managers to America so that they could study local methods. However, this initiative was finally abandoned, a subsequent US official report regretted, because of 'the obvious lack of enthusiasm of so many students in their educational experience, the weakness of British industry's support of this program, and the pedestrian administration of the projects by the British Ministry responsible'.[87] The campaign to undermine the BIM also continued unabated. During 1954, a senior figure in the BPC appealed for Ministerial help to quell 'the quite unnecessary feud' which one employers' association was 'pursuing against' the BIM. However, even this produced little result, with smears and obstruction remaining facts of life for the management organization until the 1960s.[88]

Some Conclusions

The reform movement failed, therefore, for two main reasons. Its objectives ran counter to long-established management thinking. Secondly, reform organizations became embroiled in a wider field of industrial politics, the struggle by employers to prevent state encroachment into business. Such a combination was powerful enough to produce stalemate.

As a final coda, it is worth asking whether this failure mattered. Such a question is not easy to answer, but it seems likely that what happened did impose costs. British management today is suspicious of formal training; retains a belief in leadership as more important than technical competence; and continues to have difficulty in coping with conceptual innovation. Moreover, it has not fully accepted the idea that workers should be treated as valuable assets rather than dispensable commodities, a point that firms trying to imitate Japanese human relations practices often discover.[89] All of these attitudes are widely judged to be disabling. Yet each was identified and criticized by the reform movement forty years ago. Had reformers been able to gain greater purchase, it appears likely that current problems would not exist on anything like a similar scale.

The legitimacy of this conclusion is confirmed by looking at what happened in other European countries after the War. Management reform was on the agenda in much of Western Europe at this time, usually prompted by American pressure. Change was often contested, with French managers, for example, remaining deeply ambivalent about organizations like the EPA.[90] Nevertheless, in general, reformers were much more successful than in Britain, and this was especially true of Germany and Italy.[91] By the beginning of the 1960s, therefore, observers were already beginning to notice a substantial gap between management standards in Britain and those in much of the rest of industrialized Europe, and this pattern has persisted up to the present.[92]

In overall terms, therefore, the period that has been considered here seems to have been a wasted opportunity. The reformers of the 1940s and 1950s identified what was wrong with British management and proposed a series of realistic and appropriate solutions. Their failure to induce large-scale change left a legacy of problems that is still being grappled with today.

NOTES

1. I would like to thank Terry Gourvish, Jim Obelkevich, Jim Tomlinson, and Jonathan Zeitlin for helpful comments on earlier drafts of this chapter and advice on sources.

2. B. Supple, 'British Economic Decline since 1945', in R. Floud and D. McCloskey (eds.), *The Economic History of Britain Since 1700* 2nd edn., iii: *1939–1992* (Cambridge, 1994), 324–5.

3. M. Porter, *The Competitive Advantage of Nations* (London, 1990), 502; K. Williams *et al.*, 'Facing up to Manufacturing Failure', in P. Hirst and J. Zeitlin (eds.), *Reversing Industrial Decline? Industrial Structure and Policy in Britain and Her Competitors* (London, 1989), 82–4; and Cmd. 2263, *Competitiveness* (London, 1994).

4. For example, management is largely ignored in both N. F. R. Crafts and N. Woodward (eds.), *The British Economy Since 1945* (Oxford, 1991) and Floud and McCloskey, *Economic History*.

5. M. Best, *The New Competition* (Cambridge, 1990), 144.

6. See, for example, D. C. Coleman, 'Gentlemen and Players', *Economic History Review*, 26 (1973), 92–116; I. A. Glover and M. P. Kelly, *Engineers in Britain* (London, 1987); N. Swords-Isherwood, 'British Management Compared', in K. Pavitt (ed.), *Technical Innovation and British Economic Performance* (London, 1980), 88–99; and M. Weiner, *English Culture and the Decline of the Industrial Spirit 1850–1980* (Cambridge, 1981).

7. See various contributions in B. Collins and K. Robbins (eds.), *British Culture and Economic Decline* (London, 1990).

8. Hirst and Zeitlin, 'Introduction', in Hirst and Zeitlin, *Industrial Decline*, 6.

9. See e.g. D. C. Coleman and C. Macleod, 'Attitudes to New Techniques: British Businessmen, 1800–1950', *Economic History Review*, 39 (1986), 588–611.

10. Editorial comment, *Industry Illustrated*, 11 (1943), 11; and J. Child, *British Management Thought* (London, 1969), 103.

11. For a fuller discussion of the points raised in the following paragraph, see N. Tiratsoo and J. Tomlinson, *Industrial Efficiency and State Intervention: Labour 1939–51* (London, 1993), 21–63.

12. *The Times*, 6 Nov. 1944.

13. Tiratsoo and Tomlinson, *Industrial Efficiency*, 114–15 and 131–52; European Productivity Agency, *Higher Productivity Through European Co-operation* (Paris, 1956), 3; European Productivity Agency, *Activities and Achievements* (Paris, 1958), 27–35.

14. Contemporary works advocating or explaining 'progressive' methods include J. A. C. Brown, *The Social Psychology of Industry* (Harmondsworth, 1954); G. Hutton, *We Too Can Prosper* (London, 1953); and G. Rattray Taylor, *Are Workers Human?* (London, 1950). The development of new thinking in the 1940s and 1950s is surveyed in Child, *British Management Thought*, 110–57 and N. Rose, *Governing the Soul* (London, 1991), 80–101.

15. L. H. C. Tippett, *A Portrait of the Lancashire Textile Industry* (London, 1969), 23; anon., 'Schooling for Steelmen', *Manager*, 32 (1964), 41–2.

16. I. McGivering *et al.*, *Management in Britain* (Liverpool, 1960), 80.

17. *The Economist*, 16 Aug. 1958; British Institute of Management, *Report . . . by a Committee under . . . Sir Cecil Mead* (London, 1968), 39.

18. *The Economist*, 4 Aug. 1956; Public Records Office (hereafter PRO), CAB 134/2203, M.A.C. (59) 4th Meeting, 6 Apr. 1959, 1.

19. The education and training issue is surveyed in S. P. Keeble, *The Ability to*

Manage: A Study of British Management 1890–1990 (Manchester, 1992) and R.R. Locke, *Management and Higher Education Since 1940* (Cambridge, 1989).

20. T. M. Mosson, *Management Education in Five European Countries* (London, 1965), 156.
21. G. Cunliffe, 'Trends in Management Studies', *Manager*, 28 (1960), 194–6.
22. Management Education, Training and Development Committee, *Management Training in Industrial Relations* (London, 1975), and G. Mills, 'Education for Marketing: A Programme in Action', *Advertising Quarterly* (1966), 2–8.
23. *The Economist*, 17 Dec. 1955.
24. National Economic Development Council, *Management Recruitment and Development* (London, 1965), 6.
25. Anon., 'Is Business a Profession?', *Future*, 6 (1951), 23; anon., 'Management Indicted', *Times Review of Industry and Technology* (May 1963), 3.
26. British Institute of Management, *The Making of Managers* (London, 1963), 2.
27. E. Sidney, 'Evaluating Management Training', *Industrial Welfare*, 38 (1956), 160–4.
28. Tiratsoo and Tomlinson, *Industrial Efficiency*, 115.
29. Quoted in *Business*, 81 (1951), 33.
30. Acton Society Trust, *Management Succession* (London, 1956), 28.
31. Cmnd. 902, Advisory Council on Scientific Policy, Committee on Scientific Manpower, *Scientifical and Engineering Manpower in Great Britain, 1959* (P.P. 1959–60, xx), 33–5.
32. Board of Trade, *The Machine-Tool Industry: A Report by the Subcommittee of the Machine-Tool Advisory Council* (London, 1960), 27.
33. British Productivity Council, *The Weaving Industry in the Netherlands and Western Germany: Report of a European Visit in October/November 1961, by a British Joint Management/Trade Union Team* (London, 1962), 72.
34. G. Simpson, 'The Specialist Barrier', *Scientific Business*, 1 (1963), 143–8.
35. H. Ingham, 'Inter-firm Comparison for Management', *Manager*, 27 (1959), 316.
36. Sir T. Hutton, 'Work Study', *Manager*, 28 (1960), 127; *British Business Week*, 3 May 1968.
37. E.g. K. Rogers, *Managers—Personality and Performance* (London, 1963), 38 ff.
38. C. Kapferer, *Market Research Methods in Europe* (Paris, 1956), 68; H. Wilson, 'Market Research in the British Economy', *Commentary*, 7 (1965), 4–9.
39. R. Fry, 'New Ways to Make 'em Buy', *Manchester Guardian Survey of Industry, Trade and Finance* (1958), 46–7.
40. N. Tiratsoo, 'Popular Politics, Affluence and the Labour Party in the 1950's', in A. Gorst *et al.* (eds.), *Contemporary British History 1931–1961* (London, 1991), 52.
41. Anon., 'What's Wrong with the Motor Industry?', *Director*, 9 (1956), 95.
42. Editorial comment, *BETRO Review*, 4 (1949), 79.
43. T. Burns and G. M. Stalker, *The Management of Innovation* (London, 1961), 211; Rogers, *Managers*, 138; and M. Pritchard, 'Can We Sell Our Way Out of Inflation?', *Manager* 24, (1956), 884.
44. R. Lewis and R. Stewart, 'The Men at the Top', *Encounter*, 11 (1958), 44–54.
45. Federation of British Industries, *Management Education and Training Needs of Industry* (London, 1963), 3.
46. L. Urwick, *Personnel Management in Perspective* (London, 1959), 14.

47. PRO, LAB 10/1627, Note K. Ashfold to T. Evans, 27 Jan. 1961, 1–7.
48. *New Society*, 16 June 1966.
49. P. F. Dyer, 'Presenting Financial Information to Employers', *Manager*, 25 (1957), 101–8.
50. C. Chisholm, 'New Answers and Old Problems', in C. Chisholm (ed.), *Communication in Industry* (London, 1955), 3.
51. A. P. Gray and M. Abrams, *Construction of ESSO Refinery, Fawley* (London, 1954), 38.
52. A. Albu, 'Taboo on Expertise', in A. Koestler (ed.), *Suicide of a Nation* (London, 1963), 82–93; R. Malik, *What's Wrong with British Industry* (Harmondsworth, 1964); Political and Economic Planning, *Attitudes in British Management* (Harmondsworth, 1966); and M. Shanks, *The Stagnant Society* (Harmondsworth, 1961).
53. R. W. Revans, 'Time for Franks', *Times Review of Industry* (Dec. 1963), 98.
54. Anon., 'The Squeeze is On', *Director*, 6 (1953), 833; and more generally, S. J. Wells, *British Export Performance. A Comparative Study* (Cambridge, 1964) and National Economic Development Council, *Imported Manufactures: An Inquiry into Competitiveness* (London, 1965).
55. See e.g. editorial comment, *Business* (Sept. 1946), 35–6; and *Board of Trade Journal*, 5 Jan. 1952.
56. See information in *Board of Trade Journal*, 28 July 1956; and R. Ormandy, 'The Threat of Japanese Competition', *Manchester Guardian Review of Industry, Commerce and Finance* (1952), 67, 69.
57. D. C. Platt, 'The Perils of American Business Education', *Director*, 12 (1960), 294–6.
58. For these arguments, see J. Zeitlin, 'Americanisation and its Limits: Theory and Practice in the Reconstruction of Britain's Engineering Industries, 1945–55', *Business and Economic History*, 24 (Autumn, 1995), 277–86.
59. Modern Records Centre, University of Warwick (hereafter MRC), MSS 200 F/3/T3/29/4, Interim Report for the MSA, 12 May 1953, 18.
60. British Productivity Council, *Better Ways, Nineteen Paths to Higher Productivity* (London, 1957), 34.
61. National Archives, Washington (hereafter NA), Record Group 469, Mission to the U.K., Office of the Director, Subject Files . . . Box 6, File on 'UK Productivity', Memo by F. E. Rogers to W. L. Batt, 5 Aug. 1952, 2.
62. *Director*, 9 (1956), 143.
63. Elements of this culture are discussed in Child, *British Management Thought*; M. W. Kirby and M.B. Rose (eds.), *Business Enterprise in Modern Britain* (London, 1994); P. L. Payne, 'Industrial Entrepreneurship and Management in Britain', in P. Mathias and M. M. Postan (eds.), *The Cambridge Economic History of Europe*, vii: *The Industrial Economies* (Cambridge and London, 1978), 180–230; and J. F. Wilson, *British Business History, 1720–1994* (Manchester, 1995).
64. See e.g. R. A. Brady, *Crisis in Britain* (London, 1950), 649.
65. Anon., 'Interregnum for Steel Managers', *Future*, 4 (1949), 45, 47.
66. *Director*, 6 (1955), 915.
67. *Manager*, 19 (1951), 426.
68. Federation of British Industries, *Management Education*, 3–4.

69. D. Cleghorn Thompson, 'Management Training: Some Frank Opinions', *Manager*, 21 (1953), 271.
70. D. Granick, *The European Executive* (New York, 1962), 234.
71. *Business*, 71 (1941), 13.
72. Mass Observation, *People in Production* (London, 1942), 365.
73. PRO, LAB 10/444, R.I.R.O. Midlands Weekly Report, 6 Oct. 1944, 2.
74. Tiratsoo and Tomlinson, *Industrial Efficiency*, 64–5.
75. Anon., 'No Common Aim', *Scope* (Sept. 1942), 24.
76. Anon., 'The F.B.I. Pt. 1', *Scope* (Sept. 1949), 48–55 and 77–8; 'Industrial Trade Associations', *Planning*, 25 July 1955; 'What Does the Institute of Directors Do?', *Director*, 2 (1951).
77. See material in MRC, MSS 200 F/1/1/186.
78. *Director*, 1 (1950), 3.
79. M. Frankel, 'Joint Industrial Planning in Great Britain', *Industrial and Labor Relations*, 11 (1958), 429–45 and Tiratsoo and Tomlinson, *Industrial Efficiency*, 73–88.
80. Tiratsoo and Tomlinson, *Industrial Efficiency*, 87.
81. Conservative Party Archive, Bodleian Library, Oxford, CCO4/3/249, P.O.R.D. 'Confidential Supplement' (June 1949), 2.
82. *Director*, 1 (1950), 51.
83. Editorial comment, *Scope* (July 1954), 35.
84. Editorial comment, *Director*, 6 (1955), 231.
85. D. E. Butler and R. Rose, *The British General Election of 1959* (London, 1963), 252–3.
86. MRC, MSS 200 B/4/2/3, B.E.C. Bulletin, No.76, Dec. 1957, 2.
87. NA, Record Group 469, Mission to the U.K. Office of the Director, Subject Files, Box 5, File on 'U.K. Productivity—General', Report by F. E. Rogers on the U.K. Technical Exchange and Section 115-K Program, 6 Sept. 1956, 17.
88. PRO, BT 258/96, Minute by S. A. Dakin, 28 Sept. 1954, 1 and material in MRC, MSS 200/F/3/S2/38/3.
89. See e.g. C. Hampden-Turner and F. Trompenaars, *The Seven Cultures of Capitalism* (London, 1994); C. Handy *et al.*, *Making Managers* (London, 1988); N. Oliver and B. Wilkinson, *The Japanization of British Industry* (Oxford, 1988); and T. J. Watson, *In Search of Management: Culture, Chaos and Control in Managerial Work* (London, 1994).
90. R. Kuisel, *Seducing the French* (Berkeley and Los Angeles, 1993), 70–102.
91. See e.g. NA, Record Group 469, Records Relating to EPA 1953–7, Box 3, File on Productivity and Applied Research Committee, Minutes of Committee, 37th Session, 5–6 Aug. 1955; and L. Segreto, 'Redeemed Sceptics, Ungrateful Friends vs. Dreaming Social Engineers: Italian Business Community, Italian Government, the US and the Comitato Nazionale per la Produttiva', paper presented at EU Seminar on the EPA and European Business Schools, Bertinoro, Italy, June 1995.
92. V. M. Clarke, 'Education for Management in the Common Market' *Manager*, 30 (1962), 29–34, Granick, *European Executive* and J. B. Shallenberger, 'Are European Managers Better Organised?', *Manager*, 29 (1961), 855–8; and J. L.

Barsoux and P. Lawrence, *Management in France* (London, 1990), Hampden-Turner and Trompenaars, *Seven Cultures*, C. Lane, *Management and Labour in Europe* (London, 1989) and R. Stewart *et al.*, *Managing in Britain and Germany* (London, 1994).

PART III

Education

6. Education Change and In-Firm Training in Post-War Japan

TAMOTSU NISHIZAWA

Introduction

With natural resource disadvantages but a long tradition of respect for education, human resources have been an area where Japan has created competitive advantages. Much has been written on the importance attached to education and training, or the human capital investment by the government, parents, and companies in Japan. Over 95 per cent stay on in full-time schooling until the age of 18, in contrast to 32 per cent of the 16–18-year-olds in Britain. The rate of attendance at high school (upper secondary school) has increased with economic growth; it was 70.7 per cent in 1965 and 91.9 per cent in 1975. The proportion of general courses has constantly increased at the same time. Such high intensity of schooling is explained partly by a high standard of literacy and numeracy, which supplied a mass homogeneous work-force of good quality, and seems to have contributed to the expansion of labour-intensive manufacturing and to the ability to adapt to changes in technology and world demand.[1]

In Japan, wages, promotion, and social status are basically determined by one's educational and academic qualifications, or by one's company, not by professional qualification. If someone is asked about his profession, he usually answers by referring to his company: 'he is likely to define himself as a Hitachi man first and as an engineer second'. 'Technicians' and 'craftsman' are not familiar words in a Japanese factory: instead, the terms most likely to be used are 'middle-school-graduate employee' and 'high-school-graduate employee', to make a similar distinction. Then the university degree is 'the ticket-of-entry into the managerial ranks'.[2]

The recruitment of new graduates as a source of labour has had crucial importance in Japan's labour market. It is said that about 70 per cent of upper-secondary-school leavers and 60 per cent of university graduates are not vocationally trained when they start working. In order to get the necessary skills and knowledge for their jobs they are trained by the company. Because of the lifetime employment system, what Japanese companies are most concerned about with new graduates is not their specific skills or knowledge but their lifetime potential capability. Once they get a 'golden egg', as long as they cherish it, it may be expected to be a 'golden goose' in the future.[3]

Japan's formal higher educational system administered by the Ministry of Education seems to have provided a sound foundation for later in-firm training and continual upgrading of human resources by both on-the-job and off-the-job methods, which served to promote the flexibility and all-important diagnostic skills and management techniques. This further training and upgrading in each company has been largely devised and promoted by the various business organizations and conducted by the external training centres at the initial stages.

'*Gakureki* Society' in the Making

As a late-developed country Japan has been transformed into the '*Gakureki* society' (meritocracy: literally 'impact of educational background') far more quickly than Britain, and educational qualifications are more likely to be the route to social advancement. There is a general faith in the education system as a fair ground for meritocratic competition and a valid sorting mechanism for determining life chances. The importance of higher formal education has been strongly emphasized in professional and business careers. A comparison of the proportion of university-educated business leaders in Japan, the United States, and the United Kingdom, as Figure 6.1 shows, indicates striking differences. Starting with a very low proportion, Japanese business firms soon found great value in university and college education and began to recruit future technologists and managers on the basis of educational qualifications. Whereas in Britain only half of managers had degrees by the 1970s, in Germany the figure was 62 per cent, in the USA 85 per cent, and in Japan 90 per cent. By the 1970s Japanese managers were 'the most highly educated in the world' and received systematic, company-specific technical and managerial training throughout their careers.[4]

In the 1920s and 1930s it was increasingly usual for the Japanese businessmen in the largest firms to have a degree. By the 1960s and 1970s it was almost a prerequisite for the business executives to be a graduate. An overwhelming majority (91 per cent) of the 1960s business leaders received higher education in colleges or universities. Over two-thirds (68 per cent) graduated from universities: only 9 per cent went no further than compulsory middle school. Of the 305 men who in 1967 occupied departmental chief positions and head office section-chief positions in Hitachi, only nine had not been either to a university or to one of the pre-war technical high schools of quasi-university status. The recruitment of new graduates has been the dominant mode of recruitment of technologists and managers since the 1920s.[5]

Among university graduates, there are also differences based on the reputation and prestige of the universities, which are very steeply graded.

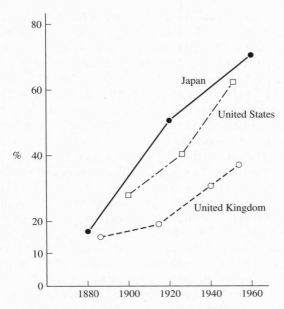

FIG. 6.1.   Proportion of university graduates among business leaders: Japan, United
States, United Kingdom, 1880–1952 (per cent).

Source: H. Mannari, *The Japanese Business Leaders* (1974).

Some of the Japanese companies recruit new graduates exclusively from
several 'prestigious universities'. Graduates from less esteemed universities
are not even given the chance to take an interview. Only 31 per cent of large
companies (more than 5,000 workers) are said not to use a university nom-
ination system. Therefore, people know that to get a high salary in a big
company, they must go to a prestigious university, which would require
them to go to a prestigious upper secondary school, which in turn would
require them to go to a prestigious lower secondary school, and so on. In
order to go up this educational ladder, everybody has to take and pass a
very competitive entrance examination, which has created the so-called
'examination hell'. Competitive entrance examinations at the top universities are very stiff indeed.[6] Consequently, Japan's formal education system
works as a sophisticated sorting-out process. In the academic qualification
society, the name of the university and its department gives little information about what students learned there. However, it indicates the level of
their general ability within society as a whole. By recruiting graduates from
'first-class' universities, employers can expect them to have 'first-class'
general ability and potential. Selection by the universities at the top of
the prestige scale would provide 'the best predictor of useful lifetime
employability'.[7]

The system of higher education, on the other hand, had not been brought into the service of business in Britain even by the 1960s. As late as the mid-1950s less than half of the directors and only about one in five managers (one in three top managers) of large British firms were graduates. Germany, Japan, and the USA had surpassed this in the 1920s.[8] G. C. Allen, who was appointed at the Higher Commercial School in Nagoya in 1922 and lived in Japan in the early 1920s, noticed 'a sharp contrast' in the educational systems of England and Japan, and remarked in his first book on Japan: 'Unless a man has received the conventional academic training appropriate to his particular career, then he has little hope of ever obtaining a good position. It is not merely the civil servants, lawyers and teachers to whom this applies, but engineers, technicians and businessmen also. The banks and business firms themselves recruit very largely from the graduates of the commercial and higher commercial schools, and one rarely meets a bank manager or an important official in a joint-stock company who has not been trained at one of these institutions.' In Britain, on the other hand, the majority of managerial and administrative posts were filled by people with a general education or self-made men who had worked their way up. Allen noted 'very clearly the contrast in intellectual quality between the typical Japanese executive or manager and his British counterpart'.[9]

Unlike British companies, companies in Japan were quick to seek and hire university graduates, and to offer them promotions and salary increases based on educational and academic qualifications. The results of a nationwide survey in 1930 showed that 72 per cent of the middle- and upper-level managers in private companies and 57 per cent of engineers were graduates of higher education institutions. There was a trend toward the bureaucratization of management after World War I along with the rapid increase of white-collar workers or the growth of the 'new middle classes'. Employees were classified into three or four categories in the big companies, and recruited respectively from different grades of the educational hierarchy. It seems that the prototype of the Japanese employment system dates back to the 1920s.

Employment was not only dependent on educational achievement, but also on the university from which a person graduated. Starting salaries (per month) of the graduates entering Nihon Yusen in 1917 were: for the graduates from Tokyo Imperial University 40–45 yen; for those from Tokyo Higher Commercial School (later Hitotsubashi University) 35–40 yen; Keio and Waseda 30 yen; and other private colleges 25 yen. The word *Gakureki-shugi* or *Gakureki-shakai* (academic qualification society) came into common use only in the 1960s. But the phenomenon had existed from the early 1920s, and had become one of the most important ways of defining a person's status and prestige in Japanese society. The 'examination hell', as it is known today, existed in Japan as early as the 1920s.[10]

Although Japan has a very high proportion of business leaders with university or college education, her business community has not recognized professional training at graduate school as an important qualification. It would be true to say that the *Gakureki* of Japan's business leaders was limited to university graduates, compared with the situation in the United States, where 44 per cent of the business élite had a graduate degree, and in Germany, where 50 per cent had a Ph.D. Instead, in Japan training after graduation has been largely entrusted to 'in-firm training'.[11] If in the USA the professional education of managers at graduate schools rather than shop-floor workers was emphasized, in Japan the firm-based education and training of all sections of the work-force was inseparable from strategies of flexible production. As technology and organizational systems became more complicated, there was an increasing demand for supplementing on-the-job by off-the-job training, and the training industry was growing. However, instead of sending managers and engineers to American-style graduate schools, there was a preference for training in-house.[12]

While American-type graduate schools for professional education have not developed in Japan, formal vocational education has been rather neglected since the age of high economic growth. The proportion of general courses at the upper-secondary-school level has steadily increased since 1970. The training which the major firms give to their new recruits both on- and off-the-job, adds more to the stock of the nation's skills than the vocational schools. 'Japan's strength as an industrial nation lies not so much in the sheer volume of vocational education in schools and universities—there are two and a-half times as many engineering graduates per capita as in Britain, etc.—but rather in its very high levels of general education'. Therefore, the lack of vocational education directly applicable to jobs did not worry Japanese employers much. What they looked for in recruitment and selection for long service, was first, general intellectual ability as indicated by school and university records, and then, candidates with the right personality and attitudes as reflected by extra-curricular activities. Vocational knowledge was useful (the more so the smaller the company) but was prized more for its mastery of the theoretical background, as a basis for further learning.[13]

Thus, an 'academic bias problem' has been generated. This bias has led over time to a smaller proportion of pupils on vocational courses (28 per cent in 1985, as compared with 40 per cent in 1955 and 1965). In the main, vocational education is overshadowed these days by the functioning of the schools and universities as mechanisms for ability labelling. There arose a demand that the vocational streams should not be final ends and that their graduates should be able to go on to universities. Hence an increasing proportion of the curriculum was devoted to general education. At the university level, the first two years of the four-year course are spent on general subjects. Specialization starts only in the third year. Thus, the standard of B.Sc. engineering graduates in Japan on average is said to be lower than that attained by British students.[14]

High Economic Growth and Educational Change

Vocational Demands in the 1950s and 1960s.

In the early 1950s the Japanese economy began to boom and the business world expected to be able to recruit many good new graduates who would be instantly useful to industry. The recognition of a serious shortage of scientific and technical manpower emerged as a major educational problem in the heyday of rapid economic growth in the 1950s and 1960s. Educational policy seems to have been consciously designed to foster economic development, and there is no doubt that the interests of business and industry have been highly influential in shaping educational policy since the mid-1950s. The business community became active in education and training, and the leading business organizations, and in particular Nikkeiren (Japan Federation of Managers Association), raised their voices of criticism against the new post-war 6–3–3–4 linear formal education system, which was guided and formed under the influence of the American education mission. Nikkeiren, founded in 1948 under the presidency of Moroi Kan-ichi, who had made great efforts to develop the Central Society for Promotion of Industrial Education (Sangyo Kyoiku Shinko Chuo-kai), thought that under the new 6–3–3–4 linear system the pre-war concept of industrial or vocational education would almost disappear (see Fig. 6.2).[15]

Nikkeiren vigorously requested the educational authorities to make several reforms. They first presented 'demands for reconsidering the new educational system' in 1952, and advocated 'the expansion of the industrial higher school' so as to be able to 'display the proper dignity of the industrial schools as the training institutes of the middle ranks of company employees'. 'The demands for improvement of the current educational system' in 1954, requested the school system to meet in particular the requirements of medium-sized and smaller businesses by: (1) promptly correcting the over-emphasis on law and literature studies in the universities; (2) eliminating the uniformity of Japanese universities; (3) adjusting the balance between general subjects and the elementary subjects of specialized courses and expanding special subjects; (4) in the higher schools in each region, enlarging the characteristic special subjects to correspond with the requirements of regional society where medium and smaller businesses were dominant.[16]

In 1956 Nikkeiren submitted to the government its famous 'Opinion on technical education to meet the needs of the new era', which was influenced

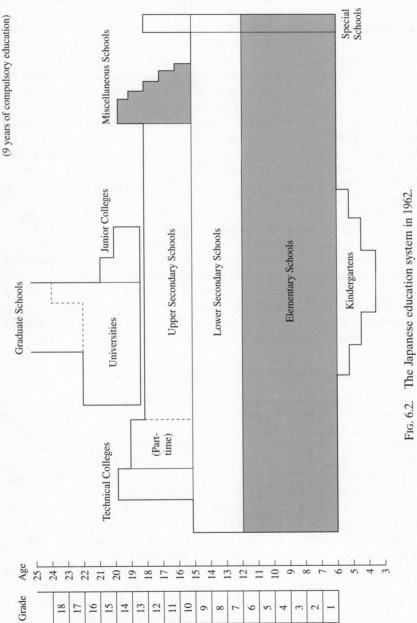

Fig. 6.2. The Japanese education system in 1962.

Source: 'Education in Japan—A Graphic Presentation', by the Education Ministry.

by Britain's White Paper on Technical Education, saying that 'the promotion of technical education is a pressing matter that will not allow a single day's delay'. To reform industrial technological education to meet the demands of the new era and to systematically cultivate scientists, technicians, and engineers, they urged the government to take the following measures: (1) promotion of science education and vocational education in compulsory education; (2) the expansion of higher technical schools for the training of technicians and supervisors (normal higher schools to be reduced as much as possible); (3) reform of science and engineering university education. Here industry felt strongly that there was a need for the kind of middle-ranking engineers which the pre-war industrial professional schools supplied. Two-year junior colleges should be merged with higher schools to establish five-year special technical colleges; in four-year universities the imbalance favouring law and literature should be corrected by an increase in government expenditure and subsidies for science and technology universities. Finally, industry was disappointed by the fall in the number of class hours given to special courses during the four-year degrees of technology-related universities, which were 30 or 40 per cent down on hours provided by the pre-war colleges.[17] It was even argued in the National Income Doubling Plan of 1960 that under the existing system of enrolment there would be a shortage of 440,000 technicians with higher technical school diplomas in the target year of the Plan. It was estimated that approximately 1.6 million school-trained technicians and approximately 1.8 million retained technicians would be needed.[18]

High Economic Growth and Manpower Development

In 1960 the Ikeda Cabinet introduced its National Income Doubling Plan, declaring that 'in order to double our national income within ten years the target of annual economic growth for three years forward should be aimed at 9 per cent on average'. In the 1960s, Japan's education policy also seems to have changed a great deal. By making education 'part of economic policy', the National Income Doubling Plan gave a crucial impetus to education policy. 'The advancement of manpower capability and promotion of scientific technology' was emphasized as follows: 'The main characteristic of the contemporary economy is that of technological innovation supported by continuous high-level economic growth and rapid advances in science and technology. It is essential to promote manpower development as part of economic policy in order to fully comprehend and utilize science and technology, and to sustain further development of our economic life.'[19]

In association with it the Sub-committee for Education and Training of the Economic Advisory Council (Keizai Shingi-kai) officially announced its 'Long-term Education Plan accompanying the Income Doubling Plan'. This stressed the expansion of upper secondary schools and the technical edu-

cation connected with general education. In addition to cultivating technical experts and skilled labour, which was stressed by Nikkeiren, a policy
was required that would seek to improve the aptitude of the general
populace. Manpower development could be attained by raising the educational standards of the nation and thereby instilling broad knowledge, the
ability to make accurate judgements, and a proper sense of values. For these
reasons, it was announced in the Income Doubling Plan that 'we must
implement the educational training of youths from 15 to 18 years old, a
world-wide task'. The rate of enrolment in upper secondary school was 57.7
per cent in 1960. It was estimated that this rate would rise in correlation
with the rise of per capita income to 72 per cent in the target year of the
National Income Doubling Plan (in 1970 the rate of enrolment was actually 82.1 per cent), (see Table 6.1.).[20]

Prime Minister Ikeda made his famous 'Hitozukuri' (formation of human
beings) speech on 25 May 1962, saying:

What brought forth the progress of our nation today, despite the fact that defeat in
war caused us to lose territory and left us surrounded by destruction, is the education which our forerunners bequeathed . . . If we are to build the nation of Japan,
we must build human beings [ningen o tsukuru]. Japan is restricted in territory and
limited in resources, but the Japanese people themselves have an excellent consti-
tution. Through education, the Japanese people can continue to cultivate this superb
character and contribute not only to their own country, but also show their fibre to
the world.[21]

TABLE 6.1. *Rates of attendance at upper secondary school and the shares of
general and vocational courses, 1955–1983 (percentages)*

Year	Rate of attendance	Share of general courses	Share of vocational courses	(1) × (2)	(1) × (3)
	(1)	(2)	(3)	(4)	(5)
1955	51.5	59.8	40.2	30.8	20.7
1960	57.7	58.3	41.7	33.6	24.1
1965	70.7	59.5	40.5	42.1	28.6
1970	82.1	58.5	41.5	48.0	34.0
1975	91.9	63.0	37.0	57.9	34.1
1980	94.2	68.2	31.8	64.2	30.0
1981	94.3	69.1	30.9	65.2	29.1
1982	94.3	70.0	30.3	66.0	28.6
1983	94.0	70.5	29.5	66.3	27.7

Source: K. Inoue, *The Education and Training of Industrial Manpower in Japan*
(1985).

In November 1962 the Ministry of Education published its White Paper on Education called 'Japan's Growth and Education'. Special attention was directed to the relationship between educational and economic developments, and its pivotal point was long-term education planning from the viewpoint of 'educational investment'. Economic growth had been emphasized to the detriment of individual or personal development. In developed countries, such human factors as scientific creativeness, technological talents, labourers' skills, and the ability to utilize fully all available resources had been recognized as affecting economic development. For future economic growth to occur it would be necessary to increase investment in the development of all available national resources. Education directed at the development of 'human resources' should be considered as one of the most important forms of investment. Hence education should be looked upon not as a mere item of consumption but as an investment in economic growth. Education was an indispensable factor in the full utilization of the fruits of rapid acceleration of technological innovation. In this context, education should be regarded as an investment.

The White Paper stressed the role of education in Japan's economic development. The remarkable recovery after the War 'has depended mainly on such human factors as knowledge and talents which had been accumulated since the pre-war period' and in particular, the spread of general elementary education to farming families who constituted the major part of the labour-force at the beginning of modernization. The diffusion of elementary education raised the quality of the people's skills, modernized their ideas, and made it possible for them to participate successfully in modern economic activities. Thus the high evaluation of the role of education in achieving economic development in Japan should be attributed to 'the effort of the people who restricted consumption and invested the money thus saved in education'. Indeed, 'the rate of education expenditure to national income in Japan was among the highest in the world'.[22]

In co-operation with the Ministry of Education the Economic Advisory Council published a report on *Problems and Strategies in Manpower Development during Economic Growth* in January 1963. First, it asserted the necessity for manpower policy. Japan had focused on manpower as labour and considered that its relationship with economic growth had always been necessary for the improvement of the national standard of living. In short, the goal of manpower policy was to develop the economic conditions for the enrichment of life and to develop manpower as an element in promoting economic growth. The existing system of educational training did not aim at developing the type of human talent that was equipped for high economic growth. In order to attain effective resource utilization it was necessary to review the various factors involved in management and labour–management relations. Considering the issue of human resource cultivation, it was essential to develop skilled workers, such as technicians and specialists, who would directly support and promote economic development, and therefore develop people with greater skills ('high talent').

The report also put emphasis on the 'improvement in education by implementing meritocracy [noryokushugi]'. The standardized system of automatically promoting pupils to higher grades should be reformed into a more flexible system that took into account individual abilities. The entrance examination should be reformed into a more rational system. To achieve this, it was necessary to administer a nation-wide qualifying entrance examination aimed at allowing entrance to schools of higher levels based upon objective criteria.[23]

This was the time when the so-called 'Japanese employment system' was establishing itself. The system of in-firm training was in the making, where new graduates or new recruits first entered the company and through on-the-job and off-the-job training advanced in accordance with the company's needs and requirements. Under such a system of employment and recruiting the standard of estimation was inclined to be scholarly attainments and school careers rather than pluralistic standards, as has been argued above.

When the life employment and seniority systems were completed, and the subordination of the work-force to the company was advanced, there was heightened consciousness that in order to obtain a better or stronger position in the company, a higher school career would be more advantageous than the acquisition of subdivided special abilities. Such a situation caused subdivided technical training to be less attractive. Thus, the Ministry of Education's diversification policy never materialized, and vocational schools were downgraded in the public's mind.[24]

The Japan Productivity Centre and the Diffusion of In-Firm Training

The post-war history of in-house management training started first with the introduction of various American management methods at the end of the 1940s and spread widely in the early 1950s. They were called CCS seminars for top management, MTP (management training programmes) for middle management, and TWI (training within industry) for supervisors or inspectors. In 1949, the Civil Communications Section of the American Occupation GHQ convened CCS management seminars, which marked a watershed in Japan's post-war management education. The CCS seminars on top management were conducted by Nikkeiren from 1953 and two years later became the responsibility of the Japan Society for Industrial Training (Nihon Sangyo Kunren Kyokai, founded in 1955 under the auspices of Nikkeiren). TWI and QC (Quality Control) were diffused most extensively in the post-war industrial world and contributed much to the recovery of the Japanese economy. In 1950 the late Dr Deming gave a series of lectures on transmitting the rudiments of statistical quality control. Also of great importance was the formation of various organizations dedicated to the promotion of diffusion of quality control such as the Japanese Union of Scientists and Engineers (Nikka Giren, founded in 1946), the Japanese Standards Association (Nihon Kikaku Kyokai, founded in 1945), and the Japan Management Association (Nihon Noritsu Kyokai), to which almost all the companies seeking to introduce quality control sent their employees for training. These organizations also did a great deal in the promotion of management education and training in general.[25]

It is said that 1955 was the first year in the age of the development of the managerial function. It marked the institutionalization of management education as part of in-firm training. On the political front the Liberal Democratic Party won the election in that year, then stayed in power until very recently, providing a stable, pro-business environment. Furthermore, two prominent external training organizations were born in 1955, with powerful backing from business organizations and government: the abovementioned Nihon Sangyo Kunren Kyokai and the Japan Productivity Centre. They met the needs of management development in industry for which the higher academic institutions were neither willing nor equipped to deal with by graduate schools. That need was essentially concerned with practical competence to manage specific and individual business problems rather than the acquisition of theoretical and abstract notions.[26]

The Japan Productivity Centre (Nihon Seisansei Honbu) was founded in 1955 as a result of a nation-wide campaign for improving productivity, against the background of a successful European productivity movement under Marshall Aid. The concept of the JPC dates back to the sixth annual meeting of Keizai Doyukai, which was founded in 1946 as a union of 'progressive businessmen'. The Keizai Doyukai's intellectual leader and its secretary, Goshi Kohei, referred to his recent experience in Europe, where he was greatly impressed by the industrial relations and co-operation of managers and workers in West Germany and the productivity movement in Britain. Graham Hutton's *We Too Can Prosper* (1953) was a major influence on Goshi, and he was deeply interested by remarks such as: 'The secret of the high productivity of the US is not in the machine . . . it lies in the unreserved collaboration of the worker and the boss.'

Goshi was also influenced by the suggestion that US technical aid for higher productivity in European countries could be extended to Japan. As a result of Doyukai's efforts, four leading business organizations in Japan—Federation of Economic Organizations, Japan Chamber of Commerce and Industry, Nikkeiren, and Doyukai—met and reached agreement that a productivity movement should be launched in Japan. In consequence, the Japan Productivity Council was set up in 1954. Japan's Labour Ministry was concerned with improving labour productivity, translating ILO reports, and MITI itself had been studying the activities of the Anglo-American Productivity Council and intended to establish a national productivity centre.

Then the Japan Productivity Council transformed itself into the Japan Productivity Centre, consisting of representatives of workers, managers, and intellectual neutrals under the vice-presidency of Nakayama Ichiro, who was then the president of Hitotsubashi University and also of the Central Labour Committee. Professor Nakayama was an earnest and theoretical advocate of Management Councils (Keiei Kyogi-kai) and Worker–Managers Joint Consultancy (Roshi Kyogi-sei) which meant in-firm organizations to help forward the collaboration of managers and workers. Worker–Managers Joint Consultancy was a crucial concept of Japan's productivity movement, and it has been introduced into some 70 per cent of all companies.[27]

In 1956 Keizai Doyukai proposed 'the recognition and practice of social responsibility by managerial persons'. They stressed the importance of fostering and training their successor managers not only for business itself, but also for society. Doyukai stated that 'business corporations are now public instruments of national economy' and that 'the eternal development of business firms is the great responsibility of the managers'. It asserted that the 'long-term development of business firms could not be expected without quantitative expansion and qualitative advancement of managerial persons', and emphasized the significance of the self-development of managers and fostering the successor managers who had both intelligence and management technique. Doyukai, who had already opened the Management Academy (Keiei Daigaku), advanced 'a policy for the development of managers' in 1958 and stressed the necessity of the institutionalization of management education by setting up a long-term education programme in business firms.

By means of the National Income Doubling Policy attention to the training of human resources was rapidly strengthened and management education was rapidly diffused. Against this background, education and training by JPC was accelerated. In 1960 JPC pronounced it would 'carry out systematic and organized management education with the idea of industry–university co-operation'. The Labour Productivity Academy was opened in 1964 to train labour problem specialists to advance the concept of industrial co-operation. In 1965 the Academy of Management Development was established as a part-time graduate business school. Its prospectus declared that 'it is not too much to say that the most important problem for today's business is the problem of manpower'.[28]

Around the year 1960 Japan's management education was in transition after a period in which it had enthusiastically devoured American management techniques. Japanese experts had begun taking over from Americans in management seminars and consultancy activities. Ueno Yoichi, a founder of the Japan Management Association, was a pioneering spirit in the development of management consultancy as a profession and established the Institute of Management Consultants in 1951, which is very highly

regarded today. In 1958 JPC started a full-time one-year Management Con-
sultant Course for training professional management consultants. The first
Karuisawa seminar for top management was also held in the same year.
Along with this trend, 'a boom in management studies' was created. The
publication of books on management was flourishing. Sakamoto Fujiyoshi
wrote a textbook in layman's language in 1958, and Peter Drucker's
Automation and New Society was translated in 1956. In the same year Keio
held its first top management seminar with the co-operation of Harvard
Business School. A more systematic approach was accompanied by the
introduction of a Japanese focus. In 1960, the fifth Anniversary Declaration
of JPC noted that it should aim at the application of new overseas management techniques to Japan's social and economic climate. 'Japanization'
was to be practised and carried out through firm-specific education and
training.

JPC has conducted a wide range of programmes of management development, embracing new recruits through to board directors, overseas study
teams, management guidance, the worker–managers co-operative committees, the Labour Productivity Academy, and Academy of Management
Development. With its philosophy of 'business depends on men', the management education section has provided various seminars and courses. In
1961, thirty-eight different seminars were conducted, and in 1962, fifty-four
seminars and six courses. The number of participants in seminars was: 1,147
in 1960, 1,285 in 1961, and 1,871 in 1962, when 367 attended courses. JPC
also conducted general orientation programmes for new recruits from university, college, and higher school, who had just begun work. The participants in the new employees training courses reached 3,147 in 1960, 4,425 in
1961, and 5,792 in 1962.[29]

As a questionnaire survey by the Japan Society of Industrial Training
in 1970 shows (see Table 6.2.), of 855 companies which replied, about 42
per cent were conducting Keieisha (executive) education and 85 per cent
Kanrisha (managers') education, while 75 per cent were involved in middle-
management education. Concerning the starting year, 75 per cent were concentrated in the period after 1961. The contents of executive education were
various seminars such as top management seminars, overseas study teams,
study meetings in the company, etc. But with the progress of management
education, executive education was achieved by programmes organized by
firms themselves: in 1965 own-company training accounted for 36 per cent
of the total.

The emphasis of management education naturally varied with the size of
firm and type of industry: and of all management education, *managerial*
education spread most extensively. The degree of diffusion amounted to 85
per cent in 1970, reaching 99 per cent in the big businesses of more than
5,000 employees. It was more than 90 per cent in the firms of more than
1,000 employees, and 70 per cent in the firms of less than 500 employees.

TABLE 6.2. *Diffusion of management education in 1970 (percentages)*

	Executives (Keieisha)	Managers (Kanrisha)	Middle-ranking employees	New recruits
1970				
In operation	41.7	84.8	74.9	96.4
Planned	6.4	3.2	6.7	0.8
Not operating	51.9	12.0	18.4	2.8
Starting-date				
Pre-war	0.3	0.4	1.1	5.7
1945–50	0.8	1.6	1.2	7.1
1951–55	2.1	8.3	4.9	18.2
1956–60	9.1	14.3	11.7	25.3
1960–65	15.2	30.4	29.0	27.5
1966–70	15.8	29.4	27.1	12.9

Source: JSIT, *The Present State of In-firm Training* (1970).

In finance and insurance the diffusion extended to 94.1 per cent, and in wholesale retail industry 90.3 per cent. With regard to the education for middle-ranking employees, the degree of diffusion was about 75 per cent in 1970, and reached 91 per cent in the big businesses. In finance and insurance it was the highest at more than 92 per cent.[30]

During the 1960s in-firm management education and training have spread extensively against the background of rapid economic growth. Many pioneering companies incorporated their own 'educational policy' or 'educational programme' to meet their own firm-specific needs under conditions of 'lifetime employment'. The diffusion of in-firm education and the formation of firm-specific training heralded the progress of Japanization. Business organizations such as Keizai Doyukai and Nikkeiren, and the external centres such as the Japan Management Association and the Productivity Centre seem to have played a vital role in the diffusion of firm-specific training in the initial stages in particular.

In-firm Training and Company Community

As companies accept a variety of graduates, who are not educated in the faculty appropriate for their jobs, it is crucial to train the new graduates and to fill the gap between university education and the special requirements of business. In-house training is being undertaken not only for new recruits, but also for staff at various levels, because companies usually take a policy of regular staff movement, and employees are often forced to accept what is called 'job rotation' every three or four years. Though this shows the adaptability of Japanese employees to new circumstances, they always need to be trained and educated intensively by the companies or by themselves.

The systematization of in-firm training and education has been extensively attempted with rapid economic growth. For example, Hitachi, in fostering its 'Hitachi industrial men' has created a variety of training institutions as shown in Figure 6.3, as well as a management school known as the 'Executives School', founded in 1960. During every April and May, all the new recruits collectively attend an induction course which includes visits to some of the Hitachi factories, lectures on the structure and history of the company, together with a few general lectures on management science and engineering technology, etc. The course is more particularly concerned with the related process of being socialized into the Hitachi community. As the official description of the course puts it, it is designed 'to enable new graduates to grasp the history of the company and of its separate establishments; further it seeks to develop within them the spirits and attitudes appropriate to Hitachi men and, while imparting certain basic knowledge and skills relevant to their professional status as technologists and managers, to promote the development of character and of their general education'. The

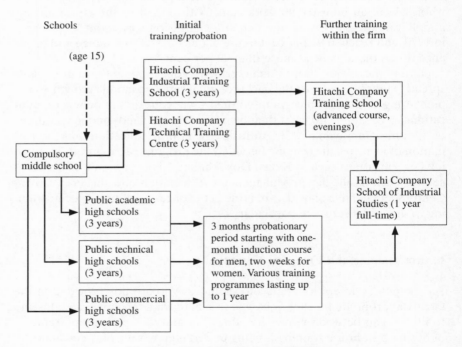

Fig. 6.3. Hitachi's training institutions.

Source: R. Dore, *British Factory—Japanese Factory* (1973).

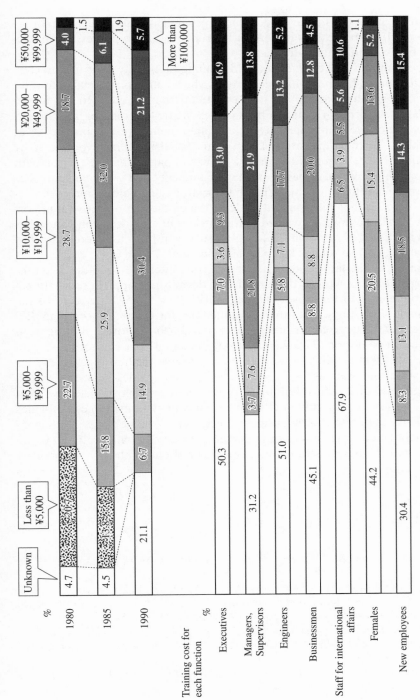

FIG. 6.4.   Annual cost of education and training per employee, 1980–1990.
Source: JSIT, *Questionnaire Survey Concerning In-Firm Training* (1990).

'Guiding Spirit of Hitachi', a document promulgated for educational purposes in 1959, represents important instruments in this process of character building and attitude formation.[31]

The comprehensive education and training of employees is a characteristic feature of Japanese management, in which companies are able to raise employees' morale and ability, and eventually to promote their productivity. Japanese firms are said to be more explicitly 'learning organizations', and some of the companies have even called themselves 'schools', such as 'Yoshida Gakko' in the case of Dentsu, an advertising company directed by Yoshida Hideo. With rapid economic growth in particular, the environment surrounding companies has been changing quickly, and every company has had to be careful to maintain flexibility with its technology and organization, in which the ability and attitude of the employees are of vital importance. Thus, the money invested in human resources by the companies has been increased as shown in Figure 6.4. A survey in 1993 discovered the ratio of training cost to total sales to be 10.8 per cent.

Almost all the large companies are offering intensive courses while providing employees with accommodation in dormitories, applying educational programmes with their own 'guiding spirit'. In 1993, 55.8 per cent of the companies questioned had their own facilities for training: more than 81.9 per cent of the large companies of more than 3,000 employees, 45.1 per cent of the companies of 1,000–2,900 employees, and 37 per cent of those with less than 1,000 employees. And 76 per cent have facilities exclusively for education and training: 49.5 per cent of the companies have the special section (Ka) or its equivalent for education and training; and 22.3 per cent have the special department (Bu) or its equivalent. Some large companies even have their own in-firm business colleges (Kigyonai College), with management creeds such as 'education is the greatest company welfare', which seems to have been instrumental in making company culture and company community.[33]

NOTES

1. R. P. Dore and M. Sako, *How the Japanese Learn to Work* (London, 1989), ch. 1.
2. R. Dore, *British Factory—Japanese Factory* (Berkeley, 1973), 48, 60.
3. K. Inoue, *The Education and Training of Industrial Manpower in Japan*, World Bank Staff Working Papers, no.729 (Washington, DC, 1985), 29.
4. H. Mannari, *The Japanese Business Leaders* (Tokyo, 1974), 197–8; M. B. Rose, 'Education and Industrial Performance: Influences on British Experience since 1945', this vol.
5. Mannari, *Business Leaders*, 199–200, 264–5; Dore, *British Factory—Japanese Factory*, 64.

6. Inoue, *Educational Training*, 25–6.
7. Ibid. 29; Dore, *British Factory—Japanese Factory*, 48–9.
8. M. B. Rose, 'Investment in Human Capital and British Manufacturing Industry to 1990', in M. W. Kirby and M. B. Rose (eds.), *Business Enterprise in Modern Britain* (London, 1995), 340.
9. G. C. Allen, *Modern Japan and Its Problems* (London, 1928), 78, 80–2; idem., *Appointment in Japan: Memories of Sixty Years* (London, 1983), 73–5; idem., *The British Disease* (London, 1976), 45–7.
10. I. Amano, *Education and Examination in Modern Japan* (trans. W. K. and F. Cummings) (Tokyo, 1983), pp. xii–xiv; Japanese National Commission for UNESCO (ed.), *The Role of Education in the Social and Economic Development of Japan* (Tokyo, 1966), 263, 295; I. Amano, *Kyusei Senmon Gakko*, (Tokyo, Nihon Keizai Shinbunsha, 1978), 154; E. Daito, 'Recruitment and Training of Middle Managers in Japan, 1900–1930', in K. Kobayashi and H. Morikawa (eds.), *Development of Managerial Enterprise* (Tokyo, 1986), 151–79.
11. M. Aso, *Nihon No Gakureki Elite* (Tokyo, Tamagawa Kaigaku Shuppanbu, 1991), 21–3.
12. M. Sako and R. Dore, 'Teaching or Testing: The Role of the State in Japan', *Oxford Review of Economic Policy*, 4/3 (1988), 78.
13. Ibid. 76–8.
14. T. Shiomi, 'Kigyo-shakai to Kyoiku', in *Sengo Kaikaku to Gendai-shakai no Keisei* (Tokyo, Iwanami-shoten, 1994), 295–6.
15. K. Toba (ed.), *Zaikai-jin no Kyoiku-kan, Gakumon-kan* (Tokyo, Daiyamondo-sha, 1970), 327–31, 338–41; Sangyo Kyoiku Shinko Chuo-kai (ed.), *50 Nen-no Ayumi* (Tokyo, 1988), 93–6; Kokuritsu Kyoiku Kenkyujo (ed.), *Nihon Kindai Kyoiku 100 Nen-shi*, x (Tokyo, 1973), 431, 588–91.
16. Nihon Keieisha Dantai Renmei, *10 Nen no Ayumi* (Tokyo, 1958), 191, 221–2.
17. Ibid. 242–4.
18. E. R. Beauchamp and J. M. Vardaman (eds.), *Japanese Education since 1945: A Documentary Study* (New York, 1994), 151.
19. Shiomi, 'Kigyo-shakai', 296–7; O. Watanabe, 'Gendai Nihon Kokka no Tokushuna Kozo', in *Gendai Nihon Shakai*, i (Tokyo, Daigaku Shuppankai, 1991), 229–30; Beauchamp and Vardaman, *Japanese Education*, 148.
20. Watanabe, 'Gendai Nihon Kokka', 230; Beauchamp and Vardaman, *Japanese Education*, 152.
21. Ibid. 154–5.
22. Shiomi, 'Kigyo-Shakai', 298–9; Watanabe, 'Gendai Nihon Kokka', 232–3; Beauchamp and Vardaman, *Japanese Education*, 156–8.
23. Shiomi, 'Kigyo-shakai', 302; Watanabe, 'Gendai Nihon Kokka', 230–2; Beauchamp and Vardaman, *Japanese Education*, 159–63.
24. Shiomi, 'Kigyo-shakai', 303–5.
25. *Nihon Kindai Kyoiku 100 Nen-shi*, 579–86; Nihon Sangyo Kunren Kyokai (ed.), *Nihon Sangyo Kunren 100 Nen-shi* (Tokyo, 1971), 333–5.
26. F. Sakamoto, *Nihon Keiei Kyoiku-shi Josetsu* (Tokyo, Daiyamondosha, 1964), 172; L. Okazaki-Ward, *Management Education and Training in Japan* (London, 1993), 34–5.
27. Nihon Seisansei Honbu (ed.), *Seisansei Undo 30 Nenshi* (Tokyo, 1985), chs. 1–2; K. Goshi, *Goshi Kohei: Seisansei to Tomoni* (Tokyo, Nihon Seisansei Honbu,

1990), 28–44, 242–54. Hutton's book was translated by S. Hasegawa in 1954. A. Carew, *Labour under the Marshall Plan* (Manchester, 1987), ch. 9. For Worker–Managers Joint Consultancy (Roshi Kyogi-sei) see *Nakayama Ichiro Zenshu*, xiii (Tokyo, Kodansha, 1972), 451–580.

28. *Keizai Doyukai 15 Nen-shi* (Tokyo, 1961), 391–7, 414–19, 422–4; *Nihon Kindai Kyoiku 100 Nen-shi*, 673–5.

29. Sakamoto, *Nihon Keiei Kyoiku-shi*, 143–4, 172–3, 180; Nihon Seisansei Honbu, *Seisansei*, ch. 3; Okazaki-Ward, *Management Education*, 35–6, 455–62. Over the thirty years following the first industrial mission of 1955, JPC sent more than 26,000 to the USA and Europe.

30. Nihon Sangyo Kunren Kyokai, *Waga-kuni no Kigyonai-Kyoiku no Genjo* (Tokyo, 1970). See also idem., *Kigyonai-kyoiku ni kansuru Sogo Anketo Chosa* (Tokyo, 1990); *Nihon Kindai Kyoiku 100 Nen-shi*, 658–62.

31. Dore, *British Factory-Japanese Factory*, 50–1.

32. *Kigyonai-kyoiku ni kansuru Sogo Anketo Chosa* (Tokyo, 1990). *Kigyo to Jinzai*, 26/603 (1993); *Kigyo no Kyoiku-tantosha Jitsumu Soran* (Tokyo, Romu Gyosei Kenkyujo, 1993).

33. As note 32.

7. Education and Industrial Performance: *Influences on British Experience since 1945*[1]

MARY B. ROSE

If modern British business is compared with the United States, Germany, and Japan, the attitude displayed towards human-capital investment by employers and workers is noticeably different. Amongst Britain's principal competitors, employers have long viewed training of their work-force as an investment, the return on which would be enhanced business performance and competitiveness. In Britain, by contrast, training has more often been viewed as a cost. It has, as a consequence, been neglected and only recently has it been viewed as a vital part of business strategy. Thus, whilst by the 1980s leading employers in Japan, West Germany, and the United States devoted 3 per cent of annual turnover to training, the comparative figure in Britain was 0.14 per cent.[2]

Until the 1950s industrial training in Britain usually meant apprenticeship. Yet its sharp decline, from 240,000 in 1964 to 179,000 in 1979, and a mere 63,700 in 1986, has left a growing skill gap in British manufacturing industry. Although some of this shrinkage came with the decline of Britain's manufacturing base, this was only part of the story.[3] Increasingly by the 1980s, in Britain both foremen and the shop-floor work-force received training which lacked both the breadth and depth of their counterparts elsewhere. Thus whereas two-thirds of German workers were trained to craftsman level, only a third of British workers were similarly qualified. Moreover, around seven times as many foremen in Germany acquire technical qualifications as in Britain.[4] It may, however, be misleading to compare experience in Britain exclusively with that in Germany. Evidence for 1982 suggests that German levels of formal technical training were matched neither in the United States nor, more revealingly, in Japan.[5] Yet, if in the United States the education of managers rather than shop-floor workers was emphasized, in Japan since the 1950s in-house training of all sections of the work-force was inseparable from distinctive strategies of flexible production. In Britain, on the other hand, post-war experience highlights the relative indifference of employers to the systematic education and training of any group of workers.

A symptom of the comparative neglect of human-resource management in Britain has been the ambivalent attitude of both managers and workers to the benefits of education. In addition close links between education and industry have been comparatively rare since World War II.[6] Between 1945 and the 1970s an anti-academic ethos amongst businessmen was reflected both in levels of graduate recruitment and in suspicion of the professional education of managers. In the 1950s, for example, only 10 per cent of mechanical engineers had degrees, whilst a mere 24 per cent of those in managerial posts were graduates. Moreover, change came only slowly so that by the 1970s the educational attainments of Britain's managers were still inferior to their counterparts in the United States, elsewhere in Europe and in Japan.[7] In the 1970s only half of British managers had degrees, while in Germany the figure was 62 per cent, in the United States 85 per cent, and in Japan 90 per cent. In contrast with the United States in particular, there was neither management education in Britain, nor detectable business pressure for its development, before the 1960s.[8] It is of course true that the same could be said of experience in Japan where professional managerial education was also largely absent. Yet by the 1970s Japanese managers were the most highly educated in the world and received systematic, company-specific technical and managerial training throughout their careers. If management education was underdeveloped in Britain before the 1960s, the post-compulsory education of the majority of school-leavers was also deficient in comparison with European and Japanese competitors. In addition, the technical competence of shop-floor workers has also been found wanting.[9]

This chapter is divided into four sections. The first outlines the development of education and training in Britain since 1945. It explores the coincidence of increasing government expenditure on education with the manifest human-capital failings detected in British business. The second section assesses the extent to which both post-war government policy and the attitudes of employers and workers were moulded by a combination of historical and contemporary influences. Negligence with respect to human resources is by no means the only supply-side explanation of the loss of competitive advantage by many of Britain's firms in the twentieth century. Nevertheless, its significance, whilst difficult to measure, should not be underrated. In the third section, therefore, the consequences of the inadequacies of post-war human-capital responses for micro- and macroeconomic performance are explored. In the final section conclusions are drawn.

The State and Education Policy Since 1945

The British industrial revolution, with its modest technical demands, was achieved without a co-ordinated government education policy.[10] This was in sharp contrast with experience in the United States, Germany, and Japan where a growing emphasis on education was associated with economic expansion. In Germany the relative backwardness of the economy, the early superiority of British manufactures and a growing government demand for technical personnel, led to a centralized and co-ordinated training and education policy.[11] 'By means of intellectual power and scientific insight'[12] Germany hoped to compensate for limited wealth and industrial experience and to enhance shop-floor training. In Japan, from 1872, the state placed education second only to national defence in its quest for economic progress. In the United States too, government support for all levels of education was considerable with 32.5 per cent of state government expenditure devoted to education.[13]

If government intervention on education proved unnecessary in the British industrial revolution, it developed only slowly in the century and a-half which followed. It took the combined pressures of foreign competition, shifts in the industrial base, technological change, and a growth in the size of firms in the late nineteenth century, to force improvements in formal technical and scientific education on to the government agenda. Legislation in 1889 and 1890 made financial provision for municipal technical colleges, while plans for junior technical colleges were aired in the 1902 Education Act.[14] Yet, if initiatives were national, implementation remained local, 'an instinct for localism' which contrasts sharply with experience in Germany and Japan.[15] With respect to university-level scientific education, on the other hand, government finance and co-ordination were even more limited. Initially financed primarily by industrialists, the new institutions reflected local industrial and commercial profiles.[16] The result of such uncoordinated development was a patchy and limited provision of scientific and technical education, which none the less proved more than adequate to meet the limited needs of industry.

World War I did not have any lasting impact on government education policy. Wartime skill shortages had prompted government-controlled initiatives, under the umbrella of the Ministry of Munitions.[17] Similarly, the spectre of a trade war after the hostilities meant that the Ministry of Reconstruction had accorded technical and scientific education a high priority. Yet the military defeat and economic collapse of Germany in 1918 drastically reduced the momentum for change.[18] The 1918 Education Act did raise the school-leaving age to 14 and required compulsory part-time continuation education. But along with other plans for post-war reconstruction, continuation education was a victim of the Geddes Axe of 1922, and further significant expansion of technical education had to await rearmament in 1938.[19] World War II marked a watershed in government attitudes towards expenditure on education and, in theory, to scientific and technical education. Manpower shortages and a concern to improve productivity placed training and education on the reconstruction agenda. The 1944 Education Act addressed the problem of compulsory education, so often shelved in the inter-war period, and left open the option of a three-tier system of grammar,

technical, and secondary modern schools to cater for the needs of both academic and non-academic pupils.[20] Similarly, the Robbins Report of 1963 sig-
nalled a dramatic expansion of the university sector. Public expenditure on
education rose accordingly, from £284 million in 1948 to £6,626 million in
1975. In the 1930s the British government devoted just 2.5 per cent of GDP
to education. By 1965 this proportion had risen to 6 per cent in 1965 and
compared favourably with leading post-war industrial powers such as Japan
and West Germany.[21]

Since World War II, and in particular since 1960, politicians and academics have often highlighted Britain's poor record on productivity, innovation, and trade. As a result attention has increasingly been directed
towards vocational education.[22] For example, the Technical Education White
Paper of 1956 emphasized the importance of education for economic
growth. It proclaimed that 'Unless we can get every intelligent youngster
on to the further education ladder, our hopes of meeting industrial needs
will not be fulfilled.'[23] Nevertheless, apprenticeship remained the favoured
preparation for the world of work until the 1960s. Aware of a growing skill
gap the government promoted firm-specific training through the Industrial
Training Act of 1964, an initiative which enjoyed only mixed success.[24]

The economic crises of the 1970s, and growing awareness of British deindustrialization, led the central government to take the lead in education and
training policy. The establishment of the Manpower Services Commission
in 1973, which had a budget of £641 million by 1978–9, was intended to
strengthen the existing industrial training structure. Yet rising unemployment meant that temporary work experience began to take priority.
Already withering on the vine, the Industrial Training Schemes became one
of the many casualties of the public expenditure cuts of the Thatcher Government between 1979 and 1981.[25] They were replaced, under the New
Training Initiative in 1981, by Youth Training Schemes which, while reducing unemployment, did little to close the skill gap with Britain's continental competitors.[26]

While youth unemployment remained a priority until the mid-1980s,
more fundamental reform of education became a corner-stone of a growing
Tory obsession with social engineering. Some innovations were nevertheless to be welcomed, if only in theory. The introduction of a National Curriculum, designed to ensure that all students study mathematics and science
until 16, was long overdue. It is also hard to fault the notion of City Technical Colleges, funded by government and industry, as an alternative secondary school route.[27] Yet differences within the Tory party concerning
educational priorities, combined with a tendency towards short-termism,
as PSBR considerations overrode educational issues, has left an overall
impression of confusion.

The evolution of British management education had been very modest before 1939.[28] In 1951 the Anglo-American Council on Productivity

favoured the establishment of US-style university business schools, to improve overall economic performance. Yet it was fourteen years, with an increasing deterioration in Britain's relative economic performance, before this was achieved. Investigating Britain's patchy provision of managerial education in 1963 the Franks Report concluded:

that there is a gap in Britain today which must be filled without delay. More and better education and training for managers, and potential managers, on the lines of what already exists is admittedly urgent, but by itself is not enough. One or more Schools of Business are needed with a scale, range of activities and quality which will produce major effects in business life and at the same time give inspiration and focus to the widely scattered efforts now going on.[29]

The foundation of first the London and then the Manchester Business School during the 1960s, in response to the Franks Report, marked the beginning of graduate management education on the American model.[30]

The Neglect of Human-Capital Investment: Cultural and Contemporary Explanations

As we have seen, the level of state intervention in, and public expenditure on, education in Britain increased in the post-war period. Yet against this background neither employers nor workers have always seemed convinced of the benefits of training and education. Indeed, it seems that industrialists lagged behind both the Ministry of Labour and educationalists in their awareness of the implications of Britain's human-capital deficiencies.[31] The FBI, for example, whilst welcoming the 1944 legislation, did not see it in terms of producing a better-educated work-force. Rather it was seen as a route to a happier world.[32] Formal education for shop-floor workers was rarely given high priority and the apprenticeship remained the preferred qualification, with both workers and employers, until the 1970s.

With respect to managerial education, scepticism within the business world was even more pronounced. The response of industrialists, in the early 1960s, to intensified government discussion of management education, was to propose a country house in the Home Counties offering remedial courses.[33] This was indicative of the indifference, not to say hostility, of the business community to managerial education programmes and undoubtedly delayed the appearance of business schools in Britain. Nor did the establishment of the London Business School and the Manchester Business School, half a century behind those in the United States, drastically transform this attitude. Only a minority of firms were, for example, prepared to provide funding for the new institutions. Moreover, as a passport to top managerial posts, the British MBA was less valid than its American counterpart, with nearly half of the students in any event coming from the public

rather than the private sector.[34] Indeed, where British managers had a
formal qualification at all, it was more likely to be in accountancy than an
MBA, as in the United States, or in engineering, as in Germany.[35]

In a world where international competitive advantage was increasingly
linked to human-capital investment, these attitudes need explanation. Differences in the post-war economic environment, the direction of educational policy, financial and labour arrangements, and macroeconomic policy
were all important influences on human-resource management in Britain.
Yet it is the complex interaction of contemporary and historical influences
which together explain Britain's distinctive experience. There has been a
long tradition of indifference to the benefits of education by employers in
Britain. It is true that cultural and institutional interpretations of economic
decline have often highlighted the deficiencies of a nineteenth-century education system which failed to meet the needs of industry.[36] Yet by 1890 the
provision of scientific and technical education, at all levels, had improved
significantly, albeit patchily, as a result of government and private initiatives.[37] By 1900, therefore, it was less the case that British education was
failing as that the majority of British industrialists were, at best, half-hearted
about its benefits for their firms.[38] In contrast to experience in the United
States, Germany, and Japan, in Britain any increase in the demand for
formal education of any kind was very modest.[39] The small scale of most
firms, the shop-floor training of many owners and the continued predominance of the staple industries, meant that pressure for educational change
did not come from industry. Instead, as in the post-1945 period, the momentum came primarily from politicians and academics.[40] Employers, and indeed
trade unionists, demonstrated an ambivalence bordering on hostility to
formal qualifications in general and to graduates in particular.[41] It was an
indifference and suspicion borne of Britain's particular experience of
industrialization.

Despite some sharp contrasts in experience, the countries in which training and education have been accorded high priority in the twentieth century
share some common characteristics. The United States, Germany, and Japan
all underwent industrialization comparatively late. In addition, indigenous
supplies of skill proved either to be inadequate or inappropriate to the
needs of increasingly technologically advanced manufacturing industry. As
a result, both employers and the state, in their different ways, were obliged
to give early precedence to human-capital investment.[42] In Britain, on the
other hand industrialization came early. The combination of the simplicity
of technology, the low skill intensity of the staple industries, and the existence of pockets of pre-industrial skill had lasting consequences for attitudes to education. In the first place the modest technical demands of the
British industrial revolution were not dependent upon a significant expansion in education.[43] Secondly, there existed in Britain, prior to industrialization, well-developed pockets of proto-industry.[44] These fundamentally

shaped attitudes to industrial training and education well into the twentieth century. As a direct consequence of the availability of craft skills, employers were able to avoid substantial human-capital investment. Instead, using both internal and external contracts early factory- and mine-owners were able to gain access to traditional skills residing in existing communities.[45] In a range of skilled activities, including shipbuilding and engineering, subcontracting was underpinned by apprenticeship. Themselves the product of custom, craft apprenticeships can be traced back to the Elizabethan Statute of Artificers. They were usually of fixed duration and provided transferable skills and formed the basis of shop-floor training during the industrial revolution.[46]

That the human-resource strategies of early nineteenth-century British family firms involved externalization rather than internalization is not surprising. This reflected a wider tendency for the boundaries of the firm to lie within the business community, with all decisions relating to finance, management, and diversification, coloured by local value systems.[47] Nor is it unexpected that pioneer factory- and mine-owners should be keen to tap existing reserves of skill within society. What is striking, in the British case, is the extent to which changing economic and social pressures in the nineteenth century reinforced this trend. They institutionalized apprenticeship, which became entrenched in the collective bargaining process.[48] Despite some adjustments in practice, apprenticeship remained widespread in engineering, textiles, iron-making, shipbuilding, mining and pottery until after World War II.[49] Britain's distinctive experience of industrialization meant that not only was practical skill preferred to academic skill, but that only a minority of firms gave priority to human-capital investment.[50] Moreover, neither employers nor trade unions argued strenuously for changes in training and education provision.[51] This attitude had become firmly embedded in British business culture by World War II and persisted, especially in engineering, for much of the post-war period. It was, nevertheless, a notable feature of the staple industries which had virtually disappeared since 1960. This decline was matched by a sharp fall in apprenticeship. There has been some change in attitude as firms have become larger and technology more complex. Nevertheless British employers have continued to lag behind their counterparts abroad in human-resource management.

Past practice may have prejudiced businessmen against the benefits of academic education as a preparation for the world of work. Yet the shortcomings of the post-war education system also influenced them. Despite the priority accorded to education by successive post-war British governments, the benefits for manufacturing industry have been comparatively limited. Indeed, in terms of human-capital investment in an industrial work-force, British education policy since 1945 has been marked more by lost opportunities than achievement.[52] In devoting a disproportionately high level of resources to the academically able, the 1944 Act did little to prepare the

majority for the world of work. Some 75–80 per cent of school pupils in the
1950s and 1960s were consigned to secondary moderns and emerged at 15
or 16 with few qualifications and even fewer skills. Nor did the shift towards
comprehensive education in the 1960s fundamentally change the balance.
In the 1980s, therefore, 40 per cent of school-leavers left without a certifi-
cate for successful completion of studies.[53] At the same time levels of mathematical competence amongst school-leavers have been inferior to their
contemporaries in Germany and Japan.[54] The shortcomings of British
general education are especially striking if experience is contrasted with
Japan. There it forms the foundation-stone upon which all future vocational
training is based. In Britain, on the other hand, its deficiencies have seriously limited the benefits of any future training.[55]

The decline and ultimate demise of the technical school has been
described as one of the most serious deficiencies of the British education
system and a major cause of Britain's skill shortage.[56] The much-heralded
technical schools declined in number from 321 in 1947 to 225 in 1962, with
only 1.2 per cent of the school population attending this type of school.
They were the victims of the shift in attitudes in both Whitehall and at the
local level in favour of the grammar school. Revived by the Tories in the
1980s, as the City Technical Colleges, technical schools have not developed
as an alternative educational route for the non-academic in Britain, as they
have for over a century in Germany.[57] Yet, if the absence of this provision
distinguishes Britain from Germany, it should not be concluded that such
schools are an essential feature of the education systems of all successful
industrial economies. In Japan, for example, it is only after nine years of
compulsory education that the over-15s receive vocational education.[58] The
problem in Britain is less that this particular dimension has been underdeveloped, as that in its absence there have been no compensatory developments in intermediate education. The form of intermediate vocational
education varies elsewhere. German firms favour formal qualifications,
while the Japanese prefer in-house training which builds on general and
vocational education.[59] In Britain, on the other hand, neither the state nor
firms have been prepared to close the education gap with regard to post-
compulsory education, so that provision has lagged behind that of other
industrial nations.[60] Moreover, although workers had the opportunity to gain
additional qualifications through day release, many completed their apprenticeship without passing any theoretical tests and employers were under no
legal obligation to provide study time.[61] It was only the larger firms, and
those with a long tradition of valuing human resources, which offered much
by way of systematic training and education. The culture of a corporation
like ICI, for example, informed as it was by the technical and scientific
requirements of its products, emphasized expertise and skill far more than
was the norm.[62]

The reforms in British higher education in the 1960s gave the impression of placing business at centre stage. It did not, however, create an American-style business education.[63] Despite the establishment of university institutes of technology and business schools, expansion of the university sector in the 1960s has been condemned for a liberal arts/social science bias, which was at the expense of technology.[64] That the higher education sector accorded low status to engineering has, Weiner suggested, contributed to 'Britain's psychological and intellectual deindustrialisation'.[65] Scholars have been justifiably sceptical of Weiner's seductive, but simplistic, cultural interpretation of British economic decline.[66] Yet the limited supply of engineering graduates and their relatively modest position in the hierarchies of British companies, at the very least, distinguishes British practice from that in Germany, the United States, and Japan.[67] Business schools, on the other hand, were viewed sceptically by educationalists.[68] If the promise of university technology and management training in the post-war period was not fulfilled, probably the greatest lost opportunity at the tertiary level lay in the development of the polytechnics in the 1970s. Their original aims of providing high-grade, tertiary, vocational education, at both degree and sub-degree level, were often subordinated as subject-mix shifted in response to academic drift.[69] The transformation of the old polytechnics into 'new' universities, with the removal of the binary funding line in 1992, has only served to confirm this move away from the continental notion of technical education in the tertiary sector. It is possible therefore to question how closely higher education met the needs of industry in the post-war period, yet this should not be exaggerated. By the late 1970s, at 3.3 per cent the proportion of the labour-force with degrees was very much in line with that in Germany.[70]

British education may not have always served the business world well, but a number of post-war economic conditions further limited interest in the value of education. One such influence was the tendency, in the 1950s and 1960s, to serve the relatively slow growing markets of the Commonwealth. Past ties to Empire contributed to British reluctance to join the European Community in the 1950s. Yet it was in the industrial rather than the primary producing world that the greatest benefits of the long boom were felt. Exclusion from the increasingly demanding, high-income markets of Europe reduced the need for employers to invest in their work-force or to value their education.

A tendency towards short-termism, by both British governments and firms in the post-war period, has further reinforced human-capital neglect. The central characteristic of government macroeconomic policy in the 1960s was the stop-go cycle, which inhibited the development of effective physical investment strategies in industry.[71] Yet in the 1960s education policy gave the impression of being strategic, even if an 'instinct for localism', born of its nineteenth-century origins, prevented any sense of national coherence.[72] Ironically, it was that most damaging of 'go' cycles, the Barber Boom

of 1972–3, which injected the short-termism in government education policy
that has been such a feature since the 1970s. The spectre of the sharp rise
in the PSBR, which was the result of this over-enthusiastic, ill-considered
boom, has haunted government policy ever since. It has contributed to the
successive rounds of public expenditure cuts which have punctuated the last
twenty years. In such an environment, cost-cutting considerations and financial uncertainty have prevented the evolution of a coherent education
policy. Short-termism in government policy has been mirrored in most firms.
Until the 1960s the availability of a growing pool of transferable skills
through apprenticeships[73] encouraged short-termism by employers. Skill
deficiency could simply be met by poaching, rather than by systematic education and training and the creation of internal labour markets as was
normal elsewhere. Moreover, the merger and take-over wave of the 1960s
further reinforced the tendency to neglect long-term investments, whether
physical or human. British business has been far more reliant on the stock
market than has been the case in Japan. As a result, businessmen constantly
face the risk of hostile take-over and the need to placate shareholders.[74] In
a world where the manager is more concerned with the bottom line of his
balance sheet in six months' time, the value of education and training has
been neglected. This is in sharp contrast to Japan, where the perspective of
manager and shop-floor worker is long-term improvement rather than
short-term gain. In addition the internal accounting procedures and managerial incentive schemes of the multidivisional firms which have come to
dominate British industry have further contributed to a short-term outlook.
With managerial bonuses tied to the monthly performance of independent profit centres, it is not surprising that the importance of long-term
commitments, such as education and training, have not always been
appreciated.[75]

From the perspective of the British work-force, and in sharp contrast to
German experience, dwindling wage differentials between skilled and
unskilled workers, and more especially between the shop-floor and
foremen, have given little incentive to gain additional qualifications. It is
interesting to note, however, that in Japan, where the emphasis is on in-
house training, wage differentials for all qualifications remain low.[76]

If economic considerations have been an important influence on attitudes
to education in Britain, socio-cultural characteristics, and in particular those
relating to the class system, are also significant and distinguish Britain from
her principal competitors. For Wiener the popularity of the public school
system for the sons of industrialists in the late nineteenth century was a
reflection of that anti-industrial spirit which he believed was the major
cause of economic decline in Britain.[77] Yet if this notion has not proved particularly robust,[78] there is evidence that the practice, if not the intent, of the
1944 Education Act may have reinforced some class differences with
respect to education. Therefore, although from 1944 the issue of compul-

sory education for teenagers was finally addressed, resources were heavily concentrated upon the academically able and in reality upon the middle classes attending grammar schools. This meant that the level of social and occupational mobility associated with the 1944 reforms was limited, the low-status secondary moderns and the technical schools being heavily working class. Nor did the shift to comprehensive education in the 1970s significantly alter the situation, since middle-class parents increasingly chose the independent school option.

During the long boom of the 1950s and 1960s the demand for unskilled labour remained buoyant, whilst apprenticeship remained popular for able working-class children, so that the shortcomings of the education system were less evident. Deindustrialization and a series of deep recessions, since the 1970s, have contributed to a long-term rise in unemployment rates, especially in blue-collar and unskilled mainly working-class occupations. In contrast to experience in Japan, where youth unemployment is exceptionally low, poor employment prospects for school-leavers, especially in working-class areas, have demotivated pupils. This effect has been further reinforced when accompanied by the long-term unemployment of a parent.[79]

Consequences of the Neglect of Human Capital for British Economic Performance

It is unclear just how far the neglect of management education, after 1950, constrained the development of the multidivisional enterprise in Britain. Yet the slow development of academic, managerial education meant that as industrial concentration rose in the 1960s, British managers were less well equipped than their American counterparts to cope with the challenges of big business. It is not, of course, the case that management education itself creates competitive advantage. Yet 'entrepreneurial spirits without state of the art managerial know-how are at a disadvantage'.[80] Since 1970, however, the situation has improved. There has been a considerable spread of management education beyond the London and Manchester Business Schools, while the growth in firm size has increased awareness of its benefits. The limited training and technical expertise of managers in this period is likely to have restricted their interest in training their work-force. Low levels of scientific and technological graduate participation at board level doubtless reinforced prejudices.[81] Yet it was primarily the inappropriateness and inadequacy of the education received by the average worker which completed the vicious circle, limiting as it did the value of any training a young shop-floor worker received.[82]

The growing productivity gap in British relative to American industry since the inter-war period, and relative to Europe and Japan between 1950 and 1980 in particular, has received growing attention.[83] By the mid-1970s, for example, German output per employee in manufacturing was about 50 per cent higher than in Britain and in the region of 80 per cent in mechanical engineering and vehicle production. Compared with Japan, the gap was even wider.[84] The precise impact of skill deficiency on productivity is difficult to quantify. Nevertheless, a series of comparative studies by the National Institute for Economic and Social Research since 1982 have explored the implications of limited education and poor training for British productivity performance.[85] They have concluded that an important explanation for Britain's twentieth-century productivity gap was a lack of technical expertise and education for managers, supervisors, and shop-floor workers. This inhibited the understanding of production techniques and reduced flexibility of outlook. Such deficiencies may, for example, have slowed down the introduction and acceptance of advanced technologies in some sectors. Moreover, poor mathematical standards on the shop floor have inhibited the introduction of the kinds of statistical controls which are central to Total Quality Control in Japan.[86] In addition, the manifest failings in intermediate education have meant that machinery breakdowns were longer in Britain than say in Germany, whilst R&D does not permeate through firms in the way that it does in Japan.[87]

The experience of foreign multinationals in Britain serves to confirm the suspicion that the key to the productivity gap must lie with human-capital deficiencies. It is undoubtedly true that the subsidiaries of foreign-owned firms operating in Britain enjoyed higher rates of productivity than equivalent British firms.[88] Yet if the productivity of foreign subsidiaries in Britain is compared with that achieved in the home economy (using identical technology, plant size, product, production-runs) the gaps are quite startling. One Japanese manufacturer reported that advanced automatic machines were produced at only 60 per cent of the rate achieved in Japan. Similarly a German multinational reported that productivity in their UK plant was between 30 and 50 per cent of the level in their German plants.[89]

The damaging impact of skill deficiency on British business performance has not merely been confined to productivity. The education system has continued to produce a work-force suited to the labour-intensive but declining staple industries and the low-skill sectors.[90] It was, however, a work-force which was patently ill-fitted for the advanced sectors which grew so rapidly in the rest of the industrialized world during the 1950s and 1960s.[91] In other words the 'education gap' between the average British worker and those in other major industrial economies, identified even before the end of the nineteenth century, was not closed in the post-war era; if anything it became wider.

From the 1950s, and especially since 1970, the most rapidly growing sectors, internationally, have been those producing technologically sophisticated, skill-intensive goods for high-income markets. These have been sectors where the flexibility of the work-force, in the face of rapidly changing markets, has held the key to competitive advantage. In Germany, for example, high levels of human-capital investment have facilitated a shift in product range to 'high-quality' goods.[92] In Japan, human resources have lain at the heart of competitive strategy. There, the skill and knowledge of an educated and skilled work-force, using computerized, lean production techniques have generated a combination of productivity gain and product flexibility.[93] In contrast, Britain, even today, remains overspecialized in product areas of low-skill intensity. In the British food and drink industries performance has been better than in manufacturing generally in the 1970s and 1980s.[94] Nevertheless, in biscuits, for example, there is evidence that where the markets served dictated variety, rather than standardization, of production, British workers lacked the flexibility to achieve the same level of productivity as Continental competitors.[95] Concentration on standardized products, however, further increases the vulnerability of British firms. This is because it is precisely in these areas where low labour-cost producers will gain competitive advantage.[96]

The macroeconomic implications for Britain of human-capital failings are manifestly clear. Hastened, it must be said, by the excesses of government monetary policy in the 1980s, there has been an absolute decline in manufacturing since the mid-1970s, which has been accompanied by a sharp rise in unemployment. At the same time the more dynamic British firms have increasingly sited their activities overseas. Inward investment, by Japanese multinationals in particular, who are looking for a springboard into European markets, has been seen as an important source of new manufacturing employment. Yet, without wide-ranging improvement in the education of her work-force, Britain may be destined to lose even that panacea.[97] The substantial education gap between shop-floor workers in Britain and those on the Continent could soon offset Britain's lower labour costs. It could mean that the UK is destined to become, or could become, an offshore producer of goods of low-skill intensity, supplying technologically sophisticated, Japanese-owned, factories elsewhere in Europe.

Conclusions

Even before 1939 British attitudes to education began to inhibit productivity growth. Yet it has been after 1945 and most especially since 1970 that the effect of Britain's human-capital deficiencies have been most damaging. Perceptions of training that had their origins in the nineteenth century lingered on in many sectors and continued to shape human-resource policies through the 1950s and 1960s. Only in those sectors such as chemicals and pharmaceuticals, where competitive advantage had long been dependent upon scientific knowledge rather than practical skill, was formal education, rather than shop-floor training, valued. Education, did, however, become a major priority of post-war governments. Yet despite a sharp rise in educational expenditure since 1945 the needs of industry, especially with respect to general and intermediate education, have not been met.

British businessmen and workers have been dubious of the direct benefits of education. This tendency, combined with the particular deficiencies in post-war British education, has had serious consequences for the international competitiveness of industry and for the sectoral mix of the economy. Britain has continued to produce a labour-force better suited to the industrial demands of a bygone age, where the majority of the workforce were unskilled or semi-skilled and where training was informal rather than dependent upon formal education. By the late twentieth century a new balance had emerged between physical and human capital where constant learning is critical to the full enjoyment of returns on investment. Despite some improvement, especially, in the level of graduate participation in industry, the ability to enjoy these returns in Britain remains sadly limited.

NOTES

1. I am grateful to the participants at the Anglo-Japanese Conference hosted by Terry Gourvish of the Business History Unit at the London School of Economics in April 1994. I am also grateful to Geoff Jones for written comments.
2. H. F. Gospel, *Markets, Firms and the Management of Labour in Modern Britain* (Cambridge, 1992), 158; R. Fitzgerald, 'Industrial Training and Management Education in Britain: A Missing Dimension', in Nobuo Kawake and Eisuke Daito (eds.), *Education and Training in the Development of Modern Corporations* (Tokyo, 1993), 97.
3. E. Keep and K. Mayhew, 'The Assessment: Education, Training and Economic Performance', *Oxford Review of Economic Policy*, 4 (1988), p. vii.
4. A. Daly, N. Hitchens, and K. Wagner, 'Productivity, Machinery and Skills in a Sample of British and German Manufacturing Plants: Results of a Pilot Inquiry', *National Institute Economic Review*, 111 (1985), 49; S. J. Prais and K. Wagner, 'Schooling Standards in England and Germany: Some Summary Comparisons Bearing on Economic Performance', *National Institute Economic Review*, 112 (1985), 53–73; G. D. N. Worswick, *Education and Economic Performance* (Aldershot, 1985).
5. C. Carr, 'Productivity and Skills in Vehicle Component Manufacturers in Britain, Germany the United States and Japan', *National Institute Economic Review*, 139 (1992), 84.
6. W. Lazonick, 'Strategy, Structure and Management Development in the United States and Britain', in K. Kobayashi and H. Morikawa (eds.), *Development of Managerial Enterprise* (Tokyo, 1986), 106.
7. D. H. Aldcroft, *Education Training and Economic Performance, 1944 to 1990* (Manchester, 1992), 42.

8. R. Locke, *Management and Higher Education since 1940* (Cambridge, 1989), 183; Keep and Mayhew, 'The Assessment', pp. vi–ix.
9. S. J. Prais, 'Educating for Productivity: Comparison of Japanese and English Schooling and Vocational Preparation', *National Institute Economic Review*, 119 (1987), 51; Daly, Hitchens and Wagner, 'Productivity, Machinery', 56.
10. M. Sanderson, 'Literacy and Social Mobility in the Industrial Revolution in England', *Past and Present*, 56 (1972), 75–104.
11. S. Pollard, *Britain's Prime and Britain's Decline: The British Economy, 1870–1914* (London, 1989), pp. 146–7.
12. Quotation from E. Hennock, 'Technological Education in England, 1850–1926: The Uses of the German Model', *History of Education*, 19 (1990), 301.
13. Lazonick, 'Strategy' , 106–7; D. Mowery, 'Firm Structure, Government Policy and the Organization of Industrial Research: Great Britain and the US, 1900–1950', *Business History Review*, 58 (1984), 523.
14. M. Sanderson, 'Education and Economic Decline, the 1890s–1980s', *Oxford Review of Economic Policy*, 4 (1988), 38–44; Pollard, *Prime and Decline*, 162–204; Hennock, 'Technological Education', 310–11; C. Barnett, *The Audit of War* (1986), 232; E. W. Jenkins, 'Junior Technical Schools, 1905–1945: The Case of Leeds', *History of Education*, 16 (1987), 116.
15. Barnett, *Audit of War*, 232.
16. M. Sanderson, *The Universities and British Industry, 1850–1970* (London, 1972), 1–30; R. Floud, *Technical Education, 1850–1914: Speculations on Human Capital Formation* (London, 1984), 7; G. W. Roderick and M. D. Stephens, *Education and Industry in the Nineteenth Century* (Newton Abbot, 1972), p. 124; Pollard, *Prime and Decline*, 162–204.
17. Fitzgerald, 'Industrial Training', 86.
18. P. Cline, 'Winding Down the War Economy: British Plans for Peacetime Recovery, 1916–19', in Kathleen Burk (ed.), *War and the State: The Transformation of British Government, 1914–1919* (London, 1982); M. W. Kirby and Mary B. Rose, 'Productivity and Competitive Failure: British Government Policy and Industry, 1914–19', in G. Jones and M. W. Kirby (eds.), *Competitiveness and the State: Government and Business in Twentieth-Century Britain* (Manchester, 1991).
19. Sanderson, 'Education and Economic Decline', 43; Kirby and Rose, 'Productivity, 32; Barnett, *Audit of War*, 233.
20. Fitzgerald, 'Industrial Training', 86.
21. P. J. A. Landymore, 'Education and Industry Since the War', in D. Morris (ed.), *The Economic System in the UK* (Oxford, 1985), 691–2; Aldcroft, *Education*, 22–3; J. Sheldrake and S. Vickerstaff, *The History of Industrial Training* (Aldershot, 1985), 61.
22. W. Taylor, 'Productivity and Educational Values', in G. D. N. Worswick (ed.), *Education and Economic Performance* (Aldershot, 1985), 106.
23. Quoted in M. Davis, 'Technology, Institutions and Status: Technological Education, Debate and Policy, 1944–56', in P. Summerfield and Eric J. Evans (eds.), *Technical Education and the State since 1850* (Manchester, 1990), 136.
24. Fitzgerald, 'Industrial Training', 93.
25. D. Finegold and D. Soskice, 'The Failure of Training in Britain: Analysis and Prescription', *Oxford Review of Economic Policy,* 4 (1988), 30–1.
26. G. Jones, 'Big Business, Management and Competitiveness in Twentieth-

Century Britain', University of Reading Discussion Paper in Economics, No. 268 (1993), 26–7.

27. Finegold and Solskice, 'The Failure', 34–5.
28. Cf. S. P. Keeble, *The Ability to Manage: A Study of British Management, 1890–1990* (Manchester, 1992), 97–124.
29. Quoted in J. F. Wilson, *The Manchester Experiment: A History of Manchester Business School, 1965–1990* (1992), 12.
30. Wilson, *The Manchester Experiment*, 4–11; Locke, *Management*, 176–8.
31. Sheldrake and Vickerstaff, *The History*, 31.
32. Fitzgerald, 'Industrial Training', 91.
33. Wilson, *The Manchester Experiment*, 11.
34. Locke, *Management*, 179–90.
35. Jones, 'Big Business', 23.
36. M. Wiener, *English Culture and the Decline of the Industrial Spirit, 1850–1980* (Cambridge, 1981); J. Wrigley, 'Technical Education and Industry in the Nineteenth Century', in B. Elbaum and W. Lazonick, *The Decline of the British Economy* (Oxford, 1986), 162–3; D. Landes, *The Unbound Prometheus* (Cambridge, 1969), 347; Lazonick, 'Strategy', 101–46; W. Lazonick, *Business Organization and the Myth of the Market Economy* (Cambridge, 1991), 48.
37. Sanderson, *The Universities*, 1–30; Floud, *Technical Education*, 7; Roderick and Stephens, *Education and Industry*, 124; Pollard, *Prime and Decline*, 162–204.
38. Sanderson, 'Education and Economic Decline', 38–40.
39. Lazonick, 'Strategy', 105–19.
40. Hennock, 'Technological Education', 300.
41. S. Pollard, *The Wasting of the British Economy* (Beckenham, 1982), 198; Keeble, *The Ability to Manage*, 85; D. C. Coleman, 'Gentlemen and Players', *Economic History Review*, 2nd ser. 26 (1973), 113.
42. I. Cohen, *American Management and British Labour: A Comparative Study of the Cotton-Spinning Industry* (Westport, Conn., 1990), 19; R. M. Tryon, *Household Manufactures in the United States, 1640–1860* (Chicago, 1917), 1; H. F Gospel, *Industrial Training and Technological Innovation: A Comparative and Historical Study* (London, 1991), 1–12; Pollard, *Prime and Decline*, 146–7; Hennock, 'Technological Education', 301; Fitzgerald, 'Industrial Training', 81.
43. Sanderson, *The Universities*, 75–104.
44. Pat Hudson (ed.), *Regions and Industries* (Cambridge, 1989), 5–38.
45. M. Berg, 'Small Producer Capitalism in Eighteenth-Century England', *Business History*, 35 (1993), 17–39; G. Timmins, *The Last Shift: The Decline of Handloom-Weaving in Nineteenth-Century Lancashire* (Manchester, 1993), 142; J. Lyons, 'Vertical Integration of the British Cotton Industry, 1825–1850', *Journal of Economic History*, 45 (1985), 419–26.
46. B. Elbaum, 'The Persistence of Apprenticeship in Britain and the Decline in the United States', in H. F. Gospel (ed.), *Industrial Training*, 196–7.
47. Mary B. Rose, 'The Family Firm in British Business, 1780–1914', EC7/93 Discussion Paper, Department of Economics, Lancaster University (1993), 21–9.
48. P. Joyce, *Work, Society and Politics* (Brighton, 1980), p. xx; Roderick and Stephens, *Education and Industry*, 117; R. A. Buchanan, *The Engineers: A History of the Engineering Profession in Britain, 1750–1914* (1989), 163; Keeble, *Ability to Manage*, 39.

49. Gospel, *Markets*, 19; Fitzgerald, 'Industrial Training', 82.
50. Fitzgerald, 'Industrial Training', 77–101.
51. Finegold and Soskice, 'The Failure of Training', 29.
52. Sanderson, 'Education and Economic Decline', 44.
53. Prais and Wagner, 'Schooling Standards', 69.
54. Daly, Hitchens and Wagner, 'Productivity', 57.
55. J.-M. Leclercq, 'The Japanese Model: School-Based Education and Firm-Based Vocational Training', *European Journal of Education*, 24 (1989), 183.
56. M. Sanderson, 'Social Equity and Industrial Need: A Dilemma of English Education since 1945', in T. Gourvish and A. O'Day (eds.), *Britain since 1945* (London, 1991), 170; M. Sanderson, *The Missing Stratum: Technical School Education in England, 1900–1990s* (London, 1994), 129–53.
57. Sanderson, 'Social Equity', 162–9.
58. Leclercq, 'The Japanese Model', 183.
59. S. J. Prais and K. Wagner, 'Some Practical Aspects of Human Capital Investment: Training Standards in Five Occupations in Britain and Germany', *National Institute Economic Review*, 103 (1983), 46; Leclercq, 'The Japanese Model', 183–96.
60. Keep and Mayhew, 'The Assessment', p. vii.
61. A. J. Peters, *British Further Education* (Oxford, 1967), 109.
62. Aldcroft, *Education*, 55.
63. Locke, *Management*, 178–9.
64. Cf. Barnett, *Audit of War*, 292.
65. Wiener, *English Culture*, 134–5.
66. See in particular the essays in B. Collins and K. Robbins (eds.), *British Culture and Economic Decline* (London, 1990).
67. Lazonick, 'Strategy', 110; Robert Locke, 'Education and Entrepreneurship: A Historian's View', and K. Yasumuro, 'Engineers as Functional Alternatives to Entrepreneurs in Japanese Industrialization', in J. Brown and M. B. Rose (eds.), *Entrepreneurship Networks and Modern Business* (Manchester, 1993), 62, 76–101.
68. Locke, *Management*, 179.
69. Landymore, 'Education and Industry', 711.
70. S. J. Prais, 'Vocational Qualifications of the Labour Force in Britain and Germany', *National Institute Economic Review*, 98 (1981), 48.
71. Pollard, *Wasting*, 124.
72. Barnett, *Audit of War*, 232.
73. Fitzgerald, 'Industrial Training', 82.
74. W. Edwards Deming, *Out of Crisis* (Cambridge, 1986), 3–4.
75. R. P. Dore, 'Financial Planning and the Long-Term View', *Policy Studies*, 6, pt. 1 (1985), 17–19.
76. Prais and Wagner, 'Productivity and Management', 40; J.-P. Jallade, 'Recent Trends in Vocational Education and Training: An Overview', *European Journal of Education*, 24 (1989), 107.
77. Wiener, *English Culture*, 80–4.
78. H. Berghoff, 'Public Schools and the Decline of the British Economy, 1870–1914', *Past and Present*, 129 (1990), 535–68.
79. Leclercq, 'The Japanese Model', 185; S. Bradley and J. Taylor, 'Education,

Human Capital Formation and Local Economic Environment in English Local Authority Areas', Lancaster University unpub. paper (1994), 9.

80. Locke, 'Education and Entrepreneurship', 65.
81. Keep and Mayhew, 'The Assessment', p. vii.
82. Idib. p. ix.
83. L. Rostas, *Comparative Productivity in British and American Industry* (Cambridge, 1948); S. N. Broadberry and N. F. R. Crafts, 'Explaining Anglo-American Productivity in the Mid-Twentieth Century', *Oxford Bulletin of Economics and Statistics*, 52 (1990), 375–402; S. N. Broadberry and R. Fremdling, 'Comparative Productivity in British and German Industry', *Oxford Bulletin of Economics and Statistics*, 52 (1990), 403; B. Van Ark, 'Comparative Levels of Manufacturing Productivity in Post-War Europe: Measurement and Comparisons', *Oxford Bulletin of Economics and Statistics*, 52 (1990), 343–73.
84. Daly, Hitchens, and Wagner, 'Productivity', 48; Carr, 'Productivity and Skills', 80.
85. A. D. Roy, 'Labour Productivity in 1980: An International Comparison', *National Institute Economic Review*, 101 (1982), 9–16; Prais and Wagner, 'Some Practical Aspects', 46–65; Prais and Wagner, 'Schooling Standards', 53–73; Prais and Wagner, 'Productivity and Management', 34–47; Daly, Hitchens, and Wagner, 'Productivity', 48; Prais, 'Educating for Productivity', 48–61; H. Steedman and K. Wagner, 'Productivity, Machinery and Skills: Clothing Manufacture in Britain and Germany', *National Institute Economic Review*, 128 (1989), 55–78; G. Mason, S. J. Prais, and B. Van Ark, 'Vocational Education and Productivity in the Netherlands and Britain', *National Institute Economic Review*, 140 (1992), 45–57.
86. W. Lazonick, *Competitive Advantage on the Shop Floor* (Cambridge, Mass., 1990), 291.
87. Daly, Hitchens, and Wagner, 'Productivity', 61; Carr, 'Productivity and Skills', 84–5.
88. John H. Dunning, *U.S. Industry in Britain* (1976), 71–4; F. Bostock and G. Jones, 'Foreign Multinationals in British Manufacturing, 1850–1962', *Business History*, 36 (1994), 89–126.
89. Carr, 'Productivity and Skills', 80.
90. J. L. Baxter and J. B. McCormick, 'Seventy Per Cent of our Future: The Education, Training and Employment of Young People', *National Westminster Bank Quarterly Review* (1984), 42.
91. Fitzgerald, 'Industrial Training', 96–7.
92. Prais and Wagner, 'Productivity and Management', 42.
93. Locke, 'Education and Entrepreneurship', 53–75.
94. V. N. Balasubramanyam, 'Entrepreneurship and the Growth of the Firm: The Case of the British Food and Drink Industries in the 1980s', in J. Brown and M. B. Rose (eds.), *Entrepreneurship Networks and Modern Business* (Manchester, 1993), 144–60.
95. Mason, Prais, and Van Ark, 'Vocational Education', 56.
96. Prais and Wagner, 'Productivity and Management', 42.
97. R. Strange, *Japanese Manufacturing Investment in Europe: Its Effect on the UK Economy* (1993), 411.

PART IV

Finance

8. A Re-examination of Japan's Post-War Financing System

CHIKAGE HIDAKA

Introduction

The economic development of post-war Japan is widely hailed as nothing short of miraculous. Despite exhausting most of its national wealth in World War II, Japan rapidly managed to rebuild its economy, largely restructuring it along modern lines in the process, and to successfully rejoin the international economy. Several valuable studies have already given us insight into the innovations and entrepreneurs who helped in Japan's post-war economic development. However, as J. A. Schumpeter noted in 'The Theory of Economic Development', in order for such innovations to be put into practice and for a nation's economy to undergo significant development, 'finance as a special act' is necessary.[1] In other words, in the absence of sufficient finance, the number of potential entrepreneurs in a nation is irrelevant; its economy will remain mired in a conventional growth pattern. Despite the crucial role of industrial finance in economic development, however, the present body of work on the development of post-war Japanese industrial finance remains relatively scant. In this paper, therefore, I have attempted to address the issue of how 'finance as a special act' played a key background role in post-war Japanese economic development.

The scope of this chapter is limited to the first two decades after the end of World War II, the era in which Japan successfully transformed its industrial structure into an advanced one based on heavy industry. The question then becomes how was this rapid transition and growth financed? We can identify two possible areas of investigation: one of degree i.e. how were such large levels of funds obtained? And one of direction i.e. how were these funds directed? It is this latter point, the direction of finance, which my study primarily emphasizes. As is widely known, industrial finance during this period was conducted mainly through indirect financing, that is business enterprises mainly raised money not through the securities market but through borrowing from financial institutions. The leading players in indirect financing are usually considered to have been the private financial institutions, particularly the major commercial banks called the city banks. It would therefore seem that Japan's post-war industrial advance can be partially credited to the extremely high levels of capital financing supplied to industry by these banks, using their own discretion. To state the question more provocatively, was Japan's post-war economic development the result of either the banks' keen loan-assessment skills, or their dauntless, risk-taking attitude? This question is the starting-point of this study.

For clarity, the chapter divides the two decades after the War, based on general economic trends, into three parts: a chaotic period, lasting for five years from the end of the War to 1950; a rehabilitation period, from 1950 to the mid-1950s; and a high-growth period, continuing from the mid-1950s into the 1960s. While industrial finance activity during this period can all be roughly categorized as 'indirect' as noted above, significant changes in context seem to have occurred.

The Japanese Economy and Industrial Finance Before 1950

General Survey of the Post-war Economy Before 1950

After the end of World War II, most nations sought to return their industrial structures to a civilian orientation. Short of natural resources, Japan was obliged to change its industrial structure so that it could develop its processing trade by importing raw materials. Immediately after the end of the War, however, Japan's economy was on the verge of breakdown. The amount of territory Japan controlled was diminished, production capacity was sharply down, foreign trade suspended, and raw materials in short supply. Before long-range policy considerations could be addressed, various steps had to be taken to resume national production in order to restore Japan's economy.

Initial post-war production was barely sustained by using war materials for civilian purposes, and supplies of raw materials threatened to be exhausted by as early as 1947. Once the stock of war materials ran out, many expected that the supply of production goods would stop, and even production of consumer goods would become impossible. Under these circumstances, the idea of the 'priority production system' was born. The intention was to supply coal, which was in constant short supply, to the steel industry exclusively, and then to return the steel produced into the coalmines, thereby increasing economic productivity gradually through mutual circulation. Priority production of coal for steel-making represented the first post-war attempt by Japan to stabilize its confused economy.

As a result of growing East–West antagonism, however, US policy toward Japan changed direction dramatically. Rather than calling for the demilitarization and democratization of Japan, the USA began encouraging Japan to transform itself into an industrial nation and to rejoin the world economy. In late 1948, in an attempt to speed restoration in Japan, the US government sent Joseph Dodge, president of the Detroit Bank, to Japan to advocate the new US policy. Dodge asserted that in order for Japan's economy to be independent, Japan should produce more goods at lower cost, accumulate capital through saving and thrift, and increase exports to allow foreign materials to be imported in order to make up for its insufficient domestic natural resources. Dodge also demanded that Japan change the direction of its economy, which had depended upon various subsidies and aids from the United States since the War's end.

This drastic change in the political environment caused Japanese government and industry to realize the importance of 'industrial rationalization'. In September 1949, with a balanced budget, single exchange rate, and healthy financial policies all firmly in place, the Japanese government extended its commitment to industrial rationalization by adopting the following four-point basic policy:

1. To provide guidance to various industries, as a prerequisite for industrial rationalization, based on future industrial goals.
2. To focus industrial rationalization efforts on bringing domestic prices into line with international prices.
3. To emphasize rationalization of enterprises based on originality and innovation, and to foster an atmosphere conducive to rationalization and the removal of obstacles, and
4. To take positive steps to improve efficiency and encourage the use of advanced technology.

To help implement these policy points, the Industrial Rationalization Council was founded in December 1949 to advise the Minister of International Trade and Industry.[2]

The Gap in the Long-term Supply of Funds

The shock imposed by the Dodge Policy provided Japan's economy with two targets: independence; and industrial rationalization. However, industrial finance in Japan, especially infrastructure funding, remained impaired, and served to inhibit development efforts. As noted earlier, post-war production resumed under an array of challenging conditions. Lack of funding was an especially serious issue. Commercial banks, themselves suffering from the after-effects of the War, could not meet businesses' borrowing needs. To solve this bottle-neck, the government established the Reconstruction Finance Corporation (RFC), which was intended to supply the funds necessary for economic restoration which could not be obtained from other lenders. Founded in January 1947, RFC actively supplied funds to industry, mainly for capital investment, and played an important role in the priority production programme.

The General Headquarters (GHQ) planned to base Japan's new post-war industrial finance system on the British and US models, wherein long-term funds are supplied from the securities markets and short-term funds from private commercial banking institutions. However, the Ministry of Finance (MOF) opposed the GHQ plan, asserting that differences between the British-US system and the existing Japanese system were too large, and that the limited availability of non-government funds in post-war Japan would make it very difficult for long-term funds to be raised on the securities markets. Despite the difference of opinion between GHQ and MOF, reform of the Japanese finance system was gradually initiated. In pre-war Japan, special banks such as the Nippon Kangyo Bank (NKB), Hokkaido Colonial Bank (HCB), and Industrial Bank of Japan (IBJ) had been in charge of long-term industrial finance. However, GHQ undertook to reform the special banks, pointing out their vague nature and asserting that they played an important role in financing the wartime economy. In June 1948, GHQ announced a 'Policy on the Special Banks' and instructed each special bank to select one of two options: (1) to become a purely commercial bank; or (2) to become a debenture-issuing company which procures funds only by issuing debentures and which engages in mortgage lending. Serious antagonism had developed between GHQ and MOF over the US contention that banks issuing debentures were not banks; the latter option served to mitigate this tension. As a result of tenacious negotiations by the Banking Bureau of MOF, the US side yielded to the Japanese position.[3] NKB and HCB then chose to become ordinary commercial banks, while IBJ chose the second option to become a financial institution to resume its activities. In April 1949 RFC, which had been a leading supplier of long-term funds since 1947, discontinued its finance activities as part of the Dodge Policy of achieving balanced public finance. Subsequently, capital investment funds were available from three sources: (1) issuing of shares and bonds; (2) collateral funding; and (3) private financial institutions. As shown below, however, these sources were insufficient to allow the goal of 'industrial rationalization' to be achieved.

GHQ placed major emphasis on the issue of shares and corporate bonds as a source of long-term funds. After giving Japan the target of 'economic independence', GHQ adopted various policies intended to develop the Japanese securities markets. However, the stock-market, which reopened in May 1949, did not function as GHQ expected. For the first few months after it reopened, the stock-market was active, due in part to a brisk influx of speculative funds and corporate stock offerings. However, basic industries such as coal, electric power, and steel, all of which needed massive capital investment funds, were unable to raise sufficient funds on the stock-market. The stock-trade market soon stagnated because of the rapid expansion of the stock-issuing market and the deepening deflation resulting from the

Dodge Policy. In late 1949, stock prices fell sharply. On the other hand, the corporate-bond market was active thanks to the Bank of Japan (BOJ), which bought actively and eased bond-issuing conditions. However, the corporate-bond market gradually became inactive after 1950, due to reduced buying by BOJ and the worsening financial situation of banks which had actively purchased large amounts of bonds.[4]

Another source of capital investment funds was the collateral fund, which held all the money obtained by sales of US aid to Japan. However, the collateral fund was controlled by GHQ, which limited access to it. Since the collateral fund operations were originally intended to help stabilize Japan's economy, very little finance to private enterprises was provided.

The third source of capital investment funds, the private financial institutions, rapidly increased in volume due to the policy of disinflation in place at the time. However, those industries which had depended upon RFC required much more funding than these banks could provide. At the end of March 1949, RFC had provided 23 per cent of all banking-related finance to industry, and 74 per cent of all capital investment funds.[5] It was very difficult for private financial institutions to immediately take over the functions of RFC. And while RFC had concentrated on lending to basic industries, the financial institutions dispersed their efforts more widely, lending to a range of industries, including textiles and chemicals, where investment led immediately to increased production. Additional funding came from IBJ, which resumed its business as a debenture-issuing bank in 1949. Helped by favourable government treatment, it actively extended financing to various industries. However, it was impossible for IBJ to compensate completely for the shortfall in long-term funds.[6]

The Korean War, which started in June 1950, provided the opportunity for Japan's economy to overcome the shortage of capital investment funds through a major increase in special procurements and exports. However, the expanded production brought about by the War was not well balanced. A large gap developed between the basic and light industries because the former required much more time and funding before production benefits became evident. This gap had effects on the finance supplied by banks, as funds flew into the textile, food, pulp, and other industries where large profits could be made. Meanwhile, the capital investment funds necessary to restore basic industries remained seriously lacking.[7] And the private financial institution had become overextended. Loan levels exceeded deposit levels, and the resulting deficits had to be covered by funds borrowed from BOJ. This situation was called 'over-loan'. In the aftermath of the Dodge Policy, the Korean War and other changes in the overall economy, however, such interim measures were no longer sufficient: a system to supply long-term funds to industry was required.

Completion of the Long-term Industrial Finance System and the Industrial Rationalization Process

Completion of the Long-term Industrial Finance System

Despite the troubling absence of sufficient long-term capital investment funds, a long-term industrial finance system was soon completed. By 1952, as the peace treaty was being concluded, Japan had successfully introduced its own financial system, which was entirely different from that outlined in the GHQ plan.

Once the target of 'industrial rationalization' was defined under the Dodge Policy and the shortage in the supply of long-term industrial funds became obvious, both industry and the banks pointed out the need for a long-term industrial finance system. In the banking industry, fears were developing that overlending might become excessive. In October 1950, MOF appealed to Dodge, stating that it was necessary to complete the finance system and to encourage normalization of banking activity by expanding government-funded special finance efforts. Since coming to Japan, Dodge had shown a strong interest in the characteristics of long-term finance in Japan, due to the poor level of capital accumulation prevailing. In response to the MOF's request, Dodge approved the use of Deposit Department funds to accept bank debentures, on the condition that the department be reformed. As a result, the Deposit Department of MOF was immediately restructured into the Fund Operation Department, which was given exclusive access to government funds. Thus, a formal route for using government funds to support industrial finance was established.[8]

In February and May 1951, respectively, two new government banking organs began business: (1) the Export Bank of Japan (EBJ), whose main role was to grant long-term credits related to plant exports; and (2) the Japan Development Bank (JDB), which was designed 'to support or encourage finance which should be carried out by conventional banking institutions, by granting long-term funds in order to promote Japan's economic reconstruction and industrial development'. Both banks were founded as independent financial institutions, and were not under direct government control. They were also expected not to compete with private financial institutions, and while they could receive government funds, neither EBJ nor JDB could borrow money from the government. The JDB was inaugurated with a capital of 10 billion yen, but soon rapidly increased its funding level by using the collateral fund and taking over the RFC's interests.[9]

Notwithstanding the establishment of these two government financial institutions as sources of long-term industrial funds, both government and industry agreed that further action was needed to correct the shortage of funds. Similar opinions were voiced during discussions on overlending by the private-sector banks. In late 1951, when control by the occupation forces was weakening as the peace treaty was near at hand, MOF announced the outline of the Long-Term Credit Bank Law. This law, enacted in June 1952, approved the establishment of banks which could procure funds by issuing debentures and lending capital investment or long-term operating funds. In accordance with this law, in December 1952, IBJ was reorganized into a long-term credit bank, and the Long-Term Credit Bank of Japan (LTCB) was founded.[10] These two private long-term credit institutions were both non-government institutions. However, in view of their nature as special banks for long-term finance, the government extended special aid to encourage their development. While both banks naturally derived their capital from non-government funds, the government, in an attempt to help them, accepted their preferred shares for a certain period. The two banks were also allowed to issue debentures up to thirty times their total capital and reserve levels for five years from their licence acquisition dates, instead of the usual twenty-times levels. In May 1952, before the Long-Term Credit Bank Law was enacted, the government announced that 'Debentures from private long-term credit institutions should ideally be purchased by private banks, using non-government funds, and by private investors. Noting the very poor levels of capital accumulation prevailing today, however, the government agrees that the MOF's Fund Operation Department would make efforts to purchase as many debentures as possible.'[11]

Through this process, the Japanese post-war system of long-term industrial finance was completed. IBJ, which participated in this process, had specialized in long-term industrial finance since the pre-war period; its experience and ability in this area were extensive. As for the other financial institutions, however, their degree of experience in long-term finance is less clear. How did they start the job? The section below investigates this issue.

The concept for RFC was developed in June 1946. As a temporary, six-month measure before preparations for RFC were completed, the government decided to establish a Restoration Finance Department in IBJ to carry out special finance activities. Due to the complexity of the special finance business, which required that optimal use be made of limited funds, it was necessary to utilize IBJ's knowledge and experience in industrial finance. The RFC, which was formally inaugurated in January 1947, took over all the duties of the Reconstruction Finance Department. Initially, 94 IBJ employees were sent to RFC, and their number increased to 124 over the next two years.[12] Relations between RFC and IBJ were co-operative, and IBJ's contributions served to ease doubts as to whether IBJ could continue to exist as a long-term finance institution. The IBJ's history indicates the reciprocal help given, which allowed IBJ to expand its activities by acting for RFC. 'Our examination and finance technologies were also preserved, thanks to the transfer to RFC of over 100 personnel. This is one of the reasons why IBJ was later reconstructed as Japan's only long-term finance institution and is now prospering as a long-term credit institution.'[13] JDB also benefited from IBJ's pre-war experience in long-term industrial finance. When JDB was inaugurated, one of IBJ's top managers became a director of JDB, and other staff members joined the central office of JDB. Furthermore, when JDB took over RFC's interests, it also took over RFC's offices as well as most of RFC's staff.

Last, let us examine the problem of LTCB. The accumulated experience of NKB, which played a comparable pre-war role to IBJ, had been utilized by LTCB. As stated above, NKB chose to become an ordinary commercial bank after the War's end. However, in 1952, when the long-term credit institution system was initiated, NKB had two potential options: (1) to establish an independent long-term credit institution as a complete subsidiary; or (2) simply to support a new long-term credit institution. NKB ultimately selected the latter option, and when LTCB was inaugurated, NKB sent 140 staff, including its vice-president, to LTCB.[14]

The role that these banking institutions played in the successful growth of the Japanese economy will be described in a separate section. As described above, however, pre-war experience and ability in long-term industrial finance were extensively transferred to the long-term industrial finance institutions established after the War's end. In other words, from the beginning, these institutions possessed the ability to function as excellent information producers for the finance system.

The Industrial Rationalization Policy and Concentrated Investment of Funds

Some five years after the end of World War II, Japan finally embarked on a full-scale rehabilitation of its economy. In February 1951, the Industrial Rationalization Council released a report entitled 'On a National Policy for Industrial Rationalization'. The report noted that while 'Japanese industries have made efforts to improve technology and to renovate machinery and equipment since 1949', in most industries except textiles, 'nothing is to be gained by simply remodelling their superannuated equipment'. Based on this analysis, the report concluded that 'rationalization can be only achieved when a national policy is put into place'. It also emphasized that the Japanese government should concentrate on the development of electric-power resources and shipbuilding, and the rationalization of the coal and steel industries.[15]

The economic situation after the Korean War boom clearly outlined the necessity of the policy recommendations in the council report. Growing production in the mining and manufacturing industries produced shortages of electric power and coal, and increased import–export activity created shortages in shipping and raised cargo rates. In addition, a steep rise in prices of imported iron ores sharply increased the price of iron and steel products and seriously influenced production costs in all industries.[16] In response to these circumstances, Japan set two policies: (1) to solve bottle-necks caused by shortages in key industries such as electric power, coal, shipbuilding, and iron and steel, through intensive investment to expand and rationalize facilities; and (2) to increase exports, expand industries in concert with one another, and promote heavy industries which provided more added value than light industries. This rationalization policy aimed to ensure sufficient capital for business through preferential treatment in tax-ation, and promote capital expenditures by concentrated mobilization of external funds. Changes in the tax code were extensive, involving: the enforcement of asset reassessment; the creation of various kinds of allowances and reserves; tax-credit exemptions, including special deduc-tions from export income; and a special depreciation system for rational-ized machinery. These benefits were substantially expanded after the Industrial Rationalization Promotion Law was passed in March 1952. The special depreciation system and asset reassessment programme proved greatly significant to rationalization efforts in many industries.[17]

In terms of the other element of rationalization policy, the supply of external funds, JDB, a governmental institution, played an important part. Initially, it provided finance to a range of industries, but the establishment of LTCB caused lending to be limited to the four industries specified in its charter. Between 1951 and 1953, 80 per cent of JDB's loans (117.4 billion yen) went to these four industries, which accounted for 18 per cent of their total capital expenditures.[18] In addition, JDB provided special, low-interest loans especially to the electric-power and shipping industries; the loans' 15-year term could not be matched by any private financial institution.[19] JDB financing was important even beyond the amounts involved. In contrast to commercial financing, it supported specific engineering programmes that introduced new and powerful equipment, in line with rationalization efforts, thereby encouraging the efficient distribution of capital investment funds.[20] JDB also helped to induce commercial banks to lend to target industries. Indeed, most of its financing activity was carried out not by JDB alone, but in co-operation with commercial banks, mainly city banks and private long-term credit institutions. For example, the breakdown of funds supplied for engineering projects (a total of about 180 billion yen), a target of JDB finance from 1951 to 1953, shows that about 35 per cent was financed by JDB and about 38 per cent by private financial institutions.[21] There is no doubt that JDB's status as a government financial institution was responsi-ble for its success in inducing commercial lending activity. Two factors seem to account largely for its influence. First, it drew much of its staff from IBJ, which specialized in long-term lending. Second, it adopted a largely com-mercial banking perspective in examining loans (i.e. selecting client enter-prises or assessing payment periods).[22] Accordingly, commercial banks considered syndicated loans with JDB to be of comparatively low risk, as well as relatively less time-consuming to examine. Moreover, JDB financed mainly large enterprises, in conformity with its policy that the promotion of productivity of leading enterprises was the first step in making the Japanese economy independent. The commercial banks desired to develop business relationships with those enterprises enjoying indirect support from the government, which became an important incentive to join in syndicated loans.

Policies on the allocation of commercial funds were not limited only to those syndicated loans led by JDB. In June 1951, a new government policy aimed at strengthening basic industries was released, which was 'intended to discourage unnecessary finance activity, to promote efficient use of funds, and to secure sufficient funds for vital sectors such as basic industries'. MOF also started redirecting commercial funds in concert with the government's policy. In July 1951, when the National Federation of Banking Associations (NFBA) were notified of the new policy, they set up a Committee for Self-Regulation of Loans with the following responsibilities: (1) to define and implement standards for discouraging unnecessary finance; and (2) to discourage capital and operating expenditures as warranted by economic and financial conditions. At first, the Committee set up an abstract and generous standard. After being asked by MOF to further decrease financing activity, however, the Committee gradually cut back on financing for all capital expenditures except those by basic industries.[23] The Committee also acted as a liaison with JDB on syndicated loans.[24] As a result of these policies, loans for capital expenditures by all commercial banks rapidly concentrated on the four basic industries indicated in Table 8.1, and investment levels in these industries remained high, accounting for more than 40 per cent of all industrial investment between 1951 and 1953.[25] Such large-scale investment greatly contributed to modernization and rationalization. There were second-order benefits as well. For example, the huge development of electric-power resources influenced the cement, machinery, and construction industries, and an expanded shipbuilding activity resulted in an increased demand for steel. This pattern was repeated across a range of industries, as concentrated investment acted as a stimulus to full-scale production throughout the Japanese economy.

Two banks, IBJ and LTCB, played the main role in financing the capital expenditure of non-basic industries. While JDB invested its funds mainly in the basic industries, these private long-term credit institutions met the capital needs for a full range of industries. Initially, most of the debentures issued by these private long-term credit institutions were accepted by the MOF's Funds Operation Department. When acceptance of bank debentures by the Funds Operation Department is taken into consideration, some 40 per cent of the capital expenditure of all industries was financed by governmental funds. Finally, efforts were made to extend commercial loans

TABLE 8.1. *Private banks' loans for capital investment, 1951–1952 (net increase in million yen)*

	Mar.–Sept. 1951	Oct. 1951–June 1952	July–Dec. 1952
TOTALS (a)	37,252	28,580	34,032
Four industries (b)	18,341	26,077	32,499
(b)/(a) (%)	49	91	95

Source: JDB, *10 Years History of JDB* (Tokyo, 1963), 72.

under the same policy used to allocate operating funds. Operating funds provided the mechanism by which pressure was applied. BOJ, which was responsible for advising the commercial banks to provide operating funds to industry, appealed to the commercial banks to extend these funds in the form of syndicated loans on the premiss that capital expenditures should be adjusted within the industries. By lending jointly, the banks could successfully assist borrowers to adjust their capital expenditures.[26] In return banks could expect BOJ to purchase their holding debentures and bonds if they co-operated in these financial mediation efforts.[27]

Industrial Financing during the Period of High Economic Growth

Industrial Financing and the Government

The Economic White Paper of 1956 contains a very famous passage: 'The post-war period has ended. . . . Economic growth throughout reconstruction is complete. Future economic growth will come through modernization.'[28] Looking back, the Japanese economy grew very strongly after the latter half of the 1950s. Sometimes dubbed the 'High Growth' period, this phase of development was led by extensive capital expenditures by private enterprise, and was supported by plentiful financing from private banks. The long-term economic forecasts prepared by the government have been credited with accelerating the effectiveness of capital investment activity. Table 8.2 indicates the flow of capital funds from 1957 to 1966. The high rate of indirect financing and large share of loans from private financing institutions can be clearly noted. This section assesses the actual conditions behind post-war industrial finance in Japan, which has been supported mainly by private financial institutions. We examine two very simple hypotheses to explain the substantial role of these institutions in industrial finance: (1) strong government control of private-sector funds; and (2) the substantial level of funds held by private financial institutions which were available to meet the needs of businesses. We shall examine these hypotheses in order.

TABLE 8.2. *Capital Flows to Japanese Industry, 1957–1966: end-year balances (billion yen, %)*

	1957	1958	1959	1960	1961	1962	1963	1964	1965	1966
Indirect finance (a)	6,622	7,733	9,156	11,035	13,469	16,113	20,326	23,741	27,781	31,753
Private banks, etc.	5,923	6,924	8,208	9,929	12,184	14,609	18,473	21,518	25,167	28,669
Government loans	699	809	948	1,106	1,285	1,504	1,853	2,223	2,614	3,084
Direct finance (b)	1,960	2,319	2,763	3,483	4,772	5,709	6,473	7,479	8,009	8,622
Bonds	337	395	540	692	1,078	1,211	1,375	1,529	1,749	1,974
Stock	1,623	1,924	2,223	2,791	3,694	4,498	5,098	5,950	6,260	6,648
TOTALS (c)	8,582	10,052	11,919	14,518	18,241	21,822	26,799	31,220	35,790	40,375
(a)/(c) (%)	77.2	76.9	76.8	76.0	73.8	73.8	75.8	76.0	77.6	78.6
(b)/(c) (%)	22.8	23.1	23.2	24.0	26.2	26.2	24.2	24.0	22.4	21.4

Source: Research Group on Finance System (Banking Bureau of MOF) (ed.), *Long-Term Finance System* (1969), 56–7.

JDB and government funds, which had taken direct strategic leadership at the beginning of the 1950s, gradually changed roles to supplement private loans during the period of high economic growth. Behind these changes was the concern by the commercial banks over fund availability. As liquidity improved in 1954 and 1955, the available commercial funds were not fully utilized due to widespread government funding activities. The banks requested a drastic retrenchment of Treasury lending and investment activity, asserting that 'large Treasury loans and investments would deter the capital accumulation in private sectors and the development of the capital markets once the economy returned to normal'. If a national industrial policy were to be established, the banks said, they would co-operate with it.[29] These criticisms focused in particular on JDB. JDB's Basic Operation Policy of 1956 features the following sentence: 'The Basic Policy calls for private funds to be procured to the extent possible. JDB will provide effective, priority financing to those cases where private funds are not practically available.'[30]

In 1955, the MOF's Funds Operation Department stopped accepting debentures from long-term credit institutions, which it had begun after 1950. In lieu of MOF, private financial institutions became the major holders of those debentures.[31] The long-term credit banks provided long-term funds to clients of banks that accepted their debentures, which effectively reduced the lending burden on banks, and also provided an inflow of loan-substituted funds in which the long-term credit banks proposed to clients that they deposit funds in their banks in return for long-term loans.[32] In this way, the relationship between the long-term credit banks and the commercial banks was strengthened.

Although the function of government funds had shifted to indirect support of the course of high economic growth, the government still sought to maintain control over the financial mechanism, seeking to 'control it as in a planned economy'.[33] As a symbolic example, the 'Funds Committee Bill' submitted to the Diet in July 1955 proposed that lending activity by commercial banks be controlled to ensure that long-term funds were invested in important industries. However, this bill failed to pass due to strong opposition from the commercial banks and industry, which feared that government controls over industry would come next. Instead, the government's strong desire to control commercial funds found expression in a new arm of MOF, the Council on Financial Institutions' Funds, which was formed to develop and strengthen collaboration between policy-makers and commercial banks. The Council was composed of representatives from the financial and industrial sectors, academia, and government. While it had no legal power, the government remained staunchly committed to the idea that private-sector lending should comply with its policies.[34] In October 1955, the NFBA established the Committee for Investment and Loans to check the trend toward managed lending of funds. This committee had a more positive mission than the existing committee, the Committee for Self-Regulation of Loans, which was designed solely to discourage unnecessary finance. The new committee had the following charter: 'To co-operate with government policy voluntarily and positively to the extent possible, and accordingly to attempt to maintain a smooth supply of industrial funds. Deliberative activity shall consist mainly of developing investment and accommodation policies toward important industries, communicating banking opinion concerning the government's investment and loan plans, and co-ordinating investments and lending activity between the Treasury and the banks.'[35]

Despite this self-administered check on the banks, in Autumn 1957, when loan competition among banks was identified as contributing to the deterioration in international payments, eager calls were again heard for some form of legal regulation of the utilization of private funds. Taking pre-emptive action, the NFBA abolished the above two committees in favour of a new 'Committee for Regulation of Funds Allocation' which had the following agenda: (1) to consider matters regarding the banks' liquidity; (2) to set up standards for use of funds; (3) to decide basic policies on investments and loans; (4) to allocate investment and lending activity between the Treasury and the banks; and (5) to consider matters regarding interest rates.[36] The Committee was formed with the following members: selected directors of the NFBA; a Standing Councillor from the Bank of Japan; and one Councillor each from the Ministry of Finance, the Ministry of International Trade and Industry, the Ministry of Transportation, the Economic Planning Agency, and JDB. When the Committee for Regulation of Funds Allocation was established by the NFBA, the Council on Financial Institutions Funds declared that the council expected it to retain responsibility for funds allocation. At the same time, the council requested industry 'to separately arrange an independent structure for allocating investments within enterprises or industries, and to maintain extremely close contact and co-operation with the parties concerned.' Relative to this request, the Federation of Economic Organizations (FEO) decided to establish a 'Special Committee for Industrial Funds'. The Committee's role was 'to consider the balance between capital accumulation and investment in industry from the aspect of efficient overall use of funds; at the same time it intends to study self-adjustment policies on funds in industries, and to clarify controversial points and discuss potential solutions'; it was also designated to keep in close contact with the relevant authorities, such as the NFBA.[37] On the other hand, in February 1958, MITI established a 'Sectional Meeting on Industrial Funds' as a lower branch of the Industrial Rationalization Council. The meeting was intended to assess whether the capital expenditure plans of major industries contradicted either long-term economic plans or the outlook for fund demand produced by the Council on Financial Institutions Funds.[38]

By establishing various organizations to handle industrial funding-related problems in late 1957 and early 1958, as shown above, a system was produced in which the government's intentions and plans concerning fund distribution for all economic activities were made known to the finance and manufacturing sectors, instead of one in which government control was strengthened.[39] In other words, industries in finance and manufacturing were finally able to achieve their independence by reshaping their systems at the request of the government. Under this co-ordination system in which the government acted as a participant, rather than a director, banks were invariably able to obtain sufficient information on the investment plans of major industries. Of course, up to that time, we may assume that stable business relations between banks and corporations had been forming, and banks had been collecting data and information on prospective client enterprises to a certain extent. However, the existence of the above-mentioned co-ordination system meant that the banks could probably reduce their lending risks and save on the labour and expense involved in the loan examination process. At the same time, one may also suppose that some industries which had passed government screening were given certain incentives to make positive capital expenditures. It seems quite likely that many enterprises reasoned that money would be available for those projects authorized by the government.

Similar incidents—bankers' strong resistance to government intervention—also occurred later. In the early 1960s, under the guidance of MITI, a bill entitled 'Special Measures to Promote Selected Industries', intended to provide partial government control over industrial finance, was introduced in the Diet. However, the financial industry continued to strongly oppose any such government intervention, and successfully lobbied to have the bill killed. The following quotation from the twenty-years' history of the NFBA is significant. 'During the first twenty years after the War, financial institutions gradually elevated their reputation, and became confident of their ability to contribute to economic stability through self-regulated adjustment with the assistance of private organizations. The killing of the bill is proof of that confidence.'[40] This incident may also be interpreted as evidence against hypothesis (1). (See p. 151.)

Let us return briefly to hypothesis (1) above. As we noted, the finance industry, which was operating in a rapidly growing economy, consistently resisted government policies on fund control, and worked to maintain or strengthen its independence. In addition, the banks gradually took over the task of discouraging unnecessary financing activity, which was the most important issue directed by the NFBA during the Committee for Self-Regulation of Loans era. We may conclude that the huge flow of funds from private financial institutions to industries was brought about through the active intention of the finance industry, rather than through their passive acceptance of government controls. Therefore, hypothesis (1) may be rejected as untenable, and we may proceed to inspect hypothesis (2). (See p. 151.)

The Lending Ability of Banking Institutions

Immediately after the War, every component of the Japanese economy—government, business, and household—was in the red.[41] In order to recover from the destruction of the War, business enterprises were entirely dependent on financing from their bankers. Commercial banks were in turn dependent on BOJ for alleviating the shortage of lending funds. For almost a decade after the end of the War, there were frequent calls to correct the banks' practice of 'overloan'. While acknowledging the dangerous threat which overloan posed to the integrity of the national economy, BOJ merely noted that sufficient accumulation of capital would eventually eliminate the issue, and that the social costs of an administrative solution would be excessive.[42] During the period of rapid economic growth which followed, the practice of overloan gradually became more prominent, especially after 1960, though progress was somewhat erratic. One particular feature of the overloan situation were the extremely high loan–deposit ratios (i.e. total loans to total deposits) which prevailed among city banks and caused them to have consistently negative net-reserve positions (i.e. total deposits plus deposits at BOJ, minus borrowings from BOJ).[43] As part of its efforts to control the distribution of funds in the market, BOJ implemented the so-called 'window guidance' operations starting in September 1953, whereby it regularly reviewed the planned lending levels of every city and long-term credit bank. As shown in Table 8.3, however, actual lending by these banking institutions far exceeded planned levels despite the BOJ's review process.[44] The foregoing clearly suggests that hypothesis (2) also fails to properly describe actual industrial finance activity by private banks during the period of rapid economic growth. In order to attempt to develop another possible hypothesis, we will look further at the historical progress of discussions about overloan.

In June 1961, the Research Committee on Financial Systems, an advisory body of MOF (hereinafter called 'the Research Committee'), concluded that 'overloan' among banking institutions, particularly the city banks, constituted 'a most unsound banking practice'. It asked one of its subcommittees, which was composed of the vice-governor of BOJ, executive officers of leading banking institutions, and a number of prominent citizens, to formulate an action plan to correct the situation. The subcommittee's report, published two years later, highlighted the principal elements which brought about the overloan problem, and identified business eagerness to make capital investments and aggressive lending practices by banks as the major contributors. With respect to the persistent corporate desire to make capital expenditures, the Research Committee identified several key motives: to

TABLE 8.3. *'Window Guidance' by BOJ and actual lending by private banks,*
1960–1962

Year: quarter	Planned amount of lending by private banks (a)	Suggested amount of lending by BOJ (b)	Actual amount of lending by private banks (c)	(b/a) (%)	(c/b) (%)
1960: 1	1,258	860	997	68.4	115.9
: 2	1,290	945	1,019	73.3	107.8
: 3	1,656	1,383	1,535	83.5	111.0
: 4	2,035	1,705	1,942	83.8	113.9
1961: 1	1,461	1,090	1,638	74.6	150.3
: 2	2,012	1,535	1,546	76.3	100.7
: 3	2,144	1,575	1,520	73.5	96.5
: 4	2,085	1,440	1,458	69.1	101.3
1962: 1	1,758	1,150	1,322	65.4	115.0
: 2	1,880	1,225	1,273	65.2	103.9
: 3	2,133	1,475	1,535	69.2	104.1
: 4	2,685	2,270	2,489	84.5	109.6

Note: Columns (a), (b), and (c): 100 million yen.

Source: Office of Historical Studies, MOF (ed.), *History of Fiscal and Monetary Policies in Japan 1952–1973* (Showa Zaisei Shi 1952–1973), ix (Tokyo, 1991), 74.

reduce production costs by adopting mass-production systems; to restructure business by modernizing or streamlining operations; and more often, to strengthen international competitiveness to respond to the ongoing liberalization of trade. The Committee also found that these motives were further spurred by competition for market share as well as by bullish sentiment over prospects for growth. The Committee also looked at the bankers' aggressive attitude toward lending, and concluded that they had no choice but to meet the requests of their corporate borrowers, in light of competitive considerations such as the strong desire to retain good borrowers and increase their base of loyal corporate clients.[45]

At the same time, however, the report noted that government administration of monetary policy had also contributed in particular to the failure to manage interest rates appropriately and thereby encourage stability in the corporate motivation to make capital expenditures. The report went on to recommend that financial administrators take more comprehensive measures, which would not only improve the financing procedures prevailing in the market, but also help to allow institutional realignment of a broad range of fiscal and financial structures as well as taxation systems. The report specifically recommended that great emphasis be placed on efforts to strengthen the corporate capital structure by implementing appropriate administrative policies.[46]

Two months after this report was published, the Banking Bureau of MOF submitted a draft proposal to the Ministry, proposing a new series of lending guidelines to be followed by banking institutions. Entitled 'Establishing Guidelines for Bankers' Lending Practices Based on Borrower Corporations' Financial Ratios', the proposal described the guidelines as intended 'to establish a series of lending procedures to be followed by bankers based on the financial ratios of borrower corporations. They will correct excessive corporate reliance on bank loans, and will encourage corporations to improve their capital and financial structures and thereby strengthen their competitiveness in the international market. Our aim is to prevent corporations from making excessive facility investments using bank debt while simultaneously acting to exert proper control over capital expenditures by corporations and to balance their demand for loans.' The actual purpose of the guidelines, however, was to encourage commercial banks to set up their own rules on lending practices rather than to enforce their conformity to the proposed guidelines.[47] Considering this issue more properly addressed by industry rather than the banks themselves, however, the NFBA referred the Bureau's proposal to the FEO. The response from industry, including FEO, was fairly negative, as objections were raised to any drastic change in established banking practices. The proposal was thus shelved.[48]

Proposed rules on lending practices continued to be studied by the Research Committee as well, where a number of specific financial bench-marks were proposed for discussion. When considering a capital investment loan to a borrower corporation, for example, certain financial bench-marks were to be established for the company's various financial ratios, such as the net cash-flow ratio, and if the borrower corporation was unable to meet the major bench-marks, the participating bankers would then meet to discuss the proposed loan. As the members of the Research Committee representing private-sector banking institutions insisted on establishing such rules by themselves, however, the actual preparation was left to the NFBA.[49]

In July 1965, the NFBA established 'General Rules for the Extension of Credit by Bankers'.[50] A preface to the Rules declared that the basic aim was to establish a basis for sound and healthy management of corporations and good financing practices by banking institutions, so as to promote orderly corporate financing practices. The Rules were as follows:

1. Banks will act on their own responsibility and will strive to improve their loan-deposit ratios.

2. Banks will pay due attention to the financial ratios and viability of cash projections supplied by borrower corporations. If a borrower corporation's capital expenditure plan is based on an extremely limited cash-flow ratio, and the borrower's ratio of fixed assets to long-term capital is either extremely weak or imbalanced, the bank will make appropriate adjustments

to the terms and conditions of the loan, and ask the borrowers to undertake appropriate corrective actions.

3. In making a loan, a bank will have a thorough understanding of the purpose to which the loan proceeds would be applied by the borrower. Based on the purposes to which the funds would be applied, banks will assign loans to one of the following categories: long-term loans, short-term loans, capital expenditure loans, and working-capital loans. Banks will then structure the loans with appropriate terms and conditions. Under no circumstances shall loan proceeds be diverted to any purpose other than the specific purpose for which the loan was made.

4. In order to ensure the establishment of orderly industrial financing practices in co-operation with industry, banks will pay due attention to the below-mentioned matters concerning capital-investment loans, and will maintain close communication and co-ordination with other lending bankers:

(a) As a general rule, a capital investment loan to a borrower company which is part of a structurally problematic sector of industry will be made only once effective, self-imposed efforts to refrain from excessive facility investment are in place. In such cases, the terms and conditions of the loan need to be structured to be within the scope of the self-imposed plan and to confirm to the bank's established credit approval criteria.

(b) In industrial sectors where effective self-imposed production facility adjustments are difficult to implement, bankers should be willing to provide indirect assistance to adjustment efforts, while maintaining a cautious attitude toward lending.

Immediately following these clauses, the preface of the General Rules continues, 'Each and every provision in the Rules represents both a commitment and a goal. Although they tend to be expressed in somewhat general terms, we believe that specific issues should be addressed with good sense and experience in the light of economic realities.' Although the Research Committee assessed the General Rules as 'provisions expressed in quite often general terms which do not satisfactorily meet our expectations for rules governing corporate finance practices', it finally decided, after much discussion, to implement them.[51]

The Relationships Between Banks and their Corporate Clients. (Why did the banks continue to lend so much?)

As discussed earlier, during the period of rapid economic growth that prevailed in Japan after World War II, the overloan issue presented a good opportunity for discussion of corporate finance practices. Indeed, many loudly advocated the need to review banking practices and corporate financial activities. However, these discussions yielded nothing substantial. Bankers refused to accept any drastic reforms to established lending practices, despite the benefits such reforms would have yielded for the entire financing system; to banking management, and to overall corporate financial strength. In this section on the relationships between banks and their corporate clients, we will explore the following questions: what was the significance of the loans made by bankers to their corporate clients? and, what specific benefits did bankers realize by making these loans?

It is difficult to gain an accurate qualitative comprehension of the significance of the relationship between a bank and one of its corporate clients. Fortunately, however, we can partly understand the significance of the relationship by assessing findings from a series of studies concerning banking management, which were administered by the Research Committee on Financial Systems during the period of public debate on banking practices.[52] The most noteworthy findings are based on answers given, in 1968, by 1,504 corporations to the questionnaires concerning financing practices.[53] The paid-up capital levels and principal banks of account for these 1,504 respondent corporations are shown in Table 8.4, which demonstrates the predominant influence of commercial banks, particularly the city banks.

To begin with, let us look at the external source of funds most preferred by corporations. In reply to the question concerning the most preferred external means of financing capital investments, 66 per cent of respondents

TABLE 8.4. *Paid-up capital and principal bank of account of 1,504 respondent companies, 1968*

Paid-up capital level (million yen)	Principal bank (%)				
	City banks	Regional banks	Long-term Credit Banks	Other banking institutions	Totals
(A) Over 1,000	68.2	4.5	8.3	19.0	100
(B) 100–1,000	62.3	15.6	6.5	15.6	100
(C) 50–100	61.0	14.3	3.0	21.7	100
(D) 10–50	49.7	12.9	0.3	37.1	100
(E) Under 10	52.2	9.0	0.6	38.2	100
TOTALS	59.9	11.1	4.5	24.5	100

Note: 'Principal bank' is the banking institution from which the respondent corporation borrows the largest amount of money.

Source: Research Group on Finance System, *Long-Term Finance System* (1969), 24–5.

identified long-term loans, which far exceeded either the issue of corporate bonds and debentures (1.6 per cent) or capital increases (9.4 per cent). With respect to the factors motivating their selection, it is noteworthy that a great majority of the respondents referred to the 'stable nature of funds' rather than 'low cost'.[54]

The next question, 'In terms of amount, which was the most significant external means of financing your facility investments during the past two-year period?', provides insight into the principal means employed by corporate treasurers to finance capital investments in those days. Answers are shown in Table 8.5. As this table indicates, corporations were highly dependent on long-term bank loans. It is, however, interesting to note that a great number of corporate borrowers (particularly smaller businesses) financed their facility investments using short-term rather than long-term loans. This form of borrowing, which is short-term in form but long-term in reality, is commonly referred to as a 'roll-over' or 'ever-green' loan, and has historically been criticized as an impediment to sound corporate finance. In terms of principal banks of account, 25.8 per cent of corporations banking principally with city banks were financing their facility investments with roll-overs of short-term loans.[55]

Taking the outcome of the questionnaires seriously, the Research Committee conducted a fact-finding investigation on lending practices by financial institutions. The results revealed significant differences at city banks and regional banks between the contractual terms of loans and the actual period of time that loans remained outstanding, thus reflecting the existence of a customary practice of extending the maturity of loans beyond their agreed-upon terms. The investigation also revealed that the difference was negligible at long-term credit banks and trust banks, the principal business of which was to provide long-term funds to industry.[56]

TABLE 8.5. *'In terms of amount, which was the most significant external means of financing your facility investments during the past two-year period?' (percentages)*

	(A)	(B)	(C)	(D)	(E)	Totals
Short-term loan	7.3	23.1	25.1	27.7	33.7	21.4
Long-term loan	73.7	61.0	55.0	47.7	35.4	57.7
Bond issue	3.8	0.0	0.0	0.0	0.0	1.8
Equity	7.3	3.1	2.2	4.2	2.2	4.2
Intercorporate credit	2.8	3.6	3.9	8.4	12.9	5.5
No answer	5.3	9.1	13.9	11.9	15.7	10.2
TOTALS	100	100	100	100	100	100

Note: (A)–(E) correspond to the classification (by paid-up capital level) in Table 8.4.

Source: Research Group on Finance System, *Long-Term Finance System* (1969), 32.

In assessing why the unsound practice of extending short-term loans was followed so widely by city and regional banks, the Research Committee pointed to the traditional notion that commercial banks, such as city and regional banks, ought to concentrate on commercial lending. It contended that these banks felt pressured not to make formal long-term loans, particularly in their front-line business offices. In addition, the Research Committee also identified the following contributing factors: (1) a fear among banks of committing themselves to any long-term risks, due to a lack of confidence in their ability properly to appraise credit propositions of a sophisticated nature; (2) agreed rates of interest on short-term loans were lower than those on long-term loans; (3) with the exception of a limited number of extremely large industrial corporations that always enjoy an advantageous position over bankers in negotiations, banks find it easier to exert pressure on ordinary corporate borrowers when short-term money is involved. Here the Committee cited the practice of requesting a corporate treasurer to increase the compensatory deposit balance maintained with the bank.[57]

Using the foregoing analysis made by the Committee as a starting-point, we look further into the lending practices followed by the banks, particularly the city banks.

We begin by reviewing credit-appraising competence noted in factor (1) above. To do so, we compare the overall strength of city banks with that of long-term credit banks in terms of the number of credit analysts employed and the number of credit proposals handled per credit analyst. Table 8.6 shows the number of credit analysts per institution and the number of credit analysts involved in assessing every 10 billion yen worth of credit proposals. Table 8.7 shows the number of credit deals handled per credit analyst during a two-month period from July to September 1968. Although it would not be realistic to evaluate the overall credit skills and competence of the

TABLE 8.6. *Number of credit analysts per bank/10 billion yen in credit proposals*

	Per bank	Per 10 billion yen of credit proposal	Experience of credit analysts in years (av.)
City banks	40	0.3	2.0
Long-term credit banks	56	0.5	4.0

Note: 'Credit analyst' is an officer who belongs to the credit examination section of a bank, examines the contents of a credit proposal, and prepares for the credit decision or actually decides it.

Source: Research Group on Finance System, *Long-Term Finance System* (1969), 198.

TABLE 8.7. *Number of credit deals handled per credit analyst*

	Number of credit deals per credit analyst		
	Long-term	Short-term	Totals
City banks	29	433	462
Long-term credit banks	16	15	31

Source: Research Group on Finance System, *Long-Term Finance System* (1969), 199.

banks under review based on these statistics, we may safely conclude that long-term credit banks, which have a greater experience in credit assessment and review, appear to be more careful in making credit decisions.

We next consider interest rates, the subject of factor (2) above. On short-term loans subject to extension on a roll-over basis, it was a widespread practice among bank lenders to extend a loan against a promissory note from the borrower company having maturity in three months. On the maturity date, the loan was rolled over against a new note deposited by the borrower to replace the previous one. This process was repeated every three months for as long as the loan was rolled over. For borrowers, the net cost of interest on these loans was more than that implied by the agreed rate of interest because of another widespread lending practice which called for short-term borrowers to pay interest on an 'up-front or discount' basis. Furthermore, at each roll-over of loan, borrowers were asked to pay interest on the day upon which the loan was rolled over. As a consequence of these practices, a loan borrowed at a ticketed interest rate of 7.3 per cent, for example, had an actual net cost to the borrower of 7.52 per cent.[58]

Our final subject, referred to in factor (3) above is the so-called compensating deposit balance requested by bank lenders. Also widespread, this practice called for bank lenders to ask borrowers to maintain a deposit balance equal to a certain percentage of the outstanding loan balance, as compensation for the loan. Customarily, short-term borrowers would be asked to maintain relatively higher deposit balances than long-term borrowers. Looking at the statistics from May 1968 on deposit balances maintained per bank as a percentage of the amount of loans outstanding, we find a wide difference between commercial banks and long-term credit providers: 11.6 per cent on average for long-term credit banks, compared with 47.0 per cent for city banks (and 42.4 per cent for regional banks).[59] Based on the assumption that short-term lenders asked borrowers to maintain 30 per cent compensating deposit balances against short-term loans, the net cost to borrowers would be as high as 9.17 per cent per annum, which is slightly higher than the net cost of a long-term loan with a 5 per cent compensating balance requirement.[60] We might also add that the questionnaires referred to above asked respondents: 'As a borrower, what specific requests would you make of bank lenders?' The third most frequent response was 'Discontinue the practice of asking for a compensating deposit balance', exceeded only by 'Reduce the interest rates on loans' and 'Allow us to borrow the actual amount we need'. (See Table 8.8.)

To conclude this part of the discussion, we review answers to another survey question, namely: 'In general, what criticisms do you have of financial institutions, including bankers, or of the way in which the banking business is administered by the authorities?' The most frequent response was 'Take corrective actions to eliminate the compulsory deposit requirement by bank lenders.' Some actual responses in this connection are appended below.[61]

The way in which bankers push forward with their deposit collection campaigns reflects the excessive competition among themselves, and is very often intolerable. Their practice of asking borrowers to open and maintain fixed deposits as an infor-

TABLE 8.8. *'As a borrower, what specific requests would you make of bank lenders?' (percentages)*

	(A)	(B)	(C)	(D)	(E)	Totals
Allow us to borrow the actual amount we need	28.3	26.7	24.6	24.5	25.2	26.2
Reduce the interest rates on loans	30.1	23.7	21.2	20.3	18.6	23.8
Discontinue asking for compensating deposit balance	24.4	26.0	22.9	17.0	13.7	21.9
Mitigate asking for mortgage	5.2	8.6	11.1	11.9	15.6	9.4
Allow us to borrow on long term	7.9	11.3	15.5	19.8	17.5	13.4
Give advice on finance and management	0.0	0.4	1.4	1.8	1.9	0.9
Do not interfere with our management	2.5	2.2	2.2	2.2	3.8	2.5
Others	1.7	1.2	1.2	2.5	3.8	1.9
TOTALS	100	100	100	100	100	100

Note: (A)–(E) correspond to the classification in Table 8.4.

Source: Research Group on Finance System, *Long-Term Finance System* (1969), 36.

mal form of collateral security for loans is totally unreasonable. The way in which they ask short-term borrowers for compensating deposit balances is highly compulsory and authoritarian.

Competition among banks is so fierce and outrageous that they seem to lend to us mostly to get deposits back in return.

The worst types of bankers are those who ask us to borrow from them and then to deposit all the loan in return. We have no choice but to entertain their request out of respect for our long-established relationship with them. Net net, we have to pay the interest differential for nothing.

As a consequence of the outrageous competition among bank lenders to increase the compensating deposit balances for borrowers, borrower corporations must pay the net cost of a hidden high rate of interest. In other words, banking institutions are enjoying their growth and high rate of return on assets by passing on a financial burden to borrower corporations.

These responses describe only a very limited aspect of the relationship between banking institutions and their corporate clients. However, from this information, we can understand that the banker–borrower relationship established under the corporate financing systems which prevailed during the period of rapid economic growth were never of a unilateral nature. It would be misguided to conclude that the banks were so devoted to responding to the unlimited corporate desire to make capital investments that they overlooked their own interests.

To understand accurately the bankers' interests and behaviour, we must examine the way in which the Ministry of Finance supervised banking institutions and their business operations. Although bankers made an effort to establish and strengthen their independence during this rapid growth period, as we discussed earlier, they achieved no more than independence within a comprehensively structured framework of stringent restrictions, as exemplified by the extent of the regulatory authorities' control and supervision over the banking business, including restrictions on interest rates and branch operations. The history of restrictions on interest rates dates back to the end of 1947, when the Law on Temporary Adjustment of Interest Rates was enacted. The Law states, 'For the time being, the Minister of Finance may as he deems necessary in light of general economic conditions, cause the Governor of BOJ to set, alter, or repeal a maximum rate of interest to be applied by banks and other financial institutions.' Despite the qualifying term 'Temporary' in its title, this law continued to regulate the interest rates that bankers could apply to deposit and loans over the succeeding several decades.[62]

To maximize their earning opportunities in a regulated interest-rate environment, bankers naturally have to capitalize upon their lending capabilities to the fullest extent, which means increasing their customer deposit base. For bankers, the most effective means of achieving this goal should be to expand their branch network. However, MOF continued to impose stringent restrictions on efforts by banks to increase their numbers of branch offices. City banks, which were the most crowded by seekers of industrial funds, were subjected to the most stringent restrictions by MOF, for the valid reason that the competitive positions of other financial institutions had to be protected. It should also be noted that the MOF based its administrative supervision in this regard on the total balance of customer deposits held by the banks.[63] Under these circumstances, it would be highly likely that bankers, especially city bankers, would make an effort to increase loan balances to corporate borrowers, with their high potential as deposit funds, in order to increase the overall balance of customer deposits at existing branches. If the bankers intended to increase the proportion of deposit balances per unit of loans outstanding, they would in turn become more aggressive in demanding larger fixed and compensating deposits. They would also strive to increase their lending presence with parent corporations, which held a controlling interest in a large number of subsidiary companies as well as exerting management influence over a great number of affiliated or related companies. Moreover, they might actively assist corporations in their efforts to make facility investments which would help to maximize their sales revenues.[64]

This leads us to a third hypothesis of development, which explains the development of industrial finance during the period of rapid economic growth as being 'a consequence of continuing aggressive lending activities by bank lenders, motivated by the desire to maximize their deposit base'. Using this hypothesis as a guide, we may be able to explain to some extent, albeit not perfectly, industrial finance activity as it occurred under the leadership of private financial institutions, particularly the city banks. Should our reasoning be correctly oriented, it becomes clear that the interests of the banks finally converged with that of their corporate borrowers, who had a strong and consistent desire to make ambitious facility investments, while operating in a market-place where a fully-fledged capital market was not available.

Reassessment of the Japanese Style of Industrial Finance

In this chapter, we have provided an overview of industrial finance in Japan over the first twenty years or so of the post-war era. Here, let us return to the question posed at the beginning of this paper: could it be said that banks worked Japan's post-war economic miracle?

In terms of the post-war volume of capital supplied to industry, particularly after government funds began to indirectly support economic development, the generous flow of capital from private commercial banks served as a major pillar in the rapid economic development of Japan. But was the actual loan assessment process carried out by those banks themselves? If we rephrased the question to ask whether the private commercial banks played the major role in producing information, the most important function in the financial go-between system, the answer would be different. Even after the co-operative financing system carried out mainly by JDB during the recovery period had lost its importance, banks were supported by the existence of the long-term credit banks, which possessed the ability to function as excellent information producers. The banks were always successful in obtaining sufficient information about prospective investments by communicating through investment planning and adjustment organizations in the political, industrial, and financial sectors. And by doing so, it seems that banks were able to lower their risks in lending and curb their assessment responsibilities.

The presence of this kind of system, which limited the assessment responsibilities of banks and paved the way for capital flows to industry, carries much significance in the economic development of post-war Japan. So, we may find 'finance as a special act' in this kind of financial system. However, at the same time, we cannot deny that its presence weakens the assessment ability of banks and can in turn impair corporate understanding of sound financial practices. This type of structure may be responsible for the element of so-called 'horizontal consciousness' which is thought to appear in Japanese major corporations as well as major commercial banks. Moreover, if we additionally consider what we know of the banks' strong appetite for lending as well as their motives in maximizing deposits behind aggressive lending activities (in spite of the lack of comprehensive evidence cited here), we may conclude that the industrial financing system during the post-war period has been something of a double-edged sword. On the one hand, this system may be viewed as effective in promoting rapid economic growth or bringing economic miracles. However, it hardly seems to promote awareness of financial risks, or to check the incidence of excessive investment.

Finally, I would like to raise several potentially controversial points not covered within this chapter. The first asks why the debate about 'overloan' failed to progress further. By pursuing this question, we will probably be able to clarify several major issues concerning post-war Japanese fiscal and financial policies. One of these problems concerns monetary policy. In order to ensure stable economic growth, the money supply must be increased at a rate equal to the expansion-induced growth in demand for cash. Three routes are available to monetary authorities to increase the money supply: (1) inflows of gold or foreign currency; (2) excessive dispersion of general public expenditures; and (3) an increase in bank lending and securities investment. As Japan focused on achieving high economic growth, only the third route was viable. Since public finance was constrained by a balanced-budget requirement, and economic growth often exceeded forecasts, general public finance activity tended to absorb, rather than supply, commercially available funds. Consequently, a pattern was created in which BOJ had to expand the money supply by expanding credit to the commercial banks. From this perspective, 'overloan' may be seen as part of the natural course of events, and the practice would have been difficult to eliminate without overall structural change. Further, since the government's fiscal policy options were somewhat limited, as noted above, commercial finance activity not only had to promote long-term economic growth; it had to adjust to short-term business cycles. In the light of this latter function, loans from BOJ were considered to be the most appropriate means of expanding the money supply to fuel economic growth, given that repayment pressures could be effectively applied.[65]

The second point concerns the failure to develop direct financing activity in post-war Japan. In reviewing in this chapter the post-war progress of indirect financing, the relative underdevelopment of the securities market has been taken as a given. The usual explanation for this underdevelopment, particularly that of the securities trading market, has been the low level of post-war household assets. For a long time after the War, most Japanese households are thought to have held insufficient assets to allow participation in the securities markets. While this interpretation is most likely correct, the more relevant question is what role did the government take to develop these markets? Given that commercial finance activity was required to compensate for the monetary gap implied by the twin goals of a balanced budget and high economic growth, we cannot dismiss the possibility that government authorities thought it best not to extend themselves in encouraging the nascent securities markets. Instead, they would appear to have opted to unify the flow of funds to industry, mainly through the commercial banks, thereby leaving room for the MOF or BOJ to carry out financial adjustment as necessary.

NOTES

1. J. A. Schumpeter, *The Theory of Economic Development* (trans. Redvers Opie) (Oxford, 1961), 70.
2. Federation of Economic Organizations, *10 Years History of FEO* (Keizai Dantai Rengo Kai Junen Shi), ii (Tokyo, 1963), 320.
3. Kaichi Shimura, (ed.), *Evidence for Post-War Industrial History* (Sengo Sangyo Shi heno Shogen), iv (Tokyo, 1978), 290.
4. Japan Development Bank, *10 Years History of JDB (Nippon Kaihastu Ginko Junen Shi)* (Tokyo, 1963), 14–15.
5. Long-Term Credit Bank of Japan, *10 Years History of LTCB* (Nippon Choki Shin'yo Ginko Junen Shi) (Tokyo, 1962), 35.
6. JDB, *10 Years History*, 15–16.

7. Ibid. 23.
8. Ibid. 29–31.
9. Ibid. 48–51, 100.
10. LTCB, *10 Years History*, 47–9.
11. Ibid. 52.
12. Industrial Bank of Japan, *50 Years History of IBJ* (Nippon Kogyo Ginko Gojunen Shi) (Tokyo, 1957), 727.
13. Ibid. 727–8. For more detailed information on IBJ, see Kent E. Calder, *Strategic Capitalism: Private Business and Public Purpose in Japanese Industrial Finance* (Princeton nj, 1993), 158–61.
14. Shimura, *Evidence*, 17.
15. JDB, *10 Years History*, 57.
16. Ibid. 22, 70.
17. Ibid. 57–9; FEO, *10 Years History*, 323-4.
18. Ibid. 71.
19. Ibid. 67. In addition, the standard interest rate of JDB's loan was substantially lower than those of private financial institutions.
20. Ibid. 3.
21. Ibid. 68–9.
22. Ibid. 3.
23. National Federation of Banking Association, *20 Years History of NFBA* (Ginko Kyokai Nijunen Shi) (Tokyo, 1965), 163–4, 331–5.
24. Shigemitsu Ashizawa, 'Corporate Finance of the Steel Industry in Japan' (Nippon Tekko Sangyo no Sikin Chotatsu), *Shoken Kenkyu*, 103 (1993), 160.
25. JDB, *10 Years History*, 71.
26. Ashizawa, 'Corporate Finance', 170, 203.
27. Ibid. 158.
28. *Economic White Paper*, i (Tokyo, 1947), 47.
29. JDB, *10 Years History*, 100–1.
30. Ibid. 95.
31. Ibid. 103.
32. LTCB, *10 Years History*, 142.
33. Office of Historical Studies, MOF (ed.), *History of Fiscal and Monetary Policies in Japan, 1952–1973* (Showa Zaisei Shi, 1952–1973), ix (Tokyo, 1991), 130.
34. NFBA, *20 Years History*, 190–3; Bank of Japan, *100 Years History of BOJ* (Nippon Ginko Hyakunen Shi), v (Tokyo, 1985), 484.
35. NFBA, *20 Years History*, 193.
36. Ibid. 194, 339.
37. Federation of Economic Organizations, *30 Years History of FEO* (Keizai Dantai Rengo Kai Sanjunen Shi) (Tokyo, 1978), 122.
38. Office of Historical Studies, MOF, *History of Fiscal and Monetary Policies*, 134–5.
39. Ibid. 26.
40. NFBA, *20 Years History*, 347. On the Special Measures Law for the Promotion of Designated Industries, see Calder, *Strategic Capitalism*, 64–5, 157.
41. Economic Planning Agency, *Economic White Paper* (1956), 42.
42. BOJ, *100 Years History*, 528.

43. Banking Bureau of MOF (ed.), *Report on Overloan Problem* (Over Loan no Zesei ni kansuru Toshin oyobi Kankei Shiryo) (Tokyo, 1964), 9.
44. Office of Historical Studies, MOF, *History of Fiscal and Monetary Policies*, 74–5. On 'window guidance' see Calder, *Strategic Capitalism*, 87–90.
45. Banking Bureau of MOF, *Report on Overloan,* 14.
46. Ibid. 1.
47. Office of Historical Studies, MOF, *History of Fiscal and Monetary Policies,* 260–1.
48. NFBA, *20 Years History,* 255.
49. Office of Historical Studies, MOF, *History of Fiscal and Monetary Policies,* 261.
50. Banking Bureau of MOF (ed.), *Report on the Corporate Finance System for Stable Economic Growth* (Antei Seicho wo Kakuho surutameno Kigyo Kinyu no Arikata ni kansuru Toshin oyobi Shiryo) (Tokyo, 1966), 9–10.
51. Ibid. 8.
52. Research Group on Finance System in Banking Bureau of MOF (ed.), *Long-term Industrial Finance System* (Tokyo, 1969).
53. Ibid. 14–37.
54. Ibid. 35.
55. Ibid. 32.
56. Ibid. 132–3.
57. Ibid. 129.
58. Ibid. 130, 145.
59. Ibid. 145, 187.
60. Ibid. 130.
61. Special Committee on the Private Financial Institutions (Research Committee on Financial System), Documents of the Sectional Meeting of the Special Committee (1969), 5–7.
62. Office of Historical Studies, MOF, *History of Fiscal and Monetary Policies,* 66.
63. Juro Teranishi, 'Main-Bank System', in Tetsuji Okazaki and Masahiro Okuno (eds.), *Origins of the Contemporary Japanese Economic System* (Gendai Nippon Keizai Shisutemu no Genryu) (Tokyo, 1993), 87.
64. Ibid. 88.
65. Banking Bureau of MOF, *Report on Overloan,* 15–19.

9.   Finance and Industry in Britain after 1945: *some issues and evidence*

FORREST CAPIE

Introduction

Has the British economy failed, and if so can the blame for failure be placed at the door of finance? This chapter surveys some of the principal issues in the alleged failure of the British financial system in the years after 1945. It outlines first the nature of the problem, then raises some questions of theory and practice such as the connection between investment and growth, and then presents some speculation based on the available evidence. The evidence is in part circumstantial and of a qualitative kind. Research upon which stronger conclusions might be based has not yet been done.

The Problem in Context

First the problem. The story of British economic decline now has a long history. It has been running for close on a century. Contributions have been made from a long list of historians as the following titles illustrate: Alan Sked, *Britain's Decline*; Sidney Pollard, *The Wasting of the British Economy*; Martin Weiner, *English Culture and the Decline of the Industrial Spirit*; B. Elbaum and W. Lazonick, *The Decline of the British Economy*; M. Kirby, *The Decline of British Economic Power since 1870*. There is a vast literature much of it making an assessment of the following kind: 'Within the span of half a lifetime, Britain has descended from the most prosperous major state of Europe to the Western European slum . . . Moscow has been reduced to quoting Britain as the proof that capitalism doesn't work.'[1]

Pollard went on in a chapter called 'The Facts' to show that by 1991 Spain would have overtaken Britain, and that by 1987 (though we must allow a misprint on this one) Greece would have overtaken Britain. Further, he argued that early in the next century 'Eastern Europe will have sailed past Britain'. It gets worse. 'None of this [these dire forecasts]', he stated, 'takes into account the wilful destruction of British industrial power under Mrs Thatcher's rule.'[2] None of this has come anywhere near to being fulfilled and yet the underlying view seems to command almost universal assent, though there have been one or two brighter accounts recently.[3]

Interestingly, the hard information that would normally be consulted for endorsement of the pessimistic view, does not bear out this tragic story. According to Maddison's figures, German and Japanese productivity, as captured in GDP per hour worked, have lagged behind British productivity since at least 1870.[4] And according to Feinstein's calculations in terms of aggregate productivity Japan is a long way behind still.[5] When we turn to income per head (for 1989—before the recent recession and German reunification) we find that Germany was a mere 4 per cent higher than Britain and Japan 8 per cent higher. (The figures for 1994 are 3 per cent and 11 per cent respectively.) Recent exercises employing a new growth-theory framework lend further support to a more optimistic appraisal. The scope for 'catch-up' by Britain was limited and the 'failure' therefore less. None of this is to say that Britain might not have done better, either at certain points or even overall. But it does damage the credibility of the stories of long-term, inexorable, and deep decline. What needs stressing is that when blame is being attributed the scale of the problem should be kept in view.

The Cause of the Problem

However, there are those who not only find decline but are able to pinpoint its source—the failure of financial intermediation. Financial institutions in Britain have been criticized for failure of many kinds, but chief among these criticisms has been that they have failed to provide long-term finance for industry. Therefore, it is asserted, British industry has been disadvantaged relative to its competitors, and this accounts for the relative decline of the British economy. The basic premiss around which this discussion takes place is that Anglo-Saxon (or perhaps Anglo-American would now be a better way of conveying what is meant) corporate finance is different (and essentially inferior) to European-Japanese. Anglo-Saxon is market-oriented with open capital markets while European-Japanese are bank-oriented. In the former the banks generally keep a distance from industry while in the latter they become closely involved. It is often presented as a contest and the conclusion drawn that the bank-oriented system is superior in terms of its contribution to the performance of the real economy.

An issue that needs to be borne in mind throughout is the contribution the banks made in terms of stability and the costs that may have been incurred in terms of inefficiency. Stability depends on several factors. One is the structure of the system. A well-branched system that allows thorough diversification across sectors will be more stable than one that is not. The structure will be a product of evolution and legal and regulatory conditions. Another factor influencing stability is the macroeconomic environment, but essentially price stability. And there will be a two-way relationship.

Investment and Growth

At the centre of this debate lies the question of the relationship between investment and economic growth. The relationship is far from certain as a recent demonstration by Eltis shows.[6] Some countries have high investment/income ratios and strong growth, while others have low ratios and good growth. This is not surprising since there is such variation in the type of investment—infrastructure investment has a different impact from investment in machinery. Matthews, Feinstein, and Odling-Smee wrote as follows: 'Unfortunately the theory of the investment function, especially in the long run, is not one of the strongest points in economic theory.'[7] Even if high investment went unambiguously with high growth, and low investment with low growth, the question would remain over which caused which.

The view that raising investment is beneficial also implicitly assumes that it raises total factor productivity (TFP). However, TFP embraces a wide range of factors that impinge on the efficiency of capital and labour, factors such as education and training, research and development, organizational structure, and managerial efficiency, as well as financial intermediation. Financial intermediation is just one of a very large number of factors affecting total factor productivity. Financial intermediation can be expected to increase welfare by facilitating the exchange between investors and savers, and by providing secure and well-priced assets; and the more efficient it is the greater will be its contribution. Recent developments in growth theory and in its application make a greater case for the role of investment, particularly in relation to human capital, though it will be some time before we have satisfactory measures with which to work.

Short-Termism

Could there be reasons why financial institutions would not undertake profitable intermediation? Might lenders be short-termist? One possibility is that British commercial banks are short-termist in outlook, this being a product of their balance sheet—the need to balance short-term liabilities with short-term assets. This militates against lending for investment projects involving a high degree of research and development expenditure requiring a long gestation period before commercial exploitation (in the electronics or aerospace industries, for instance).

Non-bank firms may also exhibit short-termist behaviour. The historical development of firms has usually followed the path of individual owner, or family firm, through to the large joint-stock corporation. In the small family firm, ownership and control are one and the same. There should be no short-termism on the part of the closely held firm. In large joint-stock companies they are separated, and problems of 'agency' can arise. A principal engages an agent to provide some service which involves delegating decision-making authority to the agent. The question is: will the firm have a lower value in these circumstances than if it were owner-managed? There is a presumption that it will, but it could be that market discipline will keep the firm in line via the market for 'corporate control'. There is a constant threat of take-over through the stock-market if firms are not performing well.

In the nineteenth century the majority of British firms had owner-managers while today the most important owners of the largest corporations are portfolio investors. Managers are not normally subject to very effective shareholder discipline, but they are under this threat of take-over by another company (which for the individual manager may carry the threat of loss of prestige or power, or even dismissal). It is in these circumstances that managers concentrate on the share price (short term). But has that attention to the share price detracted from other possible longer-term considerations that may eventually reduce the value of the firm? Moreover, there is the view that stock-market finance encourages short-termist behaviour and, in particular, reduces expenditure on research and development. Countries relying principally on this system have firms which are disadvantaged as compared with those in bank-oriented countries. In the latter there is said to be a high degree of commitment by the banks towards corporate/industrial customers—as shown in their willingness to lend over long periods, to support corporate customers in periods of financial distress and, if appropriate, to engage actively in the long-term planning and investment decision-making of corporate customers. In contrast to such a system, it is alleged, British banks have eschewed long-term commitments, been overly concerned to maintain highly liquid assets structures, and have been averse to financing industrial developments.

Some reservations can be expressed on this. For example, Edgerton and Horrocks provide a radically different picture of British R&D expenditure than the commonly accepted one, showing that much more took place than is usually thought.[8] And Mayer and Alexander showed that for the 1970s and 1980s there was no difference in R&D expenditure between private and public companies across industries, thereby casting doubt on the short-termist tendency of stock-markets.[9]

Financial Intermediation

A principal function of intermediation is to alleviate the market imperfections caused by economies of scale. These can be found in transactions in financial markets, in information gathering and in portfolio management. If there were no such imperfections, everyone could manage his or her own assets as well as the next person. There are, too, economies of scale in providing loans or new issues. The size of the loan may be too much for one person or institution—too much in the sense that a single person or institution would not want to hold such a large proportion of their portfolio in that asset. Thus banks can lend more easily than individuals because of their ability to invest at lower costs. In addition to transaction costs, there is the question of information. The small investor cannot assess the qualities of entrepreneurs or find the time to monitor the performance of a firm. Ideas on monitoring derive from the existence of asymmetric information (the imbalance in information available to different parties to the transaction), which in turn is linked to economies of scale. There could also be advantages for a bank arising from the private information it has on a firm deriving from its credit relationship. Logic would suggest that small and less well-established firms should borrow from banks, whereas large, well-known firms with a good reputation would tend to borrow from bond- or stock-markets.

Thus banks could be the source of medium-, or long-term funds for investment. They may represent the best means of providing the right balance in the desire for control on the part of both lender and borrower. Borrowers would like to raise finance on terms that are attractive to them, including control over future uncontracted outcomes. And lenders also need protection. The way that control can be exercised is through short-maturity, collateral, security or covenants.

This raises a central issue on the degree of 'commitment' between borrower and lender. Where it exists there is clearly the promise, or at least the possibility, of a long-term relationship. It is often claimed that bank-oriented systems have managed to harness this relationship for the good of long-term investment and growth. Market-oriented systems, such as that of the UK, are said to be deprived of the advantages emanating from such a symbiotic bank–industry relationship.

Sources of Finance

In the nineteenth century the bulk of firms' investment funds came from retained profits. It is not possible to be precise about the extent of this self-financing, but there can be some confidence that the bulk of funds came from such retention. It is also well-known, of course, that significant amounts came from external sources. Much the same pattern holds in the post-World War II period. Over the post-war period, although there is a lot of variation, retained profits as a proportion of total capital employed were invariably in excess of 60 per cent and on occasions more than 70 per cent. Bank borrowing as a percentage of total capital funds fluctuated around a mean of about 18 per cent leaving the balance to be found elsewhere. The relationship of retained profits to total funds has therefore been remarkably steady.

Economic Environment after 1945

The world after 1945 has been considerably different from the period 1870–1945, and a number of the differences have had beneficial consequences for the provision of industrial finance. Macroeconomic differences include the scale of personal savings, and the rate of inflation. Microeconomic differences include the new institutional arrangements for the provision of finance, and the structure of industry itself.

Apart from the War and immediate post-war years, there had been no inflation of any consequence in Britain prior to 1945. Inflation, however, has persisted throughout the world since 1945. Inflationary expectations were prevalent in most of the period and were greatly increased after 1970 when the world resorted to fiat money (i.e. where there is no backing). The temptations for government that accompany such a regime effectively make inflation inevitable. Thus rising inflationary expectations took hold at an early point after 1950. Periods of inflation affect investors and borrowers differently. The simplest view is that debt is more popular during inflationary periods. This view of course depends upon the assumptions that inflation is not being fully anticipated and is not cancelled out by rising interest rates lagging behind changes in inflation. It is also possible that inflation affects choices between bond debt and equity finance. Here the argument is more complicated but has important consequences for the question of bank provision for industry. In an inflationary period, if a firm's costs and revenues rise in line with inflation, dividends can be maintained in real terms. The value of a share would therefore be a hedge against inflation. The opposite applies to bonds: as interest rates rise bond prices fall. Therefore, one might expect a shift in the composition of assets from bonds to equity during unanticipated inflation. However, there are several reasons why a move to equities and away from debt may not occur, such as differences between relative and general prices, the effect of taxation, and so on. In 1981 the introduction of index-linked gilts was an attempt to make bonds a hedge against inflation; it was not altogether successful since supply did not match demand. But over the post-war years as a whole the pressures are likely to have been such as to make equity finance more attractive, and hence to ease the pressure on the banks to provide debt finance.

Another factor that proved favourable immediately after 1945 was that bank liquidity was very high. Substantial bank deposits and liquid-asset holdings had been built up during the War and continued in the 'cheap money' period of the mid-1940s. It was a time, in other words, when—within the confines of government controls—the banks were 'asset driven' that is, they were looking for loans to make to match their liabilities. Liquidity remained high for more than a decade and while it is difficult to make a precise estimate of the contribution this made to the banks' ability to supply finance to industry (Matthews, Feinstein, and Odling-Smee suggest it was small), at least it must have been positive. Against that, government controls on bank lending were greater in the 1950s. When the physical controls and rationing of the war and immediate post-war years were eventually dispensed with, greater reliance was placed on controls such as those on bank lending.

A separate factor that probably operated favourably over most of the post-war period was capital controls: although they were not comprehensive, controls on capital exports lasted until 1979 and probably kept the cost of capital lower than it would otherwise have been. Judgement on this issue must, however, be reserved in the absence of the necessary research. Individuals may have altered their savings habits, and foreigners may have viewed our capital market differently. These macroeconomic factors relieved the banking system of some of the demand for funds. One factor on the microeconomic side, as Rybczynski has argued, was that the changing structure of industry reduced the demand for funds, while increased financial innovation improved the supply of funds.[10]

Several new institutions were designed to ease the financing problems of the small and medium-sized firms. To the extent that they were successful, it can be seen that there would have been even less for the clearing banks to do. There had been a great deal of pressure for action in the 1930s following the identification of the 'Macmillan gap'. In the mid-1930s three potentially important institutions were set up—Charterhouse Industrial Development Co. Ltd., Credit for Industry, and Leadenhall Securities Incorporation. Several other smaller institutions also appeared, but it was not until after World War II that a serious attempt was made to establish an institution which would devote itself specifically to small industrial and commercial issues. This was called the Industrial and Commercial Finance Corporation (ICFC), whose shareholders comprised the English and Scottish banks and the Bank of England. The banks contributed according to their size (measured by deposit liabilities), but left the day-to-day management to the Corporation. The principal aim of the ICFC was to 'provide credit by means of loans or the subscription of loan or share capital . . . for industrial or commercial business . . . where existing facilities provided by banking institutions and the Stock Exchanges are not readily or easily available'.[11]

By 1958 it had five branches and by the mid-1970s following merger, that number had risen to eighteen. ICFC catered for smaller firms. The corporation was set up to cater for smaller loans—generally thought of as being in the region of £100,000–£200,000. A sibling institution, the Finance Corporation for Industry (FCI), concentrated on making loans to larger firms. These two merged in 1973 to form Finance for Industry. By the mid-1970s lending was at a rate of £25 million per annum; on average that is only 150 loans of about £167,000 per loan, or 450 loans of £55,000.[12]

Finance for Industry's resources were greatly enlarged in 1974 when £1,000 million was made available by financial institutions, (though not taken up) to enable it to provide more medium-term lending (for periods of seven to fifteen years). In the mid-1970s another institution, Equity Capital for Industry, was set up with a similar objective at the initiative of the British Insurance Association and designed to appeal to the small issuer. Interestingly, both FFI and Equity Capital developed the ability (and used it), to monitor the progress made by companies who borrowed from them. The most rapidly developing area in the 1970s and 1980s was the unlisted securities market. Bank of England estimates suggest that by 1990, venture capital was being provided to around 700 companies which employed some 1.5 million people, and the scale of lending was running at over £1 billion per year.

Many factors after 1945 helped to provide a more favourable environment for industry to borrow funds, but the favourable aspects should not be overplayed. The fact that some borrowers went to American banks operating in Britain, or to hire-purchase companies, and were paying higher interest rate charges, *could* suggest that loans for more risky ventures were more difficult to come by. But at the same time that should not be surprising.

The Commercial Banks

The commercial banks had for some time formed a hard cartel. We should therefore expect them to behave less efficiently than a perfectly competitive system. But at this point we do not know by how much. A starting-point for an examination of the banks' contribution to industrial finance, is their 'advances ratio'—the proportion of their assets allotted to loans and overdrafts. Before World War I the banks aimed for a 50 per cent ratio, which seems to be very close to what they achieved. Not surprisingly, the ratio fell during World War I so that by 1918 it was down to 29 per cent. It bounced back almost immediately after the War and for most of the inter-war years was over 40 per cent, although it was on a downward trend in the 1930s. There followed another, not surprising, steep decline in the ratio in World War II—this time down to 15 per cent. Following that War, however, the ratio did not bounce back quickly: not until the 1960s did it rise above 40 per cent. By the mid-60s it was back to what might be regarded as its normal or desired level in the high 40 per cent region. Then from the late 1960s until the late 1980s it settled at around 50 per cent (apart from a brief, sharp rise to around 70 per cent in the early 1970s which is explicable in terms of 'round tripping ' as a result of legislation). Thus, in broad ratio terms the banks behaved in a consistent fashion across a period of more than a century, aiming for (though not always successfully) an advances ratio of close to 50 per cent.

The interesting issue is about to whom the advances went, on what terms, and, importantly, for how long. Unfortunately, for much of the post-World

War II period there is limited information on how the proportions of these loans and advances made to manufacturing industry differed from previous times. There is reason to believe given some scattered evidence, that they stayed roughly in line with the pattern of the inter-war years when the banks made half of all their loans to industry, and that many or most were short term but were often rolled over to become in effect medium or long term. Still awaiting research is the question of who the recipients were and, more importantly, who the disappointed applicants were. What is certain is that in the 1960s the clearing banks became more active in medium-term liabilities and, to keep the balance sheet symmetrical, they increased their medium-term lending.

Regulation

The explanation for the pattern in the advances ratio, particularly the behaviour of the ratio after 1945, can be found in part in the subjugation of bank behaviour to the perceived greater needs of government finance. The banks held large amounts of liquid assets after the War. The government wanted to keep interest rates down and was launching its nationalization programme. Government concern for servicing and funding the enlarged national debt coloured all its policies towards financial markets, including the banks. In particular, the clearing banks were effectively obliged to hold an historically large proportion of their assets in government securities. In the immediate post-war period, too, the Capital Issues Committee (CIC) laid down the guide-lines for the use of advances. Three times in the first few years (1945, 1947, and 1949) the CIC issued directives, and this restrictive climate persisted for most of the next decade. Further, by the mid-1950s the first quantitative restrictions on bank lending were imposed, to be followed soon after by a (relatively small) call for 'special deposits'. In 1964 the Bank of England laid down loan priorities which essentially meant that the finance of exports had priority and anything that smacked of speculation should be avoided.

In addition, the bank cartel of the inter-war years continued after 1945 and was, indeed, fostered by the Bank of England which liked to use moral suasion in the exercise of monetary policy. In return for complying with the Bank's wishes the clearers were, for example, given exemption from publishing their profits. In 1958 the return to sterling convertibility had the eventual effect of opening up the London financial markets a little; at the same time other financial institutions were expanding. In 1971 the abolition of the cartel following the introduction of the policy of 'Competition and Credit Control' released the clearers from the restraints of cash and liquidity ratios which had clearly become too onerous, restrictive, and dated. New, less restrictive reserve ratios were introduced, and even though short-term economic pressures were to oblige the Bank of England to reimpose temporary restrictions on bank lending in the form of the 'corset' (1973), this was less distorting than earlier rationing. Thus the 1950s and 1960s were decades in which the activities of the banks were closely restricted by the authorities. Greater freedom arrived in the 1980s.

The banks had formed a loose cartel by the late nineteenth century and this had not been discouraged by the monetary authorities. In fact, the cartel was much tighter by the 1920s. The Bank of England's use of moral suasion in exercising monetary policy meant it found it more convenient to deal with a few bank chairmen in close proximity. The 1930s saw the cartel strengthened still further and this persisted into the post-World War II years. There were costs as a result of the deviation from competitive conditions, some borne by the monetary authorities (mainly the Treasury) and some by the banks themselves. The principal cost was the tax effectively imposed by the requirement to maintain a cash/deposit ratio of 8 per cent (and a liquid-assets ratio of some 28–30 per cent). On the basis of subsequent developments in the 1970s and 1980s, such reserve ratios now appear to have been far in excess of what the banks would have chosen for themselves if operating in a free, commercial environment. The total cost can be estimated by taking the amount of reserves held between the banks' preferred ratio and that imposed, and multiplying the difference by the return on Treasury bills. Such costs have been shown to be quite substantial. However, the main cost is the loss of social welfare in the form of the higher price paid for the product that results from lack of competition. There may not have been a very large loss here (depending on the contestability of the market) but casual assessments suggest that the banks were less efficient than they might have been.

On the positive side, as in earlier periods, the British system delivered considerable financial stability. Cash and near-cash assets were large enough to meet any likely contingency and the whole system was underpinned by the Bank of England's close concern and its traditional role of lender of last resort. Such gains for the community must offset at least some of the losses from the operation of the clearing bank's oligopoly.

Some Evidence from Inquiries

Such was the concern over industrial finance in the years after 1945 that it was the subject of regular investigation and inquiry. All the serious investigations in the period reached conclusions which were moderately favourable towards the banks. In general, they found that there was no reason to regard the cost of capital or the availability of external finance as a greater obstacle to investment in Britain than elsewhere.

The Radcliffe Committee of 1959 was generally sympathetic to the clearing banks and also praised the Industrial and Commercial Finance Corporation. At the same time, it pointed to a gap between the seven-year time limit imposed on loans by the clearing banks and the fifteen-year minimum of the finance houses.[13] The Prices and Income Board inquiry on bank charges was critical of the absence of price competition amongst the big banks.[14] However, like Radcliffe, the Bolton Committee of 1971 also absolved the clearing banks of blame for failing to provide funds.[15] The Radcliffe Committee had recommended the reduced use of overdrafts and the extended use of fixed-period loans, and by the time the Wilson Committee reported in 1980, this had indeed been done.[16] Radcliffe accepted that the facilities for financing investment had grown substantially since Macmillan reported (partly as a result of private institutions such as Charterhouse), and they did not advocate any further proliferation of institutions, either public or private. 'On the contrary, we believe that . . . the existing institutions can look after the ordinary requirements of small business for capital.'[17] Its concern was with the availability of information on the institutions. Radcliffe also accepted the bankers' own evidence of their supportive stance:

The joint-stock banks are very important in the finance of small business, not only as a major source of capital but because the ordinary business of banking establishes a close contact between businessmen and bank managers which puts the bank manager in a unique position to help and advise the businessman on his financial affairs.[18]

But more importantly from our point of view, the balance of the evidence was that 'though the bank advance is conventionally a short-term loan, the banks do in fact lend on a large scale to such customers to finance medium-term and long-term requirements'.[19]

The Wilson Committee suggested that an area of difficulty was the provision for finance to small firms and recommended further institutional change to correct for this.[20] But it also emphasized that the main new domestic source of medium-term finance had been the banking system. Medium-term finance was generally defined as loans with an initial term to maturity of more than two years. The evidence presented to Wilson by the London clearing banks showed that in late 1977 (the latest data then available), medium-term lending (including export finance) accounted for 50 per cent of all domestic advances outside the personal sector. A similar ratio seems to have held for some time before that and has continued since 1977. In the mid-1980s the CBI's City/Industry Task Force reached the unanimous conclusion that the City was not short-termist and did not inhibit industrial performance.

The 1970s and 1980s

For the more recent past, some more rigorous analysis of the relationship between banks and industry is available and specific comparisons between Germany and the UK have been made. Mayer and Alexander examined

the view that Germany has enjoyed a competitive advantage in manufacturing industry by virtue of the alleged closer relationship between banks
and industry in that country, the advantage coming from their industries
being allowed to take a longer-term perspective on investment.[21] To put it
another way, the German banking system appears to have established lower
costs of capital, in particular for long-term investment. In an examination
of the sources of corporate finance in aggregate, they find that experience
in the two countries is remarkably similar. The bulk of industry's *external*
finance is raised from the banks in both countries. In Britain over the years
1970–88, loans and short-term securities provided 23.7 per cent of
gross finance as against 21.1 per cent in Germany. There is no evidence
that bank finance has in aggregate been greater in Germany than in the
United Kingdom. Little is raised in the equity- or bond-market in either
country. The only significant difference between Britain and Germany is
that, as a proportion of total sources of finance, retentions are higher in
Britain—74.2 per cent as against 67.1 per cent in Germany over the years
1970–88.

However, Mayer and Alexander did find differences in the disaggregated
data. One difference is that found between large companies in both countries. Their findings here are that large British companies raised more external finance than did their German counterparts—a reflection of the higher
pay-out ratios of British firms—that is, a larger proportion of British firms'
profits was paid out in dividends so that more external finance was needed
for a given level of investment. In the 1980s the dividend/pay-out ratio in
Germany was around 12 per cent while in Britain it was closer to 30 per
cent. Large corporations in Britain also raised more equity finance than
did German firms but the purpose of this was to purchase other firms in
take-overs.

To return to the main hypothesis, that was also rejected at the level of
the large corporations—the predicted larger amounts of bank finance available and taken by German firms was not confirmed. Mayer and Alexander
rejected the standard explanation for these findings, such as those depending on differential taxation or on asymmetric information between management and shareholders. Instead they argue that 'control' theory
illuminates. An important difference between the two countries is that in
Britain there is an active market for corporate control whereas in Germany
there is not. There are almost no hostile take-overs in Germany: one reason
for this is that German banks have representation on companies' boards
and they also have holdings of corporate equity. Their findings on the
financing of medium-sized German companies were different. Here they
found that German firms received more bank finance than did medium-
sized British firms, apparently because of the greater influence of banks
over the development of firms—the longer-term relations that exist
between banks and medium-sized firms in Germany encourage the

provision of more long-term bank lending. In Britain, medium-sized firms had even larger pay-out ratios than large corporations (to stave off take-overs).

Studies of the 1970s and 1980s will however need to be placed in the longer-term perspective for there were great changes taking place in banking in these decades. Until 1971 British banking (and that of several other countries too) had a highly concentrated structure and a cosy relationship with the monetary authorities. After 1971 winds of change swept through the system and around the world there were moves to greater competition. This reopened discussion on the risk and return relationship in banking, and led to changes in behaviour, the final outcome of which is still not clear.

Summary

After 1945 the contribution of the banks increased as compared with earlier periods. There was more medium-term lending and closer ties were established with customers. More convincingly, for the recent past there is some more rigorous analysis which supports the view that British banks do not compare unfavourably in this respect, at least with their European counterparts. When this is coupled with the very good stability record of the British banking system, there is some evidence pointing to a measure of redemption of the much reviled London banker.

Three of the most recent publications from quite different sources all incline to a similar conclusion, one that goes much of the way to a defence of the British system. Howard Davies (1993) as Director General of the CBI rejected most of the charges that have been brought against the City. He believes there is a problem of low investment but that most of the responsibility for that rests with macroeconomic policy failures. He did, however, hold to the view that there was a problem in financing 'growth' companies.[22] Professor Harold Rose, former economic adviser to Barclays Bank, took a long-run view in his Wincott Lecture. He too is sceptical of the idea that British finance has failed. Indeed he goes further: '. . . the real fault of the British capital market is not that good firms cannot raise enough finance but that it is too easy for badly managed firms to do so . . .'.[23] Finally, the results of a major academic research project specifically on the alleged superiority of the German system over the British, and covering the period since 1945, have recently been published by Edwards and Fischer. Their strong conclusions are that 'The evidence analysed in this book refutes the view that the German system of finance for investment gives German firms greater access to external finance via the banking system than is the case in the UK.'[24] And further: 'The commonly held view of the merits of the German system of finance for investment, in terms of the supply of external finance to firms and corporate control receives no support from the analysis of our evidence.'[25]

NOTES

1. S. Pollard, *The Wasting of the British Economy* (Beckenham, 1982), 6.
2. Ibid. 7.
3. Cf. B. Supple, 'Fear of Failing: Economic History and the Decline of Britain Question', *Economic History Review*, 47 (1994), 441–58; W. D. Rubinstein, *Capitalism, Culture and Decline in Britain, 1750–1990* (London, 1993).
4. Angus Maddison, *Dynamic Forces in Capitalist Development* (Oxford, 1991).
5. C. H. Feinstein, 'Economic Growth since 1870: Britain's Performance in International Perspective', *Oxford Review of Economic Policy*, 4/1 (1988), 1–13.
6. W. A. Eltis, 'British Industrial Policy for the 1990s', in Graham Mather *et al.* (eds.), *The State of the Economy* (London, 1990), 37–56.
7. R. C. O. Matthews, C. H. Feinstein, and J. C. Odling-Smee, *British Economic Growth, 1856–1973* (Oxford, 1982), 327.
8. D. E. H. Edgerton and S. M. Horrocks, 'British Industrial Research and Development before 1945', *Economic History Review*, 47 (1994), 213–38.
9. C. Mayer and Ian Alexander, 'Banks and Securities Markets: Corporate Finance in Germany and the UK', *Centre for Economic Policy Research Discussion Paper*, 117 (1990).
10. T. M. Rybcynski, 'Industrial Finance Systems in Europe, United States, and Japan', *Journal of Economic Behaviour and Organisation*, 5 (1984).
11. R. Coopey and D. Clarke, *3i: Fifty Years Investing in Industry* (Oxford, 1995).
12. Ibid.
13. *Report of the Committee on the Working of the Monetary System* (Radcliffe Committee) (1959), Cmnd.827.
14. Prices and Incomes Board, *Report on Bank Charges* (1967), Cmnd.3292.
15. Bolton Committee, *Report on Small Firms: Report of Committee of Inquiry into Small Firms* (1971), Cmnd.4811.
16. Wilson Committee, *Report of Committee to Review the Functioning of Financial Institutions* (1980), Cmnd.7937.
17. Cmnd.827, p. 940.
18. Ibid. p. 941.
19. Ibid.
20. Cmnd.7937 p. 372.
21. Mayer and Alexander, 'Banks and Securities Markets'.
22. H. Davies, *The City and Manufacturing Industry* (Gresham College, London, 1993).
23. H. Rose, 'Finance—Villain or Scapegoat?', *Wincott Lecture* (1994), 21.
24. J. Edwards and K. Fischer, *Banks Finance and Investment in Germany* (Cambridge, 1993), 235.
25. Ibid. 240.

PART V

Case Studies: Automobiles and Electronics

10. Combining Mass Production with Variety: Itaku *Automotive Production in the 1960s*[1]

HIROMI SHIOJI

Itaku Assembly Firms

The Scale of Itaku *Production at Toyota*

It is well known that the ratio of outsourcing of automotive parts in the Japanese automotive industry is high compared with that of the industries in America and Europe. Compared to the outsourcing ratios in America, which tend to be between 40 and 60 per cent (based on the ratio of cost of goods), 60–80 per cent of the parts in Japan are not produced by the car manufacturer but are manufactured by first-tier suppliers (who actually outbase a large proportion of the parts to second-tier suppliers). An important point hitherto overlooked is the degree to which the assembly processes in automotive production (stamping, welding, painting, and assembly) are outbased to companies completely or partly specializing in such work. These companies are referred to as *itaku* assembly firms in Japan. About 40–50 per cent of Toyota's vehicles and 20–30 per cent of Nissan's are outsourced. The data in Table 10.1 and Table 10.2 clearly point out that in both 1970 and 1989 the assembly processes were outbased for about half of all Toyota vehicles. Table 10.1 shows that in 1970 the Toyota group produced about 1.677 million vehicles, of which the *itaku* assembly firms made about 859,000 vehicles, or 51.2 per cent.[2] Table 10.2 shows that Toyota's five assembly plants in Aichi prefecture had a production capacity of 2.244 million units in 1989, only 56.4 per cent of the Toyota Group's total capacity in Japan. On the other hand, the capacity of *itaku* firms was 1.732 million, 43.6 per cent of the Group total.

Figure 10.1(a) illustrates the manufacturing process of the *itaku* firms. The firms do not manufacture parts, but receive them from Toyota or parts-suppliers. Thereafter, they are responsible for the assembly process which includes stamping, welding, painting, and final assembly. After the process is finished they sell the complete vehicles to Toyota. There are basically three methods of parts procurement. The first is referred to as 'Gratuitous Supply.' Parts manufactured by Toyota are supplied directly to the *itaku* firms without charge. The main parts supplied in this manner are important

TABLE 10.1.　*Toyota's* itaku *production in 1970*

Itaku firm	Production (vehicles)	% of Toyota Group (Total 1,677,416)	Period
Toyota Shatai (Toyota Auto Body)	295,500	17.6	Business year
Kanto Jidosha Kogyo (Kanto Auto Works)	280,476	16.7	Business year
Arakawa Shatai Kogyo (Arakawa Auto Body)	41,374	2.5	Calendar year
Toyoda Jidoshokki Seisakusho (Toyoda Automatic Loom Works)	49,991	3.0	Business year
Yamaha Hatsudoki (Yamaha Motors)	71	0.004	Calendar year
Central Jidosha (Central Motors)	52,803	3.1	Calendar year
Hino Jidosha Kogyo (Hino Motors)	104,789	6.2	Business year
Daihatsu Kogyo (Daihatsu Motors)	33,993	2.1	Calendar year
TOTALS	858,997	51.2	

Sources: Yuka shoken hokokusho of Toyota Shatai, Kanto Jidosha Kogyo, Toyoda Jidoshokki Seisakusho, and Hino Jidosha Kogyo, *Arakawa Shatai 25 nenshi* (A History of Arakawa Shatai); Kazuo Tomiyama, *Nihon no Jidosha Sangyo* (Japanese Automobile Industry) (1973). Information from Central Jidosha and Daihatsu Kogyo.

parts such as engines, transmissions, and so on. The second method is referred to as 'Onerous Supply.' Parts manufactured by parts-suppliers are first purchased by Toyota and then supplied to the *itaku* firms with a charge. The third method is referred to as 'Independent Purchasing.' The *itaku* firms purchase the parts directly from the parts suppliers. In this case the *itaku* firms are sometimes directly involved in the initial design of and price negotiations for the parts. The relative importance of these three methods differs among *itaku* firms. Generally speaking, the longer their history, the higher is their ratio of independent purchasing.[3]

When the *itaku* firms deliver assembled vehicles to Toyota, the transaction is one in which the *itaku* firms sell the vehicles to Toyota. The price varies according to the type of vehicle, but is approximately 40 to 60 per cent of the suggested retail price at car dealers. However, as seen in Figure 10.1(b), even though the *itaku* firms sell the vehicles to Toyota, the actual physical flow of the vehicles is directly from the *itaku* to the dealers. Figure 10.1(c) illustrates the flow of production schedules and orders. First, car dealers agree a year-sales target proposed by Toyota. Then the dealers give

TABLE 10.2. *Production capacity of Toyota plants and*
itaku firms in 1989

Toyota plant/*Itaku* firm	Production capacity per year (1,000 vehicles)
Toyota plant	
Honsha	228
Motomachi	420
Takaoka	732
Tsutsumi	432
Tahara	432
Subtotal	2,244 (56.4%)
Itaku firm	
Toyota Shatai	396
Kanto Jidosha Kogyo	432
Araco, Gifu Shatai Kogyo, etc.	64
Toyoda Jidoshokki Seisakusho	216
Central Jidosha	84
Hino JidoshaKogyo	312
Daihatsu Kogyo	228
Subtotal	1,723 (43.6%)
TOTAL	3,976 (100.0%)

Source: 'GM o koe Shin—Jidosha Okoku zukuri eno
Fuseki' (Strategy for New Automobile Kingdom
beyond GM), *Shukan Toyo Keizai*, 29 Dec. 1990–5 Jan.
1991, Gappei-go.

monthly and ten-day orders to Toyota. Having received these orders, Toyota draws up and gives monthly and ten-day schedules to each *itaku* firm. As the ten-day orders are not final and the ten-day schedules are provisional plans, after the ten-day order car dealers may modify the ten-day order by as much as 30–40 per cent until four days before the date of actual assembly. This system is referred to as the 'Daily Modification order'.

The high degree of outsourcing among Japanese car manufacturers is not limited to the assembly processes. In fact, in the case of Toyota, 40 per cent of the functions of body development (product planning, design, drawing, prototyping, testing) and the preparations for production (mould/jig design and manufacturing, test assembly) which are essential elements of car manufacturing are outbased to the *itaku* assembly firms. For example, as

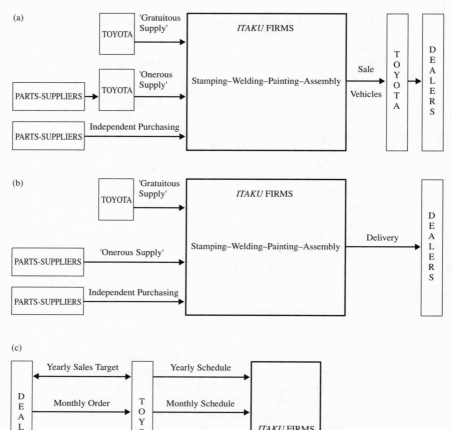

FIG. 10.1. Toyota, *itaku* firms, and parts-suppliers. (a) The manufacturing process of *itaku* firms. (b) The actual physical flow of parts and vehicles. (c) The flow of orders and production scheduling.

seen in Figure 10.2, Kanto Jidosha Kogyo develops sixteen models and assembles twelve models at present. In addition, it is interesting that five models (e.g. Windom) developed by Kanto Jidosha are assembled at Toyota and other *itaku* firms. However, the actual testing of vehicles requires the use of wind-tunnels, crash-test facilities, high-speed test tracks, and so on.

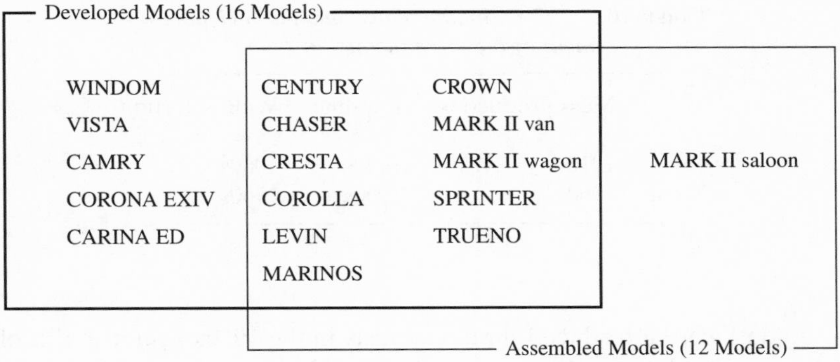

Developed Models (16 Models)

WINDOM	CENTURY	CROWN	
VISTA	CHASER	MARK II van	
CAMRY	CRESTA	MARK II wagon	MARK II saloon
CORONA EXIV	COROLLA	SPRINTER	
CARINA ED	LEVIN	TRUENO	
	MARINOS		

Assembled Models (12 Models)

FIG. 10.2. Automobile models developed and assembled by Kanto Jidosha Kogyo (as at March 1993).

Since the *itaku* firms are unable to afford such large investments, they tend to use those belonging to Toyota.

Why is the Ratio of *Itaku* Production in Japan so High?

Why has the ratio of outsourcing assembly been so high in Japan? First of all, it can be pointed out that during the 1960s, motor transport advanced rapidly and the demand for vehicles increased tenfold over the decade. The use of *itaku* firms was a measure taken in response to Toyota's inability to increase the mass production capacity of its own facilities to keep up with this explosive growth in demand. However, the importance of *itaku* production is not limited to this function of supplementary production. The key to the problem lies in the historical context of the Japanese automotive industry during the 1960s. If we compare the timing of the introduction of the following three factors, the development of mass-production of vehicles, the development of full-line production, and the development of wide-selection we find differences between Japan and the USA.[4]

As seen in Table 10.3, mass production developed in the USA during the 1910s, and in the next decade full-line production was introduced. Finally after World War II a wide selection of vehicles was offered. However, in the case of Japan, in 1960 Toyota's annual production was only about 170,000 vehicles and they did not achieve a mass-production level until later in the decade. Likewise, Toyota offered only two passenger-car models and six truck models in 1960 and full-line production was also only attained later during the 1960s. Furthermore, in the latter half of the 1960s Toyota began to offer a wide selection of each car model. Therefore, all three of the above factors (mass production, full-line production, and wide selection of each

TABLE 10.3. *The 'simultaneous and parallel development of the three factors' in Japan*

	Mass production	Full-line	Wide-selection
US	1910s	1920s	1960s
Japan	1960s	1960s	1960s

car model) were introduced simultaneously in the 1960s. I refer to this phenomenon as 'the simultaneous and parallel development of the three
factors'.

During the 1960s in Japan, along with the development of the trends
towards offering a full-line and a wide selection of vehicles, there was the
need to offer some products which could not be mass produced. Consequently, Japanese manufacturers were confronted with the problem of how
to produce a full-line and wide selection of vehicles on a small scale. In
other words, they had to find a way to combine mass production with variety
in their product line. One of the ways found to solve this problem was
the 'Toyota Production System whose premises were the Japanese-style
small-lot production of a large product variety'.[5] However, currently historians focus on 'Toyotism as a form of Post-Fordism'. I am unable to fully
support this position. During the development of a mass-production system
in Japan the trend towards offering a full-line and wide selection of products appeared in a parallel and simultaneous fashion. Under these conditions, the Toyota Production System was generated from earnest efforts
to overcome the problem of small-lot production of a large variety of
products. At any rate, in the discussion of Toyotism's place in history
and also in the search for the reasons for the miraculous growth of the
Japanese automotive industry during the post-war period, this fact cannot
be overlooked. In addition, another critical element to be considered is that
the most important solution to the problem of small-lot production of
a large variety of products faced in the 1960s was the development of outsourcing assembly. On the one hand, those vehicles which Toyota produced
in their own assembly plants (Motomachi, Takaoka, Tsutsumi, and so on)
were the saloon-type passenger vehicles produced on a large scale. On the
other hand, those vehicles for which Toyota outbased the assembly
processes were (1) passenger vehicles such as the station-wagon and
pick-up types produced on a large scale, (2) trucks, (3) passenger vehicles
produced on a small scale (for example, Century, Toyota-2000 GT, and so
on[6]), and (4) specially equipped vehicles produced on a smaller scale. This
is how the degree of outsourcing assembly developed at Toyota during the
1960s.

Trucks and Station-wagons as the Main Product of *Itaku* Production (First Half of the 1960s)

The greater part of the vehicles outbased by Toyota during the first half of the 1960s were the trucks, station-wagons, and the pick-ups. Let us now turn to the three firms (out of seven) involved in the outsourcing of these products. Toyota Shatai (Toyota Auto Body) was mainly responsible for truck production; Kanto Jidosha Kogyo (Kanto Auto Works) was responsible for the production of station-wagons and pick-ups; and Arakawa Shatai Kogyo (Arakawa Shatai Kogyo) handled the production of the Land Cruiser and other specially equipped vehicles.

Toyota Shatai (Toyota Auto Body)[7]

What was Toyota Shatai's role in Toyota's full-line-wide-selection production? First of all, let us consider the products and volume of production. Altogether Toyota Shatai was responsible for the assembly production of 74,000 trucks which included 10,000 large-size trucks, 17,000 Stouts, 33,000 Toyo Aces, and 14,000 specially equipped vehicles. These figures represented practically all of Toyota's production of the Stout and Toyo Ace as well as 85 per cent of its production of common trucks. The 74,000 trucks produced by Toyota Shatai in 1960 represented 87 per cent of Toyota's truck production and 48 per cent of its total combined production of trucks and passenger vehicles. Therefore, in 1960 Toyota Shatai was positioned as an important production base for trucks along with the No.1 Assembly Line of Toyota's Honsha plant. The brands and volume of *itaku* production four years later (in 1964) reveals that Toyota Shatai's position as an important production point for trucks had increased. This was because in 1963 Toyota shifted the production of its Dyna truck to Toyota Shatai and as a result the latter gained responsibility for the production of practically all of Toyota's truck models including the large-size trucks, Stout, Dyna, and Toyo Ace. Toyota Shatai's production of 116,000 trucks in 1964 represented 90 per cent of Toyota's truck production and 27 per cent of its total production.

Kanto Jidosha Kogyo (Kanto Auto Works)[8]

Just as Toyota Shatai was an important production base for trucks, Kanto Jidosha Kogyo was an important production base for Toyota's station-wagons and pick-ups. The total production of station-wagons and pick-ups (commercial vehicles) in 1964 was 65,000 vehicles. Excluding the Publica, Kanto Jidosha Kogyo produced almost all of Toyota's station-wagons and pick-ups. Furthermore, station-wagons and pick-ups represented 97 per cent of Kanto Jidosha Kogyo's vehicle production. This firm also performed another important *itaku* production function, although it was small in volume. It handled the assembly of non-mass-produced luxury cars and during the first half of the 1960s developed and assembled the Crown-Eight. At that time, in order to increase the efficiency of their own mass-production assembly lines, Toyota decided to outbase all its non-mass-produced vehicles. The total production of the Crown-Eight was only around 1,000 vehicles per year and this model required many distinct components for the body, interior, and engine. If it had been produced on the same assembly line as the Crowns, a mass-produced car, it would have greatly reduced efficiency. Thus, Kanto Jidosha Kogyo's position in Toyota's full-line-wide-selection production may be described as an important base for station-wagons and pick-ups as well as non-mass-produced luxury cars.

Arakawa Shatai Kogyo (Arakawa Auto Body)[9]

Arakawa Shatai Kogyo was first and foremost responsible for the production of the Land Cruiser. In 1964 the firm produced 8,000 vehicles or 88 per

Casting/Forging/Machine-shops	Assembly	Plant	Models
Honsha casting-shop	Toyota Shatai	Fujimatsu	Dyna, Toyo Ace

Honsha No.1 forging-shop
  " No.2 "
  " No.3 "
		Kariya	Large Truck, Stout, Specially equipped vehicles

Honsha No.1 machine-shop
  " No.2 "
  " No.3 "
	Arakawa Shatai	Nagoya	Specially equipped vehicles

		Honsha	Land Cruiser, Lite Bus, Publica van

Motomachi No.1 machine-shop
  "   No.2   "
  "   No.3   "
  "   No. 4   "
	Toyota	Honsha	Trucks

		Motomachi No.1	Crown saloon, Corona saloon
		Motomachi No.2	Publica saloon, Publica van
	Kanto Jidosha	Fukaura	Crown Eight, Corona pick-up, Corona van
		Taura	Master Line pick-up, Master Line van
	Central	Sagamihara	Master Line pick-up, Corona pick-up

FIG. 10.3. The division of production between Toyota and *itaku* firms in 1964.

Source: H. Shioji, 'The Factory Development of Toyota Motor in the 1960s', *Economic Review* (Kyoto University Economic Society), 37/6 (1986).

cent of the total production of this model. The Land Cruiser was the main exportable product which Toyota offered during a period marked by many failures in attempting to penetrate the North American market from the late 1950s to the early 1960s. From 1956 to 1964 the Land Cruiser represented 28 per cent of all the vehicles Toyota exported. Secondly, Arakawa Shatai Kogyo assembled the Lite Bus and the Stout van, and were responsible for 90 per cent of Lite Bus production. Thirdly, they were responsible for the production of many kinds of specially equipped vehicles such as hearses and patrol cars. In 1964, Arakawa Shatai Kogyo produced 11,000 vehicles for Toyota, or 4 per cent of the company's total production.

Figure 10.3 indicates the division of production between Toyota and the *itaku* firms in 1964. Basically Toyota produced all the saloon-type vehicles, relying on the *itaku* firms for the production of trucks, mass-produced station-wagons and pick-ups, non-mass-produced luxury cars, and specially equipped vehicles. In terms of volume, Toyota outbased 47 per cent of its vehicle production to the *itaku* firms with the following percentages: 27 per cent for Toyota Shatai, 15 per cent for Kanto Jidosha Kogyo, 3 per cent for Arakawa Shatai, and 2 per cent for Central Jidosha.

The Advent of *Itaku* Production of Saloon Vehicles (The Second Half of the 1960s)

In this section, we show how the position of *itaku* production changed during the second half of the 1960s as full-line-wide-selection production was introduced and annual production reached two million vehicles.

Toyota Shatai

As car ownership increased rapidly, the new Corona model enjoyed great success and its sales continued to rise, by fivefold from 1963 to 1965. The initial Corona saloons were made at the No.1 Assembly Line of Motomachi plant while the station-wagons and pick-ups were the responsibility of Kanto Jidosha Kogyo. In order to meet this sudden increase in demand, from 1965 the production of the Corona saloon and Corona hardtop was entrusted to Toyota Shatai. The act of entrusting the production of these mass-produced passenger cars (saloon and hardtop) represented a fundamental change in Toyota's policy for *itaku* production. Until this action was taken, Toyota had always retained responsibility for the production of mass-produced saloon cars. However, after entrusting the production of the Corona saloon and Corona hardtop to Toyota Shatai, Toyota strengthened its mass-production capacity by outsourcing the production of mass-produced passenger saloons to *itaku* firms and was thus able to satisfy the explosive demand for vehicles in the latter half of the 1960s.

In 1968 Toyota Shatai also became responsible for making the Corona Mark II hardtop and the firm's proportion of passenger car production consequently increased. In 1970 its car production volume exceeded that of trucks. Thus, Toyota Shatai was positioned as an important production base for trucks in the first half of the 1960s, and later in the second half of the decade it became an important base for mass-produced saloons. Furthermore, the latter was to become more important.[10] However, Toyota Shatai continued to be an important base for the production of trucks, and it began to handle more models in the latter half of the 1960s: the Hi Ace (production started in 1967); Massy Dyna (from 1969); and Lite Ace (from 1970).

In 1970 Toyota Shatai's vehicle production was 149,000 cars and 142,000 trucks and buses, a total of 291,000 vehicles which represented 14, 22, and 18 per cent of Toyota's production respectively. Its production of 290,000 vehicles that year was much lower than that of other auto manufacturers such as Mitsubishi Jidosha Kogyo's 470,000 vehicles, Toyo Kogyo's (Mazda) 450,000, and Honda Giken Kogyo's 380,000, but was in the same range as Daihatsu Kogyo's 320,000 vehicles, Suzuki's 280,000, and Fuji Jukogyo's (Subaru) 230,000.

Toyoda Jidoshokki Seisakusho (Toyoda Automatic Loom Works)[11]

During the 1960s, Toyoda Jidoshokki developed a diversified structure comprising an automatic loom division (30 per cent), automobile division (35 per cent), and an industrial vehicle division (33 per cent). Here we examine the position of its engine production and vehicle assembly. In 1952, Toyoda Jidoshokki produced its first engine, the S-type engine for the Toyo Ace. In 1959 the S-type was replaced by the P-type, which underwent subsequent changes to become the 2P-type in 1961 and the 3P-type in 1967. Toyoda Jidoshokki was partially responsible for the production of the P-type engine series which were used in such strongly selling models as the Corona and the Toyo Ace. Furthermore, it handled the production of all the large J-type diesel engines (used in the Dyna)[12] and the D/2D-type engines (used in large trucks). In the 1960s they were the only *itaku* company entrusted with the production of engines. Production volume in 1970 was 86,000 for the P-series, 13,000 for the J-series, and 11,000 for the D-series. The total engine production for that year was 110,000 which represented 7 per cent of Toyota's engine manufacture. Toyoda Jidoshokki's engine production was carried out at the casting-shop of its Ohbu plant and the machine-shop of its Kyowa plant. While the scale of these shops was small, the company had the same processes as in the casting-shops and machine-shops of Toyota's Kamigo plant. These Toyoda Jidoshokki shops were thus an integral part of the 'Toyota Full-Line Engine Production'.

Let us turn to the firm's vehicle production. Above all, the company was a base for specially equipped vehicles. In the first half of the 1960s it produced 1,000 to 10,000 Weapon Carriers annually, while in the latter half of the decade it produced 1,000 special vehicles annually, including small dump trucks. Thus, along with Toyota Shatai and Arakawa Shatai, Toyoda Jidoshokki was one of the three main bases of specially equipped vehicle production. Secondly, it began producing the Publica van and the Mini Ace in 1967. At first the production of the Publica van was divided between Toyoda Jidoshokki and Hino. Toyoda Jidoshokki's Nagakusa plant handled the production for western Japan while Hino's Hamura plant handled that for eastern Japan. However, later on, with decreasing demand for the Publica van, Hino ceased production in August 1970 and production was concentrated at the Nagakusa plant. Furthermore, Toyoda Jidoshokki was responsible for the entire production of the Mini Ace. In 1970, 50,000 Mini Aces were made, equivalent to 3 per cent of Toyota's vehicle production in that year.

Central Jidosha (Central Motors)[13]

Central Jidosha was first a base for pick-up type passenger vehicles, and served as a supplementary base to Kanto Jidosha, which was the main base for station-wagons and pick-up type vehicles. In 1970, Central Jidosha produced 53,000 pick-up vehicles of the Crown, the Corona, and the Corona-Mark II types. Secondly, it was a base for special vehicles and in 1968 produced 1,967 convertible-type Publica-S vehicles and 198 ambulances. Its total vehicle production in 1970 was 53,000, which represented 3 per cent of Toyota's output.

Yamaha Hatsudoki (Yamaha Motors)[14]

Yamaha was responsible for the prototyping and final assembly of the non-mass-produced Toyota-2000GT sports car. This was conceived at Toyota in 1964, but the company did not have sufficient ability to handle such a vehicle. Production was entrusted to the motor cycle manufacturer Yamaha, which had extensive experience in international racing and thus had the technical ability to handle the prototyping and production of the vehicle. The prototyping was completed in 1965 and production started in November 1966. Thereafter, annual production was 157 vehicles in 1967, 61 vehicles in 1968, 50 vehicles in 1969, and 71 vehicles in 1970.

Hino Jidosha Kogyo (Hino Motors)

Hino Motors, a motor manufacturer, ran into financial trouble in the early 1960s with the production and sales of the disappointing Contessa, the first car they designed and manufactured by themselves. In order to overcome its financial difficulties, Hino entered into a tie-up agreement with Toyota in 1966.[15] Some of the contents of the agreement were: (1) Hino would concentrate on the production of large vehicles such as large trucks and buses and give up the production of small vehicles; (2) in return, Toyota entrusted the production of its small trucks and cars to the Hino Hamura plant; and so on.

From April 1967, Hino began to perform *itaku* production for Toyota (see Table 10.4, Figures 10.4(a), (b), and (c)). First, Hino became a production base for the Toyota-Briska (later called the Hi-Lux). This vehicle was based on the Hino-Briska. Toyota's technology was applied in order to make sweeping improvements and eleven parts common to Toyota vehicles were employed. Thereafter, the vehicle changed its name to the Toyota Briska. Later, in March 1968, the vehicle became the Hi-Lux in the process of model changing and the number of common parts was increased by using

TABLE 10.4. *Toyota's share of Hino and Toyota directors at Hino, 1967–1985*

Year	Toyota's share %	Ranking of Toyota (place)	Total number of directors of Hino	Directors from Toyota	Hierarchical position of directors from Toyota
1967	2.00	7th	22	1	D
1968	2.64	5th	21	1	D
1969	4.81	3rd	21	1	D
1970	4.81	3rd	21	1	D
1971	4.81	1st	22	1	D
1972	6.75	1st	22	1	D
1973	6.79	1st	22	1	D
1974	7.05	1st	22	2	ED, D
1975	6.98	1st	22	2	ED, D
1976	6.80	1st	25	2	ED, D
1977	7.34	1st	25	2	ED, D
1978	8.07	1st	27	2	ED, D
1979	7.94	1st	28	2	VP, D
1980	9.14	1st	28	2	VP, D
1981	9.83	1st	28	2	VP, D
1982	9.75	1st	30	3	VP, MD, D
1983	10.34	1st	29	2	MD, D
1984	11.21	1st	29	2	ED, D
1985	11.31	1st	31	4	C, ED, D, A

Notes: Data are for end-March, except in 1968, which is for end-September.
C, VP, ED, MD, D, and A = Chairman, Vice-President, Executive Director, Managing Director, Company Director, and Auditor respectively.
Source: Yuka shoken hokokusho of Hino Jidosha Kogyo.

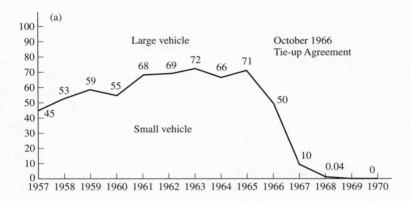

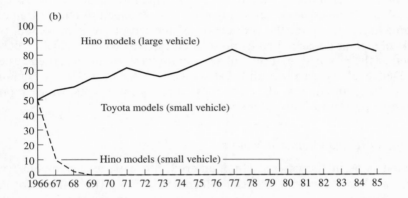

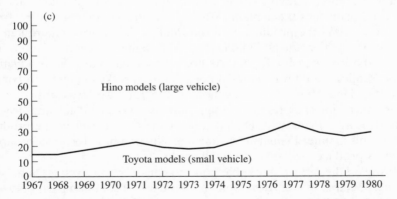

Fig. 10.4. *Itaku* production of Toyota models at Hino Jidosha Kogyo. (a) Large-vehicle/small-vehicle ratio at Hino. (b) Hino models/Toyota models ratio by volume at Hino. (c) Hino models /Toyota models ratio by sales amount at Hino.

Note: Hino models (small vehicle) were assembled in 1967, 1968, and 1978–80 but their numbers are not known (Fig. 10.4(c)).

Source: Yuka shoken hokokusho of Hino Jidosha Kogyo.

the Toyota 2R-type engine among other parts.[16] In 1969, 48,000 Hi-Lux vehicles were produced and from that point the vehicle became the truck model with the highest production volume. Secondly, Hino was made the production base for the Publica van and Publica saloon for eastern Japan. In other words, as mentioned earlier, in 1966, due to the increased production of the Corona, the production of this vehicle was moved from the No.1 Assembly Line of Toyota's Motomachi plant (where the Crown was co-produced) to the No.2 Assembly Line in order to concentrate solely on production of the Corona. Therefore, the production of the Publica, which had been assembled at the No.2 Assembly Line at Motomachi, was shifted to other plants. The Publica saloon was transferred to Toyota's Takaoka plant and the production of the Publica van for western Japan was moved to Toyoda Jidoshokki's Nagakusa plant and that for eastern Japan to Hino's Hamura plant. Later on, when the production of the Corolla was increased, the Takaoka plant dedicated all its production capacity to this vehicle. Consequently, the production of the Publica van for western Japan was entrusted to Daihatsu's Ikeda plant and that for eastern Japan to Hino's Hamura plant. In 1970, Hino produced 105,000 vehicles for Toyota, which represented 6 per cent of the latter's total production.

Daihatsu Kogyo (Daihatsu Motors)[17]

Daihatsu, as in the case of Hino, entered into a tie-up agreement with Toyota when faced with financial difficulties in 1967. The contents of the agreement were: (1) Daihatsu would focus its emphasis on mini cars and mini trucks; and (2) Toyota would outbase the production of a few cars and trucks to Daihatsu's Ikeda plant. After signing the agreement in 1967, from September 1969 the production of the Publica saloon was undertaken by Daihatsu's Ikeda plant, and in October 1970 Daihatsu began *itaku* production of the Lite Ace for Toyota. As previously mentioned, the production of the Publica saloon was shared among Daihatsu's Ikeda plant and Hino's Hamura plant. The *itaku* production of the Lite Ace was also divided according to its sales region among Daihatsu's Ikeda Plant and Toyota Shatai's Kariya Plant, with Daihatsu receiving 40 per cent of the production. In this manner Daihatsu became a production base for western Japan for mass-produced saloons and small trucks.

However, the most remarkable point to consider concerning Daihatsu's *itaku* production was the development of the use of common parts between Toyota and Daihatsu. In other words, after the tie-up between Toyota and Hino, the latter had to completely cease production of small vehicles. In contrast, after the tie-up between Toyota and Daihatsu, the latter continued the production of their own small vehicles. In order to reduce the cost of Daihatsu's small car production and increase the demand for parts made by Toyota, 80 per cent of the parts that Daihatsu used in its small cars came from Toyota. After the tie-up, 80 per cent of the parts used for Daihatsu's Consorte Berlina were common with the Publica and both vehicles were produced together on the same line at Daihatsu's Ikeda plant. In the same manner, Daihatsu's Delta introduced in 1970, and Toyota's Dyna and Daihatsu's Delta 750 of 1971 and the Lite Ace of Toyota all shared common parts. Furthermore, the Delta 750 and the Lite Ace were assembled together on the same line at Daihatsu's Ikeda plant. In 1970, Daihatsu produced 34,000 vehicles for Toyota, which represented 2 per cent of the latter's total production.

Figure 10.5 gives the distribution of *itaku* production in 1970. First, let us compare the characteristics of *itaku* production during the first half of the

Casting/Forging/ Machine-shops	Assembly	Plant	Saloon	Station-wagon and pick-up	Truck and bus	Non-mass
Honsha casting-shop	Yamaha	Iwata				Toyota 2000GT
Kamigo No.1 casting-shop " No.2 " " No.3 " " No.4 "	Toyota Shatai	Fujimatsu	Corona Mark II		Large Truck, etc.	
		Kariya			Hi Ace, etc.	Specially equipped vehicles
Tsutsumi casting-shop Honsha No.1 forging-shop " No.2 " " No.3 "	Arakawa Shatai	Sarunage			Large Truck, etc.	Specially equipped vehicles
		Honsha			Land Cruiser, etc.	
Honsha No.1 machine-shop " No.2 " " No.3 " " No.4 "	Toyota	Honsha			Trucks	
		Motomachi	Corona Mark II, etc.			
		Takaoka	Corolla, Sprinter			
Motomachi No.1 machine-shop " No.2 " " No.3 " " No.4 "		Tsutsumi	Carina, Celica			
Kamigo No.1 machine-shop " No.2 " " No.3 " " No.4 " " No.5 " " No.6 "	Kanto Jidosha	Yokosuka	Corolla, Crown	Corolla van		
		Higashifuji	Corona	Corona van		Century, etc.
	Central	Honsha		Corona pick-up		Ambulance, etc.
" No.7 " " No.8 " " No.9 " " No.10 "	Toyota Jidoshokki	Kyowa				Specially equipped vehicles
		Nagakusa	Publica	Publica van	Mini Ace	
Miyoshi No.1 machine-shop " No.2 " " No.3 "	Daihatsu	Ikeda	Publica		Lite Ace	
Tsutsumi machine-shop	Hino	Hamura		Publica van	Hi Ace	

FIG. 10.5.   The division of production between Toyota and *itaku* firms in 1970.

1960s with that in the second half. First of all, there was the beginning of *itaku* production of mass-produced saloon cars and the subsequent increase in such *itaku* production, stimulated by Toyota's inability to meet the sharply rising demand for passenger cars. Second, in the second half of the 1960s Toyota continued to increase the number of models and volume of the four types of vehicles for which Toyota relied on the *itaku* firms for production during the first half of the 1960s, namely: trucks; mass-produced station-wagons and pick-ups; non-mass-produced luxury cars; and specially equipped vehicles. As shown earlier in Table 10.1, in 1970 the *itaku* production of vehicles represented about 51 per cent of Toyota's total volume. Generally speaking, it is clear that as Toyota achieved an annual volume of 2 million vehicles and developed a full-line and wide selection of products by the beginning of the 1970s, *itaku* production had come to play an indispensable supplementary role. It is also clear that within the framework of Toyota's full-line wide-selection production system each of the *itaku* firms' production plants became an integral part of the system.

The Function of *Itaku* Production

Earlier we examined the role which *itaku* production played in Toyota's full-line wide-selection production system during the 1960s. Here we consider the function of *itaku* production while bearing in mind the peculiar historical characteristic of 'the simultaneous and parallel development of the three factors' which occurred in Japan in the 1960s.

First, by entrusting the production of non-mass-produced vehicles to *itaku* firms and concentrating on mass-production of saloon-type vehicles in its own plants, Toyota was able to reach the highest levels of efficiency and reduce costs. As we have seen earlier, Toyota entrusted to *itaku* firms not only the production of vehicles with an annual volume of only a few hundred vehicles, such as specially equipped vehicles and luxury cars (the Century among others), but also the majority of its trucks, as well as mass-produced passenger station-wagons and pick-ups. The reason for this was because, for example, it was possible to attain greater production efficiency by assembling just saloons on one production line rather than a mix of saloons and station-wagons. Second, there was also the function of 'body rotation' among *itaku* firms and Toyota to deal with fluctuations in demand for the various models. The Production Planning division of Toyota was in charge of this 'body rotation.' For example, if Toyota experienced a sudden increase in demand for a mass-produced saloon, then it was able to cover the demand by increasing the production at the various *itaku* firms which were producing the same vehicle. In this way *itaku* production functioned as a method of responding promptly to demand shifts for mass-produced vehicles. During the latter half of the 1960s, when Toyota experienced rapidly rising demand for passenger vehicles, *itaku* production played an important role in meeting the excess demand for such strategic vehicles as the Corolla.

Furthermore, this function was not limited to meeting increased demand. Rather it served to handle demand fluctuations over the long run. One example is how *itaku* production was used to deal with the fluctuations in demand for the Publica by shifting production a number of times among the plants. The production of the Publica was shifted around in the following way: The Arakawa Shatai's Toyama plant was used during the prototyping period; when the Publica was put on the market, the No.1 Assembly Line of Toyota's Motomachi plant was used; then during the first half of the Sixties, when demand for the Publica was increasing, the No.2 Assembly Line of Motomachi plant was exclusively devoted to its production; later in the latter half of the decade, when demand fell, production of the saloon was moved to the No.1 Assembly Line of Toyota's Takaoka plant (later to the No.2 Assembly Line of Takaoka plant); the station-wagon was entrusted to Toyoda Jidoshokki's Nagakusa plant and Hino's Hamura plant; by the end of the 1960s the saloon was entrusted to Daihatsu's Ikeda plant and the Hino Hamura plant; when station-wagon production was reduced, it was consolidated at Toyoda Jidoshokki's Nagakusa plant. Furthermore, through this body rotation, profit-sharing and risk-sharing were carried out among the members of the Toyota group. This can be ascertained by observing that the magnitude of the fluctuations in demand and production over the long-run for each of the firms in Toyota group does not vary to a great extent. Also it can be seen in Table 10.5 that when there was a dip in the demand for Hino's own independent large trucks and buses, Toyota intentionally increased the *itaku* production entrusted to Hino.[18]

Third, by entrusting the same model and same body type to two or more different *itaku* firms, *itaku* production served to create competition among these firms concerning such elements as cost, delivery, and quality. In other words, Toyota was able to demand that the *itaku* firms with low-performance levels brought themselves up to par with those having high-performance levels. This type of competition has been used in parts-procurement by having two or more parts-manufacturers produce the same part, and the same approach was first adopted in *itaku* production in the latter half of the 1960s.[19] Furthermore, in this type of competition, the firm with an outstanding performance during the year receives an order for an increase in volume the following year. Fourth, *itaku* production can function to reduce the cost of the parts Toyota uses by having the *itaku* firms use the same parts on their own independent vehicle models and independent products. Having Daihatsu and Toyoda Jidoshokki increase their use of the same parts used on Toyota vehicles can be given as an example.

The fifth function of *itaku* firms was the development of vehicle bodies. In other words, *itaku* firms have been responsible for developing new

TABLE 10.5. *Fluctuations in the production of Hino and Toyota models assembled by Hino at its Hamura plant, 1966–1985*

Year	66	67	68	69	70	71	72	73	74	75	76	77	78	79	80	81	82	83	84	85
Hino models	+	+	+	+	+	−	+	+	−	−	−	−	+	+	−	−	−	−	+	+
Toyota models	+	+	+	+	+	+	+	+	−	+	+	+	−	+	+	+	+	+	+	−
Opposite fluctuations						O				O	O	O	O		O	O	O	O		O

Note: + = an increase; − = a decrease compared with previous year.

Source: Yuka shoken hokokusho of Hino Jidosha Kogyo.

TABLE 10.6. *Salary gaps between Toyota and* itaku *firms in 1970*

Firm	Average monthly salary (Yen) [Average Age]	Salary index
Toyota Jidosha Kogyo (Toyota Motor)	65,294 [27.3]	100
Toyota Shatai (Toyota Auto Body)	65,934 [27.8]	101
Kanto Jidosha Kogyo (Kanto Auto Works)	69,839 [30.8]	107
Toyoda Jidoshokki Seisakusho (Toyoda Automatic Loom Works)	80,291 [34.7]	123
Yamaha Hatsudoki (Yamaha Motors)	51,733 [26.1]	79
Hino Jidosha Kogyo (Hino Motors)	51,818 [32.4]	79
Daihatsu Kogyo (Daihatsu Motors)	77,612 [32.6]	119

Source: Yuka shoken hokokusho of each company for the second half of 1970.

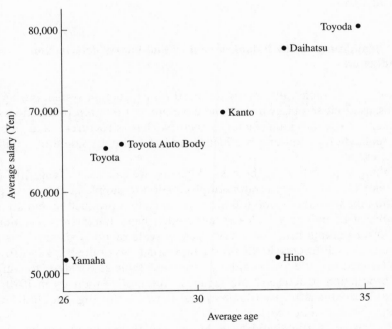

FIG. 10.6. Salary gaps between Toyota and *itaku* firms in 1970.

models and full model changes. For example, in the 1960s Kanto Jidosha Kogyo was in charge of the development of the Corona, Century, and Corona Mark II bodies. At present in 1996, around 40 per cent of all the vehicles developed are handled by *itaku* firms. As seen in Figure 10.2, in 1993 Kanto Jidosha Kogyo was in charge of the development of sixteen vehicle models, of which five were then parcelled out to Toyota and other *itaku* firms for production (a so-called 'Reverse Overture' where the *itaku* firm develops and designs the vehicle and Toyota produces it). In reference to this development function it is more appropriate to call such firms *itaku* development and assembly firms rather than simply *itaku* assembly firms.

To summarize, Toyota was not able to keep up with the sudden increase in demand by using only its own facilities, and as a result of the fast introduction of a full-line and wide selection of products there were some models and body types that could not be adapted to mass production. Under these conditions *itaku* production was indispensable and played an important role in Toyota's full-line-wide-selection production. Salary differentials were not a significant element in the process.[20] (see Table 10.6 and Figure 10.6.)

The Significance of the Establishment of Full-line-Wide-selection Production

Toyota established a full-line-wide-selection production system during the 1960s, as discussed elsewhere.[21] The development of *itaku* production supplemented Toyota's multi-factory structure. These structures made possible the realization of full-line production and an annual volume of 2 million vehicles.

Taking a quick look at the case of Nissan, we can see in Table 10.7 that just like Toyota, Nissan used *itaku* production to supplement its own production plants and develop full-line-wide-selection production and attain a volume of 1.5 million vehicles.[22] On the other hand, the *itaku* production of the lower-ranking firms was very small in scale or non-existent. This is a fundamental difference in the production structures of the Big Two (Toyota and Nissan) and the lower-ranking firms (see Table 10.8). Here, looking at the production structure of the Japanese automotive industry in 1970, the concrete existence of 'transfer barriers' between the Big Two and lower-ranking firms can be seen.

Thus, what is the significance of the establishment of full-line-wide-selection production? Here we will take a look at how Toyota was able to increase its predominance in competition with other firms in the industry and increase its dominance of the market by the creation of these structures.

First of all, based on its full-line-wide-selection production, Toyota was

TABLE 10.7. *Models produced in Nissan plants and* itaku *firms in 1970*

	Models
Nissan plant	
Oppama	President, Cedric saloon, Bluebird saloon, Sunny saloon, etc.
Zama	Sunny saloon, Cherry saloon, Datsun truck, Nissan truck, etc.
Murayama	Skyline saloon, Skyline van, Laurel saloon, Datsun truck, etc.
Tochigi	Cedric saloon, Cedric van, Gloria saloon, Gloria van, etc.
Itaku firm	
Nissan Shatai	Fairlady, Bluebird van, Sunny saloon, Sunny van, etc.
Fuji Jukogyo	Sunny coupe
Aichi Kikai	Sunny truck, Cherry cab
Isuzu	Cherry van
Press Kogyo	Nissan Bus, Patrol, Weapon Carrier
Nissan Diesel	

Source: *Nissan Jidosha shi* (History of Nissan Motor) (1975).

able to differentiate its products and thus increase competitiveness. In other words, the number of models of passenger vehicles offered by the car manufacturers was: ten for Toyota; nine for Nissan; and four for the lower-ranking firms. This difference in model ranges had a large and significant effect on the competitiveness of the manufacturers. Firms offering a full-line of products were better able to meet the needs of users and obtained a wider level of consumer demand. Furthermore, when the vehicles were replaced, the firms with a full-line selection of products were able to switch the customer to one of their other models (usually a higher-ranking model) and thus develop an exclusive sales policy. Moreover, when the demand for each model fluctuates, the firms with a full-line of products have more flexibility than those firms without a full-line or specialist firms. In light of each of these points Toyota was able to increase its domination of the market.

Second, Toyota was able to expand the scale of its mass-production based on its full-line-wide-selection production and increase its production efficiency, thus reducing costs and enabling itself to increase its price competitiveness. However, it is not the intention of this chapter to discuss the issue of the relationship between the total production scale of a firm and lower total costs. In this paper, by analysing the position and function of *itaku* production, we explain the peculiar historical characteristics of 'the simultaneous and parallel development of the three factors' in the Japanese car industry during the 1960s. In other words, we show how Toyota was able to develop a mass-production structure and increase the effects of mass production to compete more effectively with other firms under the condi-

TABLE 10.8. *Difference in the production structures of the Big Two and lower-ranking firms*

	Big Two (Toyota, Nissan)	Lower-ranking firms
Plant development	Multi plants	Single plant
Itaku production	20–50%	Small or non-existent
Production scale per year	2 million (Toyota) 1.5 million (Nissan)	Less than 0.5 million
Product Line	Full-line products	Undeveloped full-line (Mitsubishi, Isuzu, ToyoKogyo) Mini-Car, Truck (Daihatsu, Fuji, Suzuki, Honda) Large-Truck, Bus (Hino, Nissan Diesel)

tions of the trend towards product variety and small-lot production. Here, we would like to point out in particular the fact that Toyota's ability to increase the production efficiency of its own plants by entrusting the production of non-mass-produced models and station-wagon and pick-up body types to *itaku* firms was an important determining factor in its competitiveness against other firms. In the 1960s the largest market segment was that of saloons in the 800cc to 1800cc engine-size range. A firm's share in this market segment determined its competitiveness in relation to other firms. Toyota introduced strategic vehicles one after the other in this segment, such as the Publica, Corolla, Sprinter, Carina, and so on. Here it should be pointed out that the majority of the production of these strategic saloons was not entrusted to *itaku* firms, rather they were produced by Toyota in its own plants. Furthermore, when new models of these strategic vehicles were introduced, they were produced in the best and most capable Toyota plants. By doing so, Toyota was able to establish the mass production of strategic vehicles and increase its price competitiveness in this market segment. This was one of the reasons for the several price reductions of the Corona and the low cost of the Publica and Corolla in relation to the price of vehicles in the same segment offered by other firms.[23]

In consequence, Toyota was able to increase its competitiveness by establishing a full-line-wide-selection production, and raised its share in the small-size segment from 36.7 per cent in 1964 to 44.4 per cent in 1970. Nissan also raised its share from 31.9 per cent to 36.4 per cent, with the total of both firms reaching 80.8 per cent. On the other hand, among the lower-ranking firms, there were companies that exited from this segment (Hino,

Suzuki), or decreased their offerings of this segment (Fuji, Daihatsu, Isuzu), and could not avoid specializing in the mini-vehicle segment (Daihatsu, Fuji, Suzuki, Honda) or the large truck and bus segment (Hino, Nissan Diesel). Looking at the share of total production, you see that in the second

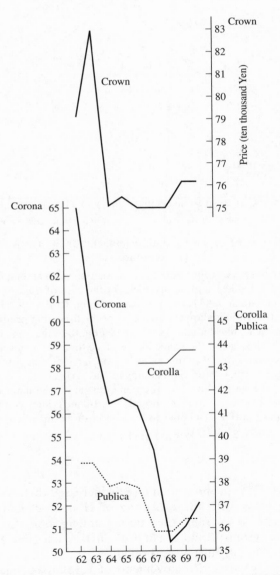

FIG. 10.7. Price movements of Toyota passenger cars, 1962–1970.
Source: Yuka shoken hokokusho of Toyota.

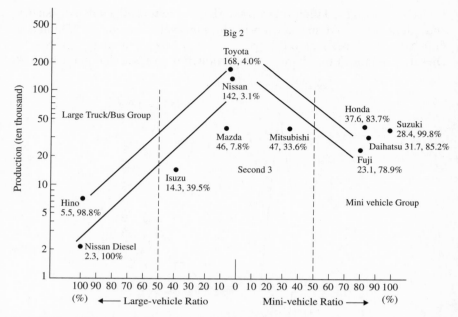

Fig. 10.8. Division of Japanese auto-manufacturers in terms of competitive structure.

Notes: The horizontal axis represents the composition ratio among three divisions: large-vehicle, small-vehicle, and mini-vehicle. In the case of the firms that produce large vehicles and small vehicles like Toyota, Nissan, Isuzu, and Hino, the large-vehicle composition ratio is shown. In the case of the firms that produce small vehicles and mini vehicles like Honda, Suzuki, and Fuji, the mini-vehicle composition ratio is shown. In the case of the firms that produce three divisions like Mitsubishi, Mazda, and Daihatsu, the absolute value of the large-vehicle composition ratio minus mini-vehicle composition ratio is shown. The vertical axis shows the production per year on a logarithmic scale. The numerals under the names of firms indicate production per year (ten thousand) (left-hand) and composition ratio (right-hand). Lines between firms indicate tie-up relations.

Source: Nihon Jidosha Kogyo kai (JAMA), 'Jidosha Tokei Geppo'.

half of the 1960s Toyota and Nissan rapidly increased their share while the lower-ranking firms, with the exception of Honda, all had stagnant or decreasing shares. At the same time, tie-ups among some firms progressed and the Toyota group (Toyota, Hino, Daihatsu) and the Nissan group (Nissan, Nissan Diesel, Fuji) were formed.

Figure 10.7 shows the price movements of Toyota passenger vehicles. It can be ascertained that from 1969, falling prices were reversed and thereafter prices were controlled by Toyota and Nissan. From there on, the price continued to rise at each model change. As pointed out in previous researches, oligopolistic competition, controlled by Toyota and Nissan, in the Japanese automobile industry was established by the end of the 1960s. Then, in 1970, as seen in Figure 10.8, each firm had established its basic position in terms of competitive structure. On the base of the establishment of this oligopolistic competition in the Japanese automobile industry, there arose a structural difference between the Big Two (Toyota and Nissan) and the lower-ranking firms in terms of the formation of full-line and wide-selection production.

NOTES

1. The term *itaku* in Japanese can be translated as 'consignment, outsourcing, sub-contracting, or entrusting'. An earlier version of this chapter appeared in *Kyoto University Economic Review*, 65/1 (Apr. 1995).
2. All of the vehicles produced by *itaku* firms are Toyota models. However, some *itaku* firms attach their own brand plate inside the vehicle, for example in the engine compartment.
3. For example, Toyota Motor Kyushu, the youngest one, has a ratio of independent purchasing of zero. On the other hand, Kanto Jidosha Kogyo, one of the oldest *itaku* firms, has a ratio of 20–40 per cent. For further details of Toyota Motor Kyushu, see Hiromi Shioji, 'Can the Development Department be Transferred to the Kyushu Area?', *Kyushu Keizai ChosaGeppo*, 47/7 (Oct. 1993).
4. Full-line production means that a particular car-maker has a variety of vehicles, especially a variety of passenger cars, from entry car to luxury car, from cheap to expensive ones. It is well known that General Motors' full-line policy started in the 1920s. Wide selection means that a particular car model has a wide variety of body types and specifications.
5. Taiichi Ohno, *The Toyota Production System* (Tokyo, 1978), 193.
6. Century was the most expensive car of the Toyota product line and Toyota 2000GT was a special sports car.
7. The Kariya plant of Toyota was separated and became Toyota Shatai, an *itaku* assembly specialist for trucks in August 1945. The data on Toyota Shatai is largely obtained from *Toyota Shatai 20 Nenshi* (A 20-year History of Toyota Auto Body) (1965) and *Toyota Shatai 30 Nenshi* (A 30-year History of Toyota Auto Body) (1975).
8. Kanto Jidosha Kogyo was founded in April 1946 and first produced electric vehicle and bus bodies. It received an order for body assembly from Toyota for the first time in December 1948 and after that concentrated on them. The data on Kanto Jidosha Kogyo is largely obtained from *Kanto Jidosha Kogyo 15 nenshi* (A 15-year History of Auto Works) (1963), *Kanto Jidosha Kogyo 25 nenshi* (A 25-year History of Kanto Auto Works) (1972) and *Kanto Jidosha Kogya 30 nenshi* (A 30-year History of Kanto Auto Works) (1978).

9. Arakawa Shatai Kogya was founded in July 1947 and designed, drew, and assembled small cars for Toyota. The data on Arakawa Shatai Kogyo is largely obtained from *Arakawa Shatai 25 nenshi* (A 25-year History of Arakawa Shatai) (1973).

10. Kanto Jidosha Kogyo also began *itaku* assembly of the Crown, Corona, and Corolla saloons, and in 1970 its car composition ratio reached 36%.

11. Toyoda Jidoshokki Seisakusho was founded in 1926 in order to produce the Toyoda automatic loom that Sakichi Toyoda invented. In 1933 it began to produce automobiles domestically and subsequently its automobile division was separated and became Toyota. After World War II, it began to produce automobile engines from 1952, specially equipped vehicles from 1953, and fork-lift trucks from 1956. The data on Toyoda Jidoshokki Seisakusho is largely obtained from *Yonju nenshi* (A 40-year History) (1967).

12. J-type diesel engines were also used for fork-lifts and shovel-loaders.

13. Central Jidosha was founded in September 1950 and began *itaku* assembly for Toyota in April 1956. The data on Central Jidosha is largely obtained from *30 nen no ayumi* (30-Year Journey) (1980).

14. Yamaha Hatsudoki was separated from Nihon Gakki and was founded in 1955. They rank second in the world as a motor-cycle manufacturer.

15. For further details of this tie-up, see Hiromi Shioji, 'An Historical Study of the Hino–Toyota Tie-up', *Japan Business History Review*, 23/2 (1988). The data on Hino Jidosha Kogyo is largely obtained from *Hino Jidosha Kogyo 40 nenshi* (A 40-year History of Hino Motors) (1980).

16. As a result of Hino's use of some parts made by Toyota or Toyota's *keiretsu* parts-suppliers, Hino's *keiretsu* parts-suppliers were damaged. Fur further details see 'Looking into the Tie-up Between Toyota and Hino', *Nikkan Jidosha Shinbun*, 26 Oct. 1966.

17. The data on Daihatsu Kogyo is largely obtained from *50 nenshi* (A 50-year History) (1957), *60 nenshi* (A 60-year History) (1967); *Daihatsu 70 nen shoshi* (A Concise 70-year History of Daihatsu) (1967), and *Moete Kakete Daihatsu 80 nen no Ayumi* (80-Year Journey of Daihatsu) (1987).

18. See Table 10.5. First, in all the twenty years from 1966 to 1985, we can ignore cases where both Hino and Toyota model production increased compared with the previous year, i.e. 1966 to 1970, 1972, 1973, 1979, and 1984. These nine years can be ignored because they presented no problem to either firm. Therefore, eleven years are left. Second, out of these eleven years, in ten years the fluctuations for the two firms were in opposite directions (see the circles in Table 10.5). For example, in 1971 Hino models decreased, but Toyota models increased, a situation repeated in 1975–7 and 1980–3. On the other hand, in 1978 and 1985, Hino models increased, but Toyota models decreased. Therefore, we can see that when Hino model production increased, Toyota decreased its *itaku* assembly from Hino, and when Hino model production decreased, Toyota increased its *itaku* assembly from Hino. Lastly, in 1974 both Hino and Toyota models decreased, but this year was an exception, the depression year affected by the first oil crisis. According to this analysis, we may assume that profit-sharing and risk-sharing were undertaken between Toyota and Hino and moreover, throughout the Toyota group. On this subject, see Haruhito Shiomi, 'The Formation of Assembler Networks in the Automobile Industry: The Case of

Toyota Motor Company (1955–1980)', in Haruhito Shiomi and Kazuo Wada (eds.), *Fordism Transformed: The Development of Production Methods in the Automobile Industry* (Oxford, 1995). Akitoshi Seike also took a detailed look at this type of body rotation in *Nihon Gata Soshiki kan Kankei no Manejimento* (*Management in Japanese Organizational Relations*) (Tokyo, 1995).

19. This type of competition in *itaku* assembly is still used. The president of Toyota, Hanai (at the time) stated 'Assembly is also competition. Profits are generated from competition' (*Shukan Toyo Keizai*, 1 July 1982). After that statement, an executive of an *itaku* firm explained how cheap the *itaku* assembly price was.
20. On the salary gap between Toyota and *itaku* firms see Table 10.6 and Figure 10.6. Excepting Yamaha and Hino, the salary gap was not so large.
21. Shioji, 'Factory Development', and Hiromi Shioji, 'The Development of the Wide-Selection Production System by Toyota in the 1960s', *Economic Review* (Kyoto University Economic Society), 141/1 (1988).
22. Nissan, like Toyota, outsourced (1) trucks, (2) station-wagons and pick-ups, and also (3) specially equipped vehicles, but they assembled the non-mass-produced luxury car, the President, at their own plant.
23. The price of the Corona was 649,000 yen in 1961. After that, Toyota continually reduced the price to 599,000 yen in 1963, 564,000 yen in 1967, 544,000 yen in 1967, and to 504,000 yen in 1968. In addition, over this period its engine was upgraded from 1000 cc to 1500 cc and, considering this point, the price reductions were even more significant.

11. From Mass-Market Manufacturer to Niche Player: *Product and Marketing Strategy at British Leyland/Rover from 1968 to 1995*

GEOFFREY OWEN

1. Introduction

When British Leyland Motor Corporation was formed in 1968, it brought together most of the best-known names in the British motor industry. On the car side, the range included Austin, Morris, Triumph, Rover, and Jaguar; Leyland was the most successful British builder of heavy trucks and buses, while Land Rover was a world leader in four-wheel-drive cross-country vehicles. With a capacity of over a million cars a year, British Leyland was the third largest car producer in Europe, behind Volkswagen and Fiat and just ahead of Renault. But it had two serious and related weaknesses. First, it produced an exceptionally wide range of models, some of which competed with each other in the same market segment; its European rivals produced fewer models in greater volume. Second, it was poorly represented on the Continent. Its predecessor firms, preoccupied with their traditional non-European markets, had been largely isolated from the rapid expansion of intra-European trade which had stimulated rationalization in the Continental motor industry during the 1950s and 1960s. Many of British Leyland's vehicles—trucks as well as cars—were not suitable for Continental customers and distribution arrangements on the Continent were weak.

Although it was not clear in 1968 whether Britain would become a full member of the European Economic Community, tariff reductions under the GATT rounds of trade negotiations were pointing towards a more open European market; car imports, which accounted for 8 per cent of domestic sales in 1968 (compared with over 20 per cent in Germany and France), seemed certain to rise. Western Europe was emerging as the principal battleground for the British motor industry and British Leyland was ill-prepared for it. Unlike Ford, its main domestic competitor, it did not have associated companies on the Continent which could form the basis of a Europe-wide manufacturing and sales organization; Ford of Europe, bringing together the US company's British and German subsidiaries, was set up a year before British Leyland.

The architects of the British Leyland merger (including the Labour government, which actively encouraged it) believed that the new company, by rationalizing its products and its manufacturing facilities, would achieve the economies of scale which its predecessor firms had lacked and thus increase its share of the world market. The outcome could hardly have been more different. Far from catching up with its Continental competitors, British Leyland continued to lose ground; by 1995 its share of the European car market was less than 3 per cent. Part of the explanation lies in the merger itself and in the way the new group was managed in the first ten years of its existence. It is an extreme example of a badly conceived, badly implemented merger which, instead of correcting the weaknesses of the participating companies, makes them harder to solve. Its aspirations—to become a world leader in all segments of the car and truck market—were almost certainly unrealistic. But even if the objective had been feasible, achieving it called for skills comparable to those of Alfred Sloan, who faced a similar set of problems when he reorganized General Motors in the 1920s.

British Leyland had to weld together five substantial car and truck makers, some of which were themselves the products of earlier, ill-digested mergers, and to do so at a time when its domestic market was under attack from imports. Yet most of its senior managers had no experience of running large companies, nor of the volume-car business which formed the biggest part of the group; Lord Stokes, chairman and chief executive, had spent his previous career with Leyland, which had only recently entered the car business by buying two of the smaller firms, Triumph and Rover. British Leyland was plagued from the start by a lack of clear strategic direction and by organizational uncertainty.

This chapter looks at the impact of these managerial weaknesses on product and marketing strategy and at subsequent attempts, starting in the late 1970s, to repair the damage. Between the creation of British Leyland in 1968 and the sale of what remained of the business to BMW of Germany in 1994 the company's share of the domestic car market fell from 40 per cent to less than 15 per cent. Three of the famous marques, Austin, Morris, and Triumph, disappeared; Jaguar was taken over by Ford; and Leyland was sold to Daf of the Netherlands. The most resilient of the original businesses was Land Rover, which retained a respectable share of the world market for four-wheel-drive vehicles. The chapter discusses how and why these misfortunes came about.

The emphasis on product and marketing strategy is not meant to imply that other factors, internal and external, did not contribute to the company's downfall. Disorderly industrial relations, from which the other British companies, including Ford, suffered almost as badly as British Leyland, are widely seen as the industry's biggest single handicap. But reforms in working practices and in collective bargaining arrangements—which were largely achieved under Sir Michael Edwardes's chairmanship between 1977 and 1982—were a necessary but not sufficient condition for the rehabilitation of British Leyland. Trade unions and shop stewards cannot be held responsible for the absence of a coherent, well-executed product strategy which matched the resources and capabilities of the company to the markets in which it was competing. That was a failure of management. Although it was partially corrected in the 1980s, the company's competitive position had deteriorated by that time to the point where it could not be preserved as an independent vehicle manufacturer.

The chapter starts by describing the inheritance which the merged company took over in 1968 (Section 2). It then considers the product and marketing strategy which was pursued in the first ten years following the merger, before and after the take-over of the company by the government in 1975 (Section 3). The next section deals with events between 1977 and 1986. In the face of mounting losses a new management team launched a drastic attack on high costs and low productivity and took a more realistic view of British Leyland's position in the market; an agreement was made to manufacture a Honda car under licence and plans for broader collaboration with the Japanese company were set in train (Section 4). Section 5 deals with the period after 1986, which saw the divestment of the truck business, the return of British Leyland (re-named Rover) to the private sector, the forging of closer links with Honda and, finally, the unexpected sale to BMW. The concluding section reviews the record (Section 6).

2. The Inheritance

By far the largest part of British Leyland's car business was the Austin Morris division, centred on two large assembly plants at Longbridge, Birmingham, and at Cowley in Oxford. Austin and Morris, the two most successful British-owned car producers in the inter-war years, had merged in 1952 to form the British Motor Corporation (BMC). Over the subsequent decade BMC remained the clear leader in Britain, with nearly 40 per cent of the market. Its main strength was in small cars and the two best-selling models were the front-wheel-drive Mini, launched in 1959, and the 1100/1300 range which came three years later; they were the work of Sir Alec Issigonis, the most innovative designer of his day. Both these models were being produced at a rate of over 250,000 units a year at the time of the British Leyland merger. But they were under-priced and yielded meagre profits; sales of the larger and potentially more profitable member of BMC's front-wheel-drive family, the 1800, were disappointing.

The rest of BMC's production was spread over a variety of models, some of them sold under the Riley, Wolseley, and MG names; although there had been some rationalization in engines following the 1952 merger, it was still making seven distinct body shells in 1968, excluding sports cars. Meanwhile it had allowed Ford to dominate the lucrative 'company car' market which emerged in Britain during the 1960s. As a result of the government's taxation and wage restraint policies, companies found it advantageous to buy fleets of cars and lease them to staff as a 'perk', which was worth more to the employee than a salary increase; the main demand was for medium-sized family cars, above the 1100/1300 range, and the Ford Cortina, launched in 1962, was precisely targeted at this sector.[1]

In 1968 the Mini and the 1100/1300 were ageing; Austin Morris lacked an effective competitor to the Cortina in the company-car sector; and on the Continent, although the Mini had achieved some success, its share of the market was small, especially in Germany. The only new model in the pipeline was the 1500 cc Austin Maxi, the least satisfactory of Issigonis's front-wheel-drive designs; launched in 1969, it was never a big seller, reaching a peak of 65,000 units in 1972. For the new British Leyland management, a renewal of the Austin Morris product range was an urgent priority.

The other three car companies, Jaguar, Rover, and Triumph, were grouped together after the merger in the specialist car division. Of the three, Jaguar, which had joined with BMC in 1966 but was still run by its entrepreneur-founder, Sir William Lyons, appeared to be the most securely placed. It produced about 30,000 luxury saloons and high-performance sports cars a year, half of which were exported, mainly to the USA; it was about to launch an attractive new model, the XJ6 saloon. Rover had pursued since the 1930s a consistent policy of building high-quality cars, below the Jaguar range. But the success of its most recent model, the Rover 2000, had taken Rover to the fringes of the mass market; there was concern within the company about whether it had the financial resources to compete in this higher league. Although Rover was profitable, its financial advisers felt that a small company in the motor industry had become an anachronism.[2] The directors hoped that, by merging with Leyland, they would obtain the financial backing which would enable them to renew and broaden their product range. They were planning two new models, a larger saloon car and a sports car, both of which would have competed directly with Jaguar.

The third member of the specialist car division, Triumph, had had a more chequered record, but since its acquisition by Leyland in 1961 it had improved its position as a manufacturer of a distinctive range of small and medium-sized cars, including a strong rival to the Rover 2000; it also had a popular line of small sports cars, sold under the TR ('Triumph Roadster') name, which competed with BMC's MG models. No significant rationalization had taken place between Rover and Triumph by the time of the British Leyland merger.

The issue for the British Leyland management in specialist cars was how to streamline this array of overlapping products and develop a coherent range which could compete against such companies as Daimler-Benz, BMW, and Volvo, all of which were producing high-quality cars in larger volume. A difficult balance would have to be struck between cutting out duplication and preserving the identity of the individual marques.

In the truck and bus division, too, there was a considerable product overlap, arising partly from the failure to rationalize earlier acquisitions. Leyland was still to some extent a federation of small companies, while BMC had its own van and truck business (the latter based at Bathgate in Scotland) as well as the heavier Guy and Daimler vehicles which had come into the group through the acquisition of Jaguar. In 1968 British Leyland trucks used thirteen different engines, nine gearboxes, eight rear axles, and five cabs. Although Leyland was the most profitable part of the division and was one of Britain's leading exporters, its overseas business was almost wholly concentrated on non-European markets, principally in the Commonwealth and in other developing countries. Not only did the division lack products which were suitable for European customers, but it was also vulnerable to competition from Continental imports. During the 1960s two Swedish companies, Volvo and Scania, took advantage of tariff reductions under the EFTA agreement to expand their sales in Britain; the construction of the British motorway network had stimulated demand for the reliable, long-distance vehicles in which the Swedish companies specialized. Like the car companies, the truck and bus division would have to adjust to competition on a European scale.

The Land Rover was in a category of its own. Introduced in 1948 as a rival to the American Jeep, this rugged cross-country vehicle had been one of the success stories of the post-war British motor industry; for the Rover company, it was a bigger source of profits than cars. The Land Rover's reliability, ease of maintenance and strong distributor organization enabled the company to win a large share of the growing world market for four-wheel-drive cars; exports, mainly in developing countries, consistently accounted for more than 75 per cent of production. Plans were well advanced in 1968 for the launch of a more luxurious vehicle, the Range Rover. But competition from the Japanese in the four-wheel-drive market was increasing; vehicles such as the Toyota Land Cruiser and the Nissan Patrol were gaining ground. Land Rover faced a different set of problems from the car and truck companies and was better placed to meet them, but it needed to upgrade the specifications of its basic utility vehicle and to improve its delivery performance.

There were strengths as well as weaknesses in this collection of businesses. British Leyland had a dominant position in the domestic car and truck market, which provided the bulk of its profits. But some erosion of market share was inevitable as tariffs came down and international competition increased. The crucial task was to expand exports, principally in Continental Europe.

3. An Excess of Ambition: Product and Marketing Strategy from 1968 to 1977

At the time of the merger the directors agreed that British Leyland would operate as a single integrated company and not as a holding company with autonomous subsidiaries. But translating this concept into practice was fraught with difficulties. What functions should be carried out at corporate headquarters? To what extent should product planning for cars be centralized? Should the manufacture of engines and other major components be entrusted to a single division, supplying all the various assembly plants? Unclear answers to these questions, partly reflecting unresolved tensions between newly recruited managers from Ford and ex-Leyland men who were used to working for small companies, contributed to a sense of organizational drift in the first few years after the merger.

Organization was closely related to strategy. What sort of business did British Leyland want to be? Did it have the resources to compete internationally in all sectors of the car and truck market, or should it concentrate in the areas where it was strongest? Lord Stokes, who had made his reputation as an export salesman, was by nature an optimist. Rather than close factories, he preferred to expand sales. To a critic who questioned whether the aim was feasible, he is said to have replied: 'We shall produce 1.5 million vehicles a year and with the same number of people, and sucks to you and everyone else.'[3] It was Stokes who decided, against the advice of some of his colleagues, to maintain Austin and Morris as two separate franchises, with Jaguar/Rover/Triumph constituting a third. Others had argued for two franchises only, consisting either of volume cars and specialist cars, or a combination of the two—perhaps Austin with Rover and Triumph, Morris with Jaguar.[4]

The franchising policy which was adopted involved a clearer separation between Austin and Morris products. The former would concentrate on innovative, front-wheel-drive cars in the Mini/1100 tradition, a sector in which Continental competition was growing, while the latter would offer conventionally engineered, rear-wheel-drive cars, but with more advanced styling than their predecessors.[5] Each would provide the dealers with a comprehensive range, as would the specialist car division in a higher-price bracket.

The first new model conceived under British Leyland management was the Morris Marina, designed as a 'Cortina killer' to regain ground lost to Ford in the company-car market. Introduced in 1970, the Marina has been described as a mediocre stylistic and engineering compromise aimed at cheapness rather than quality, reflecting British Leyland's lack of experience in rear-wheel-drive, medium-sized cars.[6] It consistently lagged behind the Cortina. Even more disappointing was the new Austin model, the Allegro, which in its best year achieved no more than 5 per cent of the domestic market; its predecessor, the 1100/1300, had accounted for over 15 per cent at its peak. The Allegro, according to one critical account, was 'a mechanically uncouth styling disaster', a 'piggy little saloon' which 'could never sell well against chic and functional hatchbacks like the Renault 5 and VW Golf'.[7]

The poor public response to the Allegro was especially serious for Austin Morris because it was aimed at private buyers who provided the bulk of the division's sales, and this was the sector most vulnerable to Continental and Japanese imports; the company-car market, dominated by Ford, remained generally loyal to British-made vehicles.[8] What Austin Morris needed, but failed to achieve, was an offsetting increase in sales to neighbouring European markets. The Mini was still selling well, but dealers needed complementary models to fill out the range; neither the Allegro nor the Marina met this requirement.

All car manufacturers have occasional new model setbacks, but the contrast between the success of the Mini and 1100 (at least in terms of market share) and the relative failure of the Allegro and Marina suggests that the 1968 merger weakened rather than strengthened the company's ability to develop good cars. The explanation appears to lie in the paucity of British Leyland's engineering resources, in the failure to deploy them effectively and in the attempt to cover too many segments of the market. John Barber, Stokes's finance director who had previously worked for Ford, thought that it was a mistake to launch a frontal attack on the Cortina; his preference would have been to move Austin and Morris somewhat 'up market' in quality and styling, drawing on the skills and resources of the specialist car companies, even at the cost of some loss of market share.[9] But that would have implied a more integrated approach to product planning and engineering across the entire range of cars and less autonomy for the individual businesses.

The absence of a clear plan for integration was a major weakness. In groping for the right balance between centralization and decentralization British Leyland sometimes ended up with the worst of both worlds, as its experience in specialist cars illustrates. Jaguar was soon recognized as a separate business in its own right and was separated from the specialist car division. Attention was concentrated on turning Rover/Triumph into a world-scale competitor in executive cars. The new models which Rover had planned when it was independent were cancelled in favour of a new medium-sized saloon car, code-named SD1, aimed at a production of 150,000 cars a year, far higher than the Rover 2000 and Triumph 2000 models which preceded it; it marked a clear break from the 'cautious pursuit of engineering excellence within a limited market niche' which had characterized Rover's product strategy in the past.[10] The project involved not only a new factory, to be built alongside the existing assembly plant at Solihull, near Birmingham, but also a new approach to product planning and production engineering which was unfamiliar to Rover's managers and work-force. It was a shock to the system which Rover found difficult to absorb; relationships between Rover and corporate headquarters were uneasy. Implementation of the SD1 project was dogged by 'the accumulated difficulties of insufficient design staff, operating in separate companies, with differing philosophies and practices'.[11] The outcome when the car reached the market in 1976 was disappointing. Serious quality problems were encountered in the rush to meet the initial demand, damaging the reputation of the car. Sales fell a long way short of target levels and the new Rover never achieved the breakthrough on the Continent which had been hoped for; its share of the domestic market was no higher than the previous model, the Rover 2000.

With the SD1 British Leyland was trying to do too much too quickly, without the resources or the organization necessary to support it. Yet it was only one element in an ambitious product development programme which was taking shape in the early 1970s; there were thoughts of increasing production to 1.5 million cars a year or even higher. There were plans for a smaller 'sporty' saloon, code-named SD2, to be sold as a Triumph in competition with the smaller BMW models. In volume cars, work was starting on a replacement to the Mini. All this, together with the modernization of factories, would require a substantial increase in capital investment. A cash crisis seemed imminent as early as 1970, a year in which losses in Austin Morris were narrowly exceeded by profits in specialist cars and the truck and bus division. Although profits and cash flow improved in the next three years and a £50 million rights issue was launched in 1972, it was clear that, even in favourable market conditions, British Leyland would have difficulty in financing an investment programme on the scale which was envisaged. This reinforced the doubts held by several senior executives about the wisdom of competing on so many fronts. Even though the two-franchise Austin Morris policy was quietly dropped, British Leyland was trying to do what no other European manufacturer was attempting—to match firms like Ford, Volkswagen, and Renault in the mass market and to fight BMW and Mercedes-Benz in specialist cars. Its starting point in both contests was weak and the slow pace of rationalization in the first five years after the merger had done little to improve the competitiveness of the group.

The financial frailty of British Leyland was exposed by the collapse in car sales following the first oil crisis of 1973–4; the company was forced to turn to the government for support. Yet the perverse consequence of government intervention was to perpetuate an unrealistic view of British Leyland as an all-purpose car and truck manufacturer. The Ryder report of 1975, accepted by the government as the basis for large-scale support from public funds, insisted that it was to British Leyland's advantage to be represented in all the major sectors of the car market. The company could compete effectively against larger volume-car producers, the report said, as long as it built on 'the reputation for quality which it enjoys in the more expensive sectors of the market'.[12] This judgement was questioned a few months later by the House of Commons Expenditure committee, which pointed to the 'signal lack of supporting argument' underlying Ryder's confidence in British Leyland's ability to compete across the board. 'A concentration on the more expensive sectors (perhaps on the pattern of Peugeot) might be successful; a concentration on the mass market might be successful. To attempt both may well be to succeed in neither.'[13]

This warning went unheeded. Although a new management team was installed and some changes were made from the pre-Ryder model programme (including cancellation of the SD2), the full-line strategy was maintained. It took two more years of continuing losses before it became evident to the government that Ryder's projections for British Leyland's market share were hopelessly optimistic and that its prescriptions for dealing with its labour relations and productivity problems—involving, among other things, an elaborate system of worker–management participation—were not working. This led to the appointment in 1977 of a new chairman, Sir Michael Edwardes, with consequences which are described in the next section.

Meanwhile the concentration of management effort on cars had distracted attention from weaknesses on the commercial vehicle side. Leyland, hit by technical problems on two of its new engines, continued to lose market share to imports and was slow to reorient its product development and marketing towards Western Europe. Its Continental rivals, taking advantage of the growth of intra-European trade, were investing in greater standardization and additional capacity. In 1969 Daimler-Benz bought two of the smaller German producers, Hanomag and Henschel, and built a large plant at Wörth with a capacity of over 100,000 vehicles a year, twice as large as any other assembly plant in Europe.[14] Fiat set up a European truck subsidiary, Iveco, which included Unic in France and Magirus-Deutz in Germany. British Leyland's truck and bus division remained uncomfortably dependent on developing country markets. The same was true of Land Rover, but the market for four-wheel-drive cars in Europe was small and most of the Continental car and truck manufacturers had ignored it. Although Japanese competition was increasing—Toyota's production of four-wheel-drive vehicles had surpassed Land Rover by the mid-1970s—the British vehicle was still the preferred choice of many armies and police forces around the world and the Range Rover had created a market niche of its own.

It was the car business—heavily loss-making, plagued by bad industrial relations, losing market share—which would determine whether or not British Leyland could survive. At the time of the change of management in 1977 British Leyland seemed to be a classic example of a company which, to use Michael Porter's phrase, was 'stuck in the middle', neither a credible contender in the mass market nor an effective challenger to the high-margin specialists like Mercedes-Benz and BMW.[15] It was a dilemma which was to dog British Leyland for the next fifteen years.

4. An Outbreak of Realism: Product and Marketing Strategy from 1977 to 1986

When Sir Michael Edwardes took over the chairmanship of British Leyland, one of his immediate priorities, as part of a drive for higher productivity, was to restore management authority on the shop floor. Edwardes became famous for his high-profile confrontations with the shop stewards, especially at Austin Morris, culminating in the imposition of new employment practices in April, 1980. At that point, he wrote later, 'thirty years of management concessions, which had made it impossible to manufacture cars competitively, were thrown out of the window'.[16] But getting the product and marketing strategy right was no less crucial.

British Leyland's capacity of 1.2 million cars a year could, in theory, be filled with four mass-market cars produced at a rate of 250,000 units a year each, an executive car (the new Rover) at 150,000, and a luxury car (the Jaguar XJ6) at 50,000.[17] But of British Leyland's existing mass-market models only the Mini, still being built at a rate of just over 200,000 units in 1977, came near to achieving the required volumes. Yet the Mini was nearly 20 years old and losing market share to more refined Continental models in the same size category. The Allegro and the Marina were running at a rate of about 100,000 cars each, while the two larger Austin Morris models, the Maxi and the Princess (successor to the 1800), together accounted for about 80,000 units. A reasonable estimate was that Austin Morris and the specialist car division would sell no more than 800,000 cars in 1978.

To reduce the burden of surplus capacity, Edwardes set about concentrating production on fewer factories. The closure of the Triumph plant at Speke, near Liverpool, early in 1978—the TR7 sports car which was made there was transferred to the main assembly plant in Coventry—was the first sign of a tougher management approach. But even with fewer factories and more efficient working practices the issue which Barber had raised some years earlier had become even more pertinent: could British Leyland compete in the mass market against companies like Volkswagen and Toyota which were producing close to 2 million cars a year?

The desirable course was to move 'up market', as Barber had urged, offsetting British Leyland's lower volumes against higher specifications and higher margins. Edwardes and his colleagues were eager to move in this direction. They spoke of giving British Leyland cars 'a better than average specification, an Austin with a pinch of Wolseley and a drop of Riley'.[18] But grafting the image of a BMW on to a company which had long been seen, at least in Britain, as a rival to Ford, was bound to take time and Edwardes could no longer count on open-ended support from the government to fund new model development. The Thatcher government, elected in 1979, was determined to stop subsidizing British Leyland and return the company to the private sector as soon as possible. Realism, rather than wishful thinking, was the order of the day, and this applied to product strategy as well as to labour relations, manning levels, and other aspects of the business.

Plans for the new Mini were well-advanced when Edwardes arrived, but there were already doubts within the company about whether the project could earn a satisfactory return. Reactions to the prototype when it was shown at customer clinics were 'discouraging in the extreme', according to Edwardes, and to carry on with what seemed likely to be a loser 'would almost certainly put the volume car operations out of business'.[19] The decision was taken in the summer of 1978 to go for a slightly larger car, known as the Metro, to be launched in 1980. The Metro has been described as the 'first wholly successful mass-production new car launched by the group for 20 years'.[20] But it was competing in a more crowded market than the one which the Mini had faced in the 1960s. Not only were the established European small car producers like Renault and Fiat producing similar models in greater volume, but the two big American companies, Ford and General Motors, were also entering this sector for the first time, with the Ford Fiesta and the Vauxhall Astra. In Vauxhall's case the new small car was part of a remarkable product-led renaissance by General Motors in Europe; its share of the British market rose from 8 per cent to 16 per cent between 1978 and 1984 and by then it was on the brink of overtaking British Leyland.

In the light- and medium-car sectors Edwardes faced an even more awkward problem. The Allegro and Marina had been outsold by Ford's Escort and Cortina in Britain and had performed poorly on the Continent. But the replacement models, known as the Maestro and the Montego, could not be launched any earlier than 1983. To bolster the position in the short term, Edwardes looked to collaboration with another manufacturer, probably building an existing model under licence. A possible solution, which arose shortly after Edwardes's arrival, was to form a partnership with Vauxhall. General Motors was looking for additional capacity as part of its plan for widening its product range in Europe. The suggestion, which came from Vauxhall, was that Longbridge and Cowley could provide the capacity that was needed, while new General Motors models would fill British Leyland's mid-range gap. As Vauxhall's chairman put it to Edwardes, 'we think that your Austin Morris problem is bigger than you think it is, for we believe you need not one, but two new models in the mid-car sector. But you don't have the people resource or the cash resource to do it. And time is against you.'[21] Although this 'imaginative concept', as Edwardes called it, did not find favour with General Motors in the USA, the diagnosis was accurate and reinforced the case for collaboration.

After abortive talks with Renault, agreement was reached in 1979 to assemble the Honda Ballade, to be sold in Britain as the Triumph Acclaim. This car was a useful addition to the British Leyland range, but it was no more than a holding operation; it accounted for just over 2 per cent of the British market in 1982, compared with 11 per cent for the Ford Escort. This first licensing agreement with Honda provided no lasting solution to the problem of where British Leyland should position itself in the world market; it was still 'stuck in the middle', weak both in volume and in specialist cars. The new Rover, planned for an output of 150,000 vehicles a year, reached a peak of just under 50,000 units in 1979 before falling back to 26,000 in the following year; the new factory at Solihull was grossly under-utilized.

As if these internal weaknesses were not enough, British Leyland was badly hit after 1979 by the appreciation of sterling, reflecting the combined effect of North Sea oil and the Thatcher government's economic policies. Export profitability was undermined and Edwardes decided in the summer of 1980 that British Leyland should plan to make itself viable on a production of 600,000 cars a year. The most painful of the closures which resulted from this review was that of the Rover plant at Solihull; production of the SD1 was transferred to Cowley, leaving Land Rovers and Range Rovers to be assembled at the other Solihull factory. The Triumph assembly plant in Coventry was closed shortly afterwards and production of the small Triumph and MG sports cars, hit hard by Japanese competition in the USA and the unfavourable exchange rate, was discontinued.

By this time the old concept of specialist cars as a separate business had lost its relevance. Rover and Triumph were subsumed within Austin Morris to form what became known as Austin Rover, while Jaguar was given greater autonomy as a free-standing business. Jaguar's performance had deteriorated during the 1970s and by the end of the decade it was making losses. The latest version of the XJ6, launched in 1979, suffered from quality defects; in that year only 14,000 cars were produced, the lowest figure since 1957. According to one account, the decline was largely due to the confused organization of British Leyland, leading to: 'a succession of senior managers imposed from corporate level, each applying widely differing policies; three debilitating corporate reorganisations; the dismemberment of Jaguar's finance, sales and marketing functions; and a crucial loss of identity within the divisional warfare in a loss-making corporation'.[22] In 1980 Edwardes appointed a new managing director, John Egan, who improved Jaguar's performance to the point where, to Mrs Thatcher's delight, it became a candidate for privatization; when Jaguar shares were floated in 1984 they were heavily over-subscribed.

Jaguar, despite its quality problems, had a well-established niche in the market which provided the basis for its rehabilitation under Egan. The same was not true of Austin Rover. It needed to move 'up market' with a coherent range of high-quality models, but it lacked the financial and engineering resources to do so on its own. The link with Honda was extended in 1981 with an agreement for the joint development of a new executive car to replace the SD1; it was launched in 1986 as the Rover 800. Edwardes and the management team which took over from him in 1982 had no intention of allowing Austin Rover to decline to the status of a mere assembler; the Honda relationship was seen as complementary to in-house engineering and product development, not a replacement for it. But the re-establishment of the company as a viable, independent car manufacturer needed more time and more money than an increasingly unsympathetic government seemed likely to give it.

A fierce argument with the government took place in 1984 over whether the company should be allowed to develop a new range of engines for small cars. As Mrs Thatcher later wrote, 'I wanted to cut back BL's investment programme and believed that one way of doing this was to buy in engines from Honda . . . rather than for Austin Rover to develop its engines.'[23] The management, backed by the Department of Trade and Industry, insisted that engine technology was a 'core competence' without which the value of British Leyland in any subsequent sale would be seriously reduced.[24] Although this argument narrowly won the day—work on the K-series engine began in 1985—it did not imply any commitment on the government's part to maintain BL as an independent British-owned car manufacturer.

At the end of 1985 Ministers encouraged two sets of negotiations—with Ford on cars and with General Motors on commercial vehicles—which might have led to the transfer of most of British Leyland's assets into American ownership. Ford's interest in Austin Rover had started with a suggestion that the two companies might collaborate in engines and this was later extended to a full-scale take-over. General Motors wanted to put together its ailing Bedford truck subsidiary with British Leyland's truck and bus division; the profitable Land Rover business was an additional attraction. Strong opposition from Conservative members of Parliament forced the government to abandon these discussions, much to Mrs Thatcher's irritation. It was a 'sorry episode', she wrote. 'Time and again I had drawn attention to the benefits Britain received as a result of American investment. The idea that Ford was foreign and therefore bad was plainly absurd.'[25]

Whatever merits a link with Ford or General Motors might have had, it was clear in the mid-1980s that the government had little confidence in an independent future for British Leyland. Its market share in Britain had continued to decline, from 24 per cent in 1977 to 18 per cent in 1985. Although the Metro had done well and the Maestro and Montego were considerable improvements on their predecessors, it was still battling in the mass market with companies which were operating on a much larger scale. Far from improving its position on the Continent, British Leyland car exports to

Common Market countries had fallen from 170,000 in 1977 to 70,000 in 1984. It was 'in the least desirable position for any late-twentieth-century major car company; it was pinned down on a domestic market where import competition was eroding its volume base and unable to find compensating volume by expanding export sales across a broad spread of foreign markets'.[26]

The outlook for the truck and bus division was even more discouraging. The appreciation of sterling had a devastating effect on the profitability of its exports, aggravated by falling demand in several of its traditional markets. Like the car companies, the division was still poorly represented in Continental Europe. Edwardes admits in his autobiography that the managers at the centre had been slow to appreciate the extent of the truck and bus division's problems, partly because of their preoccupation with cars.[27] What the division needed was new products and better distribution on the Continent, probably involving collaboration with another manufacturer. At the time of Edwardes's appointment detailed discussions with Fiat were under way; the Italian company's Iveco subsidiary, well-established in Italy, France, and Germany, was seeking to extend its operations into Britain. No agreement was reached, apparently because of reluctance on the British side to cede majority control to the Italians. Subsequent negotiations with General Motors broke down for political reasons, but in this case there was no obvious European advantage, since Bedford was as weak on the Continent as Leyland.

Land Rover was more strongly placed, mainly because of a determined effort, beginning in the early 1980s, to redirect its marketing effort away from developing countries; between 1980 and 1986 the share of production going to OECD markets rose from 37 per cent to 67 per cent. It was part of an extensive modernization of the business which included the closure of several peripheral factories, large gains in productivity and an improved version of the Range Rover which was launched in the USA in 1987. Work began on a new mid-range vehicle, to be positioned between the basic Land Rover and the Range Rover, a sector of the four-wheel-drive market which had been pioneered by Japanese products such as the Mitsubishi Shogun and the Isuzu Trooper.

While Land Rover had a coherent product and marketing strategy which built on an already strong position in the market, the same was not true of cars. Despite all the improvements which had been made since 1977, the move 'up market' was still more aspiration than reality. In financial terms, moreover, although the huge losses of the early 1980s had been brought to an end, the company was still a long way from becoming a self-supporting business capable of funding its own development. These were the circumstances in which the Thatcher government appointed a new chairman, Sir Graham Day, with a clear remit to end the losses and return the company to the private sector; he took over in May 1986.

5. From 'Honda-Ization' to BMW: Product and Marketing Strategy from 1986 to 1995

One of Edwardes's first acts when he became chairman had been to change the name of the company from British Leyland to BL. He wanted to focus public attention on the individual marques—hence the choice of a 'low-profile, uninteresting name' for the holding company.[28] Day went further by renaming the company Rover, a change which he described as a 'marker in the ground' for a new marketing strategy. He believed that, for a smaller vehicle manufacturer, a name associated with a single brand was essential. 'We had Rover cars, Land Rovers and Range Rovers. Rover was the oldest and most respected name available to us and market research confirmed its appeal.'[29] At the same time he defined what he saw as the core business, consisting of Austin Rover and Land Rover, and set about disposing of everything else.

No longer included in the core was the truck and bus division, which was 'haemorrhaging cash at the rate of £1.5 m per week'.[30] Day identified Daf of the Netherlands, one of the smaller European truck builders, as a possible buyer and in 1987 a joint company was established, with Rover holding a 40 per cent stake; this was later reduced to 16 per cent when the company went public. The deal with Daf removed a financial millstone, but proved inadequate as a long-term solution to Leyland's problems. The Dutch company was a weak player in an industry dominated by Daimler-Benz, Iveco, and Renault's RVI subsidiary, together with the two Swedish heavy truck specialists, Volvo and Scania. The mismatch between Daf's ambitions and its financial resources was exposed by a severe recession in the early 1990s and it went into receivership in 1993.

Leyland needed a European partner, but Daf was the wrong one to choose. Land Rover, by contrast, had been able to stand on its own feet even in British Leyland's darkest days—Edwardes had come under strong pressure from Mrs Thatcher to sell it—and it had become the most profitable part of the group. After the launch of the mid-range Discovery in 1989 it had an attractive three-model line-up with which it could realistically hope to raise annual production to over 100,000 units, with a spread of markets which avoided its old dependence on the Third World. The modernization of Land Rover had come just in time, since the rising popularity of 'sports-utility' vehicles like the Range Rover was attracting a number of new entrants, including some of the European and American volume-car producers. There was also competition from 'multi-purpose vehicles', such as the Renault Espace. But the Land Rover/Range Rover image seemed strong enough to take the strain.

Land Rover had a clearly defined position in its market; Austin Rover did not. As Day admitted in an interview soon after his appointment, 'we are neither a volume producer nor a specialist producer. Actually, I am not quite sure what we are. We are not a volume producer because we don't really have a full product range. What we have is a presence in four or five segments of the market. We need to redefine where we want to be.'[31] The drive 'up market', which John Barber had wanted in the early British Leyland days and Michael Edwardes had begun, was to be pursued more vigorously, with the aim of creating a viable business at an annual volume of some 500,000 cars. It was to be achieved in large measure through closer collaboration with Honda. Agreement was reached in 1987 for a new small car, which became the Rover 200/400 series, and two years later work started on the third member of the Honda/Rover family, the Rover 600.

Rover benefited from the Honda link not only by saving development costs but also by observing and imitating the Japanese company's approach to designing and making cars. After an uneasy early phase in which British managers and engineers were reluctant to accept a subordinate role, 'the organisation began to grasp fully the gulf in productivity, quality, cost, product development—in short almost every indicator—between Rover and Honda, and to realise there were lessons to be learned here'.[32] It was no longer a partnership of equals as it had seemed in 1979; since then Honda had become one of the world's leading car manufacturers and had built its own assembly plant in Britain. When the Rover 600 was launched in 1993, three of Rover's four principal models were dependent on Honda; the only exception was the Metro. The British company still had its own engine technology, through the K-series, and, as it showed with the 200/400 series, had sufficient design and engineering capacity to develop a wide range of variants based on a Honda chassis. But it was doubtful whether Rover any longer had the resources to develop an all-new mainstream car programme on its own.[33]

There were doubts, too, about whether, even after the disposal of loss-making subsidiaries and continuing efficiency gains in what remained, Rover could generate the profits needed to become financially self-supporting. Mrs Thatcher was still pressing for privatization, but flotation on the stock-market was hardly feasible, at least in the time-scale which the Prime Minister had in mind. In the autumn of 1987 Volkswagen expressed interest in buying Austin Rover and Land Rover, but, quite apart from the awkward issue of foreign ownership, the cost to the government was likely to be substantial; the Germans 'expected the government to deal with the accumulated debt, restructuring costs and forward financing on the scale envisaged in the corporate plan'.[34] Day was in any case anxious to avoid selling Rover to a competitor, which would almost certainly have led to rationalization and closures. A *deus ex machina* then appeared in the form of British Aerospace, which saw the acquisition of Rover as a way of continuing its diversification away from the aircraft industry; the sale was completed, on favourable terms to the purchaser, in 1988. From the Prime Minister's point of view, it was a satisfactory outcome. As she wrote later, 'the effects of the disastrous socialist experiment to which the company had been subject had now been overcome and Rover was back in the private sector where it belonged'. Moreover, the transaction had 'one marked political advantage: the company would stay British'.[35]

Although ownership by British Aerospace gave Rover some stability in which to continue the process of 'Honda-ization', there was no synergy between the two companies and no economies from putting them together. It was never clear how British Aerospace could compete effectively in two demanding industries, both of which required heavy and continuing capital expenditure. The failure of the diversification programme led to a financial crisis at British Aerospace, a new management was installed and by the end of 1993 Rover was up for sale again.

This time the purchaser was a competitor, a company which some British Leyland managers had seen as their role model as far back as 1968—BMW. For the German company, which paid nearly £1 billion, the attractions included Land Rover—BMW had no presence in the four-wheel-drive market—and the British company's experience in small, front-wheel-drive cars, including the K-series engine; together with BMW's planned car plant in the USA, the investment in Britain also reduced the German company's dependence on its high-cost manufacturing base in Germany. BMW's managers spoke of converting Rover into 'the premium British marque . . . with its own identity linked to the great tradition of the British motor industry'.[36]

How this objective would be achieved was unclear at the time this chapter was written. The Metro, sold on the Continent as the Rover 100, was still at a volume disadvantage compared to its European rivals and could not be magically invested with a BMW image which would justify a premium price; it was in any case nearly fifteen years old and needed to be replaced. At the higher end of the range BMW's aim was to give Rover cars a more 'exclusive' character which would clearly differentiate them from those of Honda. The Rover 600 and 800 models were made at Cowley in accordance with what the chairman of BMW described as Honda's batch-production system. 'This is a typical mass-manufacture approach', he said. 'We have to change that process because we want to sell exclusive products to the BMW 3-series market and above, but which deliver something completely different from a BMW.'[37] Despite the efforts of the preceding decade it was evident that, in BMW's view, Rover's push 'up market' still had some way to go.

The sale of Rover to BMW completed the dismemberment of the group which had been created with such high hopes in 1968. Of the businesses which had formed part of the original British Leyland the two which appeared to have the best future in 1995 were Land Rover and Jaguar. After its privatization in 1984, Jaguar continued to improve its quality and productivity; ambitious targets were set for raising output to 100,000 a year by the mid-1990s. Jaguar's experience of 'cultural change and competitive renaissance' was seen by outside commentators as a model of corporate renewal from a condition of near-bankruptcy.[38] But, like other low-volume specialists in the motor industry, Jaguar was vulnerable to external shocks. In 1989 its position in the USA, its most important overseas market, was badly affected by an unfavourable exchange rate and by Japanese competition. Looking for a partner to share the costs of development, Egan came close to a deal with General Motors, which would have taken a minority stake. But these negotiations were overtaken by a full bid from Ford, which paid £1.6 billion for the company.

Ford was widely considered to have paid too much and the business continued to make losses for several years after the take-over. But the US company had the resources to strengthen Jaguar's engineering department and to accelerate the model renewal programme.[39] In 1994 a revised version of the XJ6 saloon was launched and in the following year Ford announced plans for a smaller model, code-named X200, described by one commentator as 'Jaguar's belated answer to BMW';[40] it would use the same chassis as a new executive-car range being developed by Ford in the USA and the engine would be made at Ford's South Wales plant. After four changes of ownership—the merger with BMC in 1966, the formation of British Leyland in 1968, privatization in 1984, and the sale to Ford in 1989—Jaguar appeared to have found a secure home in which its distinctive image and skills would be put to good use.

What distinguished Jaguar and Land Rover from other parts of British Leyland in 1968 was that they were operating in profitable market niches where they were less vulnerable to competition from high-volume producers; they were also well established overseas, mainly in the USA for Jaguar, in the developing countries for Land Rover. Thus they were better equipped to withstand the difficult conditions of the 1970s and 1980s than the other car companies and the truck and bus division; in particular, the impact of Europe-wide competition, which was central to the decline of Austin Morris, the old Rover company, and Leyland, was less severe for Land Rover and Jaguar. Although they were damaged by the mismanagement of British Leyland in the first ten years of its existence and by the company's subsequent financial weakness, they were resilient enough to emerge as viable international competitors, albeit under foreign ownership.

6. Why did British Leyland Fail?

By 1995 the fortunes of the British motor industry rested almost entirely in the hands of foreign companies. Although there were good prospects that, thanks to inward investment, car production and exports would continue to rise, the outcome has to be regarded as a signal British failure. Part of that failure was the inability to make the British Leyland merger work. When every allowance has been made for disorderly industrial relations,

inconsistent and often unhelpful government policies, and a difficult economic environment, management errors must take a large part of the
blame.

Why did this merger fail when other mergers in the European motor
industry were more successful? A possible comparison is with Volkswagen
and Peugeot, both of which made acquisitions in the 1960s and 1970s. Volkswagen bought NSU in 1965 and Auto-Union in 1969; the two companies
were merged to form Audi-NSU and this division played the same 'up
market' role in relation to the volume-car operation as the specialist car
division was meant to do in British Leyland. Audi-NSU and Volkswagen
were kept largely separate in the early years after the acquisition, but when
the Beetle came to the end of its life in the mid-1970s, Audi technology
played a vital part in the regeneration of Volkswagen's product line with
the Golf/Jetta/Passat range. A similar transfer of technology from volume
to specialist cars was not seriously attempted in British Leyland, partly
because of anxiety that any such transfer 'would lead to homogenisation
and debasement of the up-market product'.[41] Yet Volkswagen managed it
without jeopardizing the separate identity of the Audi marque.

Integration along these lines was more complicated for British Leyland
because of the larger number of companies and marques involved. Moreover in the German case the volume-car business, despite Volkswagen's
financial crisis in the mid-1970s, was strong enough to lead and co-ordinate
the model replacement programme, whereas Austin Morris was the weakest
part of the British group; responsibility for reviving it was in the hands of
ex-Ford and ex-Leyland executives who had conflicting product and management philosophies.

When Peugeot took over Citroën in 1973, the acquirer was a successful,
cautiously managed company which had steadily broadened its model
range over the previous ten years.[42] Citroën competed in the same market
segments, but with an image which was quite different from that of Peugeot
and a strong dealer network; its factories, thanks to earlier investments
while Citroën had been controlled by Michelin, were generally modern and
well-equipped. Integration, consisting mainly of greater commonality in
components, proceeded cautiously; out of it emerged two complementary
ranges of models which preserved the distinctiveness of the two marques.
Much less successful was Peugeot's subsequent acquisition of Chrysler
Europe, an over-ambitious venture which contributed to severe financial
strains in the early 1980s; plans for a third family of models under the Talbot
name had to be abandoned.

Would Peugeot have survived if it had bought Citroën and Chrysler
Europe at the same time? Certainly no other European company attempted
a rationalization as complex as that of British Leyland. Any thoughts of creating a single 'national champion' in France were ruled out by Peugeot's
firm determination to keep itself independent of its state-owned rival. The

creation of British Leyland involved an extraordinarily difficult organizational transformation in a period when the company's markets were going through a profound change, arising from entry into the Common Market and the rise of the Japanese; at the same time long-standing weaknesses in industrial relations had to be corrected. The merger might have worked if rationalization had been carried out more quickly and more ruthlessly. A coherent product and marketing strategy probably would have involved two complementary product lines, based on Austin Morris and Rover/Triumph, similar to the division between Volkswagen and Audi, with a high degree of common components; Jaguar might have been given a special status, sharing some common components with the other companies but otherwise left undisturbed in its niche. Such an approach would have required an integrated structure similar to that created by Alfred Sloan at General Motors in the 1920s; instead, there was an unclear and unstable compromise between centralization and decentralization.

Would the two companies which merged in 1968, British Motor Holdings (comprising BMC and Jaguar) and Leyland Motor Corporation, have done better if they had stayed separate? By 1968 BMC needed an injection of money and management to modernize its factories, its products and its internal organization. If it had not merged with Leyland, it would have been forced to slim down, perhaps concentrating production on the Austin factory in Birmingham, developing a model range around the Mini/1100 family and building a stronger distribution network on the Continent. At that point Peugeot might have been a more appropriate role model than the established volume-car producers such as Volkswagen, Renault, Fiat, and Ford. But any such strategy would have hinged on successors to the Mini and 1100/1300 of a very different quality than the Allegro and the Marina.

As for Leyland, it has sometimes been suggested that if Rover had been allowed to pursue its incremental approach to product development, supported by Triumph at the lower end and by the profitable Land Rover operation, it could have become a viable BMW competitor. Here, too, the crucial weakness was in Continental Europe. Only Germany of the four large European countries has fostered two large specialist car companies in BMW and Mercedes-Benz. Rover lacked the large domestic demand for this type of car which the German companies enjoyed, and the volume-car makers were beginning to encroach on its territory. But Rover was probably better equipped than BMC, financially, technically, and managerially, to make the transition to a higher level of competition; the merger with British Leyland made it less likely that it would do so.

A final speculative question is whether, from the late 1970s onwards, alternative strategies were available which might have preserved British Leyland/Rover as an independent manufacturer. Some observers have suggested that Sir Michael Edwardes was over-preoccupied with labour relations at the expense of other issues which were no less vital to the company's future. According to one critic, 'management attention was almost excessively focused on one relatively minor aspect of its overall problems. No similar efforts were directed towards improving supplier relationships, worker training, quality control or renovation of marketing and distribution networks.'[43] Yet it is hard to see how British Leyland could have survived if labour relations had continued in the state they were in when Edwardes arrived; that was a nettle which had to be grasped firmly and quickly. As for product and marketing strategy, the Metro, Maestro, and Montego, introduced between 1980 and 1984, represented British Leyland's last attempt to retain an independent position in the high-volume sectors of the market. They were better than their predecessors, but not quite good enough to compete against the latest offerings from companies which had larger engineering resources.

One group of critics has argued that British Leyland's 'fatal miscalculation' in the early 1980s was its failure to invest in the marketing and distribution of the new cars on the Continent. According to this view, the company should have spent more in Europe on dealer development and support, parts back-up, advertising to establish the new products, and aggressive new entrant pricing.[44] But even if the government had made funds available for this purpose, it is far from certain that British Leyland could have regained ground in Europe that had been lost in the preceding twenty years. To succeed on the Continent it needed to offer something different from the mass-produced models of its European rivals. The Metro, Maestro, and Montego were not different enough.

With the wisdom of hindsight, it might be argued that if the move 'up market' had started in 1968 and if British Leyland had set more modest objectives for itself at that time, it might have found a defensible position in the world motor industry. On top of all the other inherited problems which the new company had to correct, the combination of wishful thinking and confused organization precipitated a decline which continued, with only occasional interludes of optimism, for the subsequent twenty-five years.

NOTES

1. The importance of the 'company-car' market is discussed in Karel Williams, John Williams, and Dennis Thomas, *Why are the British Bad at Manufacturing?* (1983), and in Karel Williams, John Williams, and Colin Haslam, *The Breakdown of Austin Rover* (Leamington Spa, 1987).
2. Graham Turner, *The Leyland Papers* (London, 1971), 82.
3. Ibid. 211.

4. Ibid. 189.
5. Jonathan Wood, *Wheels of Misfortune: The Rise and Fall of the British Motor Industry* (London, 1988), 176.
6. Steven Tolliday, 'Competition and the Workplace in the British Automobile Industry, 1945–1988', *Business and Economic History*, 17 (1988).
7. Williams, Williams, and Haslam, *Why are the British*, 240.
8. Ibid. 232.
9. Quoted in Wood, *Wheels of Misfortune*, 176.
10. Richard Whipp and Peter Clark, *Innovation and the Auto Industry, Product, Process and Work Organisation* (London, 1986), 109.
11. Ibid. 103.
12. *British Leyland: The Next Decade* (HMSO, 1975), 16.
13. *The Motor Vehicle Industry*, a Report by the House of Commons Expenditure Committee, August 1975.
14. Nicholas Owen, *Economies of Scale, Competitiveness and Trade Patterns Within the European Community* (Oxford, 1983).
15. Michael E. Porter, *Competitive Strategy* (New York, 1980), 41.
16. Michael Edwardes, *Back from the Brink* (London, 1984), 135.
17. D. G. Rhys, 'European Mass-Producing Car-Makers and Minimum Efficient Scale: A Note', *Journal of Industrial Economics*, June 1977.
18. Ray Horrocks, Managing Director (Cars), interviewed in *Motor*, 25 Aug. 1979.
19. Edwardes, *Back from the Brink,* 185.
20. Martin Adeney, *The Motor Makers* (London, 1988).
21. Edwardes, *Back from the Brink,* 201.
22. R. Whipp, R. Rosenfeld, and A. Pettigrew, 'Culture and Competitiveness: Evidence from Two Mature Industries', *Journal of Management Studies*, Nov. 1989.
23. Margaret Thatcher, *The Downing Street Years* (London, 1993).
24. Frank Mueller and Michael Roper, 'Technological Innovation and Commercial Success: The Development of the K-series Engine at Rover', *Technology Project Papers*, No. 15, London Business School, Nov. 1991.
25. Thatcher, *Downing Street Years*, 118.
26. Karel Williams, Colin Haslam, Sukhdev Johal, and John Williams, *Cars: Analysis, History, Cases* (Providence, RI, 1994), 159.
27. Edwardes, *Back from the Brink*, 178.
28. Ibid. 77.
29. Graham Day, Price Waterhouse Lecture to the Cardiff Business School, 16 May 1990.
30. Ibid.
31. Interview in *Autocar*, 17 July 1987.
32. Andrew Mair, *Honda's Global Local Corporation* (Basingstoke, 1994), 278.
33. Kevin Done, 'Road Map to the Rover's Return', *Financial Times*, 7 Apr. 1993.
34. Lord Young, *The Enterprise Years* (London, 1990), 288.
35. Thatcher, *Downing Street Years*, 680.
36. *Financial Times*, 13 Sept. 1995.
37. Interview in *Sunday Times*, 10 Oct. 1994.
38. Whipp, Rosenfeld, and Pettigrew, 'Culture and competitiveness'.
39. Haig Simonian, 'The Year of the Smaller car', *Financial Times*, 14 July 1995.
40. Ibid.

41. Steven Tolliday, 'From "Beetle Monoculture" to the "Germany Model: The Transformation of Volkswagen, 1967–1991', *Business and Economic History*, 24/2 (Winter 1995).
42. Jean-Louis Loubet, *Automobiles Peugeot: Une réussite industrielle, 1945–1974* (Paris, 1990).
43. Steven Tolliday, 'Competition and the Workplace in the British Automobile Industry 1945–1988', *Business and Economic History*, 2nd Ser., 17 (1988).
44. Williams, Williams, and Haslam, *Why are the British*.

12. Internalization and Externalization: *Organizational Strategies for Fuji Denki, Fujitsu, and Fanuc*

SEIICHIRO YONEKURA*

Introduction

The age of managerial capitalism has been closely associated with the rise of large, diversified, multidivisional companies. As Alfred Chandler has pointed out, this pattern of growth with the creation of a multidivisional structure had its origin in the United States. In the late nineteenth and early twentieth centuries, companies in capital-intensive industries internally grew or externally consolidated to form single large enterprises, through mergers or take-overs. These companies pursued economies of scale by vertically integrating organizational functions, thus optimizing the flow of raw materials, semi-finished goods and final products. The multifunctional organization emerged, along with the rise of the first generation of big businesses.

After World War I, these large integrated companies began to exploit their accumulated resources by diversifying into related or sometimes unrelated business fields. To pursue economies of scope by maximizing the internal managerial resources, these companies started diversification. Facing great difficulties in managing unrelated businesses or markets, some pioneering companies created a multidivisional organization as early as in the 1920s. The multidivisional structure did not spread immediately, however, because diversification was not so common in the business world of the 1930s and 1940s. After World War II and by the 1960s in particular, as these large multifunctional companies increasingly encountered maturing core markets and competition with newcomers from the developing countries, they were forced to move into new markets, especially those markets related to newly developed technology, such as the fields of electrical engineering and chemicals. Many of these companies achieved diversification by adding new divisions to existing ones, thus adopting a multidivisional

*This chapter is a revised version of a paper published with Hans-Jürgen Clahsen on 'Innovation by Externalization: A New Organizational Strategy for the High-Tech Industries—Fuji Denki, Fujitsu and Fanuc', in Takeshi Yuzawa (ed.), *Japanese Business Success: The Evolution of a Strategy* (London, 1994), 39–64.

organization. Over time, these companies grew bigger and bigger and came to represent what is now widely regarded as a modern industrial enterprise.[1] The multidivisional structure is also regarded as a cost-saving organization, since internal distribution and transactions of managerial resources (capital, human resources, real goods and facilities, and information) are far more rational and economical than external distribution and transactions through the market mechanism.[2] Furthermore, the multidivisional structure saves redundant indirect costs and corporate taxes, because a general corporate office is solely in charge of them.

As their organizational structure and internal hierarchy grew to become even more complex and thicker, however, these multidivisionalized firms increasingly lost the dynamism for which they had been renowned earlier on. Many of them increasingly came to be governed through complex bureaucratic procedures which did in fact hamper entrepreneurial dynamism and consequently witnessed a slowdown of economic activity. Moreover, as these complex hierarchically organized companies also came to be haunted by conflicts and struggles between the corporate office and divisions, or among divisions, the gigantic multidivisional structure itself negatively affected their ability to exploit available economic resources as fully as management would have liked.[3] Thus, while these giant multidivisional enterprises had once been regarded as the powerful driving force behind the rise of industrial capitalism in the United States and Europe, more and more they came to be associated with sluggish bureaucratic hierarchies which, rather than being at the forefront of economic and technological development, are characterized by a wasting of economic resources within their own organizations. As a result, in the 1970s and 1980s, small venture businesses and internal corporate ventures gained recognition as a useful alternative in the United States.[4]

While the pattern of big business came to present the mainstream of industrial capitalism, however, there were exceptions in the form of enterprises which, rather than integrating into giant multidivisional units, took a different approach to growth by spinning off divisions as independent companies. This spinning-off pattern of corporate growth appears to occur more frequently in Japan than in any other industrialized country. Looking at the history of many companies, which have become closely associated with the image of Japan as arguably one of the most dynamic economies of the late twentieth century, we can detect that many of these companies are members of the pre-war *zaibatsu* or the post-war industrial groups which have engaged in very different kinds of activities. Many of these companies have their origin as the offspring of former parent companies. One example is Toyota Motor Company, created by Kiichiro Toyoda, which was an offspring of Toyoda Shokki, a manufacturer of weaving looms. Another example from the car-manufacturing sector was Nissan, an automobile division of the Nissan *zaibatsu*. Hitachi and Toshiba, now Japan's leading all-round electric machinery and appliance companies, were also members of the Nissan *zaibatsu* and Mitsubishi *zaibatsu* as independent affiliate companies.[5]

There are many more examples, and without mentioning them individually, we would like to draw attention to a common pattern the vast majority of these share. Companies founded as offspring to deal with a newly developed technology, later on exceeded their parent companies in organizational dynamism, economic performance, and very often in scale too. This led to the emergence of a large company which spun off yet another new company in turn and again institutionalized the successful development and exploitation of a new technology.

Why did some Japanese firms prefer to spin off their new business units instead of adding them as new divisions? Compared with the American situation, it might be said that as there was no legal constraint against cross-shareholdings and interlocking directorships, Japanese firms whether a pre-war *zaibatsu* or post-war business groups were able to form strongly interdependent groups of firms. If there were no economic rationale, however, this spinning-off strategy would be nonsense, because these independent firms have to pay redundant corporate tax and other legal fees, and to employ their own indirect corporate staff. If there were no economic or organizational advantage in spinning off over that in a multidivisional structure, which jointly utilizes indirect corporate staff and saves these transaction costs, the latter would be far more economical. Nevertheless, the Japanese firms preferred spinning off. Why? Although the multidivisional structure saves redundant indirect costs and external transaction costs, it sometimes has diseconomies of size. Ronald Coase, when he discussed the size of the firm, pointed out the diseconomy of internalization. He picked up three major factors which limit an internalization of transactions:

(1) As a firm gets larger, there may be decreasing returns to the entrepreneurial function, that is, the cost of organizing additional transactions within the firm may rise.
(2) It may be that as the transactions which are organized increase, the entrepreneur fails to position the factors of production in the uses where their value is greatest, that is, fails to make the best use of the factors of production.
(3) The supply price of one or more factors of production may rise because the 'advantages' of a small firm are greater than those of a large firm.[6]

Coase clearly recognized entrepreneurial failure and diseconomies of size in large firms when he wrote 'The Nature of the Firm' in 1937. Some Japanese companies, unintentionally at the beginning and more strategically in recent years, by spinning off their new divisions or business units, have avoided diseconomies of upscaling.

In this chapter, we trace the history of a company which has twice spun off new enterprises which developed into world leaders in their markets by using state-of-the-art technologies: Fuji Denki, Fujitsu, and Fanuc. Fuji

Denki, a Furukawa and Siemens joint venture, spun off its telecommunications department as an independent company in 1935. This company,
which came to be known as Fujitsu, developed into a leading telecommunications manufacturer before World War II and subsequently moved into
computers in the early 1960s. Initially challenging IBM in its home market,
it grew to mount a serious challenge to IBM's predominance on a world-
wide scale. While challenging in the world market, by 1990 Fujitsu had itself
spun off 121 affiliated and 37 related companies in Japan, and 28 'affiliated'
(over 50 per cent stake) and 8 related (20–49 per cent stake) companies
abroad. Among these, Fanuc has been the most successful and important.
In 1972 Fujitsu spun off its own department dealing with computer numeric
control and automation technology, to form a new company, Fanuc, which
rapidly developed into the world leading manufacturer of computerized
numeric control technology and robotics. It achieved a market share of 50
per cent world-wide and 70 per cent in Japan. There was an extraordinary
growth in each company after spinning off. First, we give a summary of the
history of the companies involved and second, try to explain the underlying motives and factors affecting this type of corporate growth pattern.

Fuji Denki: A Japanese-German Joint Venture

Fuji Denki (Fuji Denki Seizo Kabushiki Kaisha, or the Fuji Electric Manufacturing Corporation) was established in August 1923 as a joint-venture of
Furukawa Denki Kogyo, a company belonging to the Furukawa *zaibatsu*,
and Siemens of Germany. The new company had its headquarters in Koji-
machi, Tokyo and a nominal capital of 10 million yen, a quarter of which
was paid-up at the time of foundation. Furukawa put up 70 per cent of the
capital while Siemens contributed 30 per cent. The Furukawa *zaibatsu* has
its origin in the copper-mining business started by Ichibei Furukawa in 1875.
Starting in copper-mining, he gradually diversified into silver-, gold-, and
coal-mining, and into refining. After Ichibei's death in 1903, his family business was incorporated as Furukawa Kogyo (Furukawa Mining), an unlimited partnership, in 1905. At that time, Furukawa Kogyo had expanded to
embrace twenty-three metal and six coal-mines. In the economic boom
which followed the Russo-Japanese War (1904–5), the firm started further
diversification by buying or investing in wire-cable manufacturing, railway,
and electric-light businesses.[7]

Siemens, which provided the technological knowledge for Fuji Denki,
already had a long history of business activity in Japan. In fact, it was the
first foreign manufacturing company to make direct contact after the Meiji
Restoration in 1868. As early as 1870, Siemens was considering the prospect
of doing business in Japan and, after consulting with Japanese officials in
Berlin, it sent Otto Henneberg to Tokyo in 1884 and a young engineer called

Hermann Kessler in 1887 to establish an office there.[8] In September 1887, two months after he arrived in Tokyo, Kessler went to Asio Copper Mine to meet Ichibei Furukawa and succeeded in selling an electric generator and boiler to Furukawa. Siemens then began to supply its products to Furukawa on a regular basis, and after the Sino-Japanese war (1894–5), Furukawa appointed Siemens & Halske's Tokyo branch as the sole supplier to the group. In 1905 Siemens incorporated the branch as Siemens Schuckert Denki Kabushiki Kaisha, a Japanese corporation, in anticipation of the further development of the Japanese economy. The company employed sixteen engineers, nine Japanese and seven Germans, and engaged in marketing the full line of Siemens products in Japan. The outbreak of World War I in Europe and the entry of Japan on the Allies' side against Germany forced the company to close its office and suspend business. The demand for heavy machinery and chemicals relating to the War brought an economic boom in Japan, which had been suffering from a chronic depression ever since the end of the Russo-Japanese War. Since those products had been imported from Europe and America, the interruption of the imports caused by the war forced Japan to rely on her own technological ability and she was able to enhance the technological foundations of her economy to a considerable extent. Despite this development and the eagerness to import foreign technology to Japan, especially in the fields of heavy machinery and chemicals however, the gap still remained wide and contacts with foreign companies quickly resumed after the end of the war.

German companies, on the other hand, faced economic restrictions stipulated by the Peace Treaty of Versailles, which prohibited the production and trade of goods which had a military potential. Furthermore, the German economy was witnessing a period of severe inflation. Thus, given the unfavourable conditions for the export of finished products to Japan, Siemens shifted its policy from its pre-war stance of direct exports to the export of technology, which meant the provision of licences to facilitate production in Japan. In November 1919, Siemens approached its long-standing business partner, Furukawa Gomei, the holding company of the Furukawa *zaibatsu*, with a proposal to set up a jointly owned and operated manufacturing company, which would produce electrical equipment based on Siemens' technologies. Given this long-standing relationship with Siemens, Furukawa responded positively and sent an executive, Hideo Kajiyama, to Berlin, to support the company's representative in Europe, Heitaro Inagaki, who was already engaged in talks with the Germans.[9] In his detailed study, Hisashi Watanabe revealed that Siemens was more aggressive in this negotiation process than Furukawa because the former had realized that it lagged behind its American and British competitors in the Asian market.[10] Negotiations were, however, interrupted by the speculative failure of Furukawa Shoji (Furukawa's trading company) in China. The incident led not only Furukawa Shoji but also Furukawa Gomei, the holding company, to the brink of bankruptcy and threatened the very foundations of the group. Although Furukawa was finally able to overcome this crisis, it had to stop the negotiation for two years. Furukawa resumed talks with Siemens again in late 1921 and reached a conclusion in 1923.

Fuji Denki's field of business was to be the production, assembly, and marketing of heavy and light electrical equipment. However, telecommunications technology was excluded because both parent companies had other vested interests in this field. Furukawa Denko, which had been manufacturing cables and equipment in its own factory in Yokohama since June 1920, continued its own telephone and telegraph activities, while Siemens continued to import equipment from Germany. This situation contravened the original intention of also granting Fuji Denki the right to market Siemens-made telephone and telegraph equipment. As both sides persisted in their desire to execute the original plan, after long and complicated negotiations between the German and Japanese representatives a final decision was reached in June 1925. According to this agreement, Fuji Denki was to take over the importation and marketing of telephone switchboard equipment from Siemens exclusively, and Siemens was to hand over its own telephone and telegraph division, including the entire staff, to Fuji Denki. In turn Furukawa Denko would abandon its own production, but in any case, its production facilities had been completely destroyed by the devastating Kanto earthquake. Thus, Fuji Denki became the sole importer and distributor of Siemens-made telephone and telegraph equipment.

Fuji Denki could only enjoy a short period of rapid expansion in the beginning of the 1920s. In the unstable economy of the late 1920s and early 1930s the company faltered, making a cumulative loss of 1.22 million yen by 1930. The telephone and telegraph business remained buoyant, since domestic competition was limited, and the company won several tenders for the supply of switching systems, especially in the Osaka-Kobe district. From 1924 to 1934, Fuji Denki imported and installed twelve switching stations with a total of 46,300 circuits.[11] But it suffered greatly from changed political and economic conditions in the 1930s. As the world-wide depression triggered a sharp decline in the yen, a worsening foreign trade balance, and a rapid decline of foreign currency reserves, the Japanese government called for a policy of import reductions and the fostering of exports, in order to improve the balance of payments and prevent the outflow of reserves. Successive cabinets pursued a protectionist policy and consequently industries came under increasing political pressure to reduce their dependence on foreign products and technology and to substitute home-manufactured products for imported ones.

Fuji Denki, which was particularly reliant on Siemens imports in its telephone and telegraph business, was no exception to this general trend. In the field of heavy electrical equipment, it already had a production base in Japan and continued to reduce its dependence on Siemens technology. But with telecommunications technology the company's efforts to 'nationalize' production had to start from scratch and it lagged behind other manufacturers, such as Oki and Hitachi, which had already started producing switching systems as early as 1929.

Pressure on the company to manufacture automatic switching equipment, a crucial component in Japan's national telephone network, mounted. The Ministry of Post and Communications (*Teishin-sho*) introduced a new procurement policy requiring a written oath from the manufacturer certifying that the equipment delivered had been produced in Japan. Thus, the chances of winning a government order with imported products were diminishing. The Ministry made it very clear that it would not tolerate Fuji Denki's existing policy of installing imported equipment from Siemens and strongly demanded that equipment be made in Japan.

Concerned about the company's future, Fuji Denki's executives entered into negotiations with Siemens on the 'nationalization' of switching systems and other telephone and telegraph equipment. Although the Germans were apprehensive about potential rivalry in the telecommunications field, they conceded the point. In May 1932 Fuji Denki commenced construction of a factory for automatic switching system equipment based on Siemens technology within Fuji Denki's Kawasaki plant. Thus, Fuji Denki ended the era of merely importing finished products from Siemens and entered a new phase of development.[12] The first two automatic switching systems manufactured at the new factory were successfully installed in Yokohama and Osaka. Consequently, in June 1934 Fuji Denki received official recognition as a supplier of switching system equipment to the Ministry of Post and Communications. By this time, military demand and the expansionist economic policy introduced by Takahashi Korekiyo produced an improvement in the overall economic climate, and Japanese companies including Fuji Denki enjoyed a boom period of increasing demand from both the private and the public sectors.

Amid this favourable economic climate, Fuji Denki's two main businesses, heavy electric machinery and telephone equipment, expanded rapidly. In pursuing these activities, however, an important fact regarding future development became increasingly clear: its two main fields of business bore little relation to each other. In other words, the manufacturing and marketing of turbines for electric-power generation and the production of switching system equipment for the national telephone network were very different activities. Furthermore, operating two different businesses within a single organizational structure was likely to cause friction which would impede the company's development. First, production of unrelated products forced Fuji Denki to maintain two different production facilities, separate research and development facilities, two sales departments, and consequently the company was in effect divided into two camps, unable to reap economies of scale or enjoy the benefits of technological synergy.

Second, since these two camps were managed by the same organizational hierarchy, there existed a battle for resources inside the company. By the mid-1930s, voices were calling for the separation of the telephone business as an independent company. The problems Fuji Denki encountered at this time were similar to those that multifunctional business enterprises encounter in the early stages of diversification. In the United States, for example, the Du Pont Company had the same problems within its diversified businesses. In order to solve them it pioneered the multidivisional organization to co-ordinate the different business activities.[13]

However, Fuji Denki chose to spin off its communications department as an independent company, Fuji Tsushinki Kabushi Kaisha (Fuji Communications Corporation) in June 1935. There were three reasons for adopting this course. The first was a cartel agreement. In February 1935, Fuji Denki signed a territorial business agreement with Tokyo Denki (later to become Toshiba), by which the companies agreed to co-operate in the field of communications technology. This meant that Tokyo Denki would focus on the production and marketing of wireless communications technology while Fuji Denki would focus on its expanding telephone business, with neither company invading the other's territory. The co-operation agreement included a passage which stipulated that both companies should separate their wireless and telephone businesses respectively as independent companies and exchange 20 per cent of the shares in the newly founded companies.[14] The second reason was military considerations. As the telecommunication industry was closely related to national security and defence matters, the Japanese government, having started a war in China, wanted to exclude foreign influence in this field. As a matter of fact, in the newly established company, Siemens had only a 0.7 per cent shareholding, compared with 30 per cent of Fuji Denki. It is clear that the spinning-off lessened Siemens' influence in terms of ownership. As we will see later, the newly formed corporation increased the share of munitions supply in its total sales and the military would become the largest customer.[15] Thus, in order to reduce Siemen's capital participation and attract government orders, it was important to spin off the telecommunication division as Fujitsu.

The third reason was historical. As Fuji Denki was one of the member companies of the Furukawa *zaibatsu*, it was accustomed to controlling subsidiaries as independent companies. In addition, because of the absence of an anti-trust law in pre-war Japan, there was no obstacle to prevent Fuji Denki from becoming the largest stockholder in its subsidiaries. In fact, Fuji Denki owned 94.7 per cent of Fujitsu's stock, before it exchanged 20 per cent of the shares with Tokyo Denki.[16]

This way, Fuji Denki went ahead with the separation of its telephone department and founded Fuji Tsushinki Kabushiki Kaisha. The company later changed its name to Fujitsu and we shall hereafter refer to it by this name. We now turn our attention to the development of this offspring.

Fujitsu: From Telephone Manufacturer to Computers

Fujitsu has been one of the most successful companies in post-war Japan. It is by far Japan's largest computer manufacturer and, unlike its domestic rivals, such as NEC and Hitachi, computers are its dominant field of activity, accounting for 71 per cent of total sales in 1990.[17] Moreover, Fujitsu appears to be one of the very few computer manufacturers, if not the only one, capable of challenging the supremacy of the industry's giant, IBM, which is now encountering increased competition from Fujitsu not only in Japan, but also in all major international markets. Fujitsu's ability to compete stems from its efforts in research and development, which have enabled it to supply computers that are highly competitive in terms of both performance and price. In addition, its strong performance, not only in computers but also in the field of telecommunications and semiconductors, makes it possible for the company to offer an integrated approach to transmitting, processing, and storing of data, something which IBM, for example, has yet to achieve.

When Fujitsu was established in 1935, however, it did not look as if it was set to become a forerunner in high technology. Its metamorphosis was a long and painful process. To understand the nature of this transformation, it is necessary to examine the internal circumstances of Fujitsu from its foundation and to consider the impact of its leading engineers and managers. Founded at a time of mounting international tension, Fujitsu's development up to the end of World War II was strongly shaped by the requirements of Japan's wartime economy. As pointed out earlier, the company's major customer was the Ministry of Communications, and its business activities were largely dependent on and fluctuated according to the Ministry's demand for communications equipment. Given this dependence, and the fact that, following Japan's invasion of Manchuria, resources were increasingly diverted from civilian to military projects, Fujitsu experienced a sharp fall in demand, which was only partially compensated for by increased military demand for communications equipment stemming from the territorial expansion in China. Moreover, along with other private industrial companies, the management of Fujitsu became increasingly subject to government control. Its factories were designated as Army-controlled (*gunjyu kasha*), and the purchase of raw materials and sale of finished products were subject to the imperatives of a controlled economy. Military demand in Fujitsu's total production increased from 52 per cent in 1942 to 95 per cent in 1944.[18] The period from the company's foundation to the end of World War II was thus characterized by scarce resources, labour shortages, increasing government interference and, finally, the destruction of production facilities by Allied air raids.

It may seem as if the War had a wholly negative influence on the company's development, but this was not entirely so. The company also learned how to overcome its dependence on foreign (i.e. Siemens) technology. Furthermore, a handful of young engineers, who would later become the driving force behind the development of the company's computer business, gained useful experience which made them realize the crucial importance of computer technology and its significance for Fujitsu's future. During the final years of the War, Fujitsu was involved in the development and production of a technologically complex air defence system designed to protect Tokyo from Allied air raids. It was envisaged that this system would first detect the position of enemy aircraft and then transmit the information to the anti-aircraft defences in and around Tokyo; anti-aircraft artillery would then be directed according to the data supplied. Fujitsu's development team, which included a young engineer named Taiyu Kobayashi, was in charge of the data transmission system. But although this system was brought into operation, it did not produce the intended results. While the individual parts of the system worked faultlessly, there was a fatal flaw—the absence of an adequate calculating device for the processing of data concerning the position of enemy aircraft. This meant that calculations of flight path and future position had to rely on a mechanical computer device which was far too slow. As a result, the system was a failure. This left a very strong impression on Kobayashi and the other members of the team. They realized the urgent need for such a facility, and felt an overpowering desire to develop and produce what they referred to as an 'electric computing device'. By the end of the War, then, there had emerged a small group of engineers who understood the value of speedy computers and were determined to develop them.

The main business activity of Fujitsu, however, remained that of switching and transmission systems. After the War, the company invested its scarce resources in the restoration of the telephone equipment that had been destroyed by the bombing; the interest in computers remained alive only in the minds of young engineers. The impetus behind its subsequent transformation was provided by this handful of young engineers who formed a group within the company. However, the group was not taken seriously at first, and, at worst, it was despised by those who were then the backbone of the firm, the 'communications people'. The most senior member of the group was Taiyu Kobayashi, who had joined Fujitsu in the year of its foundation. The others joined after the War. Toshio Ikeda, who died suddenly in 1964 aged 51, can, with good reason, be considered the intellectual leader of the 'computer group' and the brain behind Fujitsu's computer development. Gene Amdahl, the founder of Amdahl Corporation and Ikeda's personal friend, described his contribution to the company: 'Dr Ikeda was the driving force in computers within Fujitsu Limited, and under his persuasive leadership Fujitsu had advanced its computer activities to where they were contributing approximately half the revenues of Fujitsu.'[19]

Ikeda joined Fujitsu in 1946 and was assigned to the development section. For the young Ikeda, who had developed an interest in automatic computing technology in his student days at the Tokyo Institute of Technology, this was a rather dull assignment and he soon managed to make his way into the research laboratory and thus into the group which shared his interest in computers. He found personal support from the then head of research and development, Hanzo Omi, who became a kind of protective father-figure to the computer enthusiasts.

Shinsuke Shiokawa was another important member of the group; he was employed in Fuji Denki's research laboratory for electric-power distribution technology. In 1938 he published the results of his research on a binary digit calculation system, which later became a relay-based computing device. When he presented his research at the annual meeting of the Academy for Electric Sciences in 1938, few people understood his work, which was several years ahead of the mainstream of technological development.[20] He was supported, however, by a professor at the University of Tokyo, Hideo Yamashita, who became a promoter of computer development and a mediator between the computer industry and potential customers after the War. Fuji Denki paid little attention to Shiokawa's research activities. His research was not considered relevant to the development of military technology, and the increasingly serious shortage of parts and raw materials brought an end to his wartime research activities. Soon after the War, disappointed that he had not been given the support to develop a computing device based on his binary digit technology, Shiokawa worked for a couple of years as an instructor at a small technical training centre for Japan's national railway in Shizuoka Prefecture. One day, by chance, he read an article about IBM having developed an electric computer based on the same concept as his own research. Greatly encouraged by the fact that there was indeed the possibility of practical application for his research, he contacted Fujitsu, where he was warmly welcomed by Fujitsu's 'computer group'. The group's position, in turn, was reinforced by now having an expert of computer logics as a member.

The group surrounding Kobayashi, Ikeda, and Shiokawa represented the core and origin of Fujitsu's metamorphosis into a computer company. Since the members of this group were relatively young and inexperienced, and were considered in a sense to be outsiders within Fujitsu, they needed a high-ranking promoter in order to be able to pursue their activities within the existing organizational framework. This role was played by Hanzo Omi, chief of Fujitsu's R&D section. Omi supported the group as far as he was able. He had also realized the need for the development of computing systems and the prospects offered by a future market for data-processing technology.[21] Furthermore, he had been interested in the latent relationship between communications technology and data-processing technology. In particular, after reading a book by Dr Kelly, director of the telephone research centre at Bell Laboratories, he concluded that there was a mutual relationship between the two sectors and that it would be beneficial for the company's development as a whole to pursue business in both fields.[22]

Ikeda described the situation at the beginning of the group's effort to develop computers as follows:

For some strange reason, just at the very same time when I was getting interested in computers, Shiokawa joined the company. He had been working on relay technology based on the binary system since before the war and really did have some fantastic ideas. At that time, when Shiokawa came to Fujitsu, our group had by chance got a blueprint of the circuit diagram of the ENIAC computer, only one single page though. We found it interesting and, using about 90 vacuum tubes, constructed a counting circuit. Before long, everybody had developed a profound interest in automatic calculating devices, and the idea of creating a computer had emerged from amongst the young engineers. Thus, after Shiokawa had joined us, the idea to develop a computer quickly became the main topic within our group.[23]

At about the same time, the Tokyo Stock Exchange was considering installing an electric computer for the automatic processing of transactions in order to cope with the increased activity resulting from the economic boom which followed the outbreak of the Korean War. This involved Hideo Yamashita, the Tokyo University professor mentioned earlier, who was then an informal advisor to the Stock Exchange and mediator within the industry. Yamashita remembered Shiokawa and his research activities and contacted Ikeda's computer group. He asked them if they were interested in developing a data-processing system for the Stock Exchange. Kobayashi, then head of the research and development section, jumped at the idea, and Ikeda's computer group, with Takuma Yamamoto, the current chairman, Akinori Yamaguchi, Shiokawa, and Omi embarked on developing what was eventually to be Japan's first relay computer.[24]

To cut a long story short, the group managed to develop a data-processing system which followed the specifications laid down by the Stock Exchange Committee. This system was not selected, however, because its calculating speed was inferior to that of a system offered by the Univac Corporation of America. But this disappointment did not discourage those involved in the Fujitsu system. On the contrary, Ikeda and his team became even more motivated and went ahead with the development of a general purpose computer based on the knowledge and experience gained from the Stock Exchange project. Ikeda even managed to get the go-ahead for their computer project from the then chairman of Fujitsu, Junichi Ko. The circumstances were rather curious. Ikeda met Ko by chance during the intermission of a Russian ballet and asked him to support the venture.

Enchanted by both beautiful ballerinas and wine, Ko agreed within minutes, and the project which resulted in the development of the Facom-100 (Fujitsu Automatic Computer-100) began.[25] Ikeda explained that 'This wasn't a real decision from above to develop a computer. Rather, it took the form of something like: well, if there are some fellows within the company who are fond of computers let them go ahead. They won't do much harm.'[26]

This kind of approach appears to have been prevalent within the company, which was by then enjoying brisk business stemming from the ambitious expansion plans of the newly founded Nippon Telephone and Telegraph Public Corporation (NTTPC). Ikeda's computer group seems to have been regarded with paternalistic tolerance, and its members were given sufficient freedom to pursue their activities. There was apparently little opposition. This atmosphere of limited expectations and paternalistic protection proved to be ideal for Ikeda and his team. They were protégés, but few people seem to have taken them seriously. The general attitude prevailing within the company can best be illustrated by citing an example. At the time of the development of the Facom-100 machine, the group leader, Ikeda, was in the habit of gathering the other members at his home. Whilst listening to classical music, he would discuss the project until late into the night. Whereas the rest of the team would then be at work at nine o'clock the next morning, Ikeda himself would sleep until noon, then work at home until late afternoon, showing up eventually at the company after five. Wages at that time were, however, paid on a daily basis, so Ikeda received no income and was forced to sell his library to a second-hand book shop in order to make some money.[27] There were those in the company who demanded Ikeda's dismissal, but his direct superiors, Kobayashi and Omi, supported him. Indeed, they even changed his salary basis from a daily rate to a fixed monthly one.[28] However this episode is interpreted, the ability of the company to accommodate the eccentric behaviour of an extremely gifted engineer like Ikeda was remarkable. One wonders whether Fujitsu would have been able to nurture people like Ikeda and his computer team if the communications business had remained a part of Fuji Denki alongside its heavy electric equipment division.

Returning to Fujitsu's transformation into a maker of computers, it has to be stressed that the computers developed in the pioneering days were a technological, but not a commercial success. And although subsequent computers, like the Facom 128, 128B, 138A, 318A, 415A, 514, 524, received a positive reaction in the market, production facilities were insufficient and inefficient. There was no factory exclusively assigned to the production of computers; their manufacture was dispersed throughout the Kawasaki complex. Moreover, Fujitsu used not only relays and transistors as components for its computers, but also 'parametron' components, which were based on a technology developed and employed only in Japan. As the trend

towards transistors and, later, integrated circuits became clear, the parallel
development of relay, parametron, and transistor computers was abandoned in favour of concentration on the latter. However, this did not
happen until the early 1960s.

At the end of the 1960s Fujitsu was still almost entirely dependent on its
communications business, and hence on NTTPC's purchase programme. At
the same time, it was manufacturing technologically advanced computers
which were neither money-making nor solidly based within Fujitsu's strategy concept. Ikeda's 'crazy bunch', as they were referred to by the communications side of the company, were tolerated, but they still remained
outsiders. All this changed dramatically when Kanjiro Okada became president of Fujitsu in November 1959. Aged sixty-nine, Okada had formerly
held the post of president of the board of Furukawa Mining Company, the
central business within the Furukawa *zaibatsu*. Immediately after the War,
he had been forced to resign from all his posts as part of the purge conducted by the Supreme Commander for the Allied Powers. Prior to
his appointment at Fujitsu, he had served for more than a decade as vice-
president of Ube Kosan (one of the large mining companies) in Yamaguchi
Prefecture in southern Japan. Okada had received his business education
at Tokyo College of Commerce (now Hitotsubashi University) and had
accumulated managerial expertise through practical business experience as
president of Furukawa Mining and Ube Kosan before and after the War.
Fujitsu, facing a period of unprecedented expansion in its business activities, needed a person who was able to represent a more business-oriented
management approach. This is not to say that Okada ignored technology.
On the contrary, although not an engineer, and having little knowledge of
the technological aspects of communications and computers, he nevertheless embarked on a thorough study of the principles of electronics soon
after his appointment. In fact, this became a famous episode in the company,
and young engineers to whom Okada turned for lectures on electronics and
computer science seem to have received considerable encouragement from
it.

Despite Okada's efforts to master the technological aspects of Fujitsu's
business, it may, in retrospect, be concluded that he was not entirely sure
about the commercial prospects of the computer. Shortly after becoming
head of the company, he reorganized it, introducing a kind of multidivisional structure, with two major divisions—telecommunications and electronics. The electronics division did not have a computer department. It was
set up to deal with the whole range of the electronics business—electronics devices, semiconductors, and electronics machinery, but there was no
specific reference to the computer.[29] Over time it became increasingly
obvious, however, that Okada regarded the computer and its related technology as the company's future mainstay, and the computer business as the
market field with the most promising growth potential. He thus focused all

his energy on turning Fujitsu away from its dependence on NTTPC and into an aggressive high-technology firm. In 1962 an electric-computing department was established within the electronics division. Okada made it clear that he considered this would be the future driving force behind the firm's development, yet he also required the computer department to operate responsibly, with due regard for the company's financial position and profitability. He was not, it seems, willing to tolerate losses. Okada was a business man, not computer enthusiast.

With the firm's future thus hingeing on the development of the computer, Ikeda, Kobayashi, Yamamoto, and the other people belonging to the original computer group, found themselves in an increasingly important position within Fujitsu. Members of this group, who had hitherto been treated as children playing with expensive toys and who had been developing computers without having to worry about the economic implications of their activities, suddenly had to take into consideration, and accept responsibility for, the performance of the entire company. Ikeda described Okada's significance for Fujitsu when he said that, 'In a managerial sense, the real start of Fujitsu's computers was the time when Okada was appointed president.'[30] By the time Okada resigned as President, Fujitsu had become a quite different company from the one he had taken over eleven years previously. First of all, its name was changed from Fuji Tsushinki Seizo Kabushiki Kaisha to Fujitsu, the partial elimination of 'Tsushinki' ('communications equipment') from the new name reflecting the diminishing importance of the telecommunications division. Computers had become the main business activity, accounting for roughly 80 per cent of total sales. The company's image had changed too. Formerly regarded as a conservative supplier of telephones and switching systems to the NTTPC, the whole of Fujitsu came to be known as the 'crazy bunch', a term previously applied only to Ikeda's group.

Fujitsu became Japan's foremost computer manufacturer. In 1990 it consisted of 116 related and 35 affiliated companies in Japan, and 40 related companies abroad. Its share of the domestic market grew to surpass that of IBM Japan and it was able to compete with IBM in foreign markets as well. Fujitsu developed the Facom-230 series, which challenged IBM's 360-series and demonstrated a technological superiority, the 230-60 machine proving to be the most powerful general purpose computer of its day. This had been achieved without any technological help from the foreign companies on which Fujitsu's domestic rivals relied so heavily.[31] This metamorphosis was made possible by a set of specific circumstances within the firm and the surrounding environment.

First, Fuji Denki's decision to spin off its telecommunications department and establish Fujitsu, providing the expanding telecommunications business with the opportunity to pursue its business activities as a specialized company, was very important. Yet it was not really a well-planned decision, nor one based on a perfect understanding of the merits of decentralization. Although some people seem to have realized that heavy electric equipment and switching systems had little in common, and would be better separated into two different companies, there was certainly no clear plan or notion of the consequences. Rather the separation was the result of external factors and the historical environment. However, it was this separation that made Fujitsu's transformation possible. As already indicated, there was a clear difference between Fuji Denki's heavy electrical equipment and telephone businesses. There can be no doubt that there would have been much larger differences between heavy electric, telephones, and computers, and considerable difficulties if they had all been under one roof. The computer group, that 'crazy bunch', would not have had as much freedom had they been part of a large divisional organization. Second, Fujitsu was fortunate in having someone like Toshio Ikeda who has rightly been described as a computer genius. None the less, Ikeda would not have been able to accomplish what he did without people such as Kobayashi and Omi. It was they who realized both the potential of computer technology and of Ikeda's genius, and the need to protect and promote Ikeda even when his eccentric behaviour violated the rules of company conduct. Third, there was Kanjiro Okada, who made the business decision to transform the company into a computer manufacturer on a broad scale. Ikeda and his group were passionate about computers, but it was not a business passion. Okada had the vision to turn computers into the bread-winning business of the company.

Endowed with capable and willing people, the group surrounding Ikeda was given sufficient freedom to pursue its ideas and develop them into real projects. Its members were able to become inventors, developers, and entrepreneurs of a new technology within the existing company. They did not have to leave the firm in order to realize their plans, as for example, did Gene Amdahl. He was forced to leave IBM and establish his own company when he was not given the leeway to realize his plans with IBM.

If the theory of externalization and decentralization as agents of innovation holds true, then why, it might be argued, did Fujitsu not spin off its computer business as an independent company, rather than setting out on the painful route of transforming itself into a computer maker? The answer is that a spin-off, in this case, would not have been possible since the computer business would have been unable to develop or survive, either technologically or economically, without the telecommunications business. It was the revenue flowing in from the booming telecommunications business, which was poured into computer research and development, that enabled Fujitsu to diversify into computers. The telecommunications side, consisting largely of its business with NTTPC, fostered the computer side and provided it with sufficient funds for its costly development activities. Furthermore, computer components were partially developed and produced with the help of technology obtained from telecommunications. Thus the telecommunications business functioned as a benevolent mother to the computer business. As Matsuro Umetsu of Fujitsu has pointed out:

Fujitsu was founded as a company within the Furukawa group, which was known for copper-, silver-mining, transportation and other things, and when I joined Fujitsu in 1954, it was a totally humble company. There was Ikeda's group which was being referred to as 'the crazy bunch'. They were developing computers while generating enormous losses. Needless to say, the company's mainstay was the telecommunications with NTTPC as the dominant customer, and this might not have been a business which could be called 'business' (since NTTPC's procurement was fixed in 5-year expansion plans).[32]

Attention will now be drawn to a company spun off by Fujitsu from one of its most profitable areas of business on technological, managerial, and market-related grounds. This is the case of Fanuc, the leading manufacturer of numeric control devices and robotics.

Fanuc: A Small Giant

Fanuc's history, like that of its parent company Fujitsu, is the story of people who took the initiative in the development and application of a new technology. In the case of Fujitsu, Ikeda was the father of its computer technology. Similarly, Fanuc's history is closely connected with the name of its current president, Seiemon Inaba. Like Ikeda, Inaba had, with a small group of young engineers, been undertaking research on numeric control (NC), a new technology. They too were outside the mainstream of the firm, and they too were given enough freedom and patronage to enable them to pursue their research and development activities without being constrained by short-term financial goals.

The members of Inaba's group proved their competence as researchers and engineers by going on to develop the first numeric control in Japan in 1956, and the first continuous-path NC and the first electro-hydraulic pulse motor in the following year. The electro-hydraulic pulse motor, in particular, was a personal achievement of Inaba. When Okada became president of the company in 1959, the position of Inaba's group began to change. From that time on, and here again there were parallels with Ikeda's group, they were no longer regarded as outsiders who could play around with technology without making any contribution to the company's performance. In 1962, Okada told Inaba, then head of the N section , that 'The basis of all business activity is profit. I would like to see your section in the black.'[33] Being made accountable for corporate profitability, the attitude of Inaba and his group changed from being solely concerned with developing technologically superior NC machines to becoming 'business-oriented'.

Under Inaba's leadership, the first profits in automatic control were made in 1965. While overall turnover was small in comparison with that of the company as a whole—10 billion yen compared with 152.6 billion yen in 1970—margins were much higher. The profit-sales ratio was more than 20 per cent while that of Fujitsu as a whole was only 6.7 per cent.[34] Given these figures, it is understandable that there was considerable opposition when a plan was put forward to make the automatic-control section a separate company. The view was taken that:

The fruits of our long-term investment are finally about to ripen. At this point in time, there is no way to separate the NC business. On the contrary, the profit from the NC business should flow into computers which need any money they can possibly have. Making it a separate company would be absurd.[35]

The president, Okada, was also negative about separation, but in 1970 he was succeeded by Yoshimitsu Kora, and it was Kora who made the decision to establish Fanuc. Kobayashi, Kora's successor, described the situation thus:

President Okada's style was that of centralized control. In contrast to this, Kora favoured a decentralized management style. At the time immediately preceding the separation of the NC section, Fujitsu's business activity was heavily focused on computers. Thus, the chairman and other people involved in the decision, thought that computers and NCs, the technology and market structure of which are both different, under the same management would be detrimental to both businesses. At a time of drastic technological change, it is necessary to have a leader who is able to fully comprehend the technology involved. In the case of NC technology, the only one within the company who understood NC technology was Inaba. Therefore, Kora decided that it would be better to have something like 'Inaba NC Manufacturing Corporation'.[36]

As can be seen from these accounts, the main promoter of the plan to establish a separate company was Kora himself. Indeed, the decision to go ahead was taken on his authority, in the face of strong opposition.

In December 1972, the NC section was established as a separate company named the Fujitsu Fanuc Corporation. The president of the new company was Kora himself, president of Fujitsu. But the person in effective control was Seiemon Inaba, then a board member. From the time of its foundation, Fanuc emphasized its status as an independent company, and the influence exerted by its parent has since been in decline. For example, while Fujitsu initially owned 100 per cent of Fanuc's shares, this proportion has gradually fallen, to the present 34 per cent. As Inaba has observed, 'Fanuc is neither a subsidiary nor an affiliated company of Fujitsu. I dare say, Fujitsu is nothing more than the biggest shareholder and Fanuc is nothing more than a member of the Fujitsu group, that's all.'[37]

Kobayashi explained Fujitsu's attitude to the development of Fanuc as follows:

In order for Fanuc to continue to grow, I think it best to leave things to Inaba. If you have good people and money, you can manage any business, so it is said. However, for a company like Fanuc which is dealing with a completely new technology, this would not be enough. The top leaders have to be experts in the technology involved, as well as the conditions of the market in which the firm is operating. Thus, if the leader isn't quite a kind of superman, this would not be possible. Therefore, it is best to put such a person in charge and leave things to him. And Inaba is indeed the appropriate person for the job. From his days at Fujitsu onward, he has been responsible for the technology development, manufacturing, as well as for sales.[38]

And regarding Fujitsu's relationship with Fanuc, Kobayashi stated that:

It is desirable for Fujitsu to limit its role to that of a supplier of venture capital which has been invested in the venture business Fanuc. There have been voices saying Fujitsu shouldn't lower its shareholding below 50 per cent and retain its status as a parent company, but I think this is not necessary and would not go beyond sheer formalism anyway.[39]

Ever since it was established, Fanuc's management has been able to enjoy wide-ranging independence in its decision-making activities. The firm has developed into the world leader of NC technology and robotics. Its profit–sales ratio for the fiscal year 1990 was a phenomenal 37.1 per cent, compared with Fujitsu's 6.0 per cent.[40] Such growth has been based on the company's technological leadership, but Fanuc has been able to make full use of, and develop further this technology because it has been free to operate unfettered by the constraints of a multidivisional concern. Inaba calls his company a 'Small Giant', and declares that his managerial principle was to increase sales without increasing the work-force.[41]

Conclusion

In this chapter, we have focused on the spinning off of divisions within large business enterprises to form smaller, more innovative, less bureaucratic, independent companies. The corporate history of Fuji Denki, Fujitsu, and Fanuc serves as an excellent case-study of the process. Although this chapter set out to discuss organizational strategy, it is clear that the most important driving force behind Fujitsu's transformation from a conservative communications equipment manufacturer to its present status as an all-round information technology company was its dedicated human resources, people such as Ikeda, Kobayashi, Omi, and Okada. Fanuc's emergence as the 'IBM of the numeric-control industry' was also inspired by the strong leadership of Inaba. At the earliest stage of the computer development within Fujitsu, a number of capable engineers around Ikeda formed an informal computer group which shared a common interest in automatic computing devices. Subsequently, this group started research into computer technology and developed the first relay computer in Japan, the Facom 100. Clearly their research and development activity was not part of the firm's strategy, nor had it been ordered from above. At the very beginning, Fujitsu's top management might not even have been aware of the group's existence. However, the group managed to obtain informal permission to continue its work from the president, Ko, although its members continued to be regarded as outsiders within Fujitsu until Okada became president. Ikeda and his group can be described as entrepreneurs within the enterprise. The same can be said of Inaba and his NC research-and-development group. They too staged a 'revolution from below', pursuing their activities without recognition from, and sometime even without the consent of, the management. Why and how were these informal groups able to survive within the existing organization? It is now necessary to return to the question of organization.

When Fuji Denki separated off its communications business as a new company, those involved in the decision presumably did not realize its implications for the relationship between future innovative entrepreneurship and organizational size. Rather, the decision was part of a historical process. The crucial factor, however, was the size of organization. When Fuji Denki spun off its telecommunications division as Fujitsu, it had 4,000 employees while Fujitsu had 700. In 1945, at the end of World War II, Fujitsu employed 4,119 in four factories, while Fuji Denki employed 15,200 in six factories. Although both companies had to trim their work-forces in the chaotic period after the War, Fujitsu was sufficiently small and flexible to allow enthusiastic engineers to commit themselves to innovations. In other words, Fujitsu was more open towards new technology and less constrained by vested interests. As already mentioned, Fujitsu was able to keep its important human assets by changing, if necessary, its normal rules of work for them. Kobayashi changed the daily-rate wage to a fixed monthly one for Ikeda, whose attendance at his work-place was irregular. In addition, the proximity of the corporate office and the factory site was important. Both Fujitsu's corporate office and its operational departments were at its Kawasaki factory site. This meant that a chief executive like Okada was not a remote figure, but was conscious of everything that was going on: when necessary, he talked to Ikeda and Inaba directly. In order to pursue and adopt innovations, firms should be small and flexible enough to give their 'champions' freedom, even if this sometimes requires them to change their rules and regulations. This was also the story of Fanuc. Learning from practical experience, Fujitsu executives realized that the smaller an organization is, the more innovatively it behaves. Kora, then president of Fujitsu, delegated authority to Inaba to develop his beloved NC technology in a separated company, Fanuc. Furthermore, by reducing its ownership share, Fujitsu has given Fanuc almost total autonomy.

At the same time, however, Ikeda's computer group and Inaba's NC enthusiasts were not totally on their own. Members of these two groups had the necessary informal support and promotion of their seniors. Omi, Kora, and Kobayashi were protectors, buffers, and mentors of the creative young-sters. For innovative behaviour to succeed, both dedicated young people, so-called 'champions' and protectors, so-called 'executive champions' are necessary.[42] The expression 'the captain bites his tongue until it bleeds',[43] describes how executive champions like Omi, Kobayashi, and Kora felt when they delegated the authority to develop new products. However, to establish these two groups as business units, it was also necessary to have someone like Okada who could give them a feeling of responsibility as well as freedom. Both Ikeda and Inaba recalled that Okada had changed them from being mere technology fanatics into business-oriented leaders. Fujitsu was fortunate to have had all these talented people within the firm at the same time.

Whether Fujitsu would have become a computer company if it had remained a division of Fuji Denki is no more than a hypothetical question. Similarly, it is impossible to determine whether Fanuc would have been able to reach its current position as world leader in the NC and robotics markets had it continued to exist within the computer maker Fujitsu. However, it can be said that separating off as a smaller independent company that part of a firm which engages in a technology and market which is different from the core business, appears to be a good way of enhancing innovative behaviour and technological change. In the case of industries characterized by rapid changes in technological innovations and consumer needs, in particular, the externalization strategy which has been examined in this chapter seems to be more effective than the traditional multidivisional strategy. The current discussion about corporate entrepreneurship focuses on this point. As Burgelman and Sayles state:

Large, established corporations and new, maturing firms alike are confronted with the problem of maintaining their growth, if not their existence, by exploiting to the fullest the unique resource combinations they have assembled. Increasingly, there is an awareness that internal entrepreneurs are necessary for firms to achieve this.[44]

Regarding the growing significance of so-called 'intrapreneuring', they point out that:

It seems to us that the development currently crystallizing in American business heralds an epoch-making change. We believe the change may well be of the same magnitude as the one that occurred during the first quarter of the 20th Century, which led to the organizational innovation represented by the 'divisionalized firm' as brilliantly documented in Alfred D. Chandler's landmark study on strategy and structure.[45]

Interestingly, while this development is a current one in the United States and Europe, Japanese companies have been experiencing and practising intracorporate entrepreneurship for some hundred years.

NOTES

1. On this pattern of corporate growth see Alfred D. Chandler, Jr. *Scale and Scope: The Dynamism of Industrial Capitalism* (Cambridge, Mass., 1990).
2. See Oliver Williamson, *Market and Hierarchies* (New York, 1975).
3. On the bureaucratic decline of the large multidivisional corporations see Gifford Pinciot, *Intrapreneuring* (New York, 1985) and Robert Burgelman and Leonard Sayles, *Inside Corporate Innovation* (New York, 1986). Even Chandler, by pointing out the separation of top management in the corporate office from the middle management in the operating units, has mentioned the decline of the corporate dynamism of the large companies (see Chandler, *Scale and Scope*, 621).
4. See Pinciot, *Intrapreneuring*; Burgelman and Sayles, *Inside Corporate Innovation*; and Richard Florida and Martin Kenney, *The Breakthrough Illusion* (New York, 1990).
5. On Toyota and Nissan see Michael Cusumano, *The Japanese Automobile Industry* (Cambridge, Mass., 1983) and Udagawa Masaru, *Shinko zaibatsu* (New Industrial Zaibatsu) (Tokyo, 1984).
6. Ronald Coase, 'The Nature of the Firm', in Oliver Williamson and Sidney Winter (eds.), *The Nature of the Firm: Origins, Evolution, and Development* (Oxford, 1993).
7. Nihon Keieishi Kenkyusho (ed.), *Sogyo hyakunenshi: Furukawa Kogyo* (A 100-year History of Furukawa Mining) (Tokyo, 1976), 207–52.
8. Toru Takenaka, *Siemens to meiji nihon* (Siemens and Meiji Japan) (Tokyo, 1991) and Fuji Denki Seizo Kabushiki Kaisha Shashi Henshu Iinkai (ed.), *Fuji Denki Seizo Kabushiki Kaisha Shashi* (History of Fuji Denki) (Tokyo, 1957), 2.
9. Fuji Tsushin Kabushiki Kaisha Shashi Henshu Iinkai (ed.), *Fujitsu Shashi I* (History of Fujitsu I), (Tokyo, 1964), 4.
10. Hisashi Watanabe, 'Fuji Denki seiritsu katei no sironteki bunseki' (A Hypothetical Analysis of the Establishment Process of Fuji Denki), in Moriaki Tsuchiya and Hidemasa Morikawa (eds.), *Kigyosha katsudo no siteki kenkyu* (Tokyo, 1981).
11. Ibid. 12.
12. Ibid. 14.
13. Alfred D. Chandler, Jr. *Strategy and Structure*, (Cambridge, Mass., 1962), 83–96.
14. *Fujitsu Shashi I* (Tokyo, 1964), 23–35. Tokyo Denki also established Tokyo Denki Musen (Tokyo Electric Wireless Corporation) in October 1935.
15. Kasai Masanao has pointed out the importance of the pressure from the military to spin off the telecommunications department at Fuji Denki. See Kasai, 'Senjika niopkeru tsushinki seizo kogyo no tenkai katei' (A Development

Process of the Telecommunication Industry in the War Period), *Fuji Daigaku Kiyo*, 24/2 (1992).
16. *Fujitsu Shashi I*, 180.
17. Fujitsu Kabushiki Kaisha, *Yukashoken Hokoku-Sho* (Annual Report) (1990).
18. *Fujitsu Shashi I*, 54.
19. Gene Amdahl, 'Dr. Ikeda, the International Man,' in Fujitsu Kabushiki Kaisha (ed.), *Ikeda Kinenronbunshu* (Tokyo, 1978), 229.
20. Hiroshi Matsuo, *Daitanna Chosen* (Tokyo, 1978), 87–8.
21. Taiyu Kobayashi, *Tomokaku Yatte Miro* (Tokyo, Toyo Keizai Simposha, 1983), 41–4.
22. Hanzo Omi, 'Ikeda Toshio no Omoide,' in Fujitsu Kabushiki Kaisha (ed.), *Ikeda kinen ronbun shu* (Tokyo, 1978), 224–5.
23. 'Ikeda san no kotoba', in Fujitsu Kabushiki Kaisha (ed.), *Ikeda kinen ronbun shu* (Tokyo, 1978), 202.
24. Kobayashi, *Tomokaku Yatte Miro*, 42.
25. 'Ikeda san no kotoba', 202–3.
26. Ibid. 202.
27. Matsuo, *Daitanna Chosen*, 112–15.
28. Kobayashi, *Tomokaku Yatte Miro*, 44.
29. *Fujitsu Shashi* I, 162–3.
30. 'Ikeda san no kotoba', 208.
31. Fujitsu later took a capital stake in Amdahl Corporation, which was established by a former IBM researcher Gene Amdahl, and started a technological alliance with it.
32. Matsuo, *Daitanna Chosen*, 201.
33. Kano Akirhiro, *Fanuc-Joshiki Hazure Keieiho* (Tokyo, 1983), 59.
34. Ibid. 77 and Fuji Tsushin Kabushiki Kaisha Shashi Henshu Iinkai (ed.), *Fujitsu Shashi III* (History of Fujitsu III) (Tokyo, 1986), 44.
35. Kobayashi, *Tomokaku Yatte Miro*, 64–5 and Kano, *Fanuc*, 78.
36. Kano, *Fanuc*, 77.
37. Ibid. 79.
38. Ibid. 79.
39. Ibid. 80.
40. Fujitsu, *Yukashoken Hokoku-Sho*, 25 and Fanuc, *Yukashoken Hokoku-Sho* (Annual Report) (1990), 29.
41. Ken Mukui, *Kiiroi robotto: Fujitsu Fanuc no Kiseki* (Yellow Robot: The Miracle of Fujitsu Fanuc), (Tokyo, 1982), 75.
42. Tom Peters and Robert Waterman, *In Search of Excellence* (New York, 1981), 224–5.
43. Ibid. 226. This naval expression refers to the reaction of a captain when he allows a junior officer to bring a ship alongside the dock for the first time.
44. Burgelman and Sayles, *Inside Corporate Innovation*, 187–8.
45. Ibid. 191.

13. ICL: *From National Champion to Fujitsu's Little Helper*

MARTIN CAMPBELL-KELLY

In November 1990 ICL, Britain's national-champion computer maker became a subsidiary of Fujitsu, the world's second largest computer manufacturer. Thus ICL closed the last chapter in an eighty-year history as an independent UK supplier of information technology products.

The Pre-World War II Background

In order to understand the history of ICL, and its inheritance of organizational capabilities, it is necessary to appreciate that both ICL and IBM have a common ancestor, and that for over forty years they had something of a love-hate relationship.[1] Both IBM and ICL have their origins in the punched-card tabulating machine invented by Herman Hollerith in the 1880s. In 1896 Hollerith incorporated a small firm in New York, the Tabulating Machine Company, to market a range of punched-card office machines. In 1924 this company was renamed International Business Machines.[2] In 1907 a London-based syndicate formed the British Tabulating Machine Company (BTM) to exploit the Hollerith machines in the UK. The arrangement between the British company and Hollerith was formalized in an agreement dated 1908, which gave BTM the exclusive right to work the Hollerith patents in Britain and the Empire in exchange for a payment of 25 per cent of its revenues to the American company. This was an astonishingly high royalty rate, which did much to inhibit BTM's growth potential.

In the United States a rival punched-card machine company, Powers Accounting Machines, was formed in 1911 by the entrepreneur James Powers. A subsidiary of this company, the Accounting and Tabulating Machine Company of Great Britain Ltd., was formed in Britain in 1915. The British subsidiary was acquired by the Prudential Assurance Company in 1919, by which it secured the British and Empire rights to the Powers machines; and in 1923 a French subsidiary Société Anonyme des Machines à Statistiques (SAMAS) was formed. Thus the rivalry between Hollerith and Powers in America now spread to the British territories and to Continental Europe. The British Powers operation was later renamed Powers-Samas.

Although the Powers organization in the United States was acquired by the office-machine giant Remington Rand in 1927, the Powers machines were not nearly so successful in America as those of IBM; it was estimated that in the 1930s the American market was split 90:10 in favour of IBM. By contrast, in the British territories, the market split was approximately 50:50. Moreover, BTM was not only less successful than IBM in competing with its major competitor, it was much less successful in absolute terms. Although IBM and BTM had sales territories roughly in the proportion 2:1, throughout the inter-war period BTM's revenues were approximately one-twentieth of those of IBM. BTM attributed its slow growth to the onerous royalty rate and the weak development of the market, while IBM's President, Thomas J. Watson, Sr., blamed BTM's weak management and its poorly developed selling organization. The truth lay somewhere between these two views.

During the 1920s and 1930s, both BTM and Powers-Samas ceased to be solely importers of punched-card machines from America, and developed their own R&D and manufacturing operations. By the end of the 1930s, Powers-Samas had about 2,500 employees, and BTM (which relied more heavily on imports) had about 1,200. With the onset of World War II there was a hiatus in punched-card machine development, as the British, American, and European punched-card machine companies made over their R&D facilities to war-related research. The manufacturers also devoted a high proportion of their manufacturing capacity to producing military equipment.

Electronics and Computers (1945–59)

There were essentially two types of entrant into the British computer industry in the early 1950s: established electronics firms seeking new markets (Ferranti, English Electric, Elliott Brothers, EMI, etc.); and office-machine companies switching from mechanical to electronic technologies (BTM and Powers-Samas).[3] Unlike the United States, where there were several entrepreneurial start-ups, the only British maverick was Leo Computers Limited, a subsidiary of the J. Lyons catering company.

Emerging from World War II, the punched-card machine companies faced two formidable R&D challenges: the emergence of electronics and the invention of the stored-program computer. In the United States, IBM took an approach to electronics that was evolutionary rather than revolutionary. Thus its first electronic products were enhancements to some of the standard punched-card machines first marketed in the early 1930s.[4] These machines incorporated electronics to achieve an order of magnitude increase in calculating speed; but functionally the machines were no different from their electro-mechanical predecessors. Taking their lead from

IBM, BTM and Powers-Samas began to develop electronic multipliers and calculators that reached the market in the early 1950s. These all sold in relatively high volumes—that is to say hundreds. By contrast, the market for computers was perceived as being a small one—selling 'mathematical instruments' to a largely technical market. Both American and European punched-card machine manufacturers, long used to selling or renting a high volume of relatively low-cost machines, did not see electronic computers as being an appropriate business into which to make a major entry.

The year 1949 was a watershed for the British data-processing industry. In that year BTM and IBM decided by mutual consent to break their long-standing agreement, and go into open competition world-wide. So far as BTM was concerned the end of the agreement would mean the end of paying royalties; this would enable it to at least treble its R&D spend and develop products it believed would match any that could be made by IBM. In the following year, 1950, Powers-Samas terminated its agreement with Remington Rand. From this point onwards, the British data-processing market became very much more competitive.

Although the British punched-card machine companies had been reluctant to embark upon computer manufacture, this was not the case with the British electronics manufacturers. The computer was a very natural product for these companies, who had manufacturing and marketing capabilities that were ideally adapted to the delivery of high-cost, low-volume, electronic capital goods. For them the computer was a product that was entirely at one with their existing lines such as power-generation equipment, radar sets, radio transmitters, etc.

The early structure of the computer industry in the UK was significantly shaped by the National Research Development Corporation (NRDC) which had been formed by the Labour government in 1949 to foster the exploitation and patenting of British inventions.[5] Under its energetic managing director Lord Halsbury, the NRDC immediately targeted computers as being *the* industry in which Britain should secure a strategic position. Halsbury had recognized very early (long before IBM) that the computer market would eventually focus on electronic data-processing (EDP) computers, rather than machines for science and engineering. He also saw that no British manufacturer had the range of organizational capabilities to compete with IBM, viz. electronics and electro-mechanical design and manufacturing, marketing, and applications know-how. In 1949, he tried to foster a joint development between one of the punched-card machine manufacturers and one of the electronics manufacturers, who between them would have the necessary portfolio of capabilities to develop and market an EDP computer. However, none of the firms accepted Halsbury's judgement (which was more visionary than rational) at this time, so that BTM and Powers-Samas continued to compete in traditional accounting machine products, while the electronics manufacturers developed scientific computers.

By 1955, IBM had developed into a serious competitor for the British computer companies, both at home and in their overseas markets. But the competition was not in computers, as some commentators had feared, but in the traditional punched-card machines which still accounted for most of IBM's turnover. It was to meet this competition from IBM that in 1958 BTM and Powers-Samas decided to merge to form International Computers and Tabulators Ltd (ICT). The company had a total of 19,000 employees, making it comfortably Europe's largest manufacturer of data-processing machinery.

Establishing the EDP Mainframe (1959–65)

In terms of the social shaping of technology, around 1960 the computer was redefined as a data-processing mainframe. The key actors in this redefinition were IBM and its users. Once the demand for EDP computers was established, IBM soon dominated the market by producing computers that were acceptable, in terms of reliability and software, to its existing customer base of punched-card machine users. IBM's easy domination of the US industry caused a shake-out of EDP computer manufacturers in the second half of the 1950s, that left just IBM and a handful of competitors, the so-called 'seven dwarves'—Univac, Burroughs, NCR, Honeywell, RCA, GE, and CDC. In terms of scale, ICT was in the same league as the dwarves.[6]

The event that completely transformed the outlook for computers—for IBM as much as for its competitors—and which precipitated the collapse of the punched-card machine market, was the announcement of the IBM 1401 computer in October 1959. The 1401 was a second-generation transistorized machine that captured the American EDP-computer market to an extent that took IBM by surprise, and exceeded all forecasts: a thousand orders were taken in the first few weeks following the announcement, and the machine went on to sell a total far in excess of ten thousand installations. The success of the 1401 has often been attributed to the printer that accompanied it; printing at 600 lines per minute, it enabled a single 1401 to replace four conventional accounting machines.

The huge sales of the IBM 1401 transformed the computer industry from one which had been based on the sale of high-cost, electronic capital goods in low volume, to one selling relatively low-cost machines in a much higher volume. The selling organizations of the traditional business machine manufacturers were well adapted to this new market environment, whereas the electrical engineers and control manufacturers who had prospered in the

1950s now found themselves in a market in which it was much more difficult to compete. Thus each of the electronics and control firms was faced
with a choice: either to stay in the computer business for the long-haul and
accept short-term losses; or to withdraw from the computer business
altogether. One by one, the companies made their decisions, so that by the
end of the first merger wave of 1960–3 there were just three British
computer manufacturers: ICT, English Electric-Leo-Marconi, and Elliott-
Automation.

The result of this merger activity was to leave ICT, in particular, with an
ill-assorted range of incompatible machines which included those developed by itself and in collaboration with GEC, computers acquired from
EMI and Ferranti, as well as machines being made under licence or
imported from Univac and RCA in the United States. The software and
hardware compatibility between these machines was negligible. In autumn
1963, ICT's product planners began to try to rationalize the product line
and develop a coherent plan for the future. For the longer term, it was
intended that all of ICT's medium to large EDP computers would be made
from a single 'project set' which would have compatible software and
peripherals throughout the range. It was planned that such a range of computers should be available by 1968. English Electric, following the acquisition of Leo Computers in April 1963, had a much more manageable
portfolio of machines, but was also planning a new range.

The main reason that ICT and English Electric—as well as all the American mainframe manufacturers—were planning compatible families of computers at this time was the looming 'software crisis'.[7] This crisis was that, by
the early 1960s, software was proving more expensive for computer manufacturers to develop than hardware. Yet whenever a new computer model
was introduced, most of the existing investment in software had to be
thrown away. Computer users were also facing a software crisis in that when
they replaced their first-generation computers with new transistorized,
second-generation models, all the software had to be rewritten. This sometimes cost more than the new computer, and often resulted in horrendous
organizational disruption during the changeover from one machine generation to the next.

On 7 April 1964, IBM astounded the computer industry and computer
users by announcing System/360, a compatible family of third-generation
computers, intended to replace most of its current computers.[8] The scale of
the announcement was entirely unprecedented, and all the evidence is that
it took the rest of the industry largely by surprise. System/360 was designed
to be software compatible throughout the range, from the smallest machine
up to the largest. For IBM, this meant that it would have to write only one
set of software for the complete product line. And for IBM's customers, it
meant that their investment in software would be protected when they
upgraded to a larger machine. It also meant that once customers had bought

IBM they were 'locked in', as they could only move to another manufacturer if they were prepared to scrap their software. Of course, IBM was locked in too—it would be forced to maintain software compatibility with System/360 for the next thirty and more years.

For ICT and English Electric, as well as the US mainframe makers, the effect of the System/360 announcement in April 1964 was to oblige them to introduce new computer ranges as rapidly as possible, compressing into months development programmes that had been intended to take years. For all the companies, a key choice was whether to make a range that was IBM-compatible or develop a proprietary architecture. The former strategy offered the possibility of capturing some of IBM's established customer base, because it would be easy for users to transfer their existing software to an IBM-compatible range. The second strategy offered a higher potential reward, but with significantly higher development costs and marketing risk.

ICT, for whom IBM compatibility was a cultural anathema, decided to develop an existing computer into a range of computers to be known as the '1900 series', announced in September 1964. The first production model was delivered in January 1965—only four months after the 1900 series announcement. The short lead-time of the 1900 series proved to be a major competitive advantage over System/360, whose first machines were not delivered in Europe until spring 1966. The market acceptance of the 1900 series exceeded all expectations and orders poured in, both from Britain and around the world, making it ICT's (and ICL's) most successful ever product. English Electric did not have ICT's strong emotional commitment to being non-IBM compatible, and made use of a long-standing technology sharing agreement with RCA to manufacture RCA's IBM-compatible Spectra 70 range under licence. The full range of four machines was announced as System 4 in September 1965, with deliveries promised for early 1967.

The Formation of ICL (1964–8)

The decisions of ICT and English Electric to embark independently on their own third-generation computer ranges took place against a backdrop of growing political concern at the increasing dominance of the high-technology industries by American multinational companies. This mood was heavily influenced by media anxiety and books such as J.-J. Servan-Schreiber's *The American Challenge*, which was a best-seller in both France and England.[9] When, in October 1964, Harold Wilson's Labour government came into power, one of its first acts was to establish a Ministry of Technology, envisaged as an organization to 'guide and stimulate a major national effort to bring advanced technology and new processes into British industry'. Wilson placed the British computer industry at the very top of Mintech's agenda:

My frequent meetings with leading scientists, technologists and industrialists in the last two or three years of Opposition had convinced me that, if action was not taken quickly, the British computer industry would rapidly cease to exist, facing as was the case in other European countries, the most formidable competition from the American giants. When, on the evening we took office, I asked Frank Cousins to become the first Minister of Technology, I told him that he had, in my view, about a month to save the British computer industry and that this must be his first priority.[10]

In November 1964, the newly appointed Minister of Technology made the first of several unsuccessful attempts over the next three years to get ICT and English Electric to merge their computer interests. By spring 1967, Mintech had formed the view that the main impediment to an ICT-English Electric Computers merger was the incompatibility of their current ranges. The ministry therefore offered *inter alia* a non-repayable grant in the region of £25 million towards the development of a new range of computers for delivery in the early 1970s if the companies merged their EDP computer interests. Both recognized that, individually or together, they would not have the resources to compete with IBM's 'Future System', which was expected to be announced in the early 1970s, and that government R&D support would be necessary in order to remain in the EDP-computer business.

If ICT and English Electric had moved decisively an early merger would no doubt have been achieved; but the terms of the merger were not agreed until early 1968, and the delay—each hoping for marginally better terms— was to prove disastrous. During the autumn of 1967, the UK economic climate had worsened dramatically, culminating in the devaluation of the pound in November 1967 and the public expenditure cuts of January 1968. A government subvention of the order of £25 million was now seen as politically unacceptable, and the Treasury was thinking in terms of about half that amount—in fact, £13.5 million was eventually provided. But the merger plans were now so far advanced that there was no going back. In March 1968 the Minister of Technology presented a White Paper on the computer merger to the House of Commons; and ICL was vested on 9 July 1968. ICL was the largest non-American computer manufacturer, with a work-force of 34,000.

Government Support for the New Range (1969–77)

For ICL the scene for the 1970s was set by a mission to develop a new range of computers, but with R&D resources which were not really sufficient. The new range was to prove a financial albatross for ICL throughout the 1970s.

Unfortunately there was an emotional commitment, from both ICL and the government, that as a national champion, ICL had to produce a world-class range of mainframe computers. ICL was effectively caught in a treadmill of its own making, which was to spin faster and faster as it tried to keep pace with the ever-shortening life-cycles of semiconductor technology. And at the same time that ICL was struggling with the new range, commodification of mainframes was eroding profit margins.

ICL's New Range Planning Organization was formed in January 1969, and in early 1970 work was started on detailed planning of the new computer family. Because of the R&D funding problems, the original grand plan for a range of six mainframe processors was cut down to four in a matter of months. Even so, funding remained a problem. ICL's total R&D spend, which was projected at about £90 million for the five-year period 1968–73, had not only to support the new range development, but also the continued enhancement of the current ranges. These difficulties were compounded by the first world-wide recession in the computer industry in 1970–1.

Unfortunately for ICL, the Heath Government had recently come into office pledged to a disengagement from the direct intervention in industry that had been so much a feature of the out-going Labour administration. This was the famous 'lame duck' policy.[11] Consequently, when in early 1971 ICL faced an impending financial crisis, it had to deal with it unaided: during the first half of 1971 over 3,000 workers were laid off, and R&D spending had to be reined back. Gradually, however, the political climate began to change in ICL's favour—particularly following the government rescue of Rolls-Royce in February 1971. In early 1971, a parliamentary inquiry into the British computer industry was conducted by the Select Committee on Science and Technology, and the appearance of its report *The Prospects for the United Kingdom Computer Industry in the 1970s* provided a firm basis for government action. The report was sharply critical of the government's role, and called for a much higher level of government support for the computer industry. It was estimated that the government's total support for computer R&D had been only £30 million during 1969–73: a sum that was believed to be only one-fifth of that spent for the same purpose in France, and a tenth of that spent in Germany. It was recommended that the government should increase its funding of computer-related R&D to the extent of 'not less than £50 million per annum'.[12]

In 1973, the government finally relented and made ICL a loan (not a grant) of £40 million to help sustain the momentum of the new-range R&D for the period 1972–7. But a pre-condition of the loan was that ICL should change its top management: a new American managing director was brought in from Univac, and the former managing director of IBM (UK) was appointed chairman. Under their reign, ICL was to experience its best ever years of profitability. With ICL's long-term R&D funding finally assured, the new range took centre place in ICL's five-year strategic plan for 1973–8. In October 1974, some two years later than originally anticipated, the new range was finally announced as the '2900 series'. The full range of machines, however, would not be available for another four years due to development delays.

There is no question that if ICL had been wholly dependent on its mainframes in the 1970s, it could not have sustained a viable market share. Fortunately, in 1973 it had made a very effective entry into the small business systems market, and in 1976 it acquired the European customer base of Singer Business Machines and access to its successful small business computers. These products, which sold particularly well in Continental Europe, enabled ICL to achieve an annual growth rate of well over 20 per cent during 1973–8; this was the fastest rate of growth of any of the mainframe manufacturers, excepting only Fujitsu in Japan. However, one of the main objectives of this rapid revenue growth was to ensure the survival of ICL's mainframe R&D when the £40 million government loan terminated in 1977. During the five-year period 1974–8, ICL's annual R&D spend increased from about £22 million to £36 million, although as a proportion of revenues R&D fell from 10.8 per cent to a very respectable 7.1 per cent.

The Impact of Japanese Competition: Commodification of the EDP Mainframe Computer

Although the new ICL range was strongly differentiated from IBM-compatible mainframes, this did not protect it from the general erosion of profits that commodification produced.

While IBM had been exposed to commodity peripheral manufacturers ever since the launch of System/360 in 1964, it had been little affected by this competition by virtue of its superb organizational capability in electromechanical manufacturing, and its advantages of scale. However, IBM had never had such a strong capability in electronics manufacture, so that it was much more vulnerable to plug-compatible mainframes (PCMs), which could replace the very heart of an IBM installation. Up to 1970, the main barrier to entry to PCM manufacture, had been software; this barrier fell with IBM's decision to 'unbundle' its software in 1969. A second barrier, or risk factor, for the PCM manufacturer had been the market uncertainty of IBM's long-term mainframe strategy. However, when in 1970 IBM announced System/370, a compatible successor to its current mainframes, that risk was eliminated. The Amdahl Computer Corporation was the first company to enter the PCM market. In order to secure an electronics advantage over IBM, in 1972 Amdahl made a licensing agreement with Fujitsu to use its semiconductor technology. In 1975 the first Amdahl mainframes were delivered with a price/performance of at least twice that of IBM.

The success of the Amdahl PCM strategy was a 'turning-point for the Japanese computer industry'.[13] The Amdahl-Fujitsu connection effected the technology transfer of the IBM computer architecture to Japan. Hitachi soon followed Fujitsu in IBM-compatible mainframe manufacture, and both companies licensed their technology to European and US manufacturers. During 1977 and 1978, the plug-compatible processor industry gathered momentum, with several new entrants. Now that its entire System/370 range was under attack, IBM responded with price cuts of up to 30 per cent. The other mainframe suppliers were soon forced to follow suit.

In 1978 the central issue facing ICL, as in the past, was in selecting an appropriate level of R&D expenditure and generating sufficient business to sustain it. The R&D programmes underway in 1978 indicated swiftly rising costs, from £36 million a year in 1978 increasing to £89 million in 1983. During the previous five-year period, 1973–7, total R&D expenditure had been £123 million, and this was now set to more than double to £266 million in the next five-year period, 1978–82. ICL was now faced with a choice as to the long-term future of R&D: either it could be maintained at the projected levels, which implied a further period of sustained growth of over 20 per cent a year; or it could aim for a lower, more realistic growth rate, rein back R&D, and take the first steps towards becoming a niche supplier. In May 1978 the board opted for the former course—a high-growth, high-risk strategy. The risks were that if ICL entered a period of economic turbulence, or if price/performance norms fell rapidly, then its forward plans would be thrown into disarray and threaten the existence of the business. This is exactly what happened.[14]

In January 1979, IBM responded to the increasing competition of Japanese PCM manufacturers by replacing its System/370 mid-range processors with the 4300 series. The new machines offered an unprecedented fourfold price/performance improvement over the machines they replaced. For all the mainframe manufacturers the 4300 launch created the competitive environment of 1979. In effect, they were caught in the cross-fire between IBM and the Japanese, and during the early months of 1979 they all cut prices and announced new models. By the summer of 1979 it was clear that ICL's five-year R&D programme was seriously endangered, and it seemed likely that it would eventually have to call on the government for financial support. Unfortunately for ICL, in May 1979 Margaret Thatcher's Conservative government had been elected into power. Like the Heath Government of 1971, the Thatcher administration was pledged to a disengagement from direct involvement in industry. Early in 1980 the UK fell into a major economic recession, and by January 1981, ICL was forecasting a £50 million loss for the year and the future existence of the company was very much in doubt. It was at this point that it decided to approach the government for aid.

At this time, ICL's major problem was the widening gap between its earnings and the R&D expenditure necessary to keep its products competitive. While previous governments had provided direct R&D support, this was not the route chosen by the new Thatcher administration. Rather, the view was taken that ICL's shareholders and bankers should save it; but ICL's position was now so precarious that this was unthinkable. Finally, in March 1981, in a meeting between ICL, its bankers, and the government, a highly imaginative solution to ICL's cash problems was put forward in the form of a loan guarantee. Provided ICL's bankers would extend it the £200 million it needed, the government would guarantee the loans against ICL's defaulting. In fact a total of £270 million was provided, of which the government guaranteed £200 million for a period of two years.

ICL and the Fujitsu Connection (1981–90)

In reaching the decision to provide the loan guarantees, the government had concluded—on the advice of management consultants—that ICL's problems were in large part managerial. The loan guarantees were therefore made conditional upon ICL accepting a new management team. Within a few days of taking office in May 1981, the new management began to restructure ICL's affairs, both operationally and in terms of products. The operational measures included plant closures and lay-offs. The work-force cutting continued throughout the ICL recovery, the total headcount reducing from a peak of 33,000 in 1980 to about 20,000 by 1985. The key to ICL's survival, however, lay in its products—and these in turn depended on getting the balance of R&D right. Within six months, ICL's product strategy had been radically overhauled.

A review of ICL's mainframe products, the unprofitable core of its business, disclosed some alarming trends. The most important of these was that the 2900 series accounted for a disproportionate fraction of ICL's R&D spend: mainframes which produced about one-third of turnover, consumed two-thirds of overall R&D costs. This R&D burden was inhibiting ICL's participation in the market for small and micro computers and office systems. The short-term strategy for the 2900 series was therefore aimed at reducing the ongoing R&D commitment—particularly in software—and to divert resources to small systems. In the longer term, however, it was chip technology that was at the heart of the problems of the 2900 series. Both the new-range architecture and software were well proven and competitive, but ICL lacked the semiconductor technology to manufacture systems price-competitive with IBM. In October 1981 ICL—assisted by some behind the scenes activity from the government—succeeded in obtaining an agreement with Fujitsu to obtain access to its semiconductor technology, much as Amdahl had done in the early 1970s.

The ICL-Fujitsu agreement fell into three broad areas corresponding to three main product lines: a small mainframe processor, a medium-sized processor, and Fujitsu's large IBM-compatible mainframe, to be marketed as the Atlas 10. All the architecture, design, and software of the new-range processors would remain in Britain, with Fujitsu supplying semiconductor design tools and components, and some limited manufacturing facilities. A particular attraction of the new range's advanced architecture was that the entire mainframe range was now based on just two processors—a major advantage over ICL's competitors. The third part of the ICL-Fujitsu agreement was for ICL to market Fujitsu's largest IBM-compatible mainframes as the ICL Atlas 10 series. This agreement did not really harmonize with ICL's mainframe range, but it was part of the give-and-take between Fujitsu and ICL. In fact, the Atlas 10 was a marketing failure and ICL withdrew in 1984. This effectively closed any future likelihood of ICL becoming IBM-compatible.

The new processors based on Fujitsu semiconductor technology were launched in August 1985 as the first two members of Series 39—the successor to the 2900 series. The ICL-Fujitsu agreement was perceived as an exceptionally innovative solution to ICL's mainframe challenge, and has since come to be regarded as a classic example of technology transfer in the 1980s. There have also been obvious parallels drawn with the relationship between ICL-Fujitsu and Rover-Honda.[15] The rationalization of mainframe R&D enabled resources to be diverted to the booming market for office systems and small business computers. Although rationalization had effectively doubled the resources available for new products, it was still necessary, both for reasons of development cost and lead-times, to make collaborative or licensing agreements to fill out the product range. During 1981–3 licensing deals were made with several companies including: the Three Rivers Computer Corporation for engineering work-stations; Mitel for digital exchanges; Logica and Nexos for word-processing technology; Rair for the ICL Personal Computer; and Sinclair and Psion for the innovative One-Per-Desk computer-phone. Advantage was also taken of the emerging OSI international open networking standards.

The STC and Fujitsu Take-overs

In 1980, ICL and all the other mainframe manufacturers had been faced with two major challenges, one short-term and one medium-term. The short-term problem was to come to terms with the lower profit margins caused by the price-war between IBM and the Japanese plug-compatible mainframe manufacturers. The medium-term problem was to respond to the anticipated convergence of computers and communications: this convergence implied not merely developing networked computer systems, but also achieving strategic alliances or mergers with telecommunications firms.

During ICL's recovery period, talks were held at the top level with a number of telecommunications companies to discuss achieving technological convergence and the benefits of greater scale; but nothing materialized—and ICL was in any case then negotiating from a position of weakness. By 1983 ICL was seen to have turned the corner; it had returned to profit and was now set for growth. On 26 July 1984, entirely out of the blue, a take-over bid was received from STC. Although the STC bid came as a surprise, it was not altogether unwelcome and meshed well with the long-term direction of the information business. After the usual haggling over price, ICL recommended acceptance of the offer. In September 1984, ICL became part of the STC Group.

The concept of a computer-communications convergence is one that has ebbed and flowed throughout the history of the industry; the late 1960s, for example, saw a similar wave of alliances. However, all of these anticipated convergences have faded away after a few years. In the case of the STC-ICL merger, there was no significant merging of R&D activities nor any major new products. In the mid-1980s STC experienced major financial problems associated with the decline in the market for its traditional telecommunications products, and was itself taken over by Northern Telcom. Hence, when Fujitsu offered to take over its ICL subsidiary in 1990, there were few technological or business reasons to resist.

In November 1990, Fujitsu acquired 90 per cent ownership of ICL, and Britain's national champion mainframe maker became Japanese-owned. There were two key attractions for ICL in being taken over by Fujitsu. The first was continued access to its semiconductor technology, because the original ICL-Fujitsu agreement was due to expire in 1991. The licensing agreement had been extraordinarily successful and had enabled ICL's mainframes to remain fully price-competitive with those of every other mainframe manufacturer, including IBM. The second attraction of the Fujitsu take-over was the assurance of continuity it would give to ICL's customer base. One of the consequences of ICL's roller-coaster fortunes had been that whenever it experienced a fall-off in orders during a recession—as in the early 1970s and early 1980s—the downturn was exacerbated by cancellations of orders from customers fearful for ICL's survival. It is significant that, sheltering under Fujitsu's umbrella, ICL weathered the early 1990s recession better than any other European or American mainframe computer company.

The motives for Fujitsu's acquisition of ICL have never been explicitly stated. Clearly an assured market for its semiconductor manufacturing capacity has been important for Fujitsu, but any hopes that ICL would provide an outlet for its IBM-compatible mainframes have not materialized; nor has Fujitsu adopted ICL's products for its non-European markets. Probably Fujitsu's aims are much more long-term: through ICL it will gain access to the European computer market, and in ICL it has acquired the organizational capability to develop 'Open Standards' products that have been important in shaping the European computer market.[16]

Analysis

ICL's principal shortcoming has often been portrayed, especially by the financial and technical press, as a lack of managerial competence. It is certainly true that ICL has suffered from weak management over the years, an observation that is borne out by the fact that in both 1972 and 1981 the importation of US-trained management quickly reversed the fortunes of the company. Up to the early 1990s, IBM was always held up as the managerial paradigm to which ICL should aspire, but IBM's recent demise suggests that managerial competence is not a guarantee of success in the computer industry, and that there are other forces at work. Putting aside the question of managerial competence, at least three further factors need to be taken into account when analysing ICL's relatively poor performance: ICL's organizational capabilities; the maturing of the mainframe market; and government support for the computer industry.

Organizational Capabilities

In an award-winning paper 'IBM and Its Imitators: Organizational Capabilities and the Emergence of the International Computer Industry',[17] Steven Usselman has used the theory of organizational capabilities and evolutionary economic change, as conceptualized by Nelson and Winter,[18] to explain the comparative development of the early computer industry. Usselman argues that IBM came to dominate the early computer industry because it had a unique set of organizational capabilities that fitted it ideally for the environment of the computer market during the period 1950–80. Although in the 1940s IBM, like the rest of its competitors in the office-machine industry, had little or no electronics or computer competence, it did have superb organizational capabilities in electro-mechanical design and manufacture, a sales-force used to selling data-processing machinery, and applications know-how. These organizational capabilities turned out to be much more important than computer-building experience:

This was a market that suited IBM perfectly. The company's entire culture was dedicated to the task of meeting specific data-processing problems in the field. The only significant difference between large electromechanical data-processing installations and these machines was that computers would use vacuum tubes instead of electromechanical relays and would involve a staggering amount of wiring. But these differences appear trivial when placed in the total context of the task.[19]

Thus, it was IBM's ability to nursemaid its customers in their first experience with computers that led to its dominance of the field. The absolute confidence that IBM's customers had in its ability not to let them down overcame almost all other considerations—even cost, for IBM was notoriously uncompetitive in its prices. As a future chairman of IBM, Frank Cary, was reported as saying in 1964, 'We don't sell a product . . . we sell solutions to problems.'[20] Conversely, IBM's recent demise can be attributed to the fact that the same organizational capabilities no longer fitted the environment. In the computer world of the early 1990s, with its reliable, user-friendly hardware and software, computer users no longer needed to have their hands held by IBM, and were no longer willing to pay the premium which IBM's heavyweight sales operation demanded.[21]

Despite their common heritage, IBM and ICL's forerunner BTM had very different organizational capabilities:

On the surface, [BTM] possessed the same organizational capabilities as IBM, and for that reason many in Britain always expected it to follow a similar course in computing. In reality, however, BTM had never developed the vitality that characterized IBM before the war. In particular, it lacked the vibrant production engineering mechanism that proved so instrumental to IBM's success with computing.[22]

Hence, ICL should be seen not as a clone of IBM, but much more like its business-machine competitors such as Remington Rand, Burroughs, and NCR.[23]

The Maturing of the Mainframe Market

Although the social construction of technology is now in the mainstream of the history of technology, relatively little analysis in these terms has been done of the computer industry. However, the shaping of the mainframe computer had clearly played a major role in the success of IBM *vis-à-vis* its competitors, and in its subsequent decline.

In his classic *Networks of Power* (1983) Thomas Hughes has argued that a critical factor in ensuring the success of electricity-supply companies in the 1880s and 1890s was the totality of the system that they supplied.[24] Thus piecemeal efforts at electrification repeatedly failed, whereas a total systems approach was generally successful. In the same way, IBM's success, both as a punched-card machine supplier as well as a computer manufacturer, was a consequence of its systems-minded approach. When IBM supplied a computer, the customer was provided with reliable hardware, software, and peripherals that functioned as a complete system. Moreover, if the system was deficient in any major respect—such as applications software—IBM would usually remedy this at no additional cost to the user. No other manufacturer even came close to IBM in the robustness and comprehensiveness of its systems. Thus when IBM announced its model 1401 second-generation computer in 1959, it came complete with excellent peripherals, magnetic-tape, and disc storage units, and powerful applications

software. By contrast when, to compete with the IBM 1401, ICT announced
its model 1301 in 1961, it had only the most primitive software, it initially
lacked magnetic tape, and the system was never equipped with disc storage.
The 1301 may have been a cheaper machine than the 1401, but the customer was presented with a problem rather than the solution to a problem.

Chandler has highlighted the importance of selling and finance as components of the overall system in the early electricity-supply industry:

> The company's engineers almost always knew more about the safe and efficient use
> of the new power machinery than did their customers. In addition, because of the
> much higher cost of the equipment, these companies often found that they had to
> extend far greater amounts of credit to industrial buyers than did the producers of
> lighter machines.[25]

Analogous roles were played in the early computer industry by IBM's 'sales
engineers' and by its leasing operation. In Britain, the office-machine fore-
bears of ICL—BTM, Powers-Samas, and ICT—never had such high-quality
sales engineers as IBM (indeed, the term was never used in Britain), and
their sales forces did not enjoy a markedly better reputation than those of
their competitors. In the area of finance, all the British companies were held
back by the lack of leasing capital. In the case of ICT it was not until the
formation of Computer Leasings Limited in 1963, that the company ceased
relying on *ad hoc* solutions to the problem.

Since about 1980, the market for mainframe computers has been in
decline. IBM's failure has been not to recognize this market change, and to
find new ventures to exploit its existing capabilities. By contrast, ICL recognized the decline of mainframes in 1981, when they constituted only one-
third of its revenues, and embarked on a decade of restructuring to exploit
its organizational capabilities in other fields—particularly computer services and systems integration. Today ICL's mainframes account for just 15
per cent of its turnover (though a much higher percentage of its profits.).

Government Policies for the Computer Industry

There have been several studies in the last decade that have highlighted the
pivotal role played by government in establishing the early computer industry.[26] It is in the area of government policies that the differences between
the US, Japanese, and British experiences have been most marked.

In the USA, there has been almost no direct intervention in the industry. Rather, the government has used its massive buying power first to establish the technology through defence contracts, and then to create a market
for mass-produced goods. For example, IBM's entrée into computing came
through the development of the 'Defense Calculator' in 1950. The commercial success of this computer was effectively guaranteed by eighteen
letters of intent from defence contractors. IBM subsequently used the

Defense Calculator technology for its first mainframe computers, the 700 series, in the mid-1950s. Again, IBM's participation in the SAGE air-defence system was of enormous importance to the company. The SAGE project accounted for half a billion dollars of IBM's income in the 1950s, and at its peak about 7,000–8,000 people were working on the project—some 20 per cent of IBM's work-force.[27] IBM obtained a commanding lead in processor technology, mass-storage devices, software development, and real-time systems. This catapulted IBM into the airline-reservations market, making it the world leader, initially through the SABRE project in collaboration with American Airlines.[28]

Japan was a latecomer to computing.[29] It was not until the Electronics Industry Act of 1957 that electronics (and therefore computing) was seen as the 'core of the future of the industrial development of Japan'.[30] The 1960s saw the beginning of both supply- and demand-side policies. First, IBM was permitted to manufacture in Japan: this addressed the demand-side by giving Japanese industry in general access to data-processing machinery. Second, on the supply-side, IBM was required to license its technology to Japanese competitors and a duty of 25 per cent was imposed on all non-Japanese computers (including those made by IBM Japan). Another key measure, for both the supply- and demand-sides, was the formation of the JECC leasing corporation. This provided low-cost leasing and buy-back funds that removed the need for the manufacturers to raise capital and eliminated the risk for purchasers. Some 40 per cent of computers were funded by JECC in the 1960s.

In the 1960s, under the guidance of MITI, Japanese companies were encouraged to form alliances with Western companies to gain access to technology—Hitachi, for example, manufactured RCA mainframes under licence, while NEC used Honeywell technology.[31] Having established a viable industry in a protected market, it now remained to make the industry competitive internationally. Following the launch of the IBM System/360, MITI organized and partially funded a crash programme to develop competitive integrated circuits and by late 1965 Fujitsu, NEC and Hitachi all had integrated-circuit-based computers on the market. Following the launch of System/370 in 1970, MITI encouraged inter-firm co-operation to catch up with IBM. A key initiative was the '3.5 generation' programme, 1972–6, aimed at developing IBM-compatible computers using superior semiconductor technology.[32] Co-operation through pre-competitive research is unquestionably the aspect of technology policy that has most influenced the West in the 1980s. Thus the British Alvey initiative (1981–5), was a direct imitation of the Japanese Fifth Generation programme.

Early British policies for the computer industry were largely directed to the supply-side. In the 1950s the only government policy instrument in computing was the NRDC. John Hendry has given a very complete analysis of the NRDC in his book *Innovating for Failure*, a title that encapsulates his conclusion as to its effectiveness.[33] The central problem with the NRDC was its lack of financial muscle: its only resources were a total of £5 million which it could grant to industry, in the form of loans which had to be repaid either through a levy on sales, or through the assignment of patents. Without any effective financial power, the NRDC could do little more than 'push mules up hill'. By encouraging marginal competitors into the industry, the net result of the NRDC's intervention was to make worse the unsustainable number of under-resourced entrants in the industry.

In the 1960s, the supply-side policies culminated in the formation of ICL in 1968. This was, of course, part of a much wider industrial phenomenon once described as 'Europe's love affair with bigness', and the aim of producing a national champion computer manufacturer had its parallels in the aerospace and automobile industries.[34] The formation of ICL as a single vast enterprise reflected in part the demands made by the technology of centralized mainframe computing. ICL might well have been quite successful had the market not switched to small, decentralized computers in the 1970s. But, by focusing on mainframes and on ICL, the government missed out completely on the burgeoning markets for mini- and micro-computers. Only in 1976 did it belatedly try to recover the situation by launching Inmos.[35]

The 1960s did see a number of demand-side policies, of which ICL was the chief beneficiary, focusing on diffusion and procurement. The diffusion policies included the establishment of the National Computing Centre in 1965 to foster computer use and develop applications software; government funding was also provided to establish computer laboratories and computer education in the universities. These policies were, however, no more than was being done in every advanced nation to stimulate the use of computers. Much more interventionist was the government's procurement policy, which required all government departments and nationalized industries to buy British, unless it could be demonstrated that no UK supplier could deliver a suitable system. The effect was that, in the early 1970s, some 90 per cent of government purchases were for ICL equipment, compared with about 50 per cent in private industry. While ICL was in no position to decline this preferment, it argued to the Select Committee on Science and Technology in 1969, that:

We want orders and development contracts, not preference. . . . At the moment the Government buys from us 'once offs'. If the Government buys machines that way, we are worse off. It is well known that I.B.M. get orders for $320 million worth of computers—there was an order for 110 computers for the American Air Force. As long as the Government buys in penny packages we cannot be as efficient as we ought to be.[36]

Thus, while the government accounted for a mere 15 per cent of national computer orders, procurement was a mixed blessing. After about 1980, the procurement policy (which never had any statutory basis) gradually withered away.

Since the government rescue of ICL in 1981, there has been no direct government investment in the UK computer industry. The principal form of government funding to the industry in the early 1980s was the Alvey programme of pre-competitive research (totalling £300 million), which was formulated as a somewhat knee-jerk reaction to the Japanese Fifth Generation programme.[37] Since the completion of the Alvey programme, research funding for industry has been through EU consortia. The 1980s also saw a diminishing concern over the sovereignty of the British computer industry. During the last five years ICL has been allowed to fall into Japanese hands by its sale to Fujitsu; Inmos has been sold to Italian and French interests; and most of the major players in the UK software and services industry have been allowed to fall into French or US ownership. The importance of having a strategic information-technology industry has become a smaller political concern in recent years, for it is now argued that no nation's computer industry can be independent of Japan or America for the supply of semiconductor chips and software. While a substantial information-technology R&D activity remains in Britain, strategic control has unquestionably been lost. It is far from resolved whether this actually matters or not.

NOTES

1. M. Campbell-Kelly, *ICL: A Business and Technical History* (Oxford, 1989).
2. Emerson W. Pugh, *Building IBM: Shaping an Industry and Its Technology* (Cambridge, Mass., 1995).
3. C. Freeman, C. J. E. Harlow, J. K. Fuller, and R. C. Curnow, 'Research and Development in Electronic Capital Goods', *National Institute Economic Review*, 34 (Nov. 1965), 40–91.
4. C. J. Bashe, L. R. Johnson, and J. H. Palmer, *IBM's Early Computers* (Cambridge, Mass., 1985).
5. J. Hendry, *Innovating for Failure: Government Policy and the Early British Computer Industry* (Cambridge, Mass., 1989).
6. F. M. Fisher, J. W. McKie, and R. B. Manke, *IBM and the U.S. Data Processing Industry: An Economic History* (New York, 1983); H. R. Oldfield, *King of the Seven Dwarfs* (New York, 1996).
7. D. Mowery (ed.), *The International Computer Software Industry: A Comparative Study of Industry Evolution and Structure* (New York, 1996); M. Campbell-Kelly, 'Development and Structure of the International Software Industry, 1950–1990', *Business and Economic History*, 24/2 (Winter 1995), 73–110.
8. E. W. Pugh, L. R. Johnson, and J. H. Palmer, *IBM's 360 and Early 370 Systems* (Cambridge, Mass., 1991).

9. J.-J. Servan-Schreiber, *The American Challenge* (London, 1968).
10. H. Wilson, *The Labour Government 1964–1970* (London, 1971), 8.
11. P. Mottershead, 'Industrial Policy', in F. T. Blackaby (ed.), *British Economic Policy 1960–74* (London, 1978).
12. Select Committee on Science and Technology (SubCommittee A), Session 1970–1, *The Prospects for the United Kingdom Computer Industry in the 1970's* (London, 1971), p. lx.
13. K. Flamm, *Creating the Computer: Government Industry and High Technology* (Washington DC, 1988), 195.
14. D. C. L. Marwood, 'ICL: Crisis and Swift Recovery', *Long Range Planning*, 18 (1985), 10–21.
15. S. Caulkin, 'British Firms Resurrected by Courtesy of Japan', *Guardian*, 8 May 1993.
16. B. Gomes-Casseres, 'Computers: Alliances and Industry Evolution', in D. B. Yoffie (ed.), *Beyond Free Trade: Firms Governments and Global Competition* (Boston, 1993).
17. S. W. Usselman, 'IBM and Its Imitators: Organizational Capabilities and the Emergence of the International Computer Industry', *Business and Economic History*, 22/2 (Winter 1993), 1–35.
18. Richard R. Nelson and S. G. Winter, *An Evolutionary Theory of Economic Change* (Cambridge, Mass., 1982).
19. Ibid. 9–10.
20. G. Burck, 'Fortress I. B. M.', *Fortune*, June 1964, 112–6, 196, 198, 200, 202, 207. Quotation from p. 116.
21. As if to confirm Usselman's thesis, by 1995 IBM was well on the way to recovery with the emergence of 'network-centric' computing, in which firms are increasingly connecting together hundreds or thousands of personal computers. This is a difficult technology, and once again IBM has the opportunity of holding its customers' hands. See, for example, I. Sager, 'The View from IBM', *Business Week*, 30 Oct. 1995, 40–3, 46–8.
22. Usselman, 'IBM and Its Imitators', 19–20.
23. James W. Cortada, *Before the Computer: IBM, NCR, Burroughs, and Remington Rand and the Industry They Created, 1865–1956* (Princeton, 1993).
24. T. P. Hughes, *Networks of Power: Electrification in Western Society 1880–1930* (Baltimore, 1983).
25. A. D. Chandler, Jr., *Scale and Scope: The Dynamics of Industrial Capitalism* (Cambridge, Mass., 1990), 68–9.
26. See, for example, J. Hills, *Information Technology and Industrial Policy* (1984); J. W. Cortada, *The Computer in the United States: From Laboratory to Market 1930 to 1960* (New York, 1993); M. Fransman, *Japan's Computer and Communications Industry: The Evolution of Industrial Giants and Global Competitiveness* (Oxford, 1995); Flamm, *Creating the Computer*.
27. Pugh, *Building IBM*.
28. James L. McKenney, with Duncan G. Copeland and Richard O. Mason, *Waves of Change: Business Evolution through Information Technology* (Boston, 1995).
29. M. Anchordoguy, *Computers Inc.: Japan's Challenge to IBM* (Cambridge, Mass., 1989); J. Baranson, *The Japanese Challenge to the US Computer Industry* (Lexington, Mass., 1981); K. Flamm, *Targeting the Computer: Government Support*

and International Competition (Washington, DC, 1987); Fransman, *Japan's Computer and Communications Industry*.

30. Flamm, *Targeting the Computer*, 129.
31. Fransman, *Japan's Computer and Communications Industry*, 137–8.
32. Ibid. 147–55.
33. Hendry, *Innovating for Failure*.
34. D. Hague and G. Wilkinson, *The IRC: An Experiment in Industrial Intervention* (1982).
35. T. Blackstone and W. Plowden, *Inside the Think Tank: Advising the Cabinet 1971–83* (1988), 146 ff.
36. Select Committee of Science and Technology, *Prospects for the United Kingdom Computer Industry*, 406–7.
37. B. Oakley and K. Owen, *Alvey: Britain's Strategic Computing Initiative* (Cambridge, Mass., 1989).

INDEX

Index